EQUAL IN

MONASTIC

PROFESSION

WOMEN IN CULTURE AND SOCIETY
A Series Edited by Catharine R. Stimpson

Penelope D. Johnson

EQUAL IN MONASTIC PROFESSION

Religious Women in Medieval France

THE UNIVERSITY OF CHICAGO PRESS
Chicago and London

PENELOPE D. JOHNSON is associate professor of history at New York
University.

The University of Chicago Press, Chicago 60637
The University of Chicago Press, Ltd., London
© 1991 by The University of Chicago
All rights reserved. Published 1991
Printed in the United States of America
00 99 98 97 96 95 94 93 92 91   5 4 3 2 1

Library of Congress Cataloging-in-Publication Data
Johnson, Penelope D. (Penelope Delafield), 1938–
    Equal in monastic profession : religious women in Medieval France /
Penelope D. Johnson.
        p. cm.—(Women in culture and society)
    Includes bibliographical references and index.
    ISBN 0-226-40185-5 (alk. paper)
    1. Nuns—France—History. 2. Monasticism and religious orders for
women—France—History—Middle Ages, 600–1500. I. Title.
II. Series.
BX4220.F8J64   1991
271'.90044'09021—dc20   90-45510
                                                             CIP

⊗The paper used in this publication meets the minimum requirements
of the American National Standard for Information Sciences—Perma-
nence of Paper for Printed Library Materials, ANSI Z39.48–1984.

To my grandfather
John Allyne Gade
and my mother
Margaret Gade Delafield
for engendering in me a love of the past

A nun lives in the fires of the spirit, a thinker lives in the bright wick of the mind, an artist lives jammed in the pool of materials. (Or, a nun lives, thoughtful and tough, in the mind, a nun lives, with that special poignancy peculiar to religious, in the exile of materials; and a thinker, who would think of something, lives in the clash of materials, and in the world of spirit where all long thoughts must lead; and an artist lives in the mind, that warehouse of forms, and an artist lives, of course, in the spirit. So.)

Annie Dillard, *Holy the Firm*

CONTENTS

SERIES EDITOR'S FOREWORD

"ALAS, THAT EVER I did sin!" the medieval mystic Margery Kempe once exclaimed. "It is full merry in Heaven." Margery's delight in the glory of God is one scene in an epic history—that of human spirituality, our burning thirst for the divine.

Religious communities such as the monastery seek to gratify this thirst. Women have founded, supported, joined, led, and occasionally fled from them. Unhappily, popular culture has tended to sentimentalize or slander the nun, and history has misunderstood these religious women whether abbesses, anchorites, or ordinary members of an order. As Penelope D. Johnson writes, "Women have been and still are an integral part of monastic life, but monastic scholars have tended to see them either as aberrant or as subsidiary to the main theme of male religious life."

Judicious and richly informed, *Equal in Monastic Profession* now restores professed women to the central place they once occupied. This book will appeal to any reader who wants to know about women, gender, social change, and religion. Johnson's landscape is northern France in the central Middle Ages, the eleventh through the thirteenth centuries. Here God and the devil were neither abstractions nor metaphors nor characters in a popular melodrama, but vivid if mysterious presences. The realms of the sacred and secular hung together. Necessarily, then, the monastery, a guarantor of spiritual and physical health, was a crucial place.

In fresh and solid detail, Johnson examines the everyday life of a number of individual houses from the major medieval orders, carefully distinguishing among greater and lesser, richer and poorer, well-run and messy houses. However, all monasteries were places of prayer, their schedule structured around ritual and liturgy. The nuns took their vows of poverty, chastity, and obedience seriously, if in complex and sometimes less than perfect ways. They served the sick and the poor, the young and the old. Moreover, monasteries were socially and economically active. Nuns negotiated with ecclesiastical and political authorities, entered into commercial transactions and worried about cash flow, supervised servants and laypersons, farmed lands and repaired kitchens. Indeed, Johnson shows a correlation between such interaction with the world and the corporate health of individual nunneries.

The monastic life mattered enormously for the women who entered it. Because only wellborn women could enter, they often carried with them the confidence and security of their class. The monastery offered them cultural influence and power, especially for elected leaders, an honorable spiritual place as the bride of Christ, and a useful and respected social role other than that of wife and mother.

Legitimately, however, Johnson warns us not to confuse modern women with medieval monastics, the nunnery with a feminist utopia. For the nun did not seek a sense of psychological autonomy, of individual fulfillment, in religion. Rather, she acted as a member of two families: first her birth family, the family of origin, which might have ties to a specific monastery, and second, the corporate family of the monastic group itself, her brothers and sisters in Christ. Often the two families overlapped. A women might join a religious house because her female relatives were there or because a relative had endowed it. Kinship—of blood and faith—transcended gender. Next, although the monastery did give women a special psychological and social space, nuns seem to have thought of themselves less as "women," members of a secular gender order, than as monastics, members of a sacred order that lived both among and beyond the secular and its damnable fragilities. Such a vision of spiritual commonality was an ideal of the Benedictine Rule operative since the sixth century.

Yet as with all damnable fragilities, a gender order, which the Catholic church sustained, was in place. Ideologically, another influential tradition in the ecclesiastical literature, inherited from earlier Christian ascetics, reduced women to their sexuality and found that sexuality threatening to male purity. Institutionally, only male priests could perform essential rituals, among them the mass and, after 1228, assigning penances. Female monastics had to pay priests for these services, a financial burden that became increasingly onerous.

After a blaze of female spiritual commitment and general church renewal in the first part of the twelfth century, other historical developments joined with and intensified this gender order. Together, after the middle of the twelfth century, they sapped the social, cultural, and economic strength of the monastic women in medieval France. Female and male orders separated, and spiritual commonality degenerated into "male overseers and female underlings." As Johnson explores this erosion, an elegaic tone tinges her narrative. An exceptionally responsible scholar, she knows that she must suggest a multitude of causes for such a significant effect. Monastic women suffered because new social structures replaced the family as an economic unit; because a population increase, especially among females, both devalued women and made them objects of male anxiety; because such church reforms as the rise of the mendicant friars squeezed women out; and because the failure of the Second Crusade (1147–49) generated a xenophobic search for the malignant Other, be it Moslem, Jew, homosexual man, or woman.

A merry heaven is the design of a miserable earth. History tells us about the lineaments of such designs, the needs and natures of the designers, and the translation of design into human laws, customs, habits, and practices. *Equal in Monastic Profession* is such a history—a large accomplishment.

Catharine R. Stimpson

ACKNOWLEDGMENTS

I OWE AN enormous debt of gratitude to individuals and institutions for help in the research and writing of this book, begun almost a decade ago. New York University's Presidential Fellowship and a later NYU Research Challenge Grant allowed me to begin the research, and a National Endowment for the Humanities summer grant and a Rockefeller Fellowship supported the completion of the work. The staffs at many libraries and archives helped the research along, particularly in this country at the Sterling and Beinecke Libraries at Yale University, Bobst Library at New York University, and Neilson Library at Smith College and in France at the Bibliothèque Nationale and the departmental and municipal archives in Poitiers, La Rochelle, Rouen, and Saintes. I am grateful to the staff at the University of Chicago Press for their interest and expertise in creating this book.

My thanks go to all those individuals whose help contributed to this book, especially to Jill Ann Freeland for months of valuable research assistance, to Howard Tu for quantitative expertise, and to Patrick McMahon for translating two pieces of Latin poetry. I particularly appreciate the time and talent of busy colleagues and wish to thank Constance Berman, John Boswell, Elizabeth Carlisle, Giles Constable, Edward Roesner, Mary Skinner, Virginia Stotz, and Bruce Venarde, who have helped with suggestions, reading, and comments. Jeffrey Merrick has given me support above and beyond the call of friendship, for which I am deeply grateful, and my students have provided continued helpful suggestions and inspiration.

I gratefully acknowledge permission to reprint material from "Disreputable Nuns: Scandal in Thirteenth-Century Norman Nunneries," presented at the Sewanee Mediaeval Colloquium in 1986 (with changes here as part of chapter 4); material from "Family Involvement in Medieval Monastic Life," presented at the Sewanee Mediaeval Colloquium in 1988 and printed in *Monks, Nuns and Friars in Mediaeval Society*, ed. Edward B. King, Jacqueline T. Schaefer, and William Wadley, Sewanee Mediaeval Studies 4 (Louvain: Peeters, 1989) (with changes here as part of chapters 2 and 8); material from "*Mulier et Monialis:* The Medieval Nun's Self Image," presented at the Fordham University Conference on Gender and the Moral Order in 1988 and appearing in *Thought* 64 (1989) (with changes here as part of chapter 7); and material from "The Cloistering of Medieval Nuns: Release or Repression; Reality or Fantasy?" Seventh Berkshire Conference on the History of Women, 1987, and "La théorie de la clôture et l'activité réelle des moniales françaises du XIe au XIIIe siècle," presented at the IIe Colloque International de CERCOR in 1988 in Poitiers and appearing in the *Actes du Colloque International de CERCOR* (with changes here as part of chapter 4).

ABBREVIATIONS

BD	Bibliothèque Départementale
BM	Bibliothèque Municipale
BN	Bibliothèque Nationale
ER	*Register of Eudes of Rouen*
Jaffé	Philip Jaffé, *Regesta pontificum romanorum*
Mansi	J. D. Mansi, *Miscellanea*
MGH	*Monumenta Germaniae historica*
PL	*Patrologiae cursus completus, Series Latina*
RV	*Regestrum visitationum archiepiscopi Rothomagensis*
SC	J. D. Mansi, *Sacrorum conciliorum nova et amplissima collectio*

1

INTRODUCTION

D URING THE CENTRAL MIDDLE AGES in northern France a rider
entering a medieval city like Saintes, Rouen, or Troyes and
passing the gates of handsome convent buildings could see in the
courtyards a scene of bustling activity. Inside the walls, a layperson
might proceed to the chapter house to meet with the nuns on business, go to the hospice for care, or visit with a relative. Within the
cloister the visitor could see the nuns strolling during a recreation
period or filing into the church to sing the offices. Townsfolk were
also accustomed to the sight of nuns in the city streets, tending to
business or formally processing two by two on solemn feast days.
Outside the towns one might pass a group of nuns traveling along
the dusty roadways or see an abbess in the fields, verifying boundary
stones with her officials. Peasants in the countryside went to the
nuns of a neighboring convent to pay rents, to borrow money, and to
ask for charity in hard times. Pilgrims saw a nunnery's guesthouse
as a welcome place for a meal and to spend the night when traveling.
It is these women—the nuns of the central Middle Ages—whose
world we seek to enter.

But how can we recapture the voices of mute women from the
past? If they left no personal written record, are we doomed never to
know what they thought about themselves or the world in which
they lived? Can we compare their lives with those of their male
monastic counterparts? Can we learn about ordinary religious
women, or do we have to be satisfied with knowing the extraordinary persons who may be fascinating yet are by definition unrepre-
sentative? Novelists and playwrights sometimes manage brilliantly
to create plausible characters from centuries long gone by; but for
the historian who wants to retrieve rather than imagine lives, fiction
is not a workable solution. Despite the paucity of writing by the
ordinary medieval nuns who have been the subject of this study,

these women have become very real to me as I have worked with the documents generated by their nunneries. This book is my attempt to bring them and their world, with its satisfactions and eventual restrictions, as alive for the reader as they are for me so that they will not sink "unwept into oblivion."[1]

Preconceptions may cloud our vision, and stereotypes and prejudices clutter our minds. Although no one can entirely escape social patterning, one can at least point out some of the more egregious errors to avoid. As readers in the late twentieth century in the West, we may well stumble over or tend to discount the importance of the religious framework in which medieval people functioned. Our secularization must be consciously set aside as we enter a world where God and the devil were real and the absolute goal of human life was to move through its fragile earthly existence towards eternal bliss. The medieval nun believed in spiritual power as surely as we believe in nuclear power, despite neither one's fully understanding these forces. Therefore we will be off to a bad start if we look cynically at the religious motives of medieval nuns, assuming they were empty of real content. There is also danger in idealizing the nun: seeing her as totally pure and spiritual, above petty concerns and human failings. Extreme expectations—either that nuns only feigned piety or that they fully achieved holiness—lose the real contours of three-dimensional people. The cloistered women of the Middle Ages aimed at a demanding ideal but often fell short of the mark. Some of them were saintly—most were not. Finally, we must beware the strong desire to see the past as mirroring or echoing our own times, thereby distorting what we are attempting to understand. Women in medieval monasteries were neither dwellers in Atlantis, enjoying a golden age of feminist freedom, nor the abject victims of a patriarchal system that enslaved them.[2] Our subject is best served if we take the past on its own terms rather than attempting to use it polemically.

1. George Eliot, *Middlemarch* (Oxford: Oxford University Press, 1986), p. 3: "Many Theresas have been born who found for themselves no epic life wherein there was a constant unfolding of far-resonant action; perhaps only a life of mistakes, the offspring of a certain spiritual grandeur ill-matched with the meanness of opportunity; perhaps a tragic failure which found no sacred poet and sank unwept into oblivion."

2. Barbara A. Hanawalt, ed., *Women and Work in Preindustrial Europe* (Bloomington: Indiana University Press, 1896), p. xiv, opens with an excellent warning by the editor that we not look for an El Dorado of women's economic history in the past.

Historical Overview

Women have been and still are an integral part of monastic life, but monastic scholars have tended to see them either as aberrant or as subsidiary to the main theme of male religious life. Major studies of medieval monasticism usually leave women out or relegate them to a short section.[3] Such cultural blinders have created an entire corpus of literature about monasticism that defines the institution as male, although in the Middle Ages it was a world created and inhabited by women as well as by men.

The solitary ascetic Christian life was first led by female and male hermits in Egypt in the third century. Antony (251–56) is usually credited as the initiator of this way of life; but before he withdrew into the Egyptian desert to begin his life of severe asceticism and prayer, he placed his sister in a community of nuns in Alexandria. Therefore to cite Antony as the founder of monasticism seems questionable, since the communal life for religious women apparently existed before he took on the eremitical life. The first full-scale religious community was founded by Pachomius (286–346) at Tabenna in Egypt for both women and men who wanted to dedicate themselves to poverty, chastity, and obedience. Yet despite women's presence in the incipient movement, as monasticism spread both east and west, it carried with it in the writings of the male desert hermits a repugnance for all sexuality and a distaste for all women, whom the desert fathers feared could break the male resolve to live chastely.

Various early monastic leaders devised rules for shaping the religious life, but it was not until the rule of Benedict of Nursia (ca. 480 to ca. 547) that a balanced and truly workable document was available. At the same time in southern France, the first nuns' rule was written by Cesarius of Arles (ca. 470–542) for his sister, Cesaria, but this and other attempts to legislate specifically for women failed to gain general acceptance. It was the Benedictine Rule that won out

3. This tendency is evidenced in a new study that confines its discussion of nuns to one chapter out of thirteen, as if religious women were a furbelow rather than a functional support of Western religious experience: C. H. Laurence, *Medieval Monasticism: Forms of Religious Life in Western Europe in the Middle Ages* (London: Longman, 1984). Lucien Musset, in the introduction to *Les abbayes de Normandie* (Rouen: Actes du XIIIe Congrès des Sociétés Historiques et Archéologiques de Normandie, 1979), speaks of the immense subject of monasticism from 400 to 1530 without ever mentioning nuns.

as the great frame within which both women and men from the sixth century into the twentieth have shaped their community life. By the late sixth century, two contradictory attitudes were formed that define gender in the religious life: women were suspect as sexual threats to male chastity and hence unwelcome, while in a dizzying contradiction, spiritual commonality rather than gender differentiation was the ideal of the rule and hence of monasticism.

The history of monastic life fluctuates between peaks of idealistic reform and troughs of troubles and corruption. Although monasticism had spread rapidly throughout the West to become the paramount institution of the early Middle Ages, the incursions of raiding Magyars, Saracens, and Vikings during the eighth through the early eleventh century, coupled with the interference of lay lords, damaged or destroyed many houses. The first great reform followed the creation in 909 of the Burgundian Abbey of Cluny, instituted as an exempt house, free of episcopal or baronial interference. Cluny spun a web of houses across Europe and became famous for its beautiful churches and impressive liturgy before its sheer size and wealth began to sag and tear holes in its fabric. It yielded pride of place to the next reforming movement in the late eleventh and early twelfth centuries, when a whole group of new orders was formed. Chief among these was the Cistercian order, which, under the leadership of the fierce Saint Bernard (+1153), aggressively marked Europe with a new reforming effort. The Cistercians in their turn became wealthy and complacent as the century grew old, and the final renewing wave of our period came in the early thirteenth century when Saint Francis (+1226) and Saint Dominic (+1221) each instituted a new order of friars. Women tended to share in the enthusiasm in these cycles of renewal, but as the impulse became institutionalized, they were usually marginalized or squeezed out entirely.

The turn of the twelfth century marked an extraordinary surge of large numbers of pious women into the marketplaces and fields to listen to and then follow the charismatic preachers of the reform movement. One such preacher was Robert Arbrissel (+1117), who created a great nunnery at Fontevrault in central France to accommodate the multitude of women he had converted with his preaching. These women forced their way into the awareness of church leaders by their numbers and their zeal and were at first welcomed into new foundations, to share an extraordinary symmetry. Although negative feelings and writing about women did not totally disappear, they were overshadowed until the middle years of the twelfth century, when a hostile backlash slammed the door on female monastic equality. This book is about monastic women, the gender differences between nuns and monks, how the nuns saw themselves, and what the surrounding society thought of religious women.

Parameters of the Study

The book focuses on northern France, a linguistic unity where the *langue d'oïl* was spoken.[4] The time frame is the central Middle Ages, the eleventh, twelfth, and thirteenth centuries, and the subject is religious women: those women living under a monastic rule within a religious community—a monastery or a hospital.[5] The monasteries included were founded between the sixth and the thirteenth centuries and were in fourteen different dioceses; they belonged to the major orders represented in northern France: Benedictine, Cistercian, Fontevrist, Clarist (Poor Clares who were Franciscans), Augustinian, and Premonstratensian, (See appendix A.) A functional rather than an institutional definition governed this choice. For instance, Augustinian and Premonstratensian canonesses are included because they lived a cloistered existence similar to that of nuns, although canons were separated from monks by significant differences. Likewise, female Dominicans and Franciscans shared a monastic life virtually identical to that of traditional nuns, in contrast to their male counterparts, the friars, whose public preaching mission set them apart from cloistered monks.

Using a group of orders instead of limiting the investigation to just one order takes account of the enormous fluidity in medieval monasteries; tight definitions run the risk of forcing messy realities into

4. I am persuaded by Georges Duby's argument that "ideological systems must be studied within a homogeneous cultural and social formation": *The Three Orders: Feudal Society Imagined*, trans. Arthur Goldhammer (Chicago: University of Chicago Press, 1980), pp. 6–7. The outer geographic limits all fell within the area of the *langue d'oïl*: for Metz, see p. 125. For Namur, see Louis Remacle, "La géographie dialectale de la Belgique romance," in *Les dialectes de France au Moyen Age et aujourd'hui: Domaines d'oïl et domaine franco-provençal* (Paris: Georges Straka, 1972), p. 317. For Saintes, see Aurelio Roncaglia, *La lingua d'oïl: Profilo di grammatica storica del francese antico* (Rome: Edizioni dell'Ateneo, 1971), p. 64.

5. Medieval people used the term *monasterium*, "monastery," for communities of either women or men, and I will use it in this way too. They also termed the corporate body of these houses the *conventus*; however, because modern English uses "convent" exclusively for a house of nuns, I will avoid confusion by keeping the modern usage and will also use the English word "nunnery" only for houses of women.

tidy categories. For example, a religious house could begin its existence under one guise but later shift its allegiance, its activities, the gender of its monastic population, its name, or even its geographic location. Pont-aux-Dames began its career as a hôtel-Dieu and later housed Cistercian nuns.[6] La Cour Notre-Dame de Michery began its existence as a leper house, became Cistercian in 1226, and was handed over to monks in the fifteenth century.[7] La Magdeleine started out a the hospital of Notre-Dame, but after receiving a gift of some relics of Saint Mary Magdalen, it changed its name to honor its new patron saint.[8]

Although very small dependent cells or obediences are often of interest, I have concentrated on monasteries that had eight or more members, since it is not usually possible to live the conventual life with a smaller number.[9] Also, I have included hospitals and almshouses in which women lived under a rule, caring for the sick in conjunction with lay brothers and priests. The personnel of these hospitals can be particularly elusive. The Hospital of Saint-Jean in Angers, for example, recorded gifts given to the brothers and to the

6. Paris, BN, MS. fr. 4669, fols. 36v–37r. This process was not limited to France; Sharon Elkins discovers confused and changing institutional identities among English convents: *Holy Women of Twelfth-Century England* (Chapel Hill: University of North Carolina Press, 1988), pp. 66, 86.

7. W. C. Jordan, "The Cistercian Nunnery of la Cour Notre-Dame de Michery: A House That Failed," *Revue Bénédictine* 95(1985): 314, 320.

8. Ludovic de Vauzelles, *Histoire du prieuré de la Magdeleine-lez-Orléans de l'ordre de Fontevraud* (Paris: J. Baur, 1973), p. 233, no. 32, 1343. The story of Gérigny offers a good example of the shifting fortunes of a monastery: J.-B.-E. Carré, *Notice historique sur le prieuré de Gérigny de l'ordre de Prémontré au diocèse de Reims (1130–1789) avec plans et pièces justificatives inédites* (Reims: P. Michaud, 1885), pp. 1–27. After a very confused foundation, by 1134 the modest Priory of Gérigny housed a group of Premonstratensian canonesses. In midcentury the women were moved permanently to another convent, and the male house of Cuissy claimed Gérigny, reducing it to the status of a simple chapel. Sixty-five years later the monks traded all their lands in Gérigny for a pension for Roger, the lord of Rozoy and Chaumont. In 1219 Roger gave his holdings in Gérigny to the church of Chaumont, which was to install eight priests to celebrate commemorative masses for him and his family. But because Chaumont had reformed by becoming Premonstratensian, the little priory once again was housing religious of Prémontré, although this time canons instead of canonesses. Finally, in 1297, all the men except one were withdrawn, and soon after, even he left and the buildings were abandoned.

9. *Cartulaire de l'abbaye de Saint-Sulpice-la-Forêt, Ille-et-Vilaine*, ed. Pierre Anger, extract from *Bulletin Archéologique d'Ille-et-Vilaine*, 1911, p. 187, no. 109, 1225. If a house gets too small, "tanto numero esse non possunt quod ibi monastica servare valeant instituta," it can't keep up the offices and the common life.

poor, yet a prioress and sisters served there too.[10] Although such institutions often had a male head, there is enough evidence of women's conventual life in some to make them appropriate subjects.

Another definitional quagmire is the "double house." This term has been used by scholars for monasteries that had groups of nuns and monks living in tandem under the direction of an abbess. As scholars have struggled to make sense out of an awkward term, however, they have been increasingly reshaping it in more and more convoluted ways; enough questions have been raised about its validity to make it time for a paradigm shift.[11] In reality all women's houses were "double" insofar as they all had priests attached to them for administering the sacraments and were headed by abbesses or prioresses. I will therefore avoid the term, instead defining the particular grouping of women and men when speaking of specific institutions.

SOURCES

Since my goal is to discover the ordinary medieval nun, I have concentrated my research on "documents of practice," those documents that show the world as it was, not as it should be. The bulk of the sources is made up of pragmatic records, legal and economic charters recording transactions and activities of monastic life. The "documents of theory"—prescriptive treatises, hortatory sermons, theological tracts, and the like—reveal what church leaders thought the world should be, in contrast to what it was. Such material can be useful, particularly when compared with the documents of practice. However, charters collected by monasteries into cartularies—registers of deeds and titles of a monastery's lands—make up the bulk of my sources. I chose twenty-six women's houses to supply my documentary core, seeking a sample that would reflect in miniature the

10. *Cartulaire de l'hôpital de Saint-Jean d'Angers*, ed. Célestin Port (Paris: J.-B. Dumoulin, 1870), p. ii, no. 3, 1181, for example, and p. xxxi, no. 31, 1205.

11. See, for example, Roger Gazeau, "La clôture des moniales au XIIe siècle en France," *Revue Mabillon* 58(1974): 305, n. 56, and Jean Leclercq, "Feminine Monasticism in the Twelfth and Thirteenth Centuries," in *The Continuing Quest for God*, ed. William Skudlarck (Collegeville, Minn.: Liturgical Press, 1982), p. 115. Penny Schine Gold, *The Lady and the Virgin: Image, Attitude, and Experience in Twelfth-Century France* (Chicago: University of Chicago Press, 1985), p. 102, calls for jettisoning the term in favor of more specific discussions, as does Elkins, *Holy Women of Twelfth-Century England*, p. xviii.

range of nunneries in northern France during the central Middle Ages. My sample mirrors the diversity of French convents: it represents six orders; fourteen dioceses; a range of size from as few as fourteen to as many as sixty nuns; rural and urban settings; wealthy and impoverished institutions; foundation dates stretching from 657 to 1259; and a variety of founders both lay and religious, female and male. (See appendix A.)

In addition to charters, I have used visitation records, and in particular the extensive report of visitations made by Archbishop Eudes Rigaud in Normandy in the thirteenth century.[12] This record has offered many researchers a rich vein of data in the past, and now, in the day of computers, its thousands of entries can be mined quantitatively. (See appendix B.)

Attempting to quantify medieval data is a tricky business. Caroline Bynum warns that the findings may "obscure even while they elucidate," yet other scholars ask why this extraordinary document has not yet received thorough statistical analysis.[13] Both concerns are valid. The potential pitfalls are many, but by using data from Eudes's visitations we can actually compare women's and men's monastic life within an ecclesiastical province. No other French visitation record is anywhere near detailed enough for such a comparison, and for the central Middle Ages little else is available to make monastic gender comparison possible.

Studies of women in the Middle Ages have proliferated enormously over the past twenty years. Many scholars struggle gamely to include in their notes citations to all the background work on a subject or the many positions taken over contested points. In considering the bulk of work done in social history, Bernard Bailyn wrote: "Only a besotted Faust would attempt to keep up with even a large part of this proliferating literature in any detail."[14] Since I feel no call to emulate Faust, and since I hope this book will be read by an interested general readership as well as by students and scholars, I have attempted to limit notes to pertinent examples and necessary references. Without a doubt, there will be a surfeit of citations for some tastes and for others, too sparse a collection; I aim for the

---

12. Paris, BN, MS. lat. 1245, published as RV and ER.

13. Caroline Walker Bynum, *Holy Feast and Holy Fast: The Religious Significance of Food to Medieval Women* (Berkeley: University of California Press, 1987), p. 93. Noel Coulet, "Les visites pastorales," fasc. 23 in *Typologie des sources du Moyen Age occidental,* dir. Léopold Genicot (Turnhout: Brépols, 1977), p. 73.

14. Bernard Bailyn, "The Challenge of Modern Historiography," *American Historical Review* 87(1982): 2.

via media. Also to keep down unnecessary notes, I have used a reference citation only when a subject is first mentioned.

Let us begin listening for the voices of medieval nuns within their families before they left to enter the cloister, since the family shaped the decisions of its members and then became a supporter of the monastic way of life.

PART I
CONNECTING LINKS

2

THE SECULAR COMMUNITY

THE NUN AND HER FAMILY

T HE CHARISMATIC PREACHING of Odo of Orléans in the late eleventh century changed the lives of many who heard him speak; in fact, he converted such numbers of female followers that he had to found two convents to take in all the women who were eager to enter monastic life. Maisende, one of those whose ardor he kindled, was a young married woman when she heard Odo's call and responded with her whole heart; she then turned all the eloquence and power of her spiritual rebirth to the task of convincing her husband that they should put aside their marriage and both take religious vows. Soon after she had converted her husband, Maisende discovered to her sorrow that she was pregnant and would have to wait while her husband preceded her into the cloister. When the long nine months were past and her baby was born, then at last she could joyfully assume the habit of a nun.[1]

How are we to interpret Maisende's passion for the monastic life, which led her to give up her newborn child? Is this a reflection of reality, or is the author presenting his readers with an idealization of pious female behavior? Did medieval women choose to become nuns, responding to a strong vocational pull? Or were they consigned to the cloister by their families in a less than free oblation later romanticized by Christian culture?

Choice

Although the issue of choice is of enormous interest to modern investigators, it is a valid question only "within the framework of

1. Nicolas Huyghebaert, "Les femmes laïques dans la vie religieuse des XIe et XIIe siècles dans la province ecclésiastique de Reims," in *I laici nella "societas christiana" dei secoli XI e XII*, Miscellanea del Centro di Studi Medioevali 5 (Milan: Cath-

available opportunity."[2] For most medieval people, choice did not belong to the individual because one's life was viewed as part of a whole—the family—rather than as an autonomous entity. This social perspective was shared by the noble and the peasant, rich and poor, females and males in the medieval world, which believed that individuals benefited if their own families prospered. It behooved kinships to seek advantageous relationships through marriages, godparenthood, monastic professions, and political alliances; the whole family also had an interest in preserving its patrimony, and therefore in limiting as well as controlling the marriages of its members so as not to fragment property among too many inheritors.[3] A family might decide to give a daughter to the church or to marry her off for the useful social and economic connections her union would create. The girl might not want to enter the cloister but might have little to say in the matter; or she might disdain marriage but only in rare cases, such as the famous battle royal waged by Christina of Markyate, manage to outsmart her family and avoid an unwanted betrothal.[4] The exercise of choice by women may sometimes be hard

---

olic University of the Sacred Heart, 1968), p. 367, draws the tale from the *Liber de restauratione S. Martini* by Heriman.

2. Alice Kessler-Harris in the *Chronicle of Higher Education*, February 5, 1986, p. 8. John H. Mundy, *Europe in the High Middle Ages: 1150–1309* (New York: Basic Books, 1973), p. 211, comments that individual choice was sacrificed to the good of the family.

3. The family strategies operating to maintain the patrimony and their impact on social behavior have been the object of much investigation. One of the first and most important studies was Georges Duby, "Dans la France du Nord-Ouest. Au XIIe siècle: Les 'jeunes' dans la société aristocratique," *Annales* 19(1964): 835–46, trans. as "In Northwestern France: The 'Youth' in Twelfth-Century Aristocratic Society," in *Lordship and Community in Medieval Europe*, ed. Fredric L. Cheyette (New York: Holt, Rinehart, and Winston, 1968), pp. 198–209. The most recent working out of these theories by Duby is *The Knight, the Lady and the Priest: The Making of Modern Marriage in Medieval France*, trans. Barbara Bray (New York: Pantheon, 1983), pp. 269–76. David Herlihy, *Medieval Households* (Cambridge: Harvard University Press, 1985), puts family strategies in a much broader frame and questions some of Duby's conclusions. Jack Goody, *The Development of the Family and Marriage in Europe* (Cambridge: Cambridge University Press, 1983), presents a good broad-based picture of these developments.

4. *Life of Christina of Markyate*, ed. C. H. Talbot (Oxford: Clarendon, 1959). Christina led a Perils-of-Pauline existence punctuated with narrow escapes and long and arduous concealments to finally wear down her family and her suitor so that she could be a nun. Bynum, *Holy Feast and Holy Fast*, p. 222, points out that medieval girls were given little opportunity to "pick their husbands or their futures directly" and used fasting and self-mutilation to escape unwanted marriages.

to see when it did occur; for instance, married women and widows who entered convents may sometimes have been tardily beginning the cloistered existence previously desired but denied them by their families.[5]

Variations existed, but generally society was structured so that the well-being of the kin group was a key consideration in the major life decisions of its members, although coming of age gave an individual greater control than a child enjoyed. Attaining majority was more important for boys than for girls, since when girls reached twelve, the age of consent, they were still regarded as being for all practical purposes under the guardianship of their senior male relative. The age of legal consent for boys was considered to be slightly older than for girls, generally fourteen.[6]

To be a child—regardless of one's sex—was to be fully under family control. When Geoffrey of Rancon brought his daughter to Abbess Sibylle to be received into the abbey of Saintes, Elizabeth was a small girl (puellula).[7] It is doubtful that Elizabeth had any opportunity to exercise choice, although sometimes the child oblate ran away immediately or ultimately asserted herself by later leaving the monastery, as did a thirteenth-century nun of Villarceaux in Normandy, who as an adult quit her abbey to be married.[8] Some family pressure had economic motives: relatives might push a girl to take vows when they wanted her inheritance to remain in their hands.[9] Other times coercion might be necessary because of adult decisions, as when Peter Valdès, founder of the Waldensians, experienced a

5. *Cartulaire de l'abbaye royale de Notre-Dame de Saintes de l'ordre de Saint Benoît*, vol. 2 of *Cartulaires inédits de la Saintonge*, ed. Thomas Grasilier (Niort: L. Clouzot, 1871), p. 118, no. 169, 1117–46, for an example of a woman who is "uxor Raimundi Desticac, facta sanctimonialis." See also *Cartulaire de l'abbaye du Ronceray d'Angers (1028–1184)*, ed. Bertrand de Broussillon (Paris: A. Picard, 1900), p. 87, no. 117.

6. Shulamith Shahar, *The Fourth Estate: A History of Women in the Middle Ages*, trans. Chaya Galai (London: Metheun, 1983), p. 134.

7. *Cartulaire de Notre-Dame de Saintes*, p. 63, no. 66, 1119–34. In like fashion a noble couple, William and Ermengarde, gave their little daughter (parvula) to the same house at the time of its founding: p. 144, no. 225, 1047.

8. Huyghebaert, "Femmes laïques dans la vie religieuse," pp. 370–71. ER, pp. 131–32.

9. Michel Parisse, *Les nonnes au Moyen Age* (Le Puy: Christine Bonneton, 1983), p. 245, mentions a nun at Baume-les-Dames who charged coercion in her appeal to the pope. *Cartulaire de Saint-Sulpice-la-Forêt*, pp. 422–23, no. 224, relates that after his brother has died, a man gives his niece to the abbey "quia ipsa erat haeres terrae." An interesting English court case occurred when a guardian placed a little girl in a convent to keep her inheritance in his family. See S. F. C. Milson, "Inheritance by

powerful conversion call to live the apostolic life; before he could leave all worldly concerns for a life of poverty and preaching, he had to care for his daughters, which he did by putting them in the nunnery of Fontevrault.[10] His calling thus shaped the lives of his relatives, whatever they may have wanted.

Common practice was to place a little girl as a novice in a convent, where she would be raised until she became old enough to take her vows. Actual profession could not be done by parental proxy, since canon law insisted that only the individual becoming a monastic could make her own profession.[11] When the girl reached the age of consent, then she could take the veil.[12] The practice of child oblation was not restricted to girls; boys were also disposed of in accord with family strategies. In fact, boys could be parceled out in two ways—to monasteries to become monks as well as to the church to become priests.[13]

Not only did family plans shape the life of each medieval individual, but birth also created barriers or bridges. Entry into a convent as a choir nun was limited in the early Middle Ages primarily to the nobility, and though restrictions eased from the twelfth century on, nunneries still recruited only from the upper levels of society.[14] Burgher daughters cropped up very occasionally in convents as early

---

Women in the Twelfth and Early Thirteenth Centuries," in *On the Laws and Customs of England: Essays in Honor of Samuel E. Thorne*, ed. S. Arnold Morris et al. (Chapel Hill: University of North Carolina Press, 1981), pp. 79–80.

10. R. I. Moore, *The Birth of Popular Heresy* (London: Edward Arnold, 1975), p. 112. The control of choice by families is also seen in early Irish convents: see Lisa M. Bitel, "Women's Monastic Enclosures in Early Ireland: A Study of Female Spirituality and Male Monastic Mentalities," *Journal of Medieval History* 12(1986):21.

11. *Corpus iuris canonici*, ed. Aemilius Friedberg, vol. 2 (Leipzig: Bernhard Tauchnitz, 1881), Decretalium Gregorii IX, lib. III, tit. XXXI, cols. 571–72.

12. Christopher Brooke, "Marriage and Society in the Central Middles Ages," in *Marriage and Society: Studies in the Social History of Marriage*, ed. R. B. Outhwaite (London: Europa Publications, 1981), p. 27, points out that by the mid-twelfth century, monastics were not to enter monasteries until they reached the age of consent.

13. A whole crowd of little boys could receive orders together as an efficiency measure: "Et circa triginta pueros tonsuravit": Mansi, p. 295. See Penelope D. Johnson, *Prayer, Patronage, and Power: The Abbey of La Trinité, Vendôme, 1032–1187* (New York: NYU Press, 1981), pp. 38–39, for a discussion of child oblation at this house.

14. Scholars are generally agreed on the class limitations: Shahar, *Fourth Estate*, p. 39; Linda Eckenstein, *Woman under Monasticism* (New York: Russell and Russell, 1896; reissued 1963), p. 213; Jean Verdon, "Les moniales dans la France de l'Ouest aux XIe et XIIe siècles," *Cahiers de Civilisation Médiévale* 19(1976): 264; Frederick Marc Stein, "The Religious Women of Cologne: 1120–1320" (Ph.D. diss., Yale University, 1977); see his conclusions of marked class limitations on the religious life,

as the eleventh century, and their presence became much more common by the thirteenth century.[15] The enormous gulf between market stall and mounted warrior that existed in the eleventh century
shrank as merchants grew rich and powerful and knightly younger
sons lost status over the next two hundred years. In 1219 it was
unremarkable when two daughters of a *civis*, or townsman, of Orléans took the veil at the Abbey of Voisins, or in midcentury
when burgher daughters became nuns in Normandy; some of these
women even rose to become monastic officials, as did Margaret, the
subprioress of a house in Champagne.[16] The families of these bourgeois women were mostly mercantile, although rich artisans could
find a place for their female kin, as did a Parisian goldsmith whose
daughter entered the Abbey of Port-Royal.[17] By the end of the central
Middle Ages, entry into all but the most exclusive nunneries was
possible for women of upper and sometimes middling status. For a
peasant woman, however, the cloistered life was not even a possibility unless her family could enrich itself, become free, and acquire
some stature; choice was constricted by class.[18]

Although both women and men had to subordinate their choices
and desires to the needs and plans of their families, a woman's life
options were fewer. The medieval woman from the upper levels of
society could either marry or pursue the religious life if her family

---

pp. 236–38. However, Parisse, *Nonnes au Moyen Age*, pp. 132–34, points out one of
those regional variations—the increasingly closed noble system of the canonesses of
Lorraine—which should serve as a caution against too ready generalizations.

15. *Cartulaire de l'abbaye de Saint-Georges de Rennes*, ed. Paul de la Bigne-
Villeneuve, *Bulletin et Mémoires de la Société Archéologique du Département d'Ille-
et-Vilaine* 9 (1875): 269, no. 41, ca. 1068, and *Cartulaire de Notre-Dame de Saintes*,
p. 55, no. 54, 1079–99, give examples of bourgeois nuns whose numbers begin to
proliferate in the charters after 1200.

16. *Cartulaire de Notre-Dame de Voisins de l'ordre de Cîteaux*, ed. Jules Doinel,
Collection des cartulaires du Loiret 3 (Orléans, 1887), p. 158, no. 154, 1219; Rouen,
BD 53 H carton 1, MS. no. 61 of 1248 and no. 65; E. Carré, ed., "Histoire et cartulaire
du prieuré de Notre-Dame et Ste. Marguerite de la Presle," *Revue de Champagne et
de Brie*, 2d ser., 5(1893): 352, no. 59, 1277.

17. *Cartulaire de l'abbaye de Porrois, au diocèse de Paris, plus connue sous son
nom mystique de Port-Royal*, ed. Adolphe de Dion (Paris, 1903), p. 299, no. 305, ca.
1204–80.

18. Mary Skinner, "Benedictine Life for Women in Central France, 850–1100," in
Distant Echoes, Vol. 1 of *Medieval Religious Women*, ed. John A. Nichols and Lillian
Thomas Shank (Kalamazoo, Mich.: Cistercian Publications, 1984), p. 98, mentions
several nuns from simple stock; however, it is highly likely that each of their families
had already acquired wealth and status as drapers or millers so that their daughters
were deemed respectable by the convents that accepted them.

was amenable; generally her future as wife and mother or as nun was planned for her from her childhood, since options were minimal and selecting the one most beneficial for the kinship was the province of the group. In contrast, when a noble family decreed either marriage or celibacy for a son, the boy still had some options. If it was not in the best interests of preserving family property for him to marry, he might become either a monk or a secular cleric; he might study theology, law, or medicine; he might become the lettered administrator for a secular or an ecclesiastical lordship; or he might aspire to rise to high position in the church.

Medieval people certainly did not exercise freedom of choice as modern Western society knows it; family strategies and traditions as well as class and sex determined the latitude available for individual decision making. Since the heavy hand of family authority touched everyone, it would be misleading to think that medieval nuns generally felt more dragooned into the cloister than their male counterparts; in addition, the prevailing climate of strong religious sentiment that pervaded this world made it likely that many religious people—women as well as men—whether child oblates or adult converts, lived their lives in the conviction of the spiritual value of their vocations.[19]

Family Strategies

A common practice in the Middle Ages was for a family to create localized material and spiritual networks by concentrating its energies on one or two religious institutions, favoring these particular houses with donations and requesting spiritual benefits and economic assistance from them, bringing children to be received there as monastics, and entering these monasteries when sick to be cared for and after death to be buried within the monastic precincts. Teasing out the motives for the behavior of laypeople is difficult, and probably ultimately impossible except in particular cases, since each family and each individual functioned in a unique situation. Nevertheless, general benefits for lay supporters included increased prestige and respectability, economic advantages, and spiritual support for lay patrons, while the monasteries benefited by receiving protection, donations, and recruits.[20] The alliance of lay supporters and monastic houses was a satisfactory symbiosis.

19. Skinner, "Benedictine Life for Women," pp. 96–100, makes a strong case for the real spiritual vocations of medieval nuns.

20. In chapters 1 and 3 of *Prayer, Patronage, and Power*, I emphasize the mixed motivations for secular monastic support. Constance Bouchard, *Sword, Miter, and*

The strongest bond of any was to have a family member inside the cloister as a professed monastic, linking the lay kin group with the monastic family. The decision to give a child to a monastery was a choice to donate something of worth to God, thereby benefiting the souls of parents or guardians who offered the child for oblation. But the accrual of spiritual benefits did not stop with oblation, since the child would continue to pray for the natal family's well-being. An ongoing bond of mutual support and benefit began with the entry of a family member into the cloister. Indeed, families did not always stop with the profession of only one of their number into a house. Sometimes members assumed the monastic life together.[21]

Kin drew kin both as donors and as entrants to a religious house. Once one relative became professed, others were attracted to the same institution. Nephews often entered the house or order of their uncles.[22] Aunts also drew their nieces, although this seems to have happened less frequently. Most commonly, aunts and uncles who served as magnets had already risen to high claustral position.

The pattern was generally different when mothers and daughters were nuns in the same house. A mother might choose to enter a nunnery as an elderly woman, either when widowed or with the consent of her husband. She was apt to choose a house where a relative, such as a daughter, was already established. In this case the mother might enjoy the prestige and status of her daughter: Petronilla of Roche was an important monastic official, a *decana*, in the nunnery of Notre-Dame in Saintes; her high status relative to her mother is evident in her position in the charters, preceding her mother, and referred to by her full name while her mother was simply called by her Christian name, Avice.[23]

Cloister: Nobility and the Church in Burgundy, 980–1198 (Ithaca, N.Y.: Cornell University Press, 1987), chap. 10, emphasizes the importance of genuine religious inspiration: "It is difficult to escape the conclusion that the advantages sought in such reforms would be found not in this world but in the next" (p. 240).

21. This pattern also existed in English nunneries: see Elkins, *Holy Women of Twelfth-Century England*, p. 99.

22. The austere reformer Archbishop Eudes Rigaud attracted his nephew, Adam, into the Franciscan order and then included him in his archiepiscopal household: ER, p. xv. In some cases, but probably not Eudes's, "nephew" may have been a euphemism for an illegitimate son.

23. *Cartulaire de Notre-Dame de Saintes,* p. 100, no. 124, ca. 1146, cites Petronilla as dean. The witness list of p. 131, no. 207, ca. 1148–52, reads: "Petronilla de Rocha et matre ejus Avicia." Since order in these lists tends to correspond to status, one would expect Avice to stand before her daughter by reason of age; the reverse order reflects the superior status of the younger nun within the convent.

The most common grouping of relatives within a monastic institution was that of sisters together in a nunnery. Sometimes their
entrance was effected in one fell swoop: the knight R. Panet and his
wife Elizabeth gave a generous donation to a Poitevin abbey as the
combined dowry for several daughters.[24] The same thing was effected by one parent when Walter of Rupefort brought his three
daughters, Joanna, Alice, and Philippa, to the Abbey of Notre-Dame
in Voisins.[25] Sisters also entered nunneries serially as well as in
groups, sometimes to fill a place the family designated for one of its
members. A donation of forest rights was made to Basse-Fontaine by
Robert of Mastoil so that one of his daughters would be received as
a nun into the house, and the convent agreed that "if it should happen that in fifteen years she should die, then if the parents wished,
they could substitute another girl for that place."[26] Although brothers also became monks together, it seems to have been much less
common than for sisters to live the religious life in the same convent. For example, at the Abbey of Holy Trinity in Vendôme, of the
201 monks I can identify over 155 years between 1032 and 1187,
there is only one pair of brothers, while in one nunnery there were
often three or more pairs of sisters at one time.[27] This gender difference probably reflects the greater number of options available to
boys.

The presence of a sister already established in a convent may well
have attracted younger siblings to the monastic life. When Mechtild
of Hackeborn visited Gertrude, her older sister, at the Abbey of Ro-
darsdorf, the little girl cried piteously to remain with her professed
sibling when the scheduled visit came to an end.[28] Since such stories are common in holy women's vitae, the written lives of medieval saintly people, we might suspect them of being literary topoi.
But the persistence of this theme of emulating the admired older
sister continues in the autobiographical writing of more modern

24. Poitiers, BM, MS. 27, p. 147. This oblation is dated to 1232.
25. *Cartulaire de Notre-Dame de Voisins*, p. 79, no. 76, 1262.
26. *Cartulaire de l'abbaye de Basse-Fontaine*, ed. Charles Lalore, vol. 3, *Collection
des principaux cartulaires de diocèse de Troyes* (Paris: Thorin, 1878), p. 19, no. 14,
1166.
27. *Cartulaire de l'abbaye cardinale de la Trinité de Vendôme*, ed. Charles Métais,
5 vols. (Paris: A. Picard, 1893–1904), 1:90–91, no. 352, 1094. See, for instance, *Documents sur l'abbaye de Notre-Dame-aux-Nonnains de Troyes*, ed. Charles Lalore,
*Mémoires de la Société Académique d'Agriculture, des Sciences, Arts et Belles-
Lettres du Département de l'Aube*, 3d ser., 11(1874): 125–29, no. 200, 1269.
28. Caroline Walker Bynum, *Jesus as Mother: Studies in the Spirituality of the
High Middle Ages* (Berkeley: University of California Press, 1982), pp. 209–10.

saintly women. In the seventeenth century Saint Veronica yearned to live in the cloister with her three older sisters who had already taken the veil: "I loved them so much I thought I could not survive without them"; therefore she wrote to her father:

> Most dearly beloved father,
> I think I heard that your Excellency notified my Uncle that he and the others should try to remove from my head the thought of becoming a nun. . . . You know very well the affection I have for your Excellency and for my dear sisters. I have given up home and carnality. Already my sisters are in the monastery; and I think that for me also there remains no other desire." [29]

Even in modern times little girls have been riveted by the example of cloistered siblings. This attraction is described with particular power in the writing of the modern French saint, Thérèse of Lisieux. Her longing to join her sisters Pauline and Marie in the Carmelite life helped shape her own intense vocation.[30]

Although individual choice was often curtailed, to be offered to a monastery as a small child might mean joining relatives within the cloister or even entering at the same time as other family members. The monastery became literally a home away from home. A child oblate not only was often in the company of relatives inside the convent but was also part of the concerns and plans of her kin outside the convent, thereby staying connected to her family at large. A forceful noblewoman, Hersende, made a major donation to the Priory of Saint-Silvain in Perigord in 1010.[31] She specifies in the charter all the relatives in her extended family who are to benefit by the donation. With a fine, literary sweep the gift is made to God, the Virgin Mary, and the donor's daughter, Hildegarde, who is a nun at the priory. Hildegarde is to control the property until her death, at which time Hersende's niece or some other female relative professed at Saint-Silvain is to have tenure. At no time is the property

---

29. Quoted by Rudolph M. Bell, Holy Anorexia (Chicago: University of Chicago Press, 1985), pp. 68–69.

30. The death of her mother increased Thérèse's dependence on and admiration for her older sisters. See the excellent analysis of this attraction in Monica Furlong, Thérèse of Lisieux (London: Virago Press, 1987), and the discussion of her deep yearning to take the veil with her sisters in her autobiography, Histoire d'une âme (Paris: Editions de Cerf, 1985).

31. Cartulaire de Notre-Dame de Saintes, pp. 106–8, no. 140, 1010: "trado et concedo Domino Deo et Sancte semper virgini Marie Dei genitrici, et filie mee Aldeardi."

to leave family control. Donations made to a monastery but controlled by a family member who was a monastic in that institution were very popular during the central Middle Ages. A dying woman, Havise, willed to the Priory of la Presle a grain harvest, part of which was to go to her relative the nun Eustachia.[32] When Eustachia died this portion was to go to Eustachia's niece, Ida, who was also a nun at la Presle. After Ida's death the grain due was to be given to Havise's grandniece if the girl decided to become a nun. Only when this family progression died out completely would the entire grain due go to the nuns for purchasing their habits. Such gifts were widespread because they satisfied secular society's desire to reach into the cloister and impose family controls. Secular folk conceived of monasteries not as strictly spiritual places but as local institutions existing for the well-being of their families. Therefore it seemed appropriate to arrange that one's kin would be properly cared for and one's assets assigned to family members.

When a family decided to offer a child to a monastery, the decision could resolve a number of issues. Entrance into a convent could dispose of a child who would be a burden in secular society. The seriously handicapped child was not supposed to be accepted into the religious life, but in actual practice this did happen.[33] Generally the documents gloss over such irregular practices, but we can find professions of nuns with disabilities, like the two simpleminded girls at Bondeville or the nun of Obazine who was blind from birth.[34] Equally, for a laywoman to be so physically repulsive that she was unmarriageable was as disqualifying for her survival in the world as a real physical handicap. Beatrice became a nun at Amptenhausen against her will, so reports her hagiographer, because she was too homely and (perhaps more important) too poor to attract a husband.[35] Sometimes parents went about getting a daughter accepted into a nunnery with an anxiety that suggests the girl may have had some disqualifying problem. One knight planned his donation of dowry only "after the reception of the said Philippa, my daughter"

32. Carré, "Ste. Marguerite de la Presle," 5(1893): 42–43, no. 34, 1247. See also p. 28, no. 12, 1247, which makes the connection between Havise and her brother.

33. Pierre Riché, "L'enfant dans la société monastique au XIIe siècle," in *Pierre Abélard—Pierre le Vénérable: Les courants philosophiques, littéraires et artistiques en Occident au milieu du XIIe siècle*, Colloque International de Cluny, 1972, 546 (Paris: Editions du Centre National de la Recherche Scientifique, 1975), pp. 692–93.

34. ER, P. 395; *Vie de Saint Etienne d'Obazine*, ed. and trans. Michel Aubrun (Clermont-Ferrand: Institut d'Etudes de Massif Central, 1970), p. 166.

35. Parisse, *Nonnes au Moyen Age*, p. 237.

perhaps because he was unsure the convent would actually take her.[36] But whatever the machinations on the part of families and nunneries, the cloister was a respectable alternative for the damaged members of medieval society, both female and male.[37]

The oblation of a member also served family strategies when it had become imperative to heal a breach between the kinship and the cloister. Conflict over a tithe had become intense in the early thirteenth century between the nuns of Bourbourg and a knight, Walter of Rubrouck.[38] A settlement was finally negotiated in which the tithe was returned to the abbey and the nuns agreed to accept the knight's daughter into their midst. They stipulated that she would have to come in secular clothing until they had a vacancy, but then they would take her as a novice. Reaching a settlement depended on both sides' giving in: Walter handed over the purloined tithe, and the nuns graciously responded by taking his child as a boarder, preliminary to installing her as a novice.

Parents "weighed down by a throng of sons and daughters" looked to the monastery as a solution to the problem of feeding all their progeny, according to the thirteenth-century writer, Jacques de Vitry.[39] Giving a child to the religious life could relieve a family of some of its financial worries. One investigation found that families who offered oblates usually had three to nine children.[40] Since daughters were often not mentioned in the charters, the named sons may show us fewer than half the offspring of large families. Many children stressed a family's resources, and the cloister helped relieve the burden of superfluous offspring. Scholars generally assume that parents placed their little daughters in nunneries because it was

36. Paris, BN, MS. lat. 10998, fols. 23 v–24 r.

37. ER, pp. 436, 647. The monks of Valmont took in a simpleminded monk in 1261, and six years later they included two other handicapped men among their numbers.

38. *Cartulaire de l'abbaye de Notre-Dame de Bourbourg*, ed. Ignace de Coussemaker 3 vols. (Lille: V. Ducoulombier, 1882–91), 1:107–8, no. 109, 1215. Another interesting example of oblation to settle a conflict is in *Cartulaire de Notre-Dame de Saintes*, p. 55, no. 54, 1079–99.

39. Jacques de Vitry, "Quatre sermons *ad religiosas* de Jacques de Vitry," ed. Jean Longère, in *Les religieuses en France au XIIIe siècle*, ed. Michel Parisse (Nancy: Presses Universitaires de Nancy, 1985), p. 254. An interesting conclusion of a study of late medieval wills in the Lyonnaise is that 76 percent of the daughters fated for the monastic life came from families with five or more children: M.-T. Lorcin, "Retraites des veuves et filles au couvent: Quelques aspects de la condition féminine à la fin du Moyen Age," in *Annales de démographie historique*, ed. L. Henry (Paris: Librairie de la Nouvelle Faculté, 1975), p. 199.

40. Colette Blanc, "Les pratiques de piété des laïcs dans les pays du Bas-Rhône aux XIe et XIIe siècles," *Annales du Midi* 72(1960): 144.

cheaper to endow the girls' entry into the religious life than into the married state.[41] An absolute confirmation or refutation of this explanation is not possible, since most dowries were composed of property whose relative values cannot be compared with any exactitude. However, a small but significant number of cases involved only money; from these we can indeed conclude that girls' monastic dowries generally took less out of their parent's pockets than did their marriage portions. For example, in Poitiers in the first half of the thirteenth century, 20 pounds was considered a reasonable amount for a father to put aside for his daughter's marriage portion.[42] In contrast, a girl's monastic dowry in northern France during the central Middle Ages stayed quite constant and extremely modest, averaging 2.6 pounds of annual income.[43] At those rates, it would take over seven years for the annual monastic dowry income to equal the single marital payment—long enough so that the nun might have died and the income been transferred to support another girl. Such a low sum reflects the contemporary estimate that nuns could get by on very little, and indeed that 1 pound a year should cover a nun's clothing, although in some cases dowries did not yield even this modest annual sum.[44]

41. See, for example, Shahar, *Fourth Estate*, p. 39, who is voicing the commonly held assumption. However, Bouchard, *Sword, Miter, and Cloister*, p. 59, argues against this economic motivation lying behind child oblation, insisting rather on the importance of religious conviction as the force encouraging parents to dedicate children to the monastic life.

42. Poitiers, BM, la Trinité, MS. 27, p. 145 and p. 157, record two marriage portions of twenty pounds each. However, since these are lump payments, it is difficult to compare then with annual income.

43. All twelfth-and thirteenth-century monastic dowries for women entering the more than two dozen convents used for this study were tabulated. Nineteen of these were annual rents in coin alone (not being made up in part or in toto of property, their value can be compared). The average of these nineteen is 2.89 pounds, and the mean is 2 pounds. Study of women's dowries in the Midi yields the same conclusions: Marthe Moreau, "Les moniales du diocèse de Maguelone au XIIIe siècle," in *La femme dans la vie religieuse du Languedoc (XIIIe–XIVe s.)*, Cahiers de Fanjeaux 23 (Toulouse: Privat, 1988), p. 253. Dowries to La Celle in the Midi stayed rather constant at about 100 florins: Paulette L'Hermite-Leclercq, *Le monachisme féminin dans la société de son temps: Le monastère de La Celle (XIe–début du XVIe siècle)* (Paris: Editions Cujas, 1989), pp. 213, 219.

44. *Cartulaire de l'abbaye royale du Lieu-Notre-Dame-lès-Romorantin de l'ordre de Cîteaux publié d'après l'original avec introductions, notes et appendices*, ed. Ernest Plat (Romorantin, 1892), p. 41, no. 49, 1261. A brother endows the convent with 20 shillings "for the dressing of his sister, Petronilla, in that time in which she will receive the monastic habit from all the necessary clothes of a nun." Another charter

From early in its history the church had forbidden simony, the sale of religious offices, since these were intended to be filled by those inspired with the holy spirit rather than falling to the highest bidder. During the twelfth and thirteenth centuries, the entry dowry for monastics came to be viewed as simoniacal and thus fell under official censure.[45] By 1130 dowries had been declared criminal by the canonists; the monastic orders and the papacy joined the attack on the practice by 1170, and in 1215 Fourth Lateran Council legislated against the crime of simony in Canon 64, which was aimed specifically at religious women's dowries. In response to the authorities' criticism, men's monastic institutions gradually dropped the practice of accepting entry gifts; for instance, the last such endowment received by the male Benedictine house of Holy Trinity in Vendôme was in 1218.[46] This was not the case for women's houses, for which the entry gift stayed a pragmatic—if not an official—requirement. Indeed, it was such common practice that it seemed particularly noteworthy and holy when Vitalis of Mortain accepted a female novice without a dowry.[47] Poverty-stricken women's houses may have been loath to forgo badly needed dowries, but families also felt a strong compulsion to continue the practice of endowing their daughters and thereby assuring them a dignified life.

Little effort was made to disguise the practice. When Landry of Orbec gave a parish tithe to the convent of Saint-Saens in the twelfth century, he baldly recorded that "I made this gift freely and without contest to them . . . when I made my daughter, Eufemia, a nun in that house." [48] Well after the legislation of Fourth Lateran the practice of female monastic dowries still continued. In 1245 a father

---

specifies that it costs 1.5 pounds to pay for a religious woman's habit. See no. 146, p. 97, 1268. For a king's granddaughter 3 pounds was enough for clothes out of a total dowry of only 10 pounds. Vauzelles, *Histoire de la Magdeleine-lez-Orléans*, p. 218, no. 15, ca. 1183. English nuns fared about the same; the annual dowry in the twelfth century was 2 pounds. Elkins *Holy Women of Twelfth-Century England*, pp. 65 and 188, n. 12.

45. See Joseph H. Lynch, *Simoniacal Entry into Religious Life from 1000 to 1260: A Social, Economic and Legal Study* (Columbus: Ohio State University Press, 1976), who chronicles the development of the canonical attitudes.

46. *Cartulaire de la Trinité de Vendôme*, 3:48, no. 663, 1218.

47. R. I. Moore, *The Origins of European Dissent* (Oxford: Basil Blackwell, 1985), p. 90.

48. Rouen, BD, Saint-Saens, 56 H, carton no. 1. Although undated, this charter is in a twelfth-century hand.

directed annual rents of forty solidi to the convent of Lieu-Notre-Dame-lès-Romorantin "to pay for her clothing as long as his said daughter shall live in religion."[49] But it was not just secular people who ignored church rulings. Reginald, bishop of Chartres, recorded the profession of a girl to the convent of Port-Royal in 1218, specifying her dowry without any apology or defense.[50] Sometimes, particularly in the later period, the motive of the donor was thinly disguised by asserting that the gift went to alleviate monastic poverty: so that "my daughter, Joanna, will be received as a sister and nun of their monastery, on account of their poverty."[51] Probably no one was fooled by this rhetoric.

Although families might cajole a monastery into accepting one of their handicapped members, might use oblation as a token of the resolution of a long and often acrimonious conflict, and might endow a daughter despite ecclesiastical censure, at the heart of secular strategies for sending members into monasteries was a profound belief in the spiritual efficacy of monastic suffrages.[52] The child oblate—the gift from a family of one of its own—helped assure the giver of God's favor both as a response to the generous act of giving and in answer to the continual monastic prayers that would ensure. A father giving his little daughter to the Abbey of Saint-Georges "dedicated that nun for the salvation of his soul."[53] Older oblates also enhanced their relatives' spiritual status. The foundation by Alan, the count of Brittany, of a wealthy nunnery in Rennes around the beginning of the third decade of the eleventh century was intended for his sister, Adele, who became its first abbess. The foundation document reveals how the foundation of the nunnery and the oblation of Adele benefited her brother. First the biblical verse warning not to lay up treasure in heaven is cited; then the charter continues: "I offered to God my sister, the most precious treasure I possess under the sun, and moreover I dedicated her according to her spiritual desire to perpetual virginity."[54] Alan, his mother, Havise, and

49. *Cartulaire du Lieu-Notre-Dame-lès-Romorantin*, p. 90, no. 133, 1245.

50. Paris, BN, MS. lat. 10997, fols. 11r–v.

51. *Cartulaire de Notre-Dame de Voisins*, p. 33, no. 32, 1248. Also see p. 67, no. 67, 1259.

52. This position is argued energetically by Bouchard, *Sword, Miter, and Cloister*, pp. 59–64. Bouchard completely rejects economic and demographic motivations and rigidly espouses the spiritual motivation. Religious concerns were of paramount importance to medieval people, but they were still only part—albeit the center—of a cluster of mixed motivations for entrance into the monastic life.

53. *Cartulaire de Saint-Georges de Rennes*, 9:251, no. 22, ca. 1040.

54. *Cartulaire de Saint-Georges de Rennes*, 9:218, no. 1, ca. 1028–30.

his brother, Odo, earned divine favor by parting with their treasure, while Adele took an even more important step on the path to salvation by entering the religious life.

The medieval family knew best—or thought it did—what was good for its members, so that any modern desire to discern individual choice in a monastic profession is probably anachronistic. It would be just as misguided to assume that once a woman was veiled she became totally independent on her family. Far from it. In fact relatives made all sorts of demands on monastics. A nun might be called out of her convent to nurse a sick relation or to make periodic visits home when family sentiment or need demanded.[55]

Both female and male monastics used whatever means of suasion they had to support and advance the careers of family members. The abbot of Mont Saint-Michel was censured for dowering his nieces and educating his nephew with abbey money. The boy—so reported the outraged community—had received a magnificent copy of a collection of canon law.[56] The prioress of Bondeville and her subprioress both installed their grandnieces in the priory to live with them at the expense of the institution.[57] Superiors not only used monastery resources to maintain kin but also indulged in blatant nepotism. Yet some appointments of relatives must have seemed so advantageous for the institution that they raised no hackles, as in the nun Hilary's appointment of her brother as custodian of her abbey's salt works.[58] Perhaps in such cases disapproval existed but was only muttered behind closed doors, for when a powerful reforming archbishop like Eudes Rigaud rooted out blatant family pork barrel activities, he severely censured such finagling. The archbishop sternly reproved monastic superiors in thirty-one cases of nepotism, of which six cases involved siblings and thirteen nieces and nephews.

Motives for Women's Oblations

If we could reconstruct the thoughts of the individual women who entered nunneries as adults, probably each one had a slightly different idea of what she wanted, and probably most of them had mixed motivations. Ambivalence or a change of heart sometimes left a record of why a woman entered a house.

Eremburge of Plessys-Gassault had become a nun at the great Ab-

55. ER, p. 335, mentions a nun's going home to nurse a sick relative, and pp. 212, 383, 386, and 680 cite instances of monastics' visiting their families.
56. ER, p. 274.
57. ER, p. 237.
58. *Cartulaire de Notre-Dame de Saintes*, p. 162, no. 249.

bey of Maubuisson in Normandy in the third quarter of the thirteenth century.[59] She later made up her mind to leave the convent, however, arguing that she had been forced in and had entered because of fear of a man. The abbey responded that she had been of a sufficiently mature age to know what she was doing, whatever excuses she might later raise. Her plea that she had been too young to know her own mind eventually must have been accepted, for a compromise was effected by allowing Maubuisson to keep some of her dowry and letting her depart with the rest of her property. We cannot tell what frightened Eremburge, but surely a strong part of her motive for professing at the abbey was to flee a perceived danger.

Maybe Eremburge had been orphaned and left defenseless or was unwanted by her kinfolk, a frightening situation for a woman in the Middle Ages. Being widowed and thus vulnerable perhaps led Gila, after her husband died on crusade to Jerusalem, to present herself with her two daughters "desiring to be made nuns" ("fieri moniales desiderans").[60] Gila chose this life because it appealed to her or because she had no other options. In either case she alone made the choice (desiderans is singular), and her daughters went along willynilly to become child oblates. We cannot tell whether any of the three freely opted for the monastic life, but for all of them the convent served as a refuge from what could be a harsh life.

Although life in a medieval monastery was not luxurious, the urge for upward social mobility made monastic institutions seem particularly attractive and enhanced the appeal of professing in a house where one would associate with daughters, wives, and widows of the nobility.[61] This was particularly true for women from the lower knightly and bourgeois families, which in the central Middle Ages were aspiring to better things.

In one of his sermons, Jacques de Vitry scolds those false nuns who entered convents to lead the easy life: to have food to eat and a more delicate life-style than had they stayed in the world.[62] Escape

59. Adolphe Dutilleux and J. Depoin, L'abbaye de Maubuisson (Notre-Dame-la-Royale): Histoire et cartulaire publiés d'après des documents entièrement inédits, 4 vols. (Pontoise: A. Paris, 1882–85), 1:9; the text is translated from a copy made by Dom Estiennot.

60. Cartulaire de Notre-Dame de Voisins, p. 123, no. 116, 1220.

61. L'Hermite-Leclercq, Monachisme féminin, p. 221, posits this motivation for the nuns of La Celle.

62. Jacques de Vitry, Sermons, p. 254. Those he addressed may have been from families of limited means, whose members were increasingly recruited in the thirteenth century.

from an economically perilous situation, usually after being orphaned or widowed, may have motivated some women; others may
have seen conventual life as a comfortable existence. But since the
widowed medieval woman often retained some control over property (and certainly more than women would later in early modern
Europe), the higher number of widows who entered convents may
reflect the desire to escape an unwanted second marriage as much
as the need for economic security. The sermon has a polemical intention to attack professions made for secular reasons, yet Jacques
de Vitry had conflated two distinct and separate situations—wanting to know that one's next meal is assured, and wanting to live a
pampered life. He criticizes both as evidence of false vocations. His
lumping together choices made out of desperation and out of self-
indulgence shows how complicated it is to reconstruct motivations—even for one's contemporaries.

One attraction for many women considering profession in a nunnery was the possibility of living with family members despite theoretically giving up all worldly ties. A charter from the second half of
the eleventh century records a gift from Hersende to the powerful
Abbey of Saint-Jean d'Angély. Hersende gives the abbey a substantial
alod (land held freely and not of a superior) with the provision that
she may later become a nun and stay in Vayres with her son who is
a monk there.[63] The donation gave Hersende leverage to spend her
old age in her son's company if she should so desire. What is particularly interesting is that Saint-Jean d'Angély was a house of Benedictine monks, who in this case were ready to accept a nun to live
in an informal relationship at their abbey. Sometimes it worked a
little differently, as when Ludolf, a monk, took his sister with him
to live in the male Abbey of Saint-Laurent, where she then took the
veil.[64] These ad hoc arrangements actually occurred rather frequently in the Middle Ages, when both men's and women's monastic institutions often allowed what was probably a small number
of religious of the opposite sex to live in some sort of affiliation,
most often as *ad succurrendum* nuns and monks—those who took
the habit in old age or illness.[65] In addition, it was common practice

63. La Rochelle, BM, Saint-Jean d'Angély, MS. 128, fol. 38. I date this charter to
1068–86.
64. Huyghebaert, "Femmes laïques dans la vie religieuse," p. 369.
65. Johnson, *Prayer, Patronage, and Power*, pp. 41–43. Although convents often
routinely numbered lay brothers and priests among their personnel, sometimes they
also had monks living with them as other than staff members: *Cartulaire de Saint-*

for houses of regular Augustinian canons to have in residence several *sorores conversae,* lay sisters.[66] Many variations therefore occurred on the theme of isolation of one sex within the cloister.

Medieval people were wont to plan ahead for the possibility that they might eventually want to profess at a monastery. In the early twelfth century, the founder of the convent of Clairruissel, Hugh de Gournay, gave mill rights to the nuns so that Agnes, his wife, could later become a nun there if she chose.[67] One hundred years later a Breton woman, Joanna of Pan, donated an annual grain rent to Saint-Georges in Rennes, thereby entering into the abbey's confraternity and gaining the option of later becoming one of their nuns during her life or on her deathbed.[68] In these and the many other such cases, the person (or her family) ensured an appropriate retirement.[69]

We do not know how people like Agnes of Gournay and Joanna of Pan felt about these arrangements for their old age, but they probably experienced a range of emotions when choosing an old-age oblation. The analogous modern experiences might range from that of an elderly person who feels relegated to a nursing home with no say in the matter to that of the older individual who enjoys picking out housing in a comfortably managed retirement community. But we can say with assurance that nunneries existed as the one institutional retirement option available for woman of substance and social standing.

But the medieval nunnery offered more than just a fallback position for orphans, widows, and the elderly. The conventual life seems to have exercised a positive attraction for women, some of whom pressured relatives to found houses for them, while others just took

Sulpice-la-Forêt, p. 138, no. 60. Elkins, *Holy Women of Twelfth-Century England,* pp. xvii, 55, 87, notes women's houses that included men also.

66. The canons of Corneville, Eu, Mont-Deux-Amants, Ouville, Saint-Laurent, Sausseuse, and Beaulieu all had anywhere from one to five *conversae* in residence at one time: see ER, pp. 10, 516, 586, 492, 470, 444, 414. Occasionally a monastery of Benedictine monks also had lay sisters among its personnel: for instance, Saint-Martin in Pontoise had two *conversae* in 1262 (p. 508).

67. Rouen, BD, 53 H, MS. Inventaire de Clairruissel, pp. 3–4. This is a cartulary made in 1560.

68. *Cartulaire de Saint-Georges de Rennes,* 10:23–24, no. 16, 1208: "Johannam in sororem recepimus et, cum ipsa voluerit, sive ad vitam, sive ad mortem, habitum religionis accipere poterit."

69. This practice also existed in English convents: Elkins, *Holy Women of Twelfth-Century England,* p. 68.

the bit between their teeth and began to live as monastics informally until they could prevail on someone to regularize their community.[70] But most adult women who exercised their choice of a religious vocation in the central Middle Ages entered an established nunnery, as did Agatha of Le Mans. Agatha and her sister Margaret were the only children and heirs of their father, a rich burgher in Le Mans.[71] Margaret married during her father's lifetime and received her share of the family resources when her father gave her as her dowry her mother's marriage portion. This marriage endowment constituted the customary share that Margaret could expect to receive. Agatha, in contrast, did not decide to marry, though her inheritance from her father had made her a rich and desirable bride. Instead, she entered the Cistercian Abbey of Clairets and gave her considerable wealth as dowry to the house, acting on her own. The nuns followed customary practice for solidifying a donation by obtaining consent from the interested parties, her sister and brother-in-law, "for the donation made by Agatha." This should have closed the issue. But the value of the property changing hands and the lack of older male relatives to back up the gift brought out a pack of twenty hungry claimants; these twenty challenged Agatha's right to alienate the property and had to be dealt with by the abbey.[72] Agatha seems to have chosen the cloister. No one "gave" her to the abbey, and no one donated the dowry for her. What motivated her to enter Clairets lies outside the charters; we do not know why she became a nun, but we can see that she acted independently, apparently without coercion of family pressure or financial need.

Some women entered monasteries while still married, and on occasion wife and husband decided to enter the monastic life jointly.[73] Canon law required that both spouses agree to abandon the marriage

70. Skinner, "Benedictine Life for Women," p. 89, describes women who pressured families into establishing nunneries. Marie-Théodore Renouard de Bussière, *Histoire des religieuses dominicaines du couvent de Sainte-Marguerite et Sainte-Agnès à Strasbourg* (Strasbourg: L.-F. Leroux, 1860), pp. 5–11, describes a group of women who spontaneously founded their own nunnery.

71. *Abbaye royale de Notre-Dame des Clairets: Histoire et cartulaire par le vicomte de Souancé 1201–1790*, ed. Joseph-H.-H.-J. Guillier de Souancé (Vannes: Lafolye, 1894), pp. 89–90, no. 18, 1221.

72. Paris, BN, MS. lat. 9220, fol. 76.

73. *Cartulaire de Notre-Dame de Saintes*, pp. 149–51, no. 229, 1065, records a couple who decide that she will become a nun at Saintes and he a monk at Maillezais. *Cartulaire de Saint-Georges de Rennes*, 9:269, no. 41, ca. 1068, records another example.

vow when one or both desired a life of celibacy, but in practice this may not have always been rigorously observed. The charters that record entry gifts and oblations are more laconic on the subject of consent, but they do make it clear that women with living husbands sometimes took the veil. Stephanie, "the wife of Gerald" (not the widow), gave herself to the almshouse of Saint-Jean in Angers into a life of service to the poor, as did also Essileia, the wife of Pepin.[74] The wording of some charters suggests that married women could function quite independently, choosing to leave marriage for their own reasons. A married woman, Mayheude, "first lived as a secular woman, then having been visited by the Holy Spirit and wishing to provide for the salvation of her soul, received the monastic habit" in the Abbey of Notre-Dame in Saintes.[75] She gave the abbey a house in La Rochelle as her monastic dowry, to which gift her husband Peter dutifully gave his consent. Did leaving the married state to enter a convent necessarily mean a woman was making a positive choice to pursue a religious vocation? Mayheude acted autonomously, although her choice to enter Notre-Dame could have been motivated by a need to escape an intolerable marriage as well as to fulfill a spiritual vocation. Further, it is possible that in some of these cases women's choices were not free if husbands were actually rejecting unwanted wives—those who were barren or no longer desirable—and forcing them into nunneries. This, however, is unlikely, since the canonists forbade a husband to remarry while his wife lived as a nun, so to rid himself of a wife this way did not free a man to remarry lawfully.

After her widowhood, Guibert of Nogent's mother strenuously and successfully resisted the efforts of her husband's relatives to arrange a second marriage for her.[76] But simply escaping a marriage was not enough, and a number of years later she finally achieved her heart's content when "she resolved to retire to the monastery of Fly." [77] Fly was a male monastery, but a flexible solution was achieved by building a small house for her next to the church. Here she lived a life of devotion as a laywoman. "A few years before her

74. *Cartulaire de Saint-Jean d'Angers*, p. xi, no. 10, 1185–88.

75. *Cartulaire de Notre-Dame de Saintes*, p. 64, no. 67, ca. 1163. *Cartulaire de Saint-Georges de Rennes*, 10:40, no. 30, 1234, recounts how Adele entered the abbey by giving herself and her goods, rather than being given by her brother, Clement.

76. Guibert of Nogent, *Self and Society in Medieval France: The Memoirs of Abbot Guibert of Nogent (1064?–c. 1125)*, ed. John Benton (New York: Harper, 1970), p. 71.

77. Guibert of Nogent, *Memoirs*, p. 74.

death, she conceived a strong desire to take the sacred veil." Her son argued that widows should not become professed nuns, and Abbot Anselm of Bec joined in the effort to dissuade her. But Guibert's mother's desire for the cloistered life was more powerful than even the arguments of her son and a saint: "So she prevailed, and during the ceremony, when she gave satisfactory reasons for this act in the presence of Jean, the abbot of that place, whom she had raised as a boy, in the end she proved that in this matter she had been guided by God."[78]

To the question of what women's motives were for choosing the cloister, one scholar responds: "We know that some women took the veil not because they felt a vocation for the religious life, but because the convent afforded them relative freedom from male domination, a better schooling than they could obtain in the world, and, if they became abbesses or held other convent functions, they might wield broad authority and exercise their talents as leaders and organizers."[79] Another scholar argues for the attractive environment a medieval woman experienced in monasticism, which was a "positive road to recapturing her individual reality and self-sufficiency."[80] We can be sure that women had a variety of needs that the medieval nunnery satisfied in different ways, and though both of these descriptions may be true, they leave out the real spiritual vocation that drew women like Guibert's mother to embrace monasticism actively. In addition, the positive role of the family that enhanced the cloistered life also needs to be factored in. There is a very high probability that professed women found themselves inside the cloister because of their families' wishes and perhaps their own desire to be with other relatives or at least in a nunnery patronized by their kinfolk.

The bonds that tied individuals to their families were not slipped when a person entered the monastic life. Far from it. The choice of monastery, the entrance gift, reasons for professing, and both support for and strains on that profession were determined by family considerations. Although relatives could make unfair demands on a monastery, they could also buttress it with their financial gifts and emotional support, and both self-interested and altruistic motives galvanized this lay backing. Since family networks did not stay

78. Guibert of Nogent, *Memoirs*, pp. 133–34.
79. Shahar, *Fourth Estate*, p. 8.
80. Ida Magli, quoted by Bell, *Holy Anorexia*, p. 55.

neatly in the secular world but dangled their complications and contributions over cloister walls, the interests of the local community
became thoroughly enmeshed with those of the monastery.

THE SURROUNDING LAY SOCIETY
Foundations

Why found a house for religious women? If we could solicit an un-
guarded response from a medieval patron, it might be: "for myself,
for my family's needs, and as a home for my female relatives." From
this a modern interpreter of medieval monastic institutions for
women might justifiably conclude that they were created to meet
the founders' entirely self-interested personal or family needs. In
some cases such a conclusion may be at least partially correct.
Agnes of Burgundy's foundation of Notre-Dame in Saintes became
her place for pious retirement as an old lady; the count of Brittany
gave his foundation of Saint-Georges in Rennes into the hands of his
sister as its first abbess. Without a doubt, personal and family interest colored the creation of these two institutions. Yet the medieval
records attest almost universally to the supporters' pious intentions
for every charitable act. One might then be tempted to see a deline-
ation between self-interested and altruistic motivations, but this
would be a false dichotomy, since no neat lines separated personal
and spiritual needs.

If immediate self-interest motivated founders, then a high proportion of women's houses would have had female founders, which indeed does seem to have been the case. Of the twenty-six nunneries
that form the core of this study, eight were founded by women and
two of the joint foundations were actually by women. Thus ten
of the twenty-six, or 38 percent, were the work of women. In contrast, a parallel sample of male monasteries from the same northern
French region had only 15 percent of its houses founded by
women.[81] Such a comparison suggests that powerful ladies felt a
need for and identified with houses for religious women. But this is
far from a definitive contrast. An inclusive quantitative study of
monastic houses for nuns and monks is needed to show to what

81. Twenty-six male houses from the same areas, founded in the same period and
representing the same range of orders, were founded by twenty men, two women, and
four couples, in two of which the wives may have been the moving force in the foundations. Huyghebaert points out that in Flanders and Artois women were involved at
the origins of almost *all* eleventh- and twelfth-century monasteries, whether for
women or men: "Les femmes laïques dans la vie religieuse," p. 380.

extent this small sample would hold true in the larger context, particularly in light of Elkins's findings that in twelfth-century England female founders and their relatives seldom joined their institutions.[82]

Women patrons seem to have felt a kinship with women religious. Countess Eleanor of Vermandois supported every women's house in her region and several outside her immediate orbit, as well as founding two nunneries.[83] Yet only 20 percent of her considerable largesse went to women's houses. Eleanor's monastic patronage suggests that she—possibly like other female contemporaries—identified with religious women but had many fewer nunneries than male monasteries in the area to patronize; in fact, she had to found two convents to satisfy her urge to endow nuns. Countess Eleanor's dilemma was not unique; Constance Berman charts a similar situation in the patronage of southern French monasteries in the central Middle Ages, where she sees women supporting male houses because there were only a few nunneries in the region. Also, the weakness of these convents failed to command much lay respect or episcopal support. There were also a number of barriers that impeded women from founding more convents to redress the imbalance: "The relative weakness of women's foundations is attributable not to lack of interest but primarily to economic and social forces making it more difficult for women to amass the capital for new houses and more difficult for women to alienate land and capital of any kind where they chose."[84]

Male relatives could and did found convents for their female kinfolk, although sometimes this happened almost by default, as in the case of the re-creation of Montivilliers. In the violent days of the late ninth century, Vikings had destroyed Sainte-Marie, a Merovingian foundation for women in Normandy. When Duke Richard of Normandy rebuilt it a century later, it was almost incidental to his efforts to set up his own large, rich, prestigious community of

---

82. Elkins, *Holy Women of Twelfth-Century England*, pp. 69–70.

83. Louis Duval-Arnould, "Les aumônes d'Aliénor, dernière comtesse de Vermandois et dame de Valois," *Revue Mabillon* 60(1984): 414.

84. Constance Berman, "Women as Donors and Patrons to Southern French Monasteries in the Twelfth and Thirteenth Centuries," in *Worlds of Medieval Women: Creativity, Influence, Imagination*, ed. Constance H. Berman, Charles W. Connell, and Judith Rothschild (Morgantown: West Virginia University Press, 1985), p. 54. An analysis of the differences in social, legal, and customary practices between northern and southern France may prove an important piece of research for casting new light on the social construction of gender in the Middle Ages.

monks in the very best situation he could find.[85] But since the most desirable location in the region was Fécamp, which was already occupied by nuns, he had to play musical monastics by removing the nuns from their convent at Fécamp, putting the monks in the ladies' place, and finally resettling the nuns in the rebuilt Sainte-Marie/ Montivilliers. There must have been some very hard feelings among the women, but no evidence survives since it certainly behooved them to be discreet and act grateful that they were not being disbanded out of hand.

In the next generation, Richard's family continued to support and encourage the rebuilt nunnery at Montivilliers. His daughter-in-law, Judith, wife of Duke Richard II, took an interest in the convent and endowed it substantially, and his daughter, Beatrice, who had professed at Montivilliers, became the moving force in getting her nephew, Duke Robert the Magnificent, to make the convent independent of Fécamp. Beatrice became the first abbess of the reconstituted abbey, to be followed later into the convent by two relatives: a cousin Clare and Matilda, the bastard daughter of Henry I, who would also exercise abbatial power.[86] Robert the Magnificent and later William the Conqueror both gave the convent important privileges, acknowledging their responsibilities to a nunnery that housed female relatives.[87] A convent might originally be built as a disposal site for religious women, but once there was a family connection and female relatives found a warm reception in the cloister, men in the family tended to support the institution with growing enthusiasm.

It may well be that a number of convents generally believed to have been established by men were actually instituted by women, usually the wives of the purported founders. The erroneous designation of a man as founder comes from the tendency of medieval writers to expect a man to be the moving spirit in any important undertaking. Even if a woman conceived the idea of founding a nun-

85. Edwin Hall and James Ross Sweeney, "An Unpublished Privilege of Innocent III in Favor of Montivilliers: New Documentation for a Great Norman Nunnery," *Speculum* 49(1974): 664. Hall and Sweeney summarize the chronology of this house and the scholarship on its famous "exemption," which I deal with in chapter 3.

86. Hall and Sweeney, "Unpublished Privilege," p. 662.

87. See Paul Le Cacheux, *L'exemption de Montivilliers* (Caen: 1929); Jean-François Lemarignier, *Etude sur les privilèges d'exemption et de juridiction ecclésiastique des abbayes normandes depuis les origines jusqu'en 1140* (Paris: A. Picard, 1937); Georges Priem, "L'abbaye royale de Montivilliers," in *La Normandie bénédictine au temps de Guillaume le Conquérant (XIe siècle)* (Lille: Facultés Catholiques de Lille, 1967); and Hall and Sweeney for the support of Robert and William for Montivilliers.

nery, supplied much of the endowment, and carried forward the plans, male monastic writers would be apt to name her husband as central to the process. In addition, the documents are often vague, contradictory, or even silent on the subject of who founded a house. The Abbey of Notre-Dame des Clairets has one of these snarled tales of foundation. Matilda and Geoffrey, the countess and count of Perche, are named in the foundation charter as jointly responsible for the institution of the nuns. But though Geoffrey had originally proposed building the nunnery, he died before it could be begun. After his death Matilda carried the enterprise forward.[88] Her association with the project was so intimate that Pope Innocent III recognized her as the sole founder of the convent in his confirmation of January 1204.[89] What had happened was that Geoffrey had died before he could fulfill his vow to take the cross, and Matilda then took over the task of instituting Clairets to expiate Geoffrey's unfulfilled vow.[90] But her untimely death left the final responsibility to Thomas, their son.[91] All in all, we seem to have three possible candidates for founder. Nevertheless, in this murky situation, the connection of this comital family to the institution of an abbey is clear. Whoever it was who should most appropriately receive the honor of being founder, the family of the counts of Perche followed through on the initial idea. Family solidarity rather than individual initiative, in this instance as in so much of the monastic patronage of the Middle Ages, ordered events.

The hesitancy of some sources to name Matilda as sole founder results from medieval sensibilities, which assumed in theory (if not always in fact) that married women could not act independently. Once widowed, it seemed perfectly appropriate for the countess to carry on, but even if the desire to found a convent had originated with her during her husband's lifetime, it is unlikely that contemporaries would have recorded events in that light. This attitude reflected the realities of married women's legal submersion in their husbands' personae.[92] When a woman was widowed, she acquired a new autonomy; widows account for almost all the monastic foun-

---

88. Paris, BN, MS. lat. 17140, p. 1, contains the foundation charter of July 1204. The same scenario is contained in Paris, BN, MS. lat. 9220, fol. 70, in a charter dated 1213.

89. *Abbaye des Clairets*, p. 68, no. 3.

90. *Abbaye des Clairets*, p. 81, no. 13, 1218.

91. *Abbaye des Clairets*, p. 79, no. 12, 1218.

92. Among the scholars who examine the subjugation of medieval women to their husbands in law and in custom, see Régine Pernoud, *La femme au temps des cathé-*

dations by women acting as independent agents. Thus Countess Adele inaugurated Holy Trinity in Poitiers, Countess Herlesende created La Pommeraye, Countess Blanche started La Barre, Queen Blanche of Castille founded Maubuisson, Countess Isabelle of Chartres began Romorandin—all after they were widowed.[93]

The founding of the famous Abbey of Port-Royal is often attributed to Matthew of Montmorency, the lord of Marly, and dated to just before his departure on crusade in 1202.[94] All Matthew actually did, however, was to entrust to his wife Matilda and the bishop of Paris some income with which to make a spiritual investment. It was they who founded the convent, as William of Ferté-Arnaud noted two years later when he donated a fief to the bishop and Matilda "to institute there religious women to serve God."[95] Further, Matilda must have firmly planted a commitment to the nuns in her children, for the family became their devoted benefactors, with the children's generation making seventeen donations, the grandchildren's generation giving four gifts, and the great-grandchildren twice endowing the nunnery.

If immediate self-interest and family strategies motivated some founders, what can we make of the foundation in April 1226 of the Abbey of Pont-aux-Dames near Meaux by Hugh of Châtillon? In the year of the foundation, Hugh was heir to the county of Saint Pol, and though he eventually married three times, in 1226 he seems to have been between his first and second wives.[96] His older brother, Guy of

---

drales (Paris: Stock, 1980), part 2, chap. 6; Duby, *Knight, the Lady and the Priest*, pp. 215–16; Judith M. Bennett, *Women in the Medieval English Countryside: Gender and Household in Brigstock before the Plague* (New York: Oxford, 1987), p. 140.

93. The new status of widows and their exercise of economic power is currently receiving considerable attention. Widowhood gave landed women greater control over property than their married sisters: see Gold, *Lady and the Virgin*, p. 130. Widowhood gave working women new impetus too. See the excellent essays in Hanawalt, *Women and Work in Preindustrial Europe*.

94. *Cartulaire de Porrois*, p. 1 of the introduction. But the actual charter reads: "Ego Matheus de Montemorenciaco, dominus Marliaci, notum fieri volo tam presentibus quam futuris me ratum habere quidquid Dominus Odo, pariensis episcopus et Matildis, uxor mea, facient de quindecim libris quas debebam assignare in redditibis meis de Mellento, antequam iter suscepti peregrinationis aggrederer, sed eas assignare non potui, multis et magnis negociis impeditus. Quod ut firmum inconcussumque permaneat dignum duxi sigilli mei in munimine roborandum." Paris, BN, MS. lat. 10997, fols, 20v–21r.

95. Paris, BN, MS. lat. 10997, fol. 106v.

96. See *L'abbaye du Pont-aux-Dames (ordre de Cîteaux) assise en la paroisse de Couilly*, ed. Claude H. Berthault (Meaux: Librairie le Blondel, 1878). Berthault repro-

Châtillon, was count at that time and supported the foundation by contributing the wherewithal to institute two chaplaincies at the abbey.[97]

Hugh records that: "I founded an abbey of Cistercian nuns in the almshouse on the bridge of Couilly."[98] Several interpretations of this phrase are possible. The building in which the poor and the ill had previously been housed might have fallen into disrepair and been refurbished and reinstituted by Hugh; or an ongoing charitable concern was being turned over to a group of Cistercian nuns imported to transform the almshouse into an abbey; or a group of women, already installed at the almshouse and informally caring for the local charity cases, wanted to take on institutional legitimacy by joining the Cistercians and receiving Hugh's financial support to make possible their upgrading. The third case is most likely, arguing from the silence of the charter, which neither mentions construction projects nor names a mother nunnery that was supplying a colony of nuns from outside the community (both common in charters recording such events). A few years later in 1239 Hugh moved the nuns to Ruea "for the well-being of that abbey," which reinforces the probability that initially he had transformed a modest almshouse into an abbey; then, because the space and location were suitable for an almshouse but not a convent, it became necessary to move the nuns to a more appropriate location.[99]

Although the wording of the foundation charter is very similar to that of others establishing large and wealthy abbeys, whatever Hugh was doing was on a much smaller scale. He gave the nuns two banal monopolies—for an oven and for river usage—and land that encompassed one hundred arpents (acres) of woods, eight arpents of meadow, and two hundred arpents of arable land. The Abbey of Pont-aux-Dames began its existence with this meager endowment.

When we try to discern the motivation behind this modest foundation, tangible self and family interests do not seem to figure, since Hugh as a man could not profess at the nunnery, nor does he seem to have had a wife or daughter to have benefited. Rather, Hugh's

---

duces some of the charters in toto and others in synopses. Copies were made in 1673 by Bazin: Paris, BN, MS. fr. 4669, fols. 35v–61r. Background is contained in Paris, BN, MS. Topographie de Champagne, XXIV, fols. 271–75.

97. Paris, BN, MS. fr. 4669, fol. 48r.

98. Paris, BN, MS. fr. 4669, fol. 35v: "Fundavi abbatiam quandam monialium de ordine Cisterciensis in domo Dei de ponte Colliaci."

99. Paris, BN, MS. fr. 4669, fols. 36v–37r.

immediate goals were to gain prestige and prayers, and he involved the surrounding community, his relatives, and his vassals in a sustained commitment to the nuns' growth and well-being. Almost all the subsequent donations were also modest, but they added up. Hugh made direct gifts of fishing, pasturage, and mill rights, of income from vineyards and rents, of more woods, a vineyard, and land in Crécy.[100] His older brother gave the abbey chaplaincies, his nephew gave a tithe, and his son and heir continued the family patronage with gifts of woods and rents after Hugh's death.[101]

Even more striking evidence of his patronage than his direct gifts to the abbey were his activities for its welfare, like his five-year pursuit on behalf of the nuns of the full tithe of Bouleurs.[102] Over the years the tithe had been divided and subdivided into six parts that had fallen to lay individuals and different monastic houses. Hugh's opening move was to encourage a couple to sell the abbey their part of the tithe; then he compensated the Abbey of Fontevrault and one of its dependents for another part, which was better than what happened to the canons of La Chapelle, whom he legally hornswoggled out of their partial interest in the tithe. Later his provost and the provost's wife, who held another part of the tithe in fief from Hugh, were induced to give their bit to the nuns; and finally the local chapter of the Hospitalers had to pass over its share to the bishop, who, Hugh piously asserted, could freely choose whatever institution he desired to be its recipient. To no one's surprise, I am sure, the bishop of Meaux awarded the tithe to the nuns. With such an advocate as Hugh, it is no wonder the nuns flourished.

In light of the lack of tangible benefits Hugh derived from the abbey, his assertion that the foundation was for his soul and the souls of his family and friends must be seriously entertained.[103] Hugh was not alone in committing resources and energies to a house for women without immediate benefit for female family members; this could also be the case for a woman founder. Countess

100. *Abbaye du Pont-aux-Dames*, pp. 5, 9, 18, nos. 9, 23, 61; pp. 4, 7, nos. 5, 16; pp. 9, 14, 24, nos. 25, 46, 80.

101. *Abbaye du Pont-aux-Dames*, pp. 4–5, 23–26, nos. 6, 76, 77, 83–85; p. 28, nos. 91–92.

102. *Abbaye du Pont-aux-Dames*, pp. 5–8, 11–13, nos. 10, 13, 14, 19, 34, 36, 37, 42, 43, spanning the years 1226–31.

103. Paris, BN, MS. fr. 4669, fol. 43v: "Ego dedi et concessi in puram elemosinam si me intestutum decedere contigerit ob remedium animae meae et parentum et amicorum meorum."

Isabelle of Chartres founded the Abbey of Lieu-Notre-Dame-lès-Romorantin in the early thirteenth century.[104] Isabelle's cousin was Queen Blanche of Castille, and as far as I can tell, none of this illustrious line ever took the veil at Romorantin.

Patronage

The patron's responsibility did not end once a nunnery was founded. It behooved all the people associated with it to see that the institution flourished. The greater the holdings and influence of a house, the more beautiful its buildings, the holier its inhabitants, the more reflected glory the patrons enjoyed. Medieval patrons "would have thought it a poor reward for their munificence if they had found marks of poverty in the buildings, dress and equipment of the monks" or nuns.[105]

Patronage followed family lines in several ways. Patrons tended to make donations and bequests to monasteries that housed their female and male kin. In 1227 Siger, a knight from Dompire, donated his share of a tithe to the convent of Salzinnes, where his daughter Elizabeth was the abbess.[106] This was not an entry dowry, since Elizabeth had been abbess since at least 1220.[107] It is not always so easy, however, to distinguish endowments from entry dowries: For instance, John Bobin's donation of annual rents to the nuns of Romorantin was to the religious women who already included among their number his sister Joanna and who were about to receive two other sisters, Philippa and Eremburge.[108] This gift comprised the dowries of the two younger girls, but they and the endowment went to a house in which John Bobin already had a professed relative.

Gifts to a monastery could be made specifically because a relative was professed there, as when Havise gave the nuns of Clairruissel forty shillings annual rent "for the sake of my mother, a nun at the aforementioned house."[109] Equally, a donation could be earmarked

104. See charter no. 1, in which the countess in 1247 recapitulates all her earlier gifts to the house, which she says she founded (fundavi): Cartulaire du Lieu-Notre-Dame-lès-Romorantin, p. 7.
105. R. W. Southern, The Making of the Middle Ages (New Haven: Yale University Press, 1953), p. 161.
106. Recueil des chartes et documents de l'abbaye du Val-Saint-Georges à Salzinnes (Namur) 1196/7–1300, ed. E. Brouette, Cîteaux-Commentarii cistercienses, Studia et documenta 1 (Achel: Abbaye Cistercienne, 1971), p. 32, no. 29, 1227.
107. Recueil du Val-Saint-Georges à Salzinnes, p. 22, no. 19, 1220.
108. Cartulaire du Lieu-Notre-Dame-lès Romorantin, p. 25, no. 27, 1262.
109. Rouen, BD, Clairruissel, 53 H, carton 1, no. 120.

for the cloistered woman by a relative. Lord Robert of Miliaco gave the abbey of the Paraclete six pounds annual tolls so that "our two daughters, namely A. and E., whom we made nuns at the Paraclete, will receive that money for their clothes as long as they live; after one dies, the one who survives will receive all the rents, and after the death of both, the rents revert to the church of the Paraclete without any counterclaims."[110] This pattern of direct endowments to professed people carried enormous ramifications for the regular life. The custom became normative during the thirteenth century, and its negative impact was substantial. I will discuss the practice in chapter 5.

Although monasteries could not function without endowments, the direct gifts from patrons were only part of what abbeys received from their lay benefactors. Monastic supporters spent a great deal of energy in indirect manipulation of others—particularly their relatives—to benefit their pet institutions. Walter of Sotteghem wrote to his first cousin, Roger of Sotteghem, asking that Roger kindly release land that rightfully belonged to Walter's side of the family.[111] The land in question had been given to Walter's mother by Roger's father as her part of the family inheritance. The lady then donated it to the nuns of Bourbourg and to her daughter Alice, who was the abbess, for the celebration of the donor's anniversary. Walter had a close tie to the convent through both his family's patronage and his sister's abbacy. He therefore used all his persuasive abilities to assist the abbey through diplomacy, in a medieval version of the modern fund-raising technique where individuals write letters of appeal to particular friends and relatives. It is harder to say no to your first cousin than to a stranger.

Indirect assistance for a nunnery also came from patrons who had no kin in the house but were related to a founder. Richard of Beaumont and his wife Matilda made donations to the Abbey of Romorandin at the instigation of his mother and its founder, Countess Isabelle of Chartres. The first gift was made "at the prayers of my dearest mother and lady, Isabelle, noble countess of Chartres." The

110. *Cartulaire de l'abbaye du Paraclet*, ed. Charles Lalore, vol. 2 of *Collection des principaux cartulaires du diocèse de Troyes* (Paris: Thorin, 1878), p. 139, no. 123, 1203: "Quod due filie nostre A. et E. scilicet, quas apud Paraclitum monachavimus, illas libras ad opus vestimentorum quandiu vixerint recipient; una vero mortua, que supervixerit integrum redditum recipiet; post mortem vero utriusque, ad ecclesiam Pracliti sine reclamacione redditus redibit."
111. *Cartulaire de Notre-Dame de Bourbourg*, 1:122, no. 130, 1233.

second responded to "the earnest request and prayer" of his mother, but the third was given directly to Isabelle by her son "to be conferred in alms wherever she wished."[112] The countess was operating like a modern backer for the opera or symphony, politely shaking down relatives and friends for the worthy cause in which she believed. Apparently Richard and Matilda were so badgered by Isabelle that eventually they said the equivalent of "Here it is, do whatever you want with it; just don't bother us any more."

Maneuvering members of the church hierarchy into bestowing rights and confirmations on monasteries was another way laypeople exercised indirect patronage. Women like Countess Clemence of Flanders seem to have been particularly adept at this game of politely pressuring prelates. Clemence cared deeply about the welfare of the convent of Notre-Dame in Bourbourg, a Benedictine house she had founded around the beginning of the twelfth century.[113] She made donations to the convent and assiduously marshaled episcopal and papal support. Pope Paschal II responded to her prayers to exempt the nunnery from episcopal oversight and then seven years later confirmed all its holdings.[114] One local prelate, Lambert, bishop of Tournai and Noyon, made a gift to the nuns "at the suggestion of Clemence, venerable countess of Flanders" and in response "to the petition of Lady Godildis, abbess of Bourbourg," with whom the countess had joined forces to achieve her objective.[115] Clemence's stock as an ecclesiastical lobbyist must have shot up when her brother was elevated to the throne of Saint Peter as Calixtus II. He confirmed all the abbey's possessions in one bull, and a few years later, in a telling example of how papal politics could work, he responded to his sister's request by needling the bishop of

112. *Cartulaire du Lieu-Notre-Dame-lès-Romorantin*, p. 24, nos. 24, 1232, p. 24, no. 25, 1239, and p. 46, no. 59, 1237.

113. No foundation charter exists for this house, but the earliest donation recorded in the cartulary is from 1104. Cottineau suggests that the house was founded about 1099: L. H. Cottineau, *Répertoire topo-bibliographique des abbayes et prieurés*, 3 vols. (Mâcon: Protat Frères, 1935), 1:457. The editors of the printed cartulary suggest 1102 as the foundation date: *Cartulaire de Notre-Dame de Bourbourg*, introduction passim. Clemence is referred to as "fundatix" (1:20, no. 25, 1119).

114. *Cartulaire de Notre-Dame de Bourbourg*, 1:2, no. 2, 1106, and p. 13, no. 17, 1113.

115. *Cartulaire de Notre-Dame de Bourbourg*, 1:19, no. 23, 1116: the gift is made by "ego Lambertus . . . ad petitionem domine Gothildis, abbatisse Broburgensis ecclesie in honorem sancte Marie edificate, ad suggestionem Clementie, venerabilis Flandrensium comitisse."

Arras into confirming the convent's rights to a disputed altar.[116] The countess did not confine her persuasion to clerics; in her old age she seems to have acted with all the self-assurance of an elderly dowager, directing her husband's successors, the counts of Flanders, what gifts she thought they should make to the nuns.[117] Her advocacy for the nuns of Bourbourg must have won her a warm place in their hearts—they probably would have concurred with her son that she was "the most glorious countess."[118]

The patron also exercised indirect support for a monastery by promoting its projects. Radulf, viscount of Beaumont, took part in a complicated exchange in which he bought from one house a vineyard needed by the nuns of Fontaine Saint-Martin, thereby inducing the nuns to cede land to the Franciscans of Le Mans, who required the property for a construction project.[119] The nuns had obdurately refused to sell their land in Le Mans unless they could acquire the vineyard; Radulf stepped into the impasse, "moved by the misery and empathetic with the affliction" of the friars, and for their sakes broke the deadlock.

In addition to material endowments, an important type of support lay patrons provided for monasteries was the promise of physical protection. The services of an advocate whose role was to protect a house could be valuable in times of war and civil unrest, although in some of these cases the apparent protector was gaining as well as giving advantages. At the turn of the thirteenth century, when war broke out between Angevins and Capetians, Notre-Dame in Saintes found itself in a precarious position. In the 1140s it had enjoyed the royal protection of King Louis VII and his wife, Eleanor of Aquitaine.[120] After Eleanor's divorce from Louis and marriage to Henry

116. *Cartulaire de Notre-Dame de Bourbourg*, 1:20, no. 25, 1119, and p. 23, no. 26, s.d. (1119–21): "Robertus, Dei gratia, Attrebatensis episcopus, omnibus catholice fidei cultoribus, in perpetuum. Notum sit omnibus tam presentibus quam futuris, domini Calixti, pape, mandato ac precepto nos obedientes et domine Clementie, Flandrensis comitisse, . . . altare de Costices monasterio sancte Marie de Broburg ad usum sanctimonialium ibidem Deo famulantium, imperpetuum libere possidendum concessisse."

117. *Cartulaire de Notre-Dame de Bourbourg*, 1:26, no. 30, 1121, p. 27, no. 31, 1121, and p. 28, no. 32, 1121, were all donations made by Charles the Good at Clemence's instigation, while p. 35, no. 40, 1130, and p. 40, no. 45, 1139, were donations made by the succeeding count, Thierry of Alsace, responding to "rogatu domine Clementie."

118. *Cartulaire de Notre-Dame de Bourbourg*, 1:18, no. 22, 1116.

119. *Cartulaire de Saint-Sulpice-la-Forêt*, p. 196, no. 118, 1237.

120. *Cartulaire de Notre-Dame de Saintes*, pp. 50–51, no. 47, a privilege of Louis from 1140; p. 51, no. 48, a privilege from Eleanor dated also to 1140; three more

of Anjou, her new husband lost little time in taking over the role of protector of the nunnery, which he continued to play after being crowned king of England.[121] The nunnery was therefore swept along with Eleanor, its primary sponsor, into the Angevin orbit. Yet when King Philip Augustus invaded the Saintonge during his wars with King John of England, the French king issued a charter to the Abbey of Notre-Dame in Saintes, placing the nuns under his protection.[122] This sounds like an altruistic step to ensure the abbey's safety, but there was also something in it for Philip, who could make political use of his role as patron of the rich and powerful house. Philip's move to take the nunnery under his wing was one of many such calculated insults aimed at the Angevins, by which the French king demonstrated to his English opponents that the Saintonge with all that was in it was now subject to the French crown. Advocacy of a monastic house could protect nuns and monks. At the same time, being identified with a monastery could be beneficial to its lay protector.

The good patron was the one who guarded an abbey from all eroding forces, as did Hugh of Gornay in the late twelfth century. Hugh, a Norman noble, issued a charter of protection for the convent of Bival, which he had founded. The predators he was warning off were two powerful abbots. The charter states that "all should know that the abbot of Savigny and the abbot of Beaubec have no rights in the church or in its holdings."[123] These abbots had been interfering in the internal affairs of the convent, creating confusion and plunging the nuns into despair. Some of the religious women had left the house to start a new independent monastery at Bondeville; when Hugh saw the state to which things had come at Bival, he successfully agitated to raise the convent to abbatial status and block the abbots' meddling.[124]

privileges of Louis: pp. 35–36, no. 28, 1141, p. 52, no. 49, 1141, pp. 79–80, no. 87, 1145; and one more from Eleanor while she was still married to Louis: p. 36, no. 29, 1151.

121. *Cartulaire de Notre-Dame de Saintes*, p. 37, no. 30, 1152–54, in which Henry is described as duke of Aquitaine and Normandy and count of Anjou. Once Henry became king of England, he again issued privileges for Saintes under his new imprimatur: p. 34, no. 27, after 1154, and pp. 75–76, no. 83, 1174.

122. *Cartulaire de Notre-Dame de Saintes*, p. 67, no. 73, 1204.

123. Rouen, BD, Bival, H 51, liasse 3: "Unde sciant omnes quod abbas de Saveniis et abbas de Belbec in ecclesia vel in suis appenditiis nichil habeant."

124. J. Malicorne, *Documents et courte notice sur l'abbaye de Bival du douzième siècle jusqu'en 1789* (Rouen: L. Gy, 1897), pp. 16–17.

In the central Middle Ages wealthy and powerful patrons, both women and men, used a variety of resources and tactics on behalf of a favored monastery. The support of these donors tended to follow family patterns, although some preference for their own sex existed among female supporters. Women patrons, however, showed less partiality for their own sex than did women founders, usually drawn from the highest noble levels, who acted with an assertive independence that could respond to their personal preferences as well as to family concerns.[125] The proportion of women acting on their own as patrons of any monastery was invariably small, usually about 10 percent, but close to half of all monastic patronage involved women.[126] This was the case because women were less apt to command the disposition of wealth and privileges than were their male relatives. The comparatively small pool of female founders and donors may help explain the small proportion of religious houses for women.

Damage to the Monastery

The perfect patron for an abbey would be that person who gave both unstinting financial support and effective physical protection while demanding nothing onerous from the monastics. Such paragons of disinterested charity were as rare in the Middle Ages as they are today. Monastic patrons were numerous, but those who supported a house usually had an eye on possible benefits for themselves and often calculated that their generosity gave them license to dabble in monastic affairs. The behavior of lay patrons towards medieval monasteries ran the gamut from mild officiousness to damaging interference. Benefactors wanted to receive spiritual benefits that from time to time may have taxed the resources of monasteries.[127] More pernicious, however, was the patron's desire to dictate how a monastery

125. Elkins, *Holy Women of Twelfth-Century England*, pp. 95–97, finds that in England the status of founders of convents was usually lower than that of founders of male houses, in contrast to the high status of female founders of French nunneries.

126. "In Anjou, 11.9% of the donations and sales made in the period 1000–1249 were made by female alienors": Gold, *Lady and the Virgin*, p. 121; but p. 122 finds that "half of all transactions (44.5%) had at least one woman in a consenting role." David Herlihy, "Land, Family and Women in Continental Europe, 701–1200," *Traditio* 18(1962): 108, examines several criteria by which to assess women's status and sees women acting as principal alienators of land in northern France in 8 percent of land transfers in the eleventh century and 9 percent in the twelfth century.

127. Pensions were a problem for both monastic women and monastic men, but it was particularly the anniversary masses for the dead that became burdensome to convents. See chapter 4.

should be administered. Such manipulation might be sweetened by a gift. Constance, countess of Brittany, gave the Abbey of Saint-Sulpice grain and money, stipulating that the gifts came "under the condition that the abbess or the prioress of Saint-Sulpice can neither put in nor remove the prioress, the prior, or any other nun in that house except with our consent and agreement." [128] In essence, Constance wanted total veto power over the abbey's personnel.

The monastery could be pressured to take particular novices based on past favors or solely on the patron's prestige. The latter was a constant of medieval society, in which—even if might did not make right—it got results. Despite an episcopal limit of sixty choir nuns for the Abbey of Montivilliers, the papal legate talked the nuns into exceeding that quota and admitting the daughter of one of the king's sergeants. [129] It was diplomatic for the nuns to curry royal and papal approval by complying, yet attempting to feed and house more members than an abbey could support damaged its financial equilibrium. Political expediency would always argue that "just one more" novice could be accommodated, but financial common sense would counter that one exception leads to another, and each extra person stresses a monastery's economic well-being.

Ideally, every abbey needed an advocate strong enough to make predators think twice yet benign enough to resist when tempted by its valuable but vulnerable possessions. In the real world, most abbeys had patrons who both helped and harassed the nuns or monks under their protection. This is a scenario familiar to historians of monasticism: the family that gave was often the family that took away. [130]

All parties involved in recording transfers of property took what steps they could to close loopholes in the exchange. Great efforts were made to get the consent and signatures of all who might later claim the property. Oaths were taken to abide by the agreement, and disclaimers were recorded so that the minority of a donor, or some

128. *Cartulaire de Saint-Sulpice-la-Forêt*, p. 157, no. 74, ca. 1199/1200.

129. ER, p. 647. Another such case is recorded in Rouen, BD, Saint-Amand, H 55, carton 1, 1265. In this, Fulk urges the nuns of Saint-Amand to receive Joanna. It appears that Fulk may be a local abbot.

130. I investigate this situation in *Prayer, Patronage, and Power;* see chap. 3 and particularly pp. 91–93. Barbara H. Rosenwein argues in a paper, "Givers and Takers in Cluniac Charters," presented at the Twenty-second International Congress on Medieval Studies, Kalamazoo, Mich., May 1987, that gifts "did not constitute an irrevocable transfer of property. Rather, they were made in return for, or with the expectation of, a countergift. Or they were made between people who had a relationship of dependence."

other possible disqualifying factor, would not invalidate the transaction. Sometimes these defensive legal stratagems worked, but not
always. Numerous charters record claims, counterclaims, and
settlements over contested rights and property, and readers might
reasonably conclude that monasteries spent all their time locked in
litigation. But we must be careful not to exaggerate monastic liti-
giousness, remembering that documents proliferate in response to
conflicts but are lacking in the wake of harmonious, uncontested
transactions.

Negotiating contested property transfers was a delicate balancing
act and could involve complex legal rights. The children of Falgeria
made a donation to the convent of Holy Trinity, Poitiers, from their
share of their mother's dowry.[131] She contested this gift, probably
because it affected her income, and a settlement was effected between her and Abbess Petronilla. Falgeria kept usufruct of Villa
Folet during her lifetime, and legal responsibility for hearing cases
and collecting fines was rigorously apportioned between her and the
abbey. After Falgeria's death the whole property was to go free and
clear to the nuns. Charters can be irritatingly vague about human
relationships, as is this one; I would like to know what was going on
between the children, who seem to have jumped the gun, and their
embattled mother.

Conflicted claims more commonly came from a donor's children
than from the parents. A Breton knight, Buchard, had given some
land to the nuns of the Priory of Mary Magdelen so that they would
celebrate his anniversary.[132] Buchard's eldest son and heir, Stephen,
refused consent to the donation, saying his father had no right to
alienate this property. Settlement was eventually worked out so that
the nuns got the land and its annual rent of five shillings, but from
this income they agreed to pay one penny per arpent to Buchard and,
after his death, to Stephen. The nuns would celebrate the anniversaries of Buchard and his wife and, after the donors' deaths, of Stephen and his wife.

It was not just benefactors who became snarled in litigation with
monasteries. People outside the patronage system generated some of
the turmoil that boiled up around such claims and counterclaims.
During the late eleventh century when the nuns of Notre-Dame began to build a mill in Saintes, they had ditches dug across abutters'

131. Poitiers, BD, La Trinité, 2 H 2, carton 12, MS. 6.
132. The story of this tangle is contained in *Cartulaire de Saint-Sulpice-la-Forêt*,
p. 231, no. 142, 1264.

lands to move water to and from the mill.[133] This incensed Maria, "the fattest townswoman" in Saintes, who complained fiercely and finally dropped her claim only when the nuns took her daughter into the monastery and her son conceded defeat. After Maria's allies had been lured over to the other side, she had no choice but to give up the battle. Also, she was now part of the patronage network of the abbey simply by having a daughter within the house.

The most grimly contested fights eventually were settled, usually by giving something to the complainant. Lady Clarice's gift of an alod to the nuns of Notre-Dame occasioned two generations of conflicting claims. The persistent quarrel was resolved when the nunnery gave one of Clarice's grandsons twenty shillings and the position of abbey advocate, as well as giving twenty shillings to each of the three grandsons of the man who had owned the bailiff's fees and making them all members of the confraternity.[134] The final chapter in almost all tales of contested rights and property was the incorporation of the secular malcontent into the monastery's patronage network. Such settlements might look to modern eyes like monastic capitulation, but compromise settlements in which former adversaries became members of the nuns' prayer circle and received face-saving payments went a long way towards taming the secular wolves who worried at monastic property, turning them into domesticated rather than savage neighbors.

It made little difference to an angry layperson whether the monastic institution viewed as the enemy was peopled by nuns or monks; few shreds of chivalrous protection for the "weaker sex" adorn the medieval records. Twelfth-century literature may glamorize the lady, but actual behavior gave the cloistered woman no special treatment. In like fashion, those layfolk who brought suit against a convent, seized its goods, and troubled it privileges included women as well as men. When it came to asserting and defending rights and possessions, gender was not a decisive factor.

Benefits to the Surrounding Community

Those laypeople who visited their attentions on monasteries gained luster by the association.[135] But the positive contributions of a nun-

133. *Cartulaire de Notre-Dame de Saintes*, p. 55, no. 54, 1079–99.

134. *Cartulaire de Notre-Dame de Saintes*, pp. 76–77, no. 84, 1152–74, and pp. 77–78, no. 85, after 1174.

135. See my arguments in *Prayer, Patronage and Power*, p. 14, and Bouchard, *Sword, Miter and Cloister*, chaps. 9 and 10. Jean-François Lemarignier, "Aspects po-

nery also spilled over onto its geographic neighbors, many but certainly not all of whom were benefactors. To be in the physical orbit of a monastery—whether filled with nuns or with monks—was to reap a variety of benefits.

Monastics had a rich assortment of skills and resources for helping those around them. Sharing food and clothes with the poor was one of the forms of charity demanded of all Christians, and the rule of Benedict institutionalized charity as one of the ways the monk and nun should live the apostolic life.[136] Benefactors' gifts for the poor could be funneled through a convent. It may be that the nuns encouraged donors to use their funds this way, but in any case the cloistered women seemed reliable people to dispense charity. Thus Countess Matilda donated eight pounds annual rents to the nuns to give to the poor each year.[137]

Individual nuns instituted charitable activity, as did the abbess of Montivilliers, who established the custom of feeding thirteen poor people daily at her abbey.[138] But more common was the practice of corporate charity. Convents founded almshouses as places to care for the poor. Sainte-Croix in Poitiers established a poorhouse in 1162, and Notre-Dame in Bourbourg had a flourishing almshouse by the late thirteenth century.[139] In some cases a group of women organized themselves into a nursing order, as did the canonesses of Saint-Nicholas in Bar-sur-Aube, who adopted the rule of Saint-Victor's in Paris and in 1239 received episcopal confirmation for their almshouse.[140]

---

litiques des fondations de collégiales dans le royaume de France au XIe siècle," in *La vita comune del clero nei secoli XI e XII*, 2 vols., Miscellanea del Centro di Studi Medioevali 3 (Milan: Catholic University of the Sacred Heart, 1959), 1:19–40, sees the prestige that monastic foundations brought their patrons. Jacques Boussard, "L'origine des familles seigneuriales dans la région de la Loire moyenne," *Cahiers de Civilisation Médiévale* 5(1962): 308.

136. *The Rule of St. Benedict*, ed. and trans. Justin McCann (Westminster, Md.: Christian Classics, 1972), chap. 4, p. 27.

137. *Cartulaire du Lieu-Notre-Dame-lès-Romorantin*, p. 16, no. 10, 1256. Another such case is the gift of Gaucher of Chatillon to buy clothes and shoes for the poor: *Abbaye du Pont-aux-Dames*, p. 25, no. 84.

138. ER, p. 490.

139. *Histoire de l'abbaye Sainte-Croix de Poitiers: Quatorze siècles de vie monastique*, Mémoires de la Société des Antiquaires de l'Ouest, 4th ser. 19 (Poitiers: Société des Antiquaires de l'Ouest, 1986), p. 100. *Cartulaire de Notre-Dame de Bourbourg*, 1:227–28, no. 225, 1307. The almshouse was well established by the time it crops up in the cartulary in the early fourteenth century.

140. Paris, BN, Baluze 38, fol. 96.

In a time of limited medical knowledge, what was known about health care generally was available in monastic libraries. Nuns used this knowledge individually to help the sick and corporately to found hospitals. The Abbey of Saint-Georges in Rennes seems to have been particularly assertive in stepping in when someone was seriously ill.[141] For example, when his family despaired of Rocand's life and all his relatives abandoned him, Abbess Hodierna sent an escort to bring him to one of the nuns' houses. There he was tenderly cared for until his inevitable death. The nuns gave him burial in their own graveyard, with a full procession of nuns. A few years later Rotald, the son of Marcher, had two serious illnesses that drove him to call on Abbess Adele of Saint-Georges for help. The abbess was moved by his suffering and paid for a doctor to care for Rotald. The doctor cured the sick man, who later came in gratitude to donate a tithe to the nunnery. When someone was seriously ill, the nuns offered care that no one else was willing or perhaps able to give.

Just as nunneries were involved in the establishment of almshouses, so too they created hospitals. The two were often indistinguishable in the eleventh century and became distinctive types of charitable organizations only after our period.[142] The great Abbey of Ronceray in Angers was instrumental in founding the Hospital of Saint-Jean in that city (see fig. 1), and in the mid-thirteenth century the Abbey of Montivilliers created and endowed a hospital in Normandy.[143]

It may be that some basic nursing was part of the education of

141. See *Cartulaire de Saint-Georges de Rennes*, 9:270, no. 43, ca. 1070, p. 261, no. 32, ca. 1085, for these two cases. Note that some scholars' idea that nuns did no nursing needs to be questioned. For instance, see Stein, "Religious Women of Cologne: 1120–1320," p. 35: "The teaching or nursing sister was unknown; for women, the contemplative life was the sole choice of a regular religious life."

142. Jacqueline Caille, *Hôpitaux et charité publique à Narbonne au Moyen Age de la fin du XIe à la fin du XVe siècle* (Toulouse: Privat, 1978), p. 101. Little distinction was made in Narbonnais hospitals between the sick and the poor. Raymond Oursel, *Une fondation flamande aux carrefours des chemins de pèlerinage: Le grand hôpital d'Aubrac*, Annales de l'Ecole des Hautes Etudes de Gand 9 (Ghent: Imprimerie Van Doosselaere, 1978) p. 16. Poor and sick were still intermingled in this institution during the thirteenth century.

143. See *Cartulaire de Saint-Jean d'Angers*, pp. iv–viii, nos. 4–7, and pp. xiv–xv, no. 12, which variously attribute the founding of the hospital to King Henry II or to his seneschal, Steven. Whoever was titular founder, it was the nuns of Ronceray who administered the hospital and supplied its personnel. For Montivilliers see Yvonne Aubert, "L'abbaye Notre-Dame de Montivilliers au diocèse de Rouen des origines au XVIe siècle," in *Position des thèses de l'Ecole des Chartes* (Nogent-le-Rotrou: Daupeley-Gouveneur, 1939), p. 13.

Figure 1. Great hall of the twelfth-century Hospital of Saint-Jean in Angers.

nuns in monasteries that ran hospitals, or perhaps the common expectation that women would care for the health of family members predisposed nuns to be sensitive nurses. The attentive care given the sick by religious women is dramatically recorded in the case of King Louis IX's near death. Jean de Joinville writes: "A year or two after the events I have just recorded it happened by God's will, that King Louis, who was then in Paris, was taken very seriously ill, and came at last so near to dying that one of the two ladies who were tending him wanted to draw the sheet over his face, maintaining that he was dead. But another lady, who was on the opposite side of his bed, would not allow it, and said she was sure his soul was still in his body."[144] The editors of the cartulary of Maubuisson, a Cistercian nunnery founded by Blanche of Castille and very dear to her heart, contend that the ladies caring for the king were nuns from that convent.[145] This would make sense, since the queen mother was a deeply pious woman and would have wanted those she trusted most

144. Jean de Joinville, "The Life of St. Louis," trans. M. R. B. Shaw in Jean de Joinville and Geoffrey de Villehardouin, *Chronicles of the Crusades* (Harmondsworth, England: Penguin, 1963), p. 191.
145. *Cartulaire de Maubuisson*, p. 12.

as spiritual and physical nurturers to be at her son's bedside. In the same way but with an anonymous rather than a royal protagonist, when the nuns of Saint-Amand in Rouen found themselves with the body of an apparent suicide victim on their hands, they hovered round the body until one discerned signs of life, despite the archdeacon's admonitions to rid themselves of the polluted corpse by throwing the body in a ditch.[146]

Religious men are generally seen as the inheritors of the medical knowledge of the classical tradition, drawing on Galen, Hippocrates, Soranus of Ephesus, and the eleventh-century translations of Arabic works by Constantine the African, all of which were generally found in monastic libraries.[147] Monastic women, although seldom mentioned, also partook of that knowledge and its application. For instance, the attention directed at Hildegard of Bingen's extraordinary medical writings and contributions reveals a world in which monastic women shared in the medical knowledge of their day and "in hospital work . . . were almost as important as men." [148] Moreover, as the hospitals began to proliferate in the second half of the twelfth and in the thirteenth century, a division of labor became apparent, with the physical care of the ill falling to nursing sisters, the care of their souls to the resident priests or canons, and heavy labor to lay brothers.[149] Medieval sensibilities that valued the spiritual over the corporal automatically divvied up the tasks so that those deemed less important fell to women and uneducated men. Whatever the stereotypes that structured the system, they produced an environment in which professed women offered their skills to the sick and

146. Valenciennes, BM, MSS. 500 and 502. Transcribed by Henri Platelle, "Les relations entre l'abbaye Saint-Amand de Rouen et l'abbaye Saint-Amand d'Elnone," in *La Normandie bénédictine au temps de Guillaume le Conquérant (XIe siècle)* (Lille: Facultés Catholique de Lille, 1967), p. 106.

147. Charles H. Talbot, "Medicine," in *Science in the Middle Ages*, ed. David C. Lindberg (Chicago: University of Chicago Press, 1978), pp. 391–96.

148. See, for instance, Barbara Newman, *Sister of Wisdom: St. Hildegard's Theology of the Feminine* (Berkeley: University of California Press, 1987), chap. 4. Also see the forthcoming work of Sister Prudence Allen on Hildegard, and Mundy, *Europe in the High Middle Ages*, p. 210.

149. To cite one such example, the Hospital of Mary Magdalen in Rouen was visited a number of times by Archbishop Eudes Rigaud. He notes that all the canons who served the house were priests. In addition there were twenty-seven *sorores*, nursing sisters, and five *conversi*, lay brothers who did the heavy work around the hospital: ER, p. 468. In essence this is the model that shaped our modern hospitals: male doctors and administrators, nurses who do the patient care, and male orderlies for strenuous work.

wounded, giving them nurturing not available from any other source.

Even when a hospital was owned and administered by men, as was the hôtel-Dieu at Laon, which was under the management of the canons of Laon, the nursing was in the hands of professed women.[150] These *sorores* were immediately supervised by the *magistra hospitalis* (director of nursing), but neither she nor the other sisters had any input into decision making.[151] The sisters worked hard. They washed each new beggar or patient, brought disinfected water so pilgrims could bathe their tired feet, and prepared food and distributed it to all the inmates.[152] The sisters were not cloistered, nor were they forbidden to own private property, but in keeping with the usual medieval attitudes about women, they were literally shortchanged on food and wine. For instance, one pittance accorded each brother a half measure of wine, but gave each sister only a third measure.[153] But whatever the inequities of their position, there must have been great satisfaction in the comfort they gave to the sick and needy, who responded thankfully when they could with grateful gifts for the sisters whose services they valued.[154]

The exact status of these sisters is hard for us to discern, but we can be sure some confusion existed even in the minds of their own contemporaries. When Helvide of Avin professed as a sister at the hôtel-Dieu she made a donation to the poor, part of which she designated for the nuns of Sauvoir-sous-Laon after her death.[155] The abbess of Sauvoir had a sharp, legalistic mind and saw a ripe opportunity to claim that her convent should receive this income immediately, since the monastic profession of Helvide—just like that of a choir nun—equaled juridical death. The outcome of the case is unknown, but the abbess's challenge suggests Helvide saw herself as a nursing sister, with a status somewhat different from that of a nun.

Although medieval people wanted care for the sick and dying,

150. Alain Saint-Denis, *L'hôtel-Dieu de Laon, 1150–1300* (Nancy: Presses Universitaires de France, 1983), p. 82 and passim.
151. Saint-Denis, *Hôtel-Dieu de Laon*, pp. 84–85, 99.
152. Saint-Denis, *Hôtel-Dieu de Laon*, pp. 100–105.
153. Saint-Denis, *Hôtel-Dieu de Laon*, pp. 98–99. The feeling that women needed less sustenance than men was widespread, being noted, for instance, by Heloise: *The Letters of Abelard and Heloise*, trans. Betty Radice (Harmondsworth, England: Penguin, 1974), p. 166.
154. Saint-Denis, *Hôtel-Dieu de Laon*, p. 99.
155. Saint-Denis, *Hôtel-Dieu de Laon*, p. 91.

burial of the dead in the hallowed ground of a monastery was even more important. An unusual group of charters for the Priory of Saint-Silvain point out the concern layfolk had for ensuring a holy burial. Forty-one consecutive charters copied into the cartulary deal with the priory's affairs and show something of the significance burial arrangements had in people's lives. Fifteen charters recorded gifts made for the redemption of the soul of the donor, three settled conflicts, two were oblations, and twenty-one were gifts made for the privilege of burial in the nuns' graveyard.[156] For instance, "Girgerba, called Norves, the sister of Sequin of Gardona and Ebrard the Spaniard, for her burial gave to God, the Blessed Virgin and Saint-Silvain, a house which is called Ricardecs, in the parish of Saint-Martin of Moscola." In a world that viewed the afterlife as critical, a hallowed resting place and prayers for one's soul were paramount.

Monasteries were places of refuge and help for people facing all sorts of danger and deprivation. Nuns, like monks, assisted widows and orphans, those most vulnerable members of society who were without adult male protection. Widows could receive reassurance that they would be cared for if their resources proved insufficient for their needs; orphans were protected and supported.[157] When Arnald Pharon was dying he made a donation to a convent, remembering "that it had nurtured him as a boy" with kindness and generosity he wanted to repay.[158] Monastery walls could offer a home to the homeless and a shelter to the threatened. During the communal uprising in the city of Laon, a woman fleeing the mob thought "she would be safe among the nuns," for to think of a cloister was to envision a place of safety.[159]

Charitable assistance constituted a large part of the monastic contribution to society, but the monastic women of the central Middle Ages combined practical skills and expertise with their charitable resources. It was to nuns, as to monks, that their neighbors turned for administrative help. For instance, an abbey might be called upon to administer a bequest. The beguine Ida of Nil-Saint-Vincent left all her goods to her niece, Havise.[160] The Abbey of Salzinnes was to

156. These are charters nos. 160 through 201, contained in the cartulary of Notre-Dame in Saintes. See the text of the following chapter, *Cartulaire de Notre-Dame de Saintes* p. 117, no. 166, before 1131.

157. *Cartulaire de Saint-Jean d'Angers*, p. xiii, no. 11, 1185–88. *Documents de Notre-Dame-aux-Nonnains*, p. 59, no. 84, 1237.

158. *Cartulaire de Notre-Dame de Saintes*, p. 44, no. 39, before 1134.

159. Guibert of Nogent, *Memoirs*, p. 180.

160. *Recueil du Val-Saint-Georges à Salzinnes*, p. 171, no. 137, 1264.

see to the property and pay Havise the annual rent of one muid of wheat as long as she lived. After her death the income devolved to the nuns. Ida must have felt she could trust the nuns to be careful and honorable stewards of her property for the benefit of her niece.

Nuns also functioned as the executors of wills and recorders of the affairs of others. The prioress of the hôtel-Dieu at Pontoise served as one of the four executors for a long and complicated will in which a widow left many particular bequests both to monasteries and to individual laypeople. These bequests include an annual income of forty-two shillings to the hospital, and the woman asked to be buried where the sisters were interred.[161] In the early thirteenth century when a noble couple finally settled a contested claim with a neighbor, the charter resolving the fight was sealed with the seal of the abbess, who was not an interested party, except as recorder of deeds and transactions.[162] Nuns, like monks, were generally literate in the central Middle Ages so that monastic women had the skills to act in various public administrative capacities.

It would be looking at the past through rose-colored glasses to envision medieval nuns acting in totally disinterested ways at all times. Much conventual activity was aimed at consolidating the economic power of a house by creating a network of benefactors and friends. It was good public relations to assist lay neighbors, since the institution could then enjoy friendly relations with those who had reason to be grateful. We live with an analogous situation today. When the Red Cross hurries to the scene of a disaster, society benefits and the agency gets the credit. The Red Cross acts out of humanitarian ideals, but without a good press and the resulting public support, the agency would wither away. So too the medieval monastery. Caring for the surrounding community was living out the precepts of the Christian and monastic ideal, but the motives for such charity and involvement with lay society might not always be purely altruistic.

The root of monastic charity was the gospel, reinforced for monastic women and men by chapter 4 of the Benedictine Rule, the "Tools of Good Works," which includes the directions for professed people to follow: "To relieve the poor. To clothe the naked. To visit the sick. To bury the dead. To help the afflicted."[163] It was a pain-

---

161. *Cartulaire de l'hôtel-Dieu de Pontoise*, ed. J. Depoin (Pontoise: Société du Vexin, 1886), p. 71, no. 104, 1287. Also see *Abbaye des Clairets*, pp. 190–92, no. 91, 1340, for another interesting example.

162. *Documents de Notre-Dame-aux-Nonnains*, p. 29, no. 34, 1217.

163. *Rule of St. Benedict*, p. 27.

fully demanding goal set before professed people, a goal that was taken seriously. Religious women worked "to give an abundance of all things to the weak, the weary, pilgrims, orphans, widows, those traveling, and foreign folk."[164] Whatever the faults and failings of individual nunneries, whatever the ancillary benefits of good publicity, the interactions of religious women with the surrounding lay community made them "our good friends" in the minds of their grateful neighbors.[165]

Power and Control

If monastic people—both nuns and monks—did not win the friendship, protection, and support of their community, they had no recourse in times of violent upheaval and war. Monasteries were virtually defenseless, for though they did have servants who would take up cudgels on their behalf, they did not regularly have men-at-arms in their pay. Probably nothing more catastrophic ever afflicted a religious house than to be caught in a region wracked by war. In the mid-twelfth century a widowed noblewoman, Almode, and her daughter became nuns at Notre-Dame in Saintes.[166] The abbess urged Almode to talk her sons into donating a sizable piece of woods to the abbey, which they did. The local viscount, Peter, gave consent for the gift, and Almode began building in the woods a little house topped with a cross, presumably to serve as a small priory. Soon after, her sons fell out with Peter, the local lord, and when his men tried but failed to apprehend the sons, they turned their frustration on the mother and threatened her. She was so frightened that she abandoned the little obedience and returned to the mother house, where shortly afterwards she died. While the conflict raged in the area, the nuns of Notre-Dame had to abandon construction, which allowed the monks of Limoges to take advantage of the vacuum and seize the building for themselves.

Although the conflict in this instance was small and localized, it threatened both life and property. Much greater danger accompanied large-scale warfare, such as the Angevin-Capetian struggles for power in the twelfth and early thirteenth centuries. Notre-Dame was particularly vulnerable, situated as it was in Saintes, astride the uneasy line dividing the two spheres of interest. When Henry II of England laid waste the city of Saintes, the nuns lost a mill and other

164. *Cartulaire de Notre-Dame de Saintes*, p. 27, no. 20, 1047–61.
165. *Cartulaire de Notre-Dame de Bourbourg*, 1:173, no. 182, 1271.
166. *Cartulaire de Notre-Dame de Saintes*, p. 61, no. 62, ca. 1148.

property.[167] In the general breakdown of law and order that followed the sack, various opportunists made off with whatever abbey goods were unprotected. It took a good deal of time and litigation to reclaim some of what was lost in that disaster. In 1204 Philip Augustus put the abbey under his protection, partly to shield the nuns against Angevin attack, partly to bolster his own position by showing he could dominate the Saintonge. The long-term danger to the abbey during these unsettled years was the risk of being dissolved or turned over to another house if the nuns became associated with the losing side. Abbeys had to play politics with a wary eye on their own interests if they were to avoid retribution for unwise loyalties, but the immediate threat was more to property than to lives. Indeed, the lives of nuns and monks were much less at risk than in the early Middle Ages. By the central Middle Ages, warfare seldom claimed monastics as its victims; this was true generally in Europe. When Bolognese soldiers invaded Florence, they carried off "everything in the monastery except for the clothes the nuns wore all the time."[168] The nuns themselves escaped injury.

When riots and civil disturbances occurred, danger was more real, and all manner of violence and even death might be inflicted on monastics of both sexes. When Bruges erupted in 1127–28, no one was safe from harm. The cells of the monks of one abbey were "so completely sacked that neither a book nor chalice of the Mass was left there."[169] A few years earlier when Laon experienced civil upheavals, the nunnery of Saint-Jean was burned and the abbess of a local house was killed by one of her serfs.[170] Uprisings of the lower classes continued into the thirteenth century, always threatening harm to monasteries, which as landlords were likely targets for fury. In 1258 a popular movement in the Namurois led by the *blousons dorés* wreaked its wrath on the upper levels of society, including the nunnery of Salzinnes, whose buildings were burned, forcing the nuns to flee for their lives.[171] By the central Middle Ages warfare waged by kings and barons had developed some restraints against savaging religious persons; the convulsions of class hatred were

167. *Cartulaire de Notre-Dame de Saintes*, p. 48, no. 44, after 1174.
168. "Life of St. Umilta, Abbess of the Vallombrosan Order in Florence," ed. and trans. Elizabeth Petroff, in *Consolation of the Blessed* (New York: Alta Gaia Society, 1979), p. 133.
169. Galbert of Bruges, *The Murder of Charles the Good, Count of Flanders*, trans. James B. Ross (New York: Harper, 1967), p. 303.
170. Guibert of Nogent, *Memoirs*, pp. 180, 207.
171. *Recueil du Val-Saint-Georges à Salzinnes*, p. x.

more dangerous because they involved not only the general loss of inhibitions when fighting but also the anger of the lower classes against all those in control.

Although nuns and monks were physically helpless in the path of an advancing army or a violent mob, in all but the most frenzied situations monastics had a potent weapon for defending themselves: they controlled spiritual benefits that could help ensure salvation and eternal life for recipients of their prayers. The desire to be in good odor and included in the suffrages of monastics fueled donations made to monasteries. Geoffrey of Flocinère gave a mill to the nunnery of Saint-Sulpice "for the sake of charity, for my soul, and the souls of both my forebears and my descendants." [172] In return for this gift, Geoffrey requested that two nuns of the abbey should pray for his soul and for his family. The fears and hopes of medieval people created a climate in which the prayers of monastic had worth, and the withdrawal of monastic approval and suffrages was to be avoided.

Monks and nuns used this spiritual clout to influence behavior. For instance, a troublesome situation developed after the duke of Aquitaine donated a tithe and some newly cleared woods to the Abbey of Notre-Dame in Saintes, when two brothers, Geoffrey of Pons and Peter of Neuil, violently seized this property from the nun who was administering the gift.[173] The nuns immediately protested this seizure to the count of Poitou and received satisfaction in his court. Having been awarded the rights to the property was hollow, however, since the two brothers paid no heed to the court's ruling, but an opportunity shortly came for the nuns to agitate for their rights when Geoffrey, one of the two malefactors, died. The body of the deceased was laid out in the Church of Saint-Eutrope across the river from Notre-Dame. The nuns "prepared their procession" and then proceeded in formal array across town to Saint-Eutrope. When they arrived, they confronted the grieving brothers, Peter and William, a cleric, over the bier in the chapter house. The moral force of a stern procession of nuns, intent on righting the wrongs done to their abbey, carried the day, and Peter and William resigned their claim. The nuns then graciously promised the brothers annual commemorations for the souls of their family members. The nuns made no physical threats; they wielded no weapons save their disapproval. Yet

172. *Cartulaire de Saint-Sulpice-la-Forêt*, p. 195, no. 117, 1237.
173. *Cartulaire de Notre-Dame de Saintes*, pp. 98–99, no. 122, 1133, for the description of this interaction.

they prevailed because nuns and monks in the Middle Ages exercised spiritual force with their prayers.

Nuns could protect the well-being of their institution by threatening recalcitrant individuals with a spiritual stick. They could also wield the stick on the behalf of the community at large. One summer a fierce drought afflicted Poitou, burning up crops, withering the vineyards, drying up streams, and baking the ground rock hard.[174] In a preindustrial, agrarian society with a tiny margin of survival, the drought threatened human existence. Faced with possible disaster, the local viscount organized a penitential pilgrimage with relics. The procession stopped along the way at a priory of nuns. After the bearers placed the relics on the altar, clerics conducted a service. The procession then formed up to continue on its way, but the relics proved intractable and twice could not be moved from their position. This clear signal of God's wrath terrified the people, who cried out imploring to know the cause of the divine punishment. Into this electrically charged scene stepped the chaplain and the prioress, who explained that God's judgment was aimed at the viscount as punishment for oppressing the people of the region. Thus publicly chastened, the viscount and his barons swore to behave, after which the relic bearers could raise the reliquary from the altar and lead the procession joyfully to its ultimate destination.

We can never know what really happened, but it is clear that the nuns used an emotional situation to discipline a bullying baron who was making the lives of local peasants unbearable. No one—much less a headstrong eleventh-century nobleman—would have listened to the prioress had religious women not commanded respect through their lives and involvement in the *Opus Dei* (divine offices), by which they wove an almost continuous fabric of prayer. In this instance nuns wielded their spiritual clout for the good of the community at large in highly visible circumstances. It is likely that a more muted moral suasion, mostly hidden from our eyes, went on quite commonly between monastics and the undisciplined and unruly nobility. Pierre Cotheu's words are not simply formulaic when he writes that he endows the religious women because he is "full of respect for their upright lives and honesty, and wants to benefit from their prayers day and night."[175]

174. *Cartulaire de Notre-Dame de Saintes*, pp. 139–40, no. 217, 1098, tells the story of this miraculous event.

175. "L'abbaye de la Barre et son recueil de chartres," ed. Alexandre-Eusèbe Poquet, *Annales de la Société Historique et Archéologique de Château-Thierry* 58(1884): 170, no. 58, 1303.

CONCLUSION

Above all, it was because of the intercession nuns offered for their patrons, friends, and confreres that society supported nunneries. The function of a nun was to work towards the salvation of humanity, to help wrest souls from the devil's toils. Women and men in the Middle Ages deemed that function critical for their salvation. Hugh of Apigneio started for the Holy Land in 1096 comforted and protected by the knowledge that the nuns of Saint-Georges would pray for him and celebrate his anniversary after his death.[176] If the anxieties of the townsfolk of Troyes were eased by knowing that the abbess of Notre-Dame possessed the physical key to the graveyard so that "if any burgher or his wife of the parish should choose burial in the small cemetery, he or she ought to be buried there," how much greater was their relief knowing that the nuns' prayers were the spiritual keys that were operating day and night to open the door to eternal life?[177] Further, it must have been enormously comforting to know that the prayers would outlast one's own life. As nuns aged and died, new professed women took their place and assumed the obligation of suffrages. The ties of nuns even to those long dead were reinforced by annual commemorations when the names of patrons, written in the obituary of a monastery, came up for remembrance. Those bonds could mean a great deal, even to the new generations of religious women in a convent. When the church of Notre-Dame in Saintes was expanded and embellished in the twelfth century, its founders, Agnes of Burgundy and Geoffrey Martel, had been dead a century. Yet the planners included what may well be portraits of the founding couple on the magnificent Romanesque tower.[178] Institutional memory is long—much longer than individual memory—which brought solace to those people encircled by the prayers of the nuns and monks who in the central Middle Ages provided salvific insurance.

176. *Cartulaire de Saint-Georges de Rennes*, 9:270, no. 42, 1096.

177. *Documents de Notre-Dame-aux-Nonnains*, p. 41, no. 51, 1222, and *Cartulaire de Saint-Sulpice-la-Forêt*, p. 146, no. 66, 1164: "Sanctimonialibus ibi Deo nocte dieque famulantibus."

178. Portraits of a noble couple separated by the icon for a castle adorn the northwest corner of pier 4 on the tower dated 1134–51. Virginia Stoltz pointed this out to me and suggests that the representation could well be of Agnes and Geoffrey.

3

THE ECCLESIASTICAL

COMMUNITY

RELATION TO THE CHURCH HIERARCHY
The Bishop as Authority

Houses of monastic women were an integral part of the machinery of the church in the central Middle Ages, rather than being ancillary as they would later become. Linkage to the ecclesiastical engine was generally through the drivetrain of episcopal oversight for monasteries of both women and men. Bishops' official visitations, episcopal courts, and informal interchanges created multiple connections between regular communities (those that followed a rule) and the secular church. If one part of the system malfunctioned, another generally took over, bypassing the breakdown. The record of interchanges between prelates and monastics may seem at a glance to have consisted only of hostile confrontations, since it was controversy that generated many of the documents we use to reconstruct the past. But orderly relations were probably the norm, although they did not produce stacks of letters, court decisions, and appeals.

Bishops had two responsibilities towards monastics: to minister to them sacramentally and to oversee and, if necessary, reform their individual lives as well as the corporate conventual life of the house.[1] Interactions between monasteries and bishops might occur sporadically, but the expectation was that there would be an official annual or biennial visitation for supervision and correction. Sometimes the episcopal responsibilities were exercised by an appointed

---

1. John Nichols, "English Cistercian Nuns," in *Distant Echoes*, vol. 1. of *Medieval Religious Women*, ed. John A. Nichols and Lillian Thomas Shank, Cistercian Studies Series 71 (Kalamazoo, Mich.: Cistercian Publications, 1984), categorizes bishops' responsibilities toward nuns as confirming elections, appointing chaplains and priests, and reforming both temporal and spiritual failings. French bishops functioned much as did their English confreres except that they do not seem generally to have appointed clerics to monastic positions.

stand-in, usually the archdeacon of the diocese. Exempt houses—monasteries that had been granted freedom from episcopal control—usually owed allegiance directly to the pope. Although exemption theoretically placed an abbey under the pope's direct supervision, an abbey at a considerable distance from Rome actually was free of the constraints of annual visitation and accountability. Yet even exempt houses required the bishop's sacramental services to consecrate monastics and his juridical powers to adjudicate legal cases.

During the early Middle Ages bishops had evolved into princes of the church, who generally came from the aristocracy and exercised both temporal and spiritual powers. But it was the bishop's liturgical functions that made him both indispensable to and dominant over medieval monasteries. Since only a bishop could consecrate holy places and objects, it took the sacramental actions of a prelate to make a building a church. It was an important moment, then, when the bishop of Paris came to consecrate the abbey church of Maubuisson in the presence of Queen Blanche of Castille and King Louis IX.[2] By the central Middle Ages bishops consecrated nuns and monks and received their vows, as well as consecrating those who became abbesses and abbots. Exempt houses might have the right to choose which local bishop they wanted to perform these ceremonies, but all abbeys and priories needed a bishop's sacramental powers to regularize their members and validate their leaders.

The service for consecrating monastics had many local variants in the Middle Ages, but it was always a solemn ceremony incorporated into the mass.[3] There were actually two services, one for nuns that drew heavily on the imagery of marriage and one for monks that centered on the idea of *renovatio* of the whole person.[4] The differences by gender emphasize the hierarchy's view of women as dependent and men as autonomous, of nuns as living as spouses of Christ and monks as "putting on the new Christ"—thereby identifying themselves directly with Christ.

The consecration ceremony for nuns usually began after the gradual, with the entry of the novices. The wording that followed varied, but it involved a formal dialogue between bishop and novices in which they were bidden to approach the seated bishop, who inquired whether they were promising fidelity; he then blessed habits, veils,

2. Dutilleux and Depoin, *Abbaye de Maubuisson*, p. 7.
3. René Metz, *La consécration des vierges dans l'église romaine: Etude d'histoire de la liturgie* (Paris: Presses Universitaires de France, 1954), p. 350.
4. Metz, *Consécration des vierges.*

and rings and invested each novice with them. The bishop spoke to the novices: "Come, come, come daughters, listen to me; I will teach you the fear of the Lord," to which the novices replied: "We now follow with our whole hearts"[5] The solemn beauty of the service must have deeply impressed those who participated in the liturgy, while the role of the bishop, who symbolized Christ, the bridegroom—espoused by each novice as she took her vows, received her ring, and promised her whole being to Him—could not but underline for her his indispensable function. As father and head of the family, he had questioned her suitability for the match. As Christ's representative, he had received her vows and accepted her as Christ's bride. The bishop acted symbolically as parent and as spouse for each nun. The nun might feel awe and gratitude for the figure who made her a nun, perhaps even affection; she might also transfer to the prelate whatever negative feelings she felt towards dominant men in her family, since the bishop seemed to exercise over her the power of the male patriarch. Whatever positive feelings might exist, acrimonious conflicts still developed between nuns and prelates, usually involving the resistance or even rebellion of women against those who wielded spiritual and bureaucratic authority over them.

Although exempt houses might want to see bishops as fungible, the prelates had a vested interest in maintaining personal authority over the houses in the diocese or province. The obedience of a monastery increased the episcopal power base and added to the diocesan's income through court fees and procurations—the customary fees houses paid to the official visitor. To emphasize their authoritative role and ensure compliance, bishops often exacted oaths of obedience from monasteries. In 1118 the abbess of Saint-Avit in Châteaudun promised "subjection and obedience according to the practices of the Fathers" to the bishop of Chartres and his successors.[6] A little over a century later, the oath had become more detailed; the abbess recited: "I promise that I will demonstrate subjection and obedience constituted by the Holy Fathers according to the rule of Saint Benedict to you, Father Matthew, bishop, and to your successors canonically installed in the church of Chartres and to the Holy See forever, and sign it with my own hand."[7] This second

5. Metz, *Consécration des vierges*, p. 351.

6. C. Cuissard, ed., "Sommaire de chartes de l'abbaye de Saint-Avit de Châteaudun," *Bulletin de la Société Dunoise Archéologique, Histoire, Sciences et Arts* 9(1987–1900): 172.

7. Cuissard, "Sommaire de Saint-Avit," pp. 180–81. The key words stay the same: *subjectio* and *obedientia*, which are in most formulae of abbatial submission to a

oath is a sweeping affirmation of the dominance of the bishops of Chartres over the nunnery of Saint-Avit, an abbey that was dwindling in power and wealth throughout the period. The bishops of Chartres were able to exact a general submission from the nuns in the absence of other patrons, but in return they themselves became the protectors of the house.

Many monasteries of women and of men were pressured into accepting the full authority of the diocesan, but the implied trade-off was that in doing so the houses would also acquire a powerful advocate. The evidence from Saint-Avit suggests that the bishop's dominance did not necessarily help the monastics. From the late twelfth century, the nuns were embroiled in escalating litigation, which usually resulted in losses for the abbey. It appears that secular patrons were more protective of the abbey than was the bishop. For instance, in 1183 papal support and the pressure of the count and countess of Blois maneuvered the bishop into giving the abbey the right to name its own chaplain and to remove him at will.[8] Later even though the bishops of Chartres officially still held sway over Saint-Avit, they seem to have lost interest during the thirteenth century, leaving the nuns to fend for themselves.

Medieval people believed in the efficacy of oaths to structure society, and they used them in public ceremonies to dramatize relationships. When the balance of power was such that a monastery could establish its rights and customs vis-à-vis the diocesan, the monastics, both female and male, sometimes required from him an oath respecting their privileges. This was done by the nuns of Notre-Dame-aux-Nonnains, to whom the ordinary promised: "I, ———, bishop of Troyes, do swear that I will observe for the nuns the laws, franchises, liberty, and privileges of the monastery of Saint Mary, with the aid of God and of the holy Gospels."[9] The nuns were taking no chances that the diocesan would interfere with their autonomy. The complexity of their relationship—comprising much more than

---

bishop. See the oath of the abbess of Notre-Dame-aux-Nonnains, *Documents de Notre-Dame-aux-Nonnains*, p. 184, n. 1.

8. Cuissard, "Sommaire de Saint-Avit," pp. 174–75.

9. Paris, BN, MS. lat. 9894, front endpaper verso. The hand in which the oath is inscribed is late twelfth or early thirteenth century. The liturgical drama is transcribed in a late Gothic hand in fols. 29v–30v. But since reference is made in a charter from 1300 to the custom that the bishop donated his horse to the abbess, it is likely that the ceremony evolved during the thirteenth century: *Documents de Notre-Dame-aux-Nonnains*, pp. 133–37, no. 208.

simply adversarial actions and reactions—can be seen in the intricate ceremony that had evolved by the end of the thirteenth century to administer the oath to each new bishop of the city of Troyes.

All the ecclesiastics in town were part of the elaborate liturgical drama that solemnized the prelate's oath. When the new bishop prepared to come and take possession of his see, his very first act was to ride with his retinue of clerics and servants to the Abbey of Notre-Dame-aux-Nonnains. He entered the forecourt of the nunnery, there to be met by the abbess and nuns, who had processed in state out of their cloister to receive him. The abbess formally greeted the bishop after he dismounted and received from him the gift of his horse, which she sent off to her stables. She then conducted him to the chapter house, where he vested in full pontificals—silken cope, miter, and crozier—before proceeding to the high altar of the abbey church. There, before the entire monastic community, he made his solemn oath orally and in writing to respect the abbey's rights, after which the abbess led him to his apartments, where he and his attendants could sleep in comfort. She reciprocated his gracious gift of his horse by making him a present of the cushion-strewn bed.

The next morning the second part of the ceremony unfolded. Prime and terce were sung across town at the cathedral church, after which processions of clerics, choirboys, and acolytes came from religious establishments all over the city, converging on the cathedral. They came two by two, dressed in their most magnificent liturgical robes, bearing crosses, censers, candles, and Gospels. The procession formed up with the least important contingent leading off, followed by the groups carefully arranged in ascending order of status. The final figure was the most important personage, the deacon of the cathedral. The gorgeous parade made its way through the city intoning psalms. When the procession arrived at the nunnery of Notre-Dame, the doors of the abbey church were open, and as the marchers entered they could see the lord bishop in full regalia, standing before the nuns' high altar. The deacon read the oath aloud, and for the benefit of the assembled crowd and particularly for the notaries who meticulously recorded the event, the bishop repeated his promise to uphold it. When this was finished he took his seat in a sedan chair covered in gold cloth, and the whole procession reformed, still in reverse hierarchical order. The cortege returned to the cathedral with four members of the town council exercising their right to bear the bishop through town.

Notre-Dame-aux-Nonnains was an ancient foundation, dating back to the mid-seventh century. It had survived numerous vicissitudes and had developed a strong corporate presence. Individual prelates and abbesses came and went, but the nunnery continued. The institution had learned to establish at the outset of each episcopal reign its freedom from any infringements of its rights, in which effort the nuns received substantial support from all the religious in the city. The nuns needed the goodwill of the bishop, and the bishop wanted the support of the powerful convent and its backers. Therefore the bishop inaugurated his episcopacy by going to the nunnery, making a gift to the abbess, and publicly taking an oath to respect the convent's customs. Yet the ceremony was divided into two parts: one in which bishop and nuns participated away from the public eye, and a second in which the entire drama was repeated for the city's religious establishment in the absence of the nuns. Professed women might feel and act more like professed men than like secular women, but by the thirteenth century their gender was becoming the rationale for restricting their participation in public ceremonies.

The second vital episcopal responsibility was to watch over nuns and monks and correct them if they wandered from their vows. Prelates acted as spiritual advisers of the regular religious under their care during formal visits, but also ad hoc, responding to questions as they came up. Simon Beaulieu, archbishop of Bourges in the thirteenth century, listened to the problems of a Fontevrist nun when she traveled to him at Limoges, where he was holding a visitation.[10] The nun came from the Priory of Borueul, where her excessive fasting was causing concern. She came with her mother as chaperone to obtain episcopal approval for her fasting. The two women seem to have followed the archbishop around until they caught up with him at Limoges.

Letters came to prelates from the congregations in their diocese when the houses needed some response that could not wait until the bishop next came to their region. The prioress of Bival wrote to the diocesan to inform him that the election of a new abbess had taken place.[11] The nuns had received his permission to hold the election, and now they were reporting the outcome and requesting his confirmation. His response, after he had "diligently examined both the manner of the election and the elected person," was to confirm their choice. In the same way, a bishop received official notification when a monastic superior died or resigned from office. Also

10. Mansi, pp. 270–71.
11. ER, p. 7.

he might stop for a meal, spend the night, or bless a new superior when traveling. Thus, although the formal visitations were infrequent, a variety of interactions kept bishops in touch with monasteries.

The bishop's visits to monasteries in his official capacity as visitor were splendid affairs: bells pealed and clerics and monastics singing psalms and dressed in their best habits wended their way out of their precincts to greet the arriving prelate with all possible pomp.[12] The feelings of monastics before a visitation are not recorded, but for nuns and monks these visits must have been exciting breaks in the daily round of prayers. The arrival and reception of the bishop set the stage on which he would be the principal actor. For a nun or monk with a clear conscience, all the bustle might have been stimulating, not threatening; for a disgruntled monastic, the visitor's coming offered a chance to complain and blame others; and for religious who knew they had transgressed the rule, apprehension may have marked the approaching time of reckoning.

Not many visitation records survive from the central Middle Ages, and when they do, the contents are often terse. For instance, in 1304 when Archbishop Bertrand de Got visited the nuns of Albug, we know only that he preached to them and then inquired into the state of the house and its inmates.[13] The only other information recorded is that Bertrand assumed the expenses of his visit himself rather than requiring the nuns to pay procuration. The record gives no other details, but it is reasonable to assume that the prelate was acknowledging the nuns' worthiness and financial need and that they appreciated his generosity and consideration.

When the records are more complete, we can see that visitations were made up of two parts. First the visitor gathered information, then he issued orders. The workings of an inquiry are not always spelled out in the surviving records, but the technique and process of a visitation are particularly clear in this case:

> With God's grace, we preached the word of God in the chapter of Evreux to the resident canons and clerks-choral. When this was finished they all left the chapter room, leaving us and our companions behind. A little later, desiring to make visitation as our office requires us

12. Mansi, p. 270, for an example of the pomp that could accompany the visitor on his rounds.

13. "Droits de visite au diocèse d'Agen," ed. M. Rabanis, in *Clément V et Philippe le Bel* (Paris: A. Durand, 1858), p. 166.

to do, we called in those venerable men, the dean, the treasurer, and Stephen, the archdeacon of the said place, one by one, and diligently inquired from each of them whether the Divine Office was performed at the proper hours and with required modulation both by day and by night; whether they had ornaments, books, and vestments suitable for the Divine Service; whether the lighting of the church was well and competently attended to by those responsible for this duty; whether the priest-canons willingly celebrated their masses in the church. All three replied unanimously that all of these matters were very satisfactory. Item, we asked them whether any canon, cleric, or even chaplain in that church were publicly known for the vice of incontinence, for any business undertakings, or for anything else; they replied that, through God's grace, there was none at present, and that when anyone connected with the church, whether canon or clerk-choral, was defamed of the vice of incontinence, of inebriety, or any act that brought notoriety, the hebdomadary and the chapter punished him most severely. They believed that all ill fame had ceased. Item, some of the seniors grumbled and claimed that we were not empowered to visit the province until after we had visited the prominent places of our own diocese. However, we showed them our charter of privilege, and had it read aloud in full chapter, whereby we may do this without any interruption, or, even if we are interrupted by a summons from the king, the queen, or the Pope, we may resume and enter upon our (suspended) visitation. With God's grace, we found everything else to be in good condition, and we received procuration from them this day at the palace of the bishop.[14]

Visitations to female and male monasteries were very similar; the process, the questions, and the directions were mostly gender-neutral and appropriate to all monastics. Some gender differences did exist and became more marked during the thirteenth century, particularly in levels of literacy. At midcentury in Normandy, Eudes Rigaud had to warn two nunneries and three male monasteries to obtain and use the Benedictine Rule and the Statutes of Pope Gregory both in Latin and in French.[15] But by the latter part of the cen-

14. ER, pp. 346–47.
15. ER, pp. 85, 199, 423, for nunneries and 63, 85, 133, 709 for male houses.

tury in the diocese of Bourges, Archbishop Simon of Beaulieu responded to a disparity in levels of learning by generally preaching to canons and monks in Latin and to nuns in French.[16]

Only one northern French document surviving from the central Middle Ages allows us to go below the surface of the events to recreate some of the complexities of how a bishop interacted with houses of nuns and monks. This is the register of Archbishop Eudes Rigaud, which covers twenty-one years, from 1248 to 1269, of Eudes's official visitations in the province of Rouen, Normandy. In this period the archbishop made a conscientious effort to inquire into the temporal and spiritual well-being of all the parishes, deaneries, and monasteries under his care. If we exclude the tiny nonconventual obediences (those cells with fewer than eight monastics), he cared for eighty-two regular houses: fourteen nunneries, sixty-one male monasteries, and seven hospitals tended by nuns and monks. Eudes's register goes into a detail that is unique among such French documents of the period, relating his inquisitorial findings and his orders to and feelings about monasteries he visited. We never hear the other side; the nuns and monks he visited are mute, so we must be careful to remember that we are listening to one side of the dialogue.

Not often did Eudes conclude a visit to a house of either religious women or religious men with complete satisfaction, although his unqualified approval was meted out more often to male houses than to female ones.[17] Sometimes, however, he might give only one mild warning, as when he told the nuns of Villarceaux not to take in any novices but noted otherwise: "With God's grace we found everything else to be in good condition"; both visitor and visited must have felt pleased.[18] More commonly he made a variety of recommendations how a house should change its worship or its business affairs, or both, and on occasion he angrily scolded the monastics for their faults. Although neither the nuns nor the monks of Normandy had a monopoly on their visitor's displeasure or satisfaction, one house of religious women particularly tried his equanimity.

16. The archbishop preached to the canons of Clermont in Latin, to the monks of Saint-Jean d'Angéley in both French and Latin, and to the nuns of Holy Cross, Poitiers, in French: Mansi, pp. 279, 271, 270.

17. In fact only one convent, Montivilliers, received totally uncritical visits, and those were *before* Eudes broke down the rule that only the abbess could be visited. In contrast, once during his series of visits Eudes recorded unqualified approval for eleven male monasteries, and twice he found nothing critical to say of Jumièges.

18. ER, p. 558.

In midsummer 1259 the archbishop came to the small Cistercian Priory of Saint-Saens in the countryside northeast of the city of Rouen. He must have steeled himself for what he might encounter, since on previous visits he had uncovered a number of offenses in a generally slack environment.[19] The nuns of Saint-Saens did not seem able to reform and renew the spirit of their little house, although in the past few years nothing had been horrendously wrong. Maybe it was the heat; maybe the prelate was suffering from his arthritis, but he blew up at the nuns in the chapter house. The offices were not being performed with due solemnity, and the finances of the priory were in total disarray. To add insult to injury, one of the nuns had borne two children, one of whom was being raised by the woman's sister. But Eudes had visited Saint-Saens six times since 1251, so a nun who had twice been pregnant should not have come as a surprise. Maybe he had previously censured her, but no mention of such a dressing-down appears in his records. Perhaps her fellow nuns had shielded her until this day of reckoning. The broken vow of chastity, however, was not the last straw. Rather, the final indignity in the catalog of sins and peccadilloes was that the community had drawn up letters for four of its nuns promising to receive as novices their four nieces. When Eudes had last visited the priory just a year before, he had sternly warned the nuns not to expand, since their finances were already dicey.[20] Yet here they were, blithely ignoring his directions. Eudes could not endure such wrongheaded insubordination; he lost control and in a fury dramatically shredded the letters in front of all the nuns gathered in the chapter house. One wonders who had the temerity to say anything in the silence that must have followed.

In the wake of this scene, we might expect a radical improvement. Yet when the archbishop next came to Saint-Saens a year and a half later, although things were better, there still was much to correct.[21] Eight years later he still found financial mismanagement, gossip about sexual lapses, and nuns lying to cover up for each other. In the light of all his exhortations, punishments, and appeals, the archbishop felt enormously depressed that so little had changed for the better; he left the priory "sad and out of patience."[22]

19. For the visit of July 9, 1259, see ER, p. 383, and for the previous visits, see pp. 114, 158, 187, 199, 306, 353.
20. ER, p. 353.
21. ER, p. 430.
22. ER, p. 687.

The saga of Saint-Saens is a useful corrective to the misapprehension that episcopal visitors were necessarily awesomely frightening to and hence effective with those they visited. Eudes's impact on the nuns of Saint-Saens was paltry. They seem to have been a tightly bonded community that drew together in solidarity against the visitor, making it extraordinarily difficult to reform the priory. The archbishop could punish individuals, as he did by giving the prioress penances to perform; he could fulminate against errors and plead for *renovatio*. But when all was said and done, the community that chose to stand firmly together could often—like the nuns of Saint-Saens—go its own (perhaps wrong-headed) way.

From time to time Eudes lost his temper at the congregations under his care, whether nuns, monks, canons, or priests. But it was specifically religious women whose behavior could defeat him and whose piety could win his admiration. The nuns of Saint-Saens came closer to getting the better of Eudes than any other community of unrepentant religious in his care. On one of the last of his visits, he found them "living in disorder and not according to the rule": they recited the offices badly, missed confession, failed to live communally, owed money, and had bare larders.[23] Maybe it was late in the day, or perhaps the trauma of coping with the sisters daunted him, but Eudes acknowledged the mess and put off to the next day yet one more effort to sort out the priory's problems.

However unsettling visitations might be to the archbishop, he seems to have developed respect for some of his female charges, such as Comtesse, prioress of the Cistercian house of Bondeville on the outskirts of the city of Rouen. Her two predecessors had been unsatisfactory administrators, and when the second resigned in 1258, Eudes was pleased to confirm Comtesse as superior.[24] Bondeville may have had a record of poor leadership, but it also seems to have been a difficult community to handle. Over the next three years, the archbishop visited twice and found much to criticize. When she received the second critical assessment in September 1261, the poor prioress quit. She brought out her seal of office, symbol of her position as superior of Bondeville (see fig. 2), and begged Eudes to relieve her of the burden of trying to control her unruly flock.[25] The prelate dissuaded her and, one assumes, gave her some encouragement to carry on. Five years later, when Eudes came to the priory, he was

23. ER, pp. 595–96.
24. ER, p. 337.
25. ER, p. 468.

Figure 2. Seal of Prioress Odelina of Bondeville, Rouen, successor to Prioress Comtesse, Courtesy of Bibliothequé Départementale de Seine-Maritime.

pleased with the state of affairs.[26] He recognized, however, that Prioress Comtesse had aged and had become too frail to run the house any longer. It had taken half a decade of what must have been taxing work to get Bondeville on an even keel, an effort that had sapped the strength of its leader. Eudes eased the old lady out of office, softening the blow by noting that even in her enfeebled state "she was worthily acquitting herself of this position and had done so for many years."

The Nuns' Perspective

Eudes's visitation record gives us a taste of the relationship between one bishop and the congregations he visited from the visitor's perspective. But not one of our nuns reports whether she saw the diocesan as just a gorgeously appareled prelate, a friend and supporter, or the outside quality-control expert from whom lapses should be hidden. However, we do have records of how the nuns acted, which suggest that for them the authorities—the bishops—could be either an important court of help and appeal or a power to be avoided.

The ordinary was the natural ally of religious women and men when they were negotiating with or defending themselves against secular folk. When Countess Herlesende wanted to found her own monastery in the twelfth century, she discussed her wishes with Heloise, the abbess of the Paraclete. The women worked out an arrangement whereby the abbey would cede the area of Pommeraye as a building site for the new house.[27] In exchange, the abbess of Pommeraye would acknowledge the Paraclete as mother house, with certain rights over the new monastery. This elaborate negotiation is recorded in a chirograph written by Archbishop Hugh of Sens, who accepted in his own hand the agreement of both women and then confirmed it with his seal.

In the late thirteenth century, Bishop Milo of Soissons came to the aid of the canonesses of La Barre, who were burdened by their lay patrons with more new members and servants than they could support.[28] Milo took pity on the religious women, who were having great difficulty refusing those foisted on them, even though La Barre was too poor to feed and clothe additional people. The bishop reduced the size of the house by setting new limits of thirty canonesses and eight lay sisters. The bishop had a sensitive understand-

26. ER, p. 584.
27. Paris, BN, MS. Baluze XLVI, pp. 143–44.
28. "Abbaye de la Barre et son recueil," pp. 165–66.

ing of the bind in which the women found themselves; he gave them the ammunition of an episcopal fiat but left it to the abbess to effect a gradual diminution as and when she deemed proper.

The bishop figured for the monastic in important ways. He was the logical person to ratify the actions between an abbess and a lay-woman. He was also the figure to whom an individual religious could turn for support against their monastic superiors. When Constance, a nun at Montivilliers, felt aggrieved by the punishment inflicted by her abbess, she appealed to the archbishop, Robert Poulain.[29] He responded by removing her from her abbey and putting her in another house.

But perhaps most significant in the day-to-day existence of regular institutions was the bishop's authority to adjudicate conflicts in which monasteries became embroiled. Monasteries were constantly having to defend themselves against claims and outright seizures of their property, a process in which members of the church hierarchy acted as judges and recorders. When the nuns of Saint-Avit in Châteaudun had a nasty spat over some tithes with Fulk of Montfort, a canon of Le Mans, a resolution was worked out informally by the bishop of that city with the consent of the legate.[30] In addition to such ad hoc negotiating, the ordinary could act officially as judge. Bishop Haimar of Saintes adjudicated a settlement of 1174 over the disputed land of Saint-Palladius.[31] His charter outlines the historical background: the conflict had originated when Constantine Grassus appropriated a large piece of reclaimed land and the nuns of Notre-Dame objected, saying it was theirs. Bernard, at that time the bishop of Saintes, heard the case and found for the abbey. When the nuns sent their people to take control, Constantine ignored the court ruling and violently seized the property, to which the bishop promptly responded by excommunicating him. Constantine died unrepentant, and his son, William Helias, continued his father's claim and attempted to appropriate the land of Saint-Palladius. That was too much for the abbess of Notre-Dame, the formidable Agnes of Barbezieux, who would tolerate no erosion of her abbatial holdings. This proud woman came of the highest nobility of southern France. She was descended from the dukes of Aquitaine and was connected to the royal houses of England and France through her relative

---

29. Le Cacheux, *Exemption de Montivilliers*, pp. 8–9.

30. Cuissard, "Abbaye de Saint-Avit," p. 172.

31. *Cartulaire de Notre-Dame de Saintes*, pp. 73–75, no. 82. Abbess Agnes is described in this charter as "filia Guidonis comitis."

Eleanor of Aquitaine. Agnes had been elected abbess of Notre-Dame in Saintes in 1134, an office she held for forty years. During her abbacy the monastery grew in size, wealth, and power; William Helias did not stand a chance against this adversary.

The abbess moved swiftly by sending off an appeal to the pope to regain what she saw as purloined abbey property. The papal legate, Bishop John of Poitiers, was then empowered to deal with the contested case, which he initiated by sending notice to the abbess and to William Helias to appear before him at the Abbey of Saint-Jean d'Angély. When the day for the hearing came, the abbess presented herself, but William got cold feet and did not show up, thereby incurring a sentence of excommunication. A second date was set, and both parties were again notified. This time a somewhat chastened William appeared to argue his side of the case. Apparently he barely got to open his mouth. Agnes took command, asserting that there was no issue, since the land had previously been judged by Bishop Bernard to belong to the abbey. Thereupon she produced three witnesses: two priests and one layman. William contested their testimony, complicating and thereby prolonging the hearing. The delay forced the legate to delegate two clerics to carry on the inquiry in his stead when he had to leave, but they deftly sidestepped the whole sticky mess by handing the case over to Bishop Haimar of Saintes.

Haimar set a new court date. When all were assembled on that day, he heard testimony from both sides and then ruled for the abbey. This decision exhausted all hope for the case of William and his brothers. They realized they had no recourse but to give in, so they swore in the bishop's hands to resign their claim to the land. The bishop then reinforced the finality of their submission by having William join him in the ceremony of investing the abbess with a ring as symbol of her receipt of tenure. William's final act of renunciation was to swear on the Gospels that he would allow the nuns uncontested enjoyment of the land. All his bravado extinguished, William humbly begged Abbess Agnes to intercede with the bishop on behalf of his deceased father, who having died while excommunicated, had perforce been buried in unconsecrated soil without benefit of prayers or masses for his soul. Agnes graciously complied, and Bishop Haimar obliged her by lifting the ban of excommunication from Constantine Grassus. The nuns gave William further concessions: they wrote him into the abbey's book of the rule so that his anniversary would be celebrated, and they agreed that if he were to father a legitimate daughter, they would accept her as a nun.[32] The abbess sealed the interchange with a gift to William of sixteen shillings and a silver cup—a sort of consolation prize.[33]

This case demonstrates the role the church hierarchy could play in settling conflicts. Even though Abbess Agnes enjoyed prestige and high office, unruly knights like Constantine and his son William were willing and able to challenge abbey rights and privileges. Without the backing of pope, legate, and bishop, recovery of the land would have been an uphill fight for the nuns. But for some monastic superiors of lesser birth and competence, the system could not be galvanized so adroitly. The princes of the church were natural allies of monastic women and men but were most ready to assist when the monastic supplicants had connections.

The connection that carried most weight was shared kinship. Because prelates and abbots and abbesses tended to be drawn from the same social strata and families, it was not unusual for bishops and monastic superiors to be related.[34] The first abbess of Saint-Amand in Rouen was Emma, the sister of both the bishop of Bayeux and the archbishop of Rouen.[35] It is probable that the relationship between Abbess Emma and her brother, Archbishop Jean d'Avranches, was the foundation for part of the nunnery's long-lasting prestige. The custom developed that, before taking office, the archbishop-elect spent the night at Saint-Ouen and then stopped at Saint-Amand, where the abbess gave him a ring. When he died his body was brought to Saint-Amand to lie in state, and the abbess solemnly removed the ring. First mention of the ring comes in 1444, so this part

32. The abbey house book survives with its obituary of those for whom anniversaries were celebrated. Yale, Beinecke Library, MS. Marston 25, Kalendarius liber. William Helias is recorded on March 29 (fol. 11v), but this is probably a different person, because he is noted as a burgher. Two entries record Constantine C[G]rassus, the first on January 1 (fol. 1r), and the second on January 3 (fol. 1v), which suggests that this is the same person, erroneously entered twice. Constantine is noted as a *miles*, a knight, so his son, William Helias, would not be apt to be entered as a burgher. Did the nuns, then, renege on their promise of an anniversary for William Helias, or is it possible that the son slipped downward socially?

33. The battle over the land of Saint-Palladius is also a good example of how medieval litigation resolved conflicts with face-saving and ego-salving gifts for the loser, a tendency that will be discussed further in chapter 5.

34. Bouchard, *Sword, Miter, and Cloister*, p. 67 and passim, notes that ecclesiastical leaders were drawn from the nobility.

35. Marie-Josèphe Le Cacheux, *Histoire de l'abbaye de Saint-Amand de Rouen des origines à la fin du XVIe siècle* (Caen: Société d'Impression de la Basse-Normandie, 1937), p. 40

of the ceremony may well have been a later accretion. The custom of receiving the archbishop's body, however, probably had begun much earlier when Emma exercised her family right to lay out her brother's corpse, thereby instituting a prestigious precedent for the convent.[36]

The renown one member of a family enjoyed in the church lent credence to another relative's bid for church office. When Maria was elected abbess of the Paraclete in the mid-thirteenth century, it is likely that the position of her eminent brother, Eudes Rigaud, as archbishop of Rouen enhanced her candidacy. After her election, Eudes traveled to the Paraclete and had the joyous responsibility of installing his sister as abbess.[37] True to Eudes's personality, what survives in the cartulary of the Paraclete is not a description of the consecration but rather a careful list of the abbey's goods from Maria's first computation. In some cases a relative in a powerful position may have manipulated what was supposed to be a free election so that a family member was chosen as monastic superior. Archbishop Hartwig of Bremen used his influence to secure election as abbess of his sister, Richardis von Stade; but women also engaged in pressure tactics: Countess Adele of Apulia prevailed upon Pope Paschal II to make her niece abbess of Messines.[38]

Family connections could aid a variety of monastic strategies. Abbess Imene, head of the Cistercian Abbey of Salzinnes in Namur during the mid-thirteenth century, was determined to increase the visibility of her house. She managed, at least temporarily, to house at Salzinnes the saintly Juliana of Cornillon; she also cultivated the patronage of the local countess, and she looked around for some highly respected relics to enhance the reputation of her convent.[39] Some of the most talked-about holy remains in vogue at that moment were the bones of the Eleven Thousand Virgins of Cologne, which had been discovered early in the twelfth century. These were quickly snapped up by eager institutions, so that none were going

36. Le Cacheux, *Histoire de Saint-Amand*, pp. 71–75. The author comes to the conclusion, which I find persuasive, that Emma began as an individual kinswomen's responsibility what became an institutional right for the nuns of Saint-Amand.

37. ER, p. 42. Also see *Cartulaire du Paraclet*, p. 222, no. 246, June 11, 1249.

38. Newman, *Sister of Wisdom*, p. 222. Huyghebaert, "Femmes laïques dans la vie religieuse," pp. 371–72.

39. *Recueil du Val-Saint-Georges à Salzinnes*, p. 158. Also see "Abbaye de Salzinnes," in *Monasticon Belge*, vol. 1, *Province de Namur et de Hainaut*, ed. Ursmer Berlière (Liège: Centre National de Recherches d'Histoire Religieuse, 1961), and Guillaume Simenon, *Julienne de Cornillon* (Brussels: Presses Universitaires de Belgique, 1946).

begging. Imene knew some of the bones had ended up in the keeping of the nuns of Saints Maccabees in Cologne. She asked her brother, Conrad, who held the three influential positions of archbishop of Cologne, papal legate, and archchancellor of Italy, to see what he could arrange. Needless to say, the hapless nuns of Saints Maccabees were persuaded to send Salzinnes some of their precious relics as a favor to Conrad. Having powerful relatives in the church was definitely an asset to a monastery.

The power of secular ecclesiastical authority that could support and assist a monastery was the same clout that could restrict it—or so it might appear to the monastics. Protecting the traditional liberties of a house mattered as much to monks as it did to nuns, and male monasteries also could chafe under episcopal controls.[40] Consequently, although monasteries often called on bishops for assistance, they also used other avenues to fend off unwelcome episcopal authority. The abbess of Holy Cross in Poitiers brought her case against the ordinary before a church council.[41] At issue was Bishop Gilbert de la Porrée's insistence that he had the right to install the prior of the canons of Sainte-Radegonde, the chapter that served the nuns' liturgical needs. Abbess and bishop appeared at a synod and laid their evidence before the legate, who in an unusual ruling found for the nuns. The religious women of Holy Cross kept this control until 1308, when an interdict forced them to relinquish their jealously guarded privilege.

Some of the territorial battles between prelates and monastics were resolved by compromise. The Abbey of Saint-Sulpice negotiated with the bishop of Quimper over procuration fees for its dependent priory of Locmaria.[42] Passions ran high over this issue, and the compromise had to go to ecclesiastics outside the conflict: two friars of Quimper were to judge claims of exemption and adjudicate a binding settlement for abbey and bishop in case of a stalemate. In this case both sides were partially correct. Sometimes, however, the clash between bishop and convent seems to have been very one-sided and possibly even a thinly cloaked episcopal shakedown of the

40. Sally Vaughn, *The Abbey of Bec and the Anglo-Norman State* (Woodbridge, England: Boydell Press, 1981), pp. 30 ff., demonstrates the passionate commitment of both Anselm and Lanfranc to protecting the liberties of Bec.

41. Yvonne Labande-Mailfert, "Les débuts de Sainte-Croix," in *Histoire de Sainte-Croix de Poitiers: Quatorze siècles de vie monastique*, Mémoires de la Société des Antiquaires de l'Ouest, 4th ser., 19 (Poitiers: Société des Antiquaires de l'Ouest, 1986), pp. 97–99. The author suggests that Bernard of Clairvaux, who was present and possessed enormous persuasive capacities, was not a supporter of Gilbert.

42. *Cartulaire de Saint-Sulpice-la-Forêt*, pp. 440–42, no. 242, 1239.

nuns. For instance, Stephen, bishop of Meaux, argued that he held advocacy over the convent of Faremoutiers, but he retracted this rather unlikely claim with alacrity for the hefty payment of 150 pounds from the nuns.[43]

The most commonly essayed but not always successful end run around episcopal authority was to appeal to Rome. The Abbey of Saint-Sulpice secured a papal bull from Eugenius III after a conflict had erupted over whether the diocesan had free access to its church to say mass.[44] The pope supported the nuns and gave them a guarantee that the bishop had no right to say mass at their church unless they expressly invited him. Some monastic superiors, like Abbess Imene of Salzinnes, eschewed the piecemeal approach and actively embarked on a program of piling up papal confirmations and privileges.[45] Imene garnered a whole raft of papal advantages for her nuns. Superiors like Imene enjoyed personally exerting pressure on behalf of their houses, but in other cases a monastery paid a lobbyist to go to Rome to represent its interests. The Abbey of the Paraclete paid its lobbyist ten pounds to represent the nuns at the Roman curia.[46] Male houses also sent representatives to Rome, but these were more apt to be members of their chapter than salaried outsiders as they had to be for nuns.[47] It was a costly business for nuns to have to pay a lobbyist but increasingly necessary as papal politics became more complex during the central Middle Ages.

Exemption from episcopal control was the single-shot answer to the monastic's desire for autonomy. The practice of exempting religious houses from episcopal oversight had begun with Cluny's foundation and exemption in the early tenth century, and the custom had expanded to non-Cluniac houses in the following centuries.[48] In Normandy the dukes originally awarded this privilege to houses

43. Paris, BN, MS. n.a. lat. 928, p. 39.

44. *Cartulaire de Saint-Sulpice-la-Forêt*, p. 101, no. 42, 1146.

45. From August 1245 to December 1258 she secured ten papal privileges from Innocent IV, Alexander IV, and her brother Conrad, the papal legate.

46. *Cartulaire du Paraclet*, p. 266, no. 304, 1294.

47. ER, p. 646; two of Saint-Wandrille's monks were at the Roman curia.

48. See Noreen Hunt, *Cluny under Saint Hugh, 1049–1109* (Notre Dame, Ind.: University of Notre Dame Press, 1968), p. 39, for Cluny. Barbara Rosenwein, *Rhinoceros Bound: Cluny in the Tenth Century* (Philadelphia: University of Pennsylvania Press, 1982), pp. 20–21, looks at the historiography of the subject. See Lemarignier, *Privilèges d'exemption*, pp. 231–32, for a summary of the development of exemption in Normandy and pp. 84–86, 116 for other parts of France. Archbishop Eudes Rigaud describes his relationship to an exempt house in the following terms: "They are exempt, and in consequence we cannot visit them fully. However, we warned them to

so that abbeys would assume peacekeeping and police functions, whereas in the rest of France it was the bishops who endowed favored monasteries with freedom from their control. By the mid-twelfth century the popes had firmly gathered the valuable authority to grant exemption into their own hands, preempting the power from other lords temporal or spiritual.[49]

A monastery that had been granted exemption by whatever power was theoretically freed from all the ordinary's customary rights over it and any dues owed to him. In addition, the bishop could not visit an exempt house, although in the thirteenth century nunneries of exempt orders often came to be considered fair game by the visitor.[50] For instance, Eudes visited three Cistercian convents but no Cistercian male houses in his province. From the viewpoint of the monastics, obtaining a sweeping individual exemption from the control of the diocesan must have seemed preferable to extracting bits and pieces from a reluctant prelate or trying to use the general exemption of the order. The nuns of Saint-Amand had freed themselves from paying procuration, although they accepted the authority of the ordinary to visit them; in much the same way, the nuns of Saint-Avit had jockeyed for and won the right to name their own chaplains, although they too acknowledged the diocesan's power in other areas.[51] Arguing and bitter feelings accompanied such skirmishes for each petty privilege. To such houses, winning exemption must have looked like an enormous advantage, however, even being fully exempt did not preclude the need for a monastery, particularly one of women, to maintain a vigilant guard over its rights against a variety of challenges.

The story of the exemption of Montivilliers is an interesting example of the complexity of the whole issue. In January 1035 Duke Robert the Magnificent of Normandy had concluded Christmas festivities and was readying his entourage for a pilgrimage to the Holy Land, from which he would never return; on January 13, in the company of Archbishop Robert, other bishops and abbots, counts and

live as uprightly as they could, since in the event of crime we can deal with them" (ER, p. 635). In other words, if a house got into serious trouble, even if it were exempt, the diocesan could intervene.

49. Lemarignier, Privilèges d'exemption, p. 232.

50. C. R. Cheney, Episcopal Visitation of Monasteries in the Thirteenth Century (Manchester: Manchester University Press, 1931), p. 40.

51. Le Cacheux, Histoire de Saint-Amand, p. 72, and Cuissard, "Abbaye de Saint-Avit," p. 174.

viscounts, he presided over a court held at the great Abbey of Fé-camp.[52] One piece of business was to issue a charter freeing the nuns of Montivilliers from the control of the abbot of Fécamp and grant-ing them exemption from the ordinary:

> We constitute the same church of Saint-Mary with all the churches itemized below, unconditionally immune and wholly free from all episcopal custom, which, indeed, is done not by the violence of our power, but it is estab-lished and confirmed by the gift, free choice, and agree-ment of Lord Robert, archbishop of Rouen.

> In primis eamdem sancte Marie ecclesiam, cum aliis sub-ter scriptis ecclesiis, ab omni episcopali consuetudine ab-solutam, immunem et omnino liberam constituimus, quod quidem non nostrae potestatis violentia agitur, sed donatione, voluntate et concessione domini Rotbert, Rothomagensis archiepiscopi, constituitur et confir-matur.[53]

Exactly what this meant in the eleventh century is not clear, but at the very least it granted the abbey ecclesiastical jurisdiction over the twelve parish churches listed at the end of the document.

The charter was subsequently reissued by William the Conqueror in a panchart—a collection of charters—sometime between 1068 and 1076, with five additions. Possibly the nuns were augmenting their property by falsifying the document, or they were bringing the record up to date after the time of Duke Robert. Hall and Sweeney, using the fresh evidence from a newly discovered papal bull, make a convincing case that in four of these additions the nuns simply in-troduced into the panchart wording to cover property acquired since 1035.[54] The fifth interpolation attempts to explain the original ducal

52. David Douglas discusses the contest for this decision, which has often baffled modern scholars: *William the Conqueror: The Norman Impact upon England* (Berke-ley: University of California Press, 1967), p. 35.

53. The discussion and interpretation of the diploma from this court and of its later recension can be found in Le Cacheux, *Exemption de Montivilliers*; Lemarignier, Privilèges d'exemption, app. 1; Auber, "Abbaye de Montivilliers," pp. 13–14; Priem, "Abbaye de Montivilliers," pp. 156–58; Hall and Sweeney, "Unpublished Privilege." Lemarignier reproduces a critical edition of the whole text on pp. 240–45 of the ap-pendix, where this exemption is found on p. 242. His case for the authenticity of the document is persuasive, as are the arguments of Hall and Sweeney that the five addi-tions to the panchart of 1068–76 represent insertions covering new acquisitions by the abbey rather than being a forgery.

54. Hall and Sweeney, "Unpublished Privilege," pp. 670–71.

immunity by comparing it to the privileges enjoyed by the Abbey of Fécamp, so that the nuns' exempt lands are "to be held in every way just as the church of Fecamp exercises tenure."[55] This wording, Hall and Sweeney suggest, reflects the intent of the duke's original charter bestowing freedom from episcopal customs on Fécamp.[56] Therefore it too may represent an effort of Montivilliers to explain its rights more fully, although the possibility remains that it may describe what the nuns wished were the case.[57] Either way, the abbey felt a need to clarify its freedoms, which minimally involved some diminution in episcopal control over them and their churches.

For more than a century the abbey sailed smoothly along, apparently untroubled by importunate bishops, or perhaps content to accept the authority of the archbishop of Rouen with the exception of their immunity. Indeed, Montivilliers is mentioned in a bull of Adrian IV (1154–59) listing the nunnery among the abbeys under the oversight of the archbishop of Rouen.[58] Whatever the reasoning, the abbesses seem to have felt no need to reiterate privileges until the very end of the twelfth century, when Abbess Adeline secured a charter from Pope Celestine III (1191–98).[59] Either she was extremely casual or the papal chancery was sloppy, but the bull failed to mention a large hunk of the abbey's endowment and omitted any attempt to clarify the abbey's exemption.

Political upheaval between Angevins and Capetians may have encouraged the next superior of Montivilliers, Abbess Alice, to request in 1203 a new confirmation charter from Innocent III in order to make up for the omissions in the bull of Celestine.[60] Innocent's charter begins by repeating Celestine's bull but then fills the lacunae by naming the previously omitted property.

The halcyon days came rudely to an end early in the thirteenth century. Whatever privileges the nuns of Montivilliers had believed they enjoyed, their customs came under sustained attack by a series of Norman prelates. These clashes left in their wake a string of papal

55. Quoted by Hall and Sweeney, "Unpublished Privilege," p. 666: "In omni tenetura, sicut tenet Fiscannensis ecclesia."
56. Hall and Sweeney, "Unpublished Privilege," p. 667.
57. See Leonard C. Hector, *Paleography and Medieval Forgery* (London: St. Anthony's Press, 1959), pp. 6–10, and Eleanor Searle, "Battle Abbey and Exemption: The Forged Charters," *English Historical Review* 83(1968): 449–80.
58. Priem, "Abbaye de Montivilliers," p. 156.
59. Jaffé 16975, whose date Hall and Sweeney, "Unpublished Privilege," p. 663, no. 9, believe should be April 1193.
60. Hall and Sweeney, "Unpublished Privilege," p. 669.

bulls, responses to demands from both sides for papal support.[61] First at issue was how the ordinary was to visit the house. This was temporarily resolved by a bull of May 19, 1215, in which the pope ordered the archbishop to take with him on visits only a few followers, who were to behave in a seemly fashion; not to demand procuration; and to visit only once a year. The second battle raged over the control of clerics and officials in parish churches held by Montivilliers. A bull of May 4, 1215, fixed the rights for both sides, but apparently not to the nuns' satisfaction. The archbishop subsequently complained to Rome that when he attempted to visit the abbey, armed men barred the way to most of his entourage. When his archdeacon tried to preach, the nuns marched out. A few returned, but hardly in a friendly state of mind, for they came to threaten the prelate and make frightening gestures at him. The pope finally resolved the conflict by establishing that the abbess could place her own clerics in the three contested churches, but otherwise the priests would be under the authority of the archbishop.[62]

A lull followed this heated phase in monastic-episcopal relations, to be broken when Archbishop Eudes Rigaud became primate in midcentury and squared off with the nuns. Their interactions began calmly enough when Eudes first visited Montivilliers in 1248 and "found everything connected with it to be in good condition."[63] But his visit was somewhat unusual: he conducted the inquiries entirely through the abbess, since it seems this practice had come to be part of the way the abbey interpreted its exemption. In January 1260, after seven uneventful visits during which Eudes had questioned just the abbess, he changed his approach. He writes:

> We entered the chapter of the nuns and with God's aid preached His Word to them in chapter. Then, desiring, with God's help, to perform our duty of making a complete visitation, both in head and in members, as our office requires of us, it was urged on the part of the abbess and community that the archbishop of Rouen had never been in the habit of visiting them as a community, but only through the abbess. After a great deal of altercation, we asked them collectively and singly whether they would receive us for the purpose of making a full visita-

---

61. Le Cacheux, *Exemption de Montivilliers*, pp. 7–13, spells out the particulars of each of these bulls of May 4, 1215, May 19, 1215, March 22, 1217, April 26, 1217, and June 16, 1219.

62. Le Cacheux, *Exemption de Montivilliers*, p. 12.

63. ER, p. 2.

tion; through their spokesman, Master Robert, their cleric, they replied, "No," adding that they would never consent that we exercise the office of visitation there, except in the matters concerning the abbess alone, and they rested their case upon charters, custom, and privilege. However, we warned them to make us amends for this disobedience, rebellion, and contempt before the coming Ash Wednesday.[64]

It is likely that Eudes's challenge to the custom of visiting only the abbess resulted from the discovery of earlier papal bulls, for when he next came to Montivilliers a year later, he came armed with an old charter of Innocent III. After a heated exchange, he managed to exact compliance.[65] The nuns must have spent a good deal of time in preparation for the confrontation, for they too were armed with a written statement. Although they capitulated, they did so mulishly, "saving the right of our liberty and of our abbey in all other matters in which it should be saved." (A somewhat convoluted effort to establish a loophole for wiggling out of possible future episcopal constraints.) Eudes, however, nailed down his advantage with a written statement asserting that he possessed "the full right of visitation over the said nuns," and then he briskly set to questioning the members as well as the head.

Did the twelfth-century abbesses let slip a golden opportunity to parlay Montivilliers's original enigmatic charter from Duke Robert into a full exemption?[66] Probably not; for if the nunnery had interpreted its eleventh-century privilege as a general exemption, the abbey would surely have objected forcefully to Pope Adrian IV's earlier bull listing the nunnery as under the jurisdiction of the archbishop of Rouen. A more likely interpretation of the evidence would be that the nuns had always understood their original privilege simply to be greater control than usual over the clerics in their parish churches and a limitation of the ordinary's visitation rights to questioning only the abbess. In that case the clashes of the thirteenth century grew out of a new hostility from a church hierarchy seeking to curb a rich and powerful nunnery.

Montivilliers is not an isolated example but rather a vivid representation of what seems to have been a trend in France as a central-

---

64. ER, p. 401.
65. ER, pp. 434–35.
66. Hall and Sweeney, "Unpublished Privilege," p. 671, make this suggestion.

izing ecclesiastical organization attempted to bring the regular religious under the full control of the secular religious.[67] Male as well as female houses experienced more monastic-episcopal clashes, for the desire to establish order was a general drive in the hierarchy.

We have few modern parallels to help us understand what a bishop meant to a house of medieval monastic women or men. We can read canonical legislation about episcopal responsibilities for regular communities; we can discover whether a monastery was exempt; we can track arguments about myriad rights and privileges; we can chart dates of official visitations. But none of this gets to the heart of why the relation of prelate to monastery was so important yet problematic and why it might be particularly difficult for nunneries. In general the bishop's importance for all professed religious was that he exercised institutional power; he was both a potential support and a possible threat, depending on how he managed that power. In addition, the bishop represented the personal power of men over women during the Middle Ages; the ordinary may have figured unconsciously for religious women in the role of male relative, since when a prelate consecrated a nun he acted both as the head of her family in leading the bride to her intended and as her spouse in accepting her vows. The tension this produced, jarring against the corporate independence of religious women, may explain the periodic fierce fights waged by nunneries against particular bishops.

Rome was the force all members of the church turned to for a righting of wrongs, confirmation of possessions, and support against enemies. For medieval French nuns, the papacy was a distant but potent power that they attempted to harness in order to preserve and augment their rights and privileges. The popes did not always weigh in on the side of religious women, nor did they routinely discriminate against them; rather, the larger political picture shaped the context in which the claims and petitions of religious women and religious men were decided, usually without any notable gender bias. When a particular pope had an objective he wished to pursue—be it political or personal—a monastic house might find itself in the path of the papal policy, as did the nuns of Notre-Dame-aux-Nonnains, who fell afoul of Pope Urban IV.

67. The patterns varied in different parts of Europe, with much papal intervention in Italian monasteries in contrast to more stability and less interference in the great English Benedictine houses. See Robert Brentano, *Two Churches: England and Italy in the Thirteenth Century*, rev. ed. (Berkeley: University of California Press, 1988), pp. 288–90.

Everything started out happily enough. Urban IV had been born the son of a cobbler in the city of Troyes, that affluent locus of one of the great medieval fairs in the county of Champagne. Even after becoming pontiff, Urban continued to nourish a warm spot in his heart for his hometown and all his fondly remembered roots. Soon after his elevation to the papacy he issued two bulls in favor of the nuns of Notre-Dame: he donated a forty-day indulgence to the nuns and issued a bull against those who would hurt the abbey's holdings.[68] The nunnery had been an ecclesiastical home to Urban: he had been baptized in its church, and both his parents had been laid to rest in its cemetery; in fact he had already donated his family home to the nunnery in recognition of all he owed the religious women.[69] But apparently the more Urban thought about the dizzying heights to which he had risen from his humble origins in Troyes, the more he wanted to impress on the folks back home what a success he had become. He wanted his countrymen to remember him long after his body had withered away, which he could effect by emulating his predecessor, Pope Gregory IX, and building a church where he grew up.[70] Urban's plan was simple but selfish: he wanted to take back from the nuns the family house he had given them so he could build a church on that plot of land and dedicate it to his patron, Saint Urban. He promised to reimburse the abbey for the house, its courtyard, and all the rights vested in the property that they were to hand over to his surrogates—John Garsi, his chaplain, and Thibald of Acenai, a citizen of Troyes. The high-handed papal approach must have come as a shock to the nuns of Notre-Dame-aux-Nonnains. They inhabited an enormously powerful monastery that cast even the cathedral of Troyes into the shade; they were not used to such cavalier treatment.[71] The nuns ceded the property to the pope, but with an ill will that time would reveal.

The building of a collegiate church dedicated to Saint Urban proceeded but was incomplete at the time of Pope Urban's death in 1264. Perhaps the nuns thought that with the papal patron out of

68. *Documents de Notre-Dame-aux-Nonnains*, pp. 112–13, no. 184, March 14, 1262, p. 113, no. 185, March 15, 1262. Urban was pope from 1261 to 1264.

69. Paris, BN, MS. Moreau 1208, fol. 266v; and *Documents de Notre-Dame-aux-Nonnains* p. 119, no. 191, 1263, p. 113, no. 186, 1262.

70. *Documents de Notre-Dame-aux-Nonnains* pp. 114–15, no. 186, May 20, 1262.

71. Patrick Geary points out that the nunnery dominated the economy of the city to the detriment of the cathedral and its chapter: "Saint Helen of Athyra and the Cathedral of Troyes in the Thirteenth Century," *Journal of Medieval and Renaissance Studies* 7(1977): 152.

the way interest in the new foundation would wane. If so, they were sadly in error. Whatever their reasoning, the abbess and the nuns of the monastery yearned to demolish the church.[72] They incited their servants and supporters to break down the church doors, overturn the altar, and seize the workmen's tools. As soon as the canons had recovered from this startling attack, they responded by installing new doors, only to have them smashed and carried off again by the nuns and their supporters. When news of the attack reached the new pontiff, Clement IV, he addressed himself in outraged tones to episcopal officials in the city, ordering them to secure satisfaction in two weeks from the clerics and layfolk who had perpetrated the outrage. The vandals may have sought forgiveness, but their instigators, the nuns, were far from repentant.

Two years later, when Archbishop Giles of Tyre came to Troyes to bless the canons' cemetery, the nuns swung into action again.[73] This time they did not hesitate to act directly: the abbess and some of the nuns led armed men to the canons' church so they could bar the door to the prelate. Giles warned them to open under threat of excommunication; they refused. The archbishop tried again later to execute his mandate, but the nuns stopped him, this time in the public street, and said they would exert themselves to the utmost to protect their rights. When apprised of what had happened, the pope set a two-week time limit for making amends under threat of excommunication. But the nuns knew how to manage this challenge and immediately sent off their own counterappeal. Eventually, after some delaying tactics, the case came before the local deacon and archdeacon for settlement. The nuns were found guilty, and nine of them together with twenty-three men were excommunicated. Apparently the defiant religious women of Notre-Dame-aux-Nonnains lived under the ban for fourteen years until it was lifted when they made restitution with a hefty payment of one hundred silver marks to the canons.[74] The power of the church hierarchy had finally squelched their rebellion, but probably without any diminution of their feeling that it was they—not the canons—who had been wronged.

It made no difference to Rome whether it was a community of

---

72. *Documents de Notre-Dame-aux-Nonnains* p. 121, no. 194, October 1, 1266.

73. *Documents de Notre-Dame-aux-Nonnains* pp. 123–24, no. 199, July 15, 1268.

74. *Documents de Notre-Dame-aux-Nonnains*, pp. 125–29, no. 200, March 15, 1269, relates the legal manipulations that followed, and pp. 130–32, nos. 203, 204, 205, all of 1283, outline the lifting of the excommunication and the restitution made by the nuns.

religious women or men who thwarted a papal scheme; such opposition would not be countenanced. When monasteries sought benefits and restitution from or rebelled against the Holy See, their gender was a matter of indifference. What mattered was that the majesty of Peter's successor not be diminished. Thus papal politics responded to the needs and behavior of a regular house much more than to the gender of its inhabitants, often protecting its freedoms but sometimes suppressing them.

The Abbot as Authority

The bishop was not the only church leader to exercise authority over monasteries. By the central Middle Ages the power to oversee, visit, and correct as well as to appoint officials in monasteries could also belong to abbots of orders to which individual houses belonged. With abbots as with bishops, authority over a monastery could be used either positively or negatively. But in practice, from the mid-twelfth century, abbots developed a growing tendency to deal harshly with the convents in their care. Often, in fact, fueled by their growing hostility to the *cura monialium*, the responsibility of caring for nuns, an abbot and his male house treated a dependent nunnery as a carcass to be picked over for tasty tidbits.

In the early part of the central Middle Ages a definite warm feeling had been expressed by monastic men for their female counterparts. Some monks and hermits chose to found houses for women or to accept the oversight of a nunnery. A discussion among a group of holy men is recorded in the life of Pons of Léras: "An argument therefore broke out among them as to which order was the greater, some praising the Cistercians, others the Carthusians, some even saying that it would be good to build a house for nuns. Then it was decided to lay the whole matter before the Carthusians and to leave the decision to them." [75] Although Pons and his circle did not start a house for religious women, it was an acceptable part of their deliberations in the first half of the twelfth century. Other men in this period not only considered starting women's foundations but also followed through: Robert Arbrissel founded the famous nunnery of Fontevrault at the turn of the twelfth century, and Steven of Obazine established Coyroux at midcentury.

Perhaps the most famous case of a monk's creating a community for nuns is that of Abelard, giving over his oratory of the Paraclete

---

75. Quoted by Henrietta Leyser, *Hermits and the New Monasticism: A Study of Religious Communities in Western Europe, 1000–1150* (London: St. Martin's Press, 1984), p. 93.

to Heloise and her displaced nuns from Argenteuil.[76] Whatever the personal aspect of this act, in one of the letters of direction to Heloise Abelard voices the belief that it is appropriate for monks to be responsible for nuns. Though he found this responsibility reasonable, as the century grew old it began to weigh more and more heavily on many other male monastics.[77] Pierre-Roger Gaussin notes, for instance, that relations between the nunneries in the order of la Chaise-Dieu and their mother house were excellent until the end of the thirteenth century, when trouble began to brew.[78] Some sense of this pattern can also be discerned in the history of the Priory of Jully-les-Nonnains.

Jully was founded by Milo, the count of Bar-sur-Seine, around 1115 in such a way that "the women should serve God quietly under the order of the abbot of Molesme."[79] Abbot Guido of Molesme and his monks were to see that the nuns had physical and spiritual sustenance, for since the nuns observed strict claustration, they could not manage property and tenants without male assistance.[80] The documents show no major difficulties until an enigmatic charter issued by the archdeacon of Tonnerre in 1240.[81] Archdeacon Peter states that the prioress of Jully has confirmed that she and her

76. The famous correspondence of Heloise and Abelard contains rich material for understanding the lives of nuns in France's heartland during the central Middle Ages. This marvelous source has been the subject of several scholarly sieges, during which arrows and rocks have been rained on its authenticity. The most recent attack comes from Georges Duby, who terms the correspondence a "pastiche": Thirteenth Sewanee Mediaeval Colloquium, April 1986. If in fact the letters contained in Troyes MS. 802 were first written in the thirteenth century or were rewritten and edited then, they still represent attitudes about monastic women in the central Middle Ages. In full awareness that the correspondence may not be what it purports to be, I will still use it to understand attitudes from the latter part of the period, and so as not to get into hopeless convolutions, I will attribute the ideas to the putative authors.

77. *Letters of Abelard and Heloise*, p. 210. A little farther on (p. 212) Abelard argues that abbots should rule over religious women, a policy that never was instituted at the Paraclete.

78. Pierre-Roger Gaussin, "Les religieuses de la congrégation de la Chaise-Dieu," in *Les religieuses en France au XIIIe siècle*, ed. Michel Parisse (Nancy: Presses Universitaires de Nancy, 1985), p. 113. This friction was being generated all over western Europe. See Catherine Boyd, *A Cistercian Nunnery in Mediaeval Italy: The Story of Rifreddo in Saluzzo, 1220–1300* (Cambridge: Harvard University Press, 1943), pp. 113–18.

79. *Cartulaire du prieuré de Jully-les-Nonnains*, ed. Ernest Petit, *Bulletin de la Société des Sciences Historiques et Naturelles de l'Yonne* 34(1880): 256, no. 1.

80. *Cartulaire général de l'Yonne*, ed. Maximilien Quantin (Auxerre: Perriquet et Rouillé, 1854), p. 398, no. 248, 1145.

81. *Cartulaire de Jully-les-Nonnains*, p. 293, dated 1240.

flock would accept no one to run their affairs except the prior and chamberlain sent by the abbot of Molesme. Jurisdiction apparently was becoming a concern, and by the beginning of the next century it had become a burning issue when the nuns adamantly refused to accept the officials sent them by the abbot of Molesme.[82] Because the nuns resisted the abbot's appointments, two other abbots had to step in and act as arbitrators. The settlement proved fragile, and seventeen years later outright revolt by the nuns brought excommunication down on their heads.[83] The fourteenth century was a time of uneasy compromises punctuated by the nuns' almost unceasing resistance to the control of Molesme. The inevitable end came in 1413 when, excusing their actions as necessary because of the nuns' evil ways, the abbot and prior of Molesme successfully petitioned the bishop for permission to close the nunnery and absorb its revenues.[84] Were the nuns unreasonable? Was the monastery of Molesme a poor administrator? No definite answer is possible, although there does seem to have been a tendency from the late twelfth century on for the controlling abbey either to lose interest in its caretaker functions or to take over the dependent female priory.

The convent of La Celle, dependent on the monks of Saint-Victor, suffered from such neglect.[85] Near the end of the thirteenth century the nuns had to call in the count to help them, charging that the monks of Saint-Victor were hurting their property. L'Hermite-Leclercq argues that this was an accurate perception, since as the century wore on a series of ambitious priors had begun using their position as a stepping-stone to higher office, and their evident lack of interest in and concern for the nuns of La Celle was indeed damaging the priory.

Some male monastic overseers did a good job of tending the religious women in their care, even during the troubled thirteenth century. Simone Roisin argues that the Cistercian monks in the area of Liège had a positive feeling about their female charges that proved beneficial for the spiritual growth of both nuns and monks.[86] But in general the *cura monialium* seems to have been perceived as oner-

82. *Cartulaire de Jully-les-Nonnains*, p. 300, dated 1312.

83. *Cartulaire de Jully-les-Nonnains*, pp. 330–31, dated 1330.

84. *Cartulaire de Jully-les-Nonnains*, p. 302, dated 1413.

85. Paulette l'Hermite-Leclercq, "Le monastère de La Celle les Brignole, (Var) au XIIIe siècle," in *Les religieuses en France au XIIIe siècle*, ed. Michel Parisse (Nancy: Presses Universitaires de Nancy, 1985), pp. 83–84.

86. Simone Roisin, "L'efflorescence cistercienne et le courant féminin de piété au XIIIe siècle," *Revue d'Histoire Ecclésiastique* 39(1943): 354, 364.

ous after the first flush of early twelfth-century enthusiasm had faded.[87]

If we compare how nuns fared with the ecclesiastic hierarchy, the relations of nuns and secular prelates seem to have worn better over time than those of nuns and their overseeing monks. This difference can be explained in terms of cost. The bishop had little to lose in exercising his right to visit and correct nuns. He was committed to traveling around his diocese anyway to keep tabs on secular clerics and male monastics, and the houses he visited paid him procuration to cover expenses.

An abbey charged with a dependent house of nuns, in contrast, had to give up some of its personnel to fill positions at the women's priory. Priors, chamberlains, confessors, chaplains, all might have to be provided by the monks. The Abbey of Molesme was supposed to send four monks to staff the dependent Priory of la Presle but found that obligation too heavy.[88] Instead one monk went to do the work of four, and the nuns were instructed to be content with the arrangement. In addition, although an abbot had to visit dependent male houses as well as female ones, he did not need to deplete his own manpower to staff a male priory; it could provide men itself to perform the liturgical services and attend to financial affairs. The drain of manpower from a male house to female dependent priories could be a painful loss, particularly as the number of monastic vocations dwindled in the later Middle Ages, creating a smaller pool of monks. Finally, some of the nunneries under the care of monks, like Marcigny under Cluniac oversight, had been founded to absorb the wives of men entering monasteries. This meant that such women's houses could be resented as institutional necessities rather than welcomed as spiritual partners by those monks responsible for them. Overseer-abbots and dependent nuns were in an unequal relationship that generated a sense of being ill used on both sides. The final act in these monastic dramas was often a repeat of Jully's fate:

87. See, for example, Sally Thompson, "The Problem of the Cistercian Nuns in the Twelfth and Thirteenth Centuries," in *Medieval Women*, ed. Derek Baker, Studies in Church History, Subsidia 1 (Oxford: Basil Blackwell, 1978), and Gold, *Lady and the Virgin*, pp. 84–93. Bruce L. Venarde is preparing a dissertation at Harvard to be titled "The Crisis of Female Monasticism in the High Middle Ages: Nunneries and Societies in France, Belgium, and England," which will further support this picture of a growing resistance to monastic women in the mid-twelfth century.

88. Carré, "Ste. Marguerite de la Presle," 4(1892): 11–14: "Statuimus ut . . . moniales uno monacho sint contentae."

the male house evicted the nuns and took over the troublesome female priory. In contrast to the abbot-superiors of nunneries, who had much to lose and little to gain from overseeing religious women, the bishop was a natural ally for the female religious under his care. From the bishop's perspective, nuns were not necessarily more costly to oversee than were monks. From the vantage of both religious women and men, the ordinary who kept records, held courts, and adjudicated conflicts was the natural authority to turn to for help. Like Bishop Milo of Soissons, he could both protect and respect a house in his care; like Eudes Rigaud, he might work with a superior to reform a monastery. Many prelates were kin of monastic superiors and thereby felt particular concern for the communities linked to them by blood. But at the same time, regular houses of nuns and monks often were at loggerheads with the diocesan in their drive to achieve greater communal autonomy. The experience of a monastery could be that of Montivilliers, battling for ill-defined customs and privileges with a long line of obdurate prelates, or that of the nuns of Troyes, taking on no less than the pontiff himself. In brief, prelates could be a mixed blessing for the congregations in their charge, and after the mid-twelfth century overseer-abbots generally had a negative impact on their female charges.

RELATIONS WITH OTHER CLERICS

Not all the clerics the nuns had dealings with were empowered to control them. Far from it. Most of the men in orders who interacted with religious women were priests, monks, or canons who were confreres, not superiors. Rather than serving as overseers to nuns, these clerics were associated with the nuns either by physical proximity or by spiritual bonds.

Neighborly dealings between nuns and clerics often involved property: the business could be as simple and uncharged as when a nunnery rented a house to one of the canons of the cathedral who needed a place to live, or as complicated and unpleasant as the settlement of a feud between a convent and a nearby monastery over a chapel and its tithes.[89] Interactions could be over gifts: a canon of Notre-Dame in Senlis donated a house to the nuns of Saint-Remy for his soul's sake, and the abbess of Saint-Pierre-aux-Nonnains in

---

89. *Cartulaire de Notre-Dame de Saintes*, p. 57, no. 57, 1086; *Cartulaire de Saint-Sulpice-la-Forêt*, p. 429, no. 231, 1165.

Figure 3. Town plan of the City of Metz. Phot. Bibl. Nat. Paris.

Metz gave a mill, whose income was to be shared between the nuns and the clerics, to three priests who were friends of the nuns.[90] Since urban monasteries existed in close proximity (see fig. 3), it was particularly natural for them to become involved.[91]

Monasteries could compete with their neighboring institutions or cooperate for their mutual well-being. Notre-Dame-aux-Nonnains saw the collegiate Church of Saint-Urbain as a rival. The nuns took umbrage at the upstart foundation, resisting and attacking it in every way possible. But the behavior of sister and brother institutions could be very different. In the Norman city of Rouen, a city thronged with religious institutions, the nunnery of Saint-Amand maintained a close relationship with the monastery of Saint-Ouen. When the abbess died, the monks sang the first nocturn from the office of the dead at her funeral and gave three days' pittances (an extra serving of food received by each monastic) to the poor. When

90. Paris, BN, MS. lat. 11002, fol. 19r; Paris, BN, MS. lat. 10027, fols. 17v–18r.
91. Carré, "Ste. Marguerite de la Presle," 5(1893): 441, no. 93, 1344, for a gift from Prioress Agnes of Reims to an abbatial confrere.

the abbot died, the nuns reciprocated in kind.[92] The two houses commemorated the death of each other's members by reciting psalms and giving pittances to their own congregations for the soul of their sister or brother. The brothers' generosity to the nuns was lavish: they gave the nuns seven gallons of red wine each Wednesday and celebrated on the feast of their own patron saint by sending the nuns bread, paté, and wine. (The staples of French cuisine go back a long way.) There was nothing niggling about this present: the monks gave thirty-six gallons of wine on the feast of Saint-Ouen to match the statutory number of thirty-six nuns. The nuns also had the right to receive three loads of wood a day from the monks' forests. To thank the monks and celebrate the close relationship, the nuns gave an annual feast for the abbot, forester, clerk, and three sergeants of the forests of Saint-Ouen. The long history of these two houses is notable for its cooperative rather than combative spirit.

As well as relating to houses of male monastics, nunneries sometimes had contacts with each other. For instance, established nuns could offer help to their inexperienced sisters. When a newly formed community was trying to learn the forms of worship of the Dominican order, two seasoned Dominican nuns went to them as teachers and coaches in the chant.[93] Other such short-term cooperative interactions took place between religious women, but one sharing of resources was more permanent. When a nunnery lost its superior to death or retirement, it occasionally needed to look outside its own personnel to find a replacement. One nunnery, Saint-Pierre-les-Dames in Reims, was a veritable seedbed of new abbesses during the twelfth century.[94] Saint-Pierre's nuns took over abbacies at Montmartre, Vervins, Origny, Morienval, and other houses. Saint-Pierre must have enjoyed an unusually positive reputation to have been such a major supply house of new superiors.

From time to time groups of nuns also formed colonies that split off from one house to start a new convent. When the Cistercian nuns of Bival became frustrated by what they saw as the despotic oversight of the abbot of Beaubec, small cohorts left Bival to estab-

92. Le Cacheux, *Histoire de Saint-Amand*, p. 83.

93. Renouard de Bussière, *Histoire des religieuses dominicaines*, p. 9. Elkins, *Holy Women of Twelfth-Century England*, p. 70, records a similar case in which a nun acts as instructor at a new house.

94. Françoise Poirier-Coutansais, *Gallia monastica: Tableaux et cartes de dépendances monastiques publiés sous la direction de J.-F. Lemarignier*, vol. 1, *Les abbayes bénédictines du diocèse de Reims* (Paris: Picard, 1974), pp. 483–84.

lish the new houses of Bondeville and Saint-Saens, free of the resented abbatial control.[95] Other ventures might be more cooperative than defiant, although also creating nunneries with a bond of common parenthood. The largest colonizing efforts usually involved twelve nuns, who in imitation of the apostles would begin a new religious ministry. A dozen Clarisses gathered from three established convents in 1336 to inaugurate the new house of Moncel, a migration that bonded four houses in a common effort.[96] Whether one woman went to a convent to be invested as its superior or a group of nuns became the nucleus of a new institution, the migration of women between nunneries created connections, linking religious women just as the same process bonded male colonies with shared traditions and experiences.

Nunneries established social and spiritual bonds with monks outside their region, sometimes through individual initiative, sometimes as a corporate gesture. The nuns of the important convent of Notre-Dame-aux-Nonnains communicated with major figures in the church. As early as the Carolingian period, its abbess was in touch with the great scholar Alcuin, who wrote warmly back to her praising the intellectual achievements of her nuns and thanking her for the gift of a cross she had sent him.[97] Later in the twelfth century one of its nuns wrote to Saint Bernard, seeking his support for her desire to enter a hermitage.[98] Exchanging gifts and letters between notables primarily connected the individuals, although there may have been some trickling down of the impact of this bond to the rank and file. More widespread in its effect for a monastery would have been receiving a *rotulus* and sharing the spiritual bonds of confraternity or of a mutual patron saint.

Rotuli were monastic chain letters circulated among religious institutions at the death of an abbess or abbot. A messenger would leave the monastery that had just lost its superior, bearing around his neck a roll made of parchments stitched together. The roll bearer traveled around from monastery to monastery, stopping at each one

95. Malicorne, *Documents sur l'abbaye de Bival*, p. 16. Also see Michel Desmarchelier, "L'architecture des églises de moniales cisterciennes: Essai de classement des différents types de plans," in *Mélanges à la mémoire du Père Anselme Dimier*, ed. Benoît Chauvin, Architecture Cistercienne 3, (Arbois: Benoît Chauvin, 1982), pp. 79–121.

96. A. de Sérent, "L'ordre de Sainte Claire en France pendant sept siècles," *Etudes Franciscaines*, n.s., 11(1953): 135.

97. *Documents de Notre-Dame-aux-Nonnains*, pp. 159–60.

98. Epistle 115, PL, 182:261–62.

to tell of the death and to solicit prayers for the soul of the superior and all the monastery's members who had recently died. When the messenger arrived at a house, he told his story and handed over the roll so that the monastics could write a commemorative message on it. Some of these messages are prayers or poems for the superior; some are requests for prayers for the souls of recently departed members of the writer's monastery. As the roll circulated with its bearer, it carried information and inspiration between abbeys. The often-used phrase "we pray for your members, you pray for ours" encapsulates the essential purpose, which was to create a reciprocal prayer chain.

The *rotulus* for Abbess Helvide of Saint-Amand traveled around to houses of nuns, monks, and canons of different orders. The monks of Saint-Benoît-sur-Loire added the names of six of their members who had died in the preceding year, and the monks of Saint-Aignan in Orléans wrote a piece of doggerel in her memory:

> Qui super astra sedes, Haidi fungi requie des.
> Hec bona persona tangat celestia dona,
> In regione bona celis, O Christe, corona.

> Above the stars in splendor reign!
> But unto her, your mercy deign
> to grant the crown that she has won
> and give her rest, her work is done.[99]

The roll bearer wandered around in a somewhat haphazard fashion, in some towns stopping at practically every religious institution, as he did in Nevers, Orléans, and Soissons, and at other times moving along more rapidly, bypassing a number of monasteries. He may have been systematically visiting those houses to which the nuns had sent him or—as I suspect—at least partly following his own fancy. In either case he stopped at nunneries as well as male monasteries, bearing his news to the Cistercian nuns of Lieu-Notre-Dame-les-Romorandin and to the Benedictine nuns of Saint-Pierre in Orléans. Only a few *rotuli* survive, but during the Middle Ages such manuscripts were common. They must have had a significant impact on monastic life as the messengers roamed the countryside, collecting prayers, disseminating information of all sorts, and—by

---

99. Rouen, BD, *rotulus*, Saint-Amand, H 55, titles 16, 18. The translation is by Patrick T. McMahon, O. Carm. The roll is edited in highly abbreviated form in *Rouleaux des mortes du IXe au XVe siècle recueillis et publiés pour la Société de l'Histoire de France*, ed. Léopold Deslisle (Paris: J. Renouard, 1866), pp. 401–7.

discharging their responsibilities—affirming the spiritual bonds that tied religious people together.

Confraternity, a union of prayer and privileges, linked monasteries to each other and individuals to monasteries. La Magdeleine-lez-Orléans shared confraternity with the august mother of medieval Benedictine houses, the Abbey of Cluny.[100] Although la Magdeleine was a Fontevrist priory, it was not particularly wealthy or powerful. For such a modest establishment to be tied into the unceasing round of prayers at Cluny, the largest, most famous abbey in the West, was an indication of the prestige of its order and may well have given its inhabitants an important sense of being part of the wider church.

Nunneries created confraternity among themselves as well as with male houses. The Paraclete and the Abbey of Fontevrault shared prayer fellowship between their abbesses and some of the abbey's leading clerics and nuns.[101] For the Abbey of Bourbourg, confraternity with the monks of Saint-Michael's in Wynton expanded their geographic horizons and was egalitarian.[102] The abbot extended to the nuns the promise of an annual service each Lent to commemorate all their dead, as well as a mass and fifty psalms to be sung by each brother. On hearing of the death of their abbess, the monks guaranteed to write her name in their martyrology for annual remembrance.

Although confraternity was not divided by gender lines, it tended to be elitist: wealthy and powerful houses usually prayed for similar establishments, which meant that for august male houses the nunneries that seemed worthy of confraternity might make a short list. Holy Trinity in Vendôme included only two orders of nuns among its sixty-three confreres.[103] Still, to be part of confraternity was to be in touch with other houses by correspondence as well as by circulating death rolls; it was a means of breaking down the isolation that cloistering imposed.

A shared patron saint created another spiritual connection between religious houses and across gender barriers. For instance, the nuns of Saint-Amand in Rouen were in touch with the monks of Saint-Amand at Elnone in Flanders.[104] In the memorable year 1066

100. Vauzelles, *Histoire de la Magdeleine-lez-Orléans*, p. 18.

101. *Cartulaire du Paraclet*, pp. 196–97, no. 216, 1237.

102. *Cartulaire de Notre-Dame de Bourbourg*, 1:161, no. 170, 1261.

103. The prayer list is in a late thirteenth-century hand in Vendôme, BM, MS. 100, fol. 173v. Two out of sixty-three is a paltry 3 percent.

104. Platelle, "Relations entre Saint-Amand et Saint-Amand d'Elnone," pp. 83–106, beautifully lays out the background for this argument.

the Flemish abbey burned, and twenty-two years later, in 1088, its new church was dedicated. The same year Emma, a nun of the Norman nunnery dedicated to Saint Amand, arrived in Flanders to be enclosed in an anchorhold near the saint's relics. It is probable that her arrival was timed to jibe with the dedication and must have necessitated an agreement reached by both houses. Close communication continued between the two monasteries in the next century. In 1107 Marsilia, abbess of Saint-Amand in Rouen, wrote to her confreres, the Flemish monks serving the saint at Elnone, to report a miracle. She was aware that the monks were compiling an account of the miracles performed by their mutual patron and wanted to add her tale to enhance the saint's reputation—and thereby that of her own house. Such continuing close communication between the nuns and monks resulted from the kinship felt by these monastics who revered the same saintly patron.

Shared concerns between monasteries not only could be strong and lasting but also could benefit the larger community. Lord Gaucher of Châtillon must have been well aware of the cooperative spirit between the monks of Hermières and the nuns of Pont-aux-Dames when he drew up his will in the mid-thirteenth century.[105] He left an annual rent of twenty-three pounds to the two monastic superiors and charged them to use it for the indigent. Abbess and abbot were to buy clothes and shoes and distribute them to the poor, a venture that would have been doomed to failure unless the donor knew the nuns and monks could work together amicably.

Houses of religious women and men in the same town or region had both institutional dealings and individual exchanges with each other. Gender was less apt to separate monasteries than was belonging to different orders or being radically different in size and wealth. In fact the spiritual links forged by *rotuli*, by sharing a patron saint, or by confraternity bonded houses beyond the accidents of location, order, and sex. Spiritual connection for medieval monasteries was not predicated on gender.

CONCLUSION

If we posit that medieval women in general accepted their role in patriarchal society, religious women still often challenged the authority of their male superiors. The high birth of some nuns, like that of Agnes of Barbezieux, helped create a climate in which assertive behavior seemed natural. But the presence of some noblewomen

105. Abbaye du Pont-aux-Dames, pp. 25–26, no. 84, 1248.

does not explain the common experience of the rank and file of nunneries, which routinely jockeyed with prelates over issues of control.
When women joined regular communities, they shed many of the
attitudes and much of the customary behavior of secular women.
Professed women became part of a new corporate persona. No longer
were they individual females defined primarily through the men to
whom they were related or attached; instead they became brides of
Christ who were part of the ecclesiastical establishment. By becoming participants in the church's liturgy and life, by belonging to the
church more completely than was possible for any secular person—
female or male—nuns collectively were empowered by their communal privileges and status to think and act with self-confidence.

The world of the medieval nun was not isolated from its surrounding lay community; rather, it was connected by family, regional, and
ecclesiastical ties. The strongest of all cords was shared kinship,
which bound individual nuns to their families and thereby created
obligations and loyalties on both sides. Those outside the cloister
often had a sister, aunt, or mother in the nearby convent; their parents lay buried in the nuns' cemetery, and their wills had been
drawn up at the nunnery. The convent that connected with a family
was its spiritual haven but also a resource to help meet family needs.
For nuns, therefore, support and protection—as well as pressure to
accept a novice, grant a loan, or settle a conflict—came from relatives. The mutual concerns that held families together embraced
individuals within a monastery as they did kin in the outside world.

In addition, the nuns affected their neighbors, relatives or not.
They disciplined arrogant barons; they cared for the poor and the
needy; they fielded armed attacks or legal challenges to protect their
rights and property. They dealt with patrons who meddled with
monastic peace and property as well as with those who developed
protective and supportive relations with an abbey.

Nuns also had to cooperate with or confront the ecclesiastical authorities. Churchmen from the most powerful prelate to the most
insignificant monk both bullied and benefited convents. Bishops,
however, tended to be benign supporters of the convents in their
care, whereas abbatial overseers were often unsympathetic to the
women, whose direction proved onerous. Yet the spiritual ties of
confraternity, rotuli, and shared patron saints cemented female and
male monastic houses, while differences in prestige, size, and
wealth served to separate them more than gender.

Interactions between monastic women and other people ranged

from cold and impersonal to warm and particular. Some of the connections with ecclesiastics were dictated by church politics, as for instance when popes granted privileges to houses they had never seen to recompense a powerful patron. But other interactions with clerics could be personal, like the bequest of a holy anchorite who left his anchorhold, eight manuscripts, and all his liturgical vessels to his respected neighbors, the nuns of Voisins.[106]

Some nuns stayed in close contact with their relatives outside the cloister walls, while others felt more distanced from their kinfolk in the world. But even when families dumped a little girl into a convent to avoid paying a large marriage dowry, the child often found herself in a community peopled with female relatives who probably welcomed her warmly and became a support system. Additionally, child oblates traded their natal family for an entire monastic family, since nuns who were raised in convents identified the nunnery as their home and the other nuns as their sisters. The potential pain and loneliness of being a child oblate was compensated by the strong bonding that takes place when identification with a group begins early in life.[107]

The human ecology within which medieval nuns found their niche was primarily shaped by family and spiritual concerns. The religious woman lived in this larger world where she occupied a visible and significant place. Within her cloister she lived a more private life, but one that also influenced the general social systems of her day.

Interactions of monastic women with the male clerical hierarchy generally ran parallel to the relationships their male monastic confreres had with bishops and the papacy. Notifications of the election of an abbess and of an abbot might take the same source for their model, and generally the patterns of interaction between monasteries and church leaders were similar.[108] But nunneries were always vulnerable to the powerful princes of the church, since they made up only one-quarter of all the houses and had no representation in conciliar decisions. A convent could be disbanded or seized, and unless the nuns could find a strong enough protector to defend them,

106. *Cartulaire de Notre-Dame de Voisins*, p. 135, no. 129, 1245.

107. Bynum, *Holy Feast and Holy Fast*, p. 27, points out that "women in convents and beguinages, especially those who had been raised there, had a strong sense of spiritual networks or families of women."

108. *Letters and Poems of Fulbert of Chartres*, ed. Frederick Behrends (Oxford: Clarendon Press, 1976), pp. 273–74.

they lost their home and raison d'être. This happened to the nuns of Saint-Jean in Laon.[109] The Council of Arras decided to expel the nuns and hand the house over to monks, an action King Louis VI confirmed despite Saint-Jean's status as a royal abbey. Also, monastic women had a problem of dealing with abbatial oversight unique to their gender: male abbots and orders found the *cura monialium* expensive and time consuming. In the effort to rid themselves of the burden in the later twelfth and the thirteenth centuries, male monastics suppressed, compressed, and absorbed houses of women, causing the roster of convents to shrink and forcing some women to look elsewhere for the satisfactions of a religious vocation.

109. SC, 21:371–74.

PART II
ORGANIZING STRUCTURES

4

THE SEARCH FOR PERFECTION

B Y THE CENTRAL MIDDLE AGES nuns and monks had to take much of the institution of monasticism as they found it. Rules were in place; customs and traditions were of long standing; spiritual and social expectations were fixed. Nevertheless, there was some latitude to shape and direct life within each monastery, both by rethinking spiritual directions and by restructuring the communal environment. But the essence of the institution was the understanding, gracefully expressed more than half a millennium before by Augustine of Hippo, who saw nuns "as souls whose affections are set on spiritual beauty, not as bondswomen under the law, but as free women established under grace."[1] This goal of freedom in the order of grace where there was "neither male nor female" (Gal. 3:28)—freedom from the biological and societal disabilities women experienced in the order of nature—remained as compelling in the central Middle Ages as it had been in late antiquity.

Medieval nuns were far removed from Augustine's sweltering North African world of classical cities. They lived either in a countryside dotted with lords' castles or in spire-crowned towns; but for all the exterior differences, they still shared the original spiritual ideal of the founders of monasticism. The energy of that ideal directed the medieval monastic organism's growth as well as the subsequent accretions of institutional forms and systems—the administrative carapace—that grew around it to protect and support its fragile inner substance. Sometimes the carapace assisted and protected the growth of the interior life force; sometimes it weighed so heavily that the spiritual spark was all but extinguished; sometimes metastases of interior or exterior cells destroyed the entire orga-

1. Augustine, *Letters*, vol. 32 of *Fathers of the Church* (Washington, D.C.: Catholic University of America, 1956), p. 51.

nism. If we look first at that inner spiritual ideal and then at its sheltering administrative cover, we can discern the strength of the being, from both within and without, as well as the weak systems that failed under stress, increasingly so in the latter part of our period.

Vows

The idea that someone undertaking an important new direction in life should mark that event with a promise of commitment—a vow or an oath—has had currency throughout Western civilization. Vows mark the assumption of political power and juridical and military authority, but they also accompany Christian commitments: baptism, confirmation, ordination, and marriage. Thus when a woman or man resolves to give up secular society for a life dedicated to God, it seems appropriate to promise to adhere to the precepts of divine service. Benedict required the person being professed to promise stability, conversion of life, and obedience to the superior; that is, to stay in the monastery until death, to forgo being married or owning property, and to submit entirely to the letter and spirit of the superior's direction.[2] By the central Middle Ages monastics' vows had become the famous triple promise of chastity, poverty, and obedience, omitting the commitment to stability. Eudes Rigaud commented that the nuns of Holy Trinity in Caen took these vows when they were professed but should take no further vow.[3] The possibility of a particular promise to a superior or to a monastery always existed, but it was frowned on by the church because of the danger of personalizing what needed to be broad-based loyalty. Profession was at the age of consent or majority, which for girls was generally seen as twelve in the early Middle Ages but crept up to fourteen or fifteen by the thirteenth century as the church emphasized the need for adult oblations.[4] The move to raise the age of profession may have minimized the worst abuses of child oblation, but it also reduced the bonding and modeling possible for those who entered a monastery at a young age.

2. *Rule of St. Benedict*, chap. 58, p. 130.
3. ER, p. 293. Eudes particularly warns the nuns of Saint-Amand against a fourth vow (p. 218): "They take three vows, that is to say, of obedience, poverty, and chastity; we enjoined the abbess that when they were being professed no additional vows were to be taken."
4. ER, p. 225: the nuns of Saint-Aubin took vows at fourteen; the nuns of Saint-Amand could enter the novitiate at fourteen and take vows at fifteen.

The Vow of Poverty

Poverty in all its ramifications was a major issue for religious women. They agreed at profession to take up the yoke of voluntary poverty and to own nothing themselves: no book, no bracelet, no pet, no pen. Their clothes, food, and anything necessary was to be given them by the monastery for as long as it deemed appropriate. This shedding of things, this divesting of all property, was perhaps the most difficult reformation the monastic undertook. An almost equally challenging problem was the need to avoid another variety of poverty, involuntary poverty.[5] The contradictory goals to be at one and the same time corporately solvent and personally poor created enormous tensions in monastic life, and some odd arrangements developed to ease the anxieties.

How was a monastery to survive? In the earliest years it did so by raising its own food and being economically self-sufficient. Benedict's rule divides the monastic's time into three activities: manual labor, spiritual reading, and prayer or the *Opus Dei*, the central concern of the religious life.[6] The time allotted for manual labor was intended to permit the field work necessary to produce food for the house. As time passed, however, the hours spent in corporate prayer increased so that little by little the monastics' time for laboring dwindled. A dependent peasantry filled the gap at first, but as Europe passed from a subsistence economy to a money economy, the monasteries needed not only grain for their bread but also coin to buy cloth and wine and pay laborers and lay officials.

Religious houses received donations of property and income from patrons, gifts from pilgrims, and assets from the dowries of individuals entering the cloister.[7] Since monasteries recruited from the upper levels of society, professing oblates from wealthy families could help an abbey's finances. This temptation—to take a novice for her money—was one of the recognized dangers warned against by thoughtful commentators on the religious life like Jacques de Vitry.[8] In addition, some individual monastics, primarily nuns, received

5. See Lester K. Little, *Religious Poverty and the Profit Economy in Medieval Europe* (Ithaca, N.Y.: Cornell University Press, 1978), a work that examines the development of the goal of voluntary poverty in the central Middle Ages.
6. *Rule of St. Benedict*, chaps. 47 and 48, pp. 108–10.
7. *Rule of St. Benedict*, chap. 58, p. 132, tells the novice to give away property before entering a monastery or to donate it to the house.
8. Jacques de Vitry, *Sermons*, p. 254.

gifts or bequests of property or income. In December 1010 Hersende, a strong-minded matron, gave her daughter Eldearde, a nun at the Priory of Saint-Silvain, the alod her parents had given Hersende as dowry on her wedding day.[9] Hersende made this gift in the knowledge that Roman law guaranteed her the right to alienate property even though she was a woman and for the sake of her soul and the souls of her parents, husband, sons, brother, some clerics, and her nephews. She specified in her charter that the gift was to be controlled absolutely by her daughter, "with no one gainsaying it." When Eldearde died, the alod was to go next to Hersende's niece Olga or some other female relative at that time in the convent. She reiterated her intent lest anyone be in doubt: "Truly, at no time should it go out of the control of our kin." Then Hersende describes the alod, which used to be called Mons Caprarius but which she has seen fit to rename Alasvernias. Finally, she closes with a powerful malediction on anyone foolhardy enough to interfere with the rightful tenure of this property in the female branch of her family.

Hersende's charter vividly shows one of the ways women sworn to own nothing often ended up tenured with personal property. Families had holdings earmarked for female inheritors, and convents found their members willy-nilly receiving such donations. In the mid-thirteenth century when Lady Havise lay dying, she bequeathed to the convent of Sainte-Marguerite de la Presle twelve sesters of wheat, of which eight were to go to her relative the nun Eustachia and four to the priory for clothes for all the nuns. The charter considers contingencies: when Eustachia dies, Havise's niece, Ida, is to receive the eight sesters. The testatrix makes further provisions: when Ida dies the grain is to go to the next generation of the family, Havise's great-niece, *if* she chooses to become a nun. The imagination of the testatrix ran out at that stage of four generations; when the great-niece departs life, all the grain is to become income for the priory.[10]

Sometimes the donations were clearly for the support of a nun during her lifetime and were to revert to the family at her death. These gifts amounted to family allowances for a nun's pocket money but were not intended to support the monastery itself. William Chervel gave his daughter Alice, a nun at Saint-Sulpice-la-

9. *Cartulaire de Notre-Dame de Saintes,* pp. 106–8, no. 140, 1010.

10. Carré, "Sainte-Marguerite de la Presle," 5(1893): 42–43, no. 34, 1247. This charter does not name Eustachia and Ida as nuns, but p. 51, no. 49, 1239 notes that Eustachia is a nun, and p. 53, no. 52, 1256 mentions that Ida is also professed.

Forêt, the rents from a parish in his fief during her lifetime.[11] At her death the income was to revert to William's heirs. In fact, if a family felt its wishes were ignored, it might react furiously: in a different instance, William Haimar of Oleron had seized the tithes of Bona-mia because he asserted that they had been only a lifetime allowance granted by his grandfather to his aunt; at her death the tithes should have come back to the kinship and not been appropriated by the convent.[12] The nunnery fiercely defended its version that the tithes had been given outright to the abbess and convent and not temporarily granted just to the nun. In this case the pressure of the diocesan, weighing in with all his authority on the side of the nuns, won them the argument. Some parents were less protective of family property. Houdeborch, a widow in the village of Tyou, settled a lifetime allowance of eighteen sesters of grain on her daughter Mabille.[13] After Mabille's death, twelve sesters were to return to the family, but six were to remain with the nuns to fund anniversary prayers for Houdeborch.

Often the private property a nun enjoyed was hers only as a temporary loan from her family, contributing to the sense that such income did not deform the intention of the vow of poverty. Sometimes, however, it was clear that a religious woman exercised full control over land and income: Sister Martine d'Attamville bequeathed nine solidi of her property to her nunnery of Clairruissel to fund a pittance for her fellow nuns after her death, and in like manner the abbess of Holy Trinity in Poitiers purchased property with her funds to finance the annual celebration of the claustral prioress's anniversary.[14] Even more telling was a bequest to or a purchase by a nun that she could use entirely at her discretion.[15] When a convent openly admitted that its members enjoyed income from private property, it was faced with a contradiction. This tension

11. *Cartulaire de Saint-Sulpice-la-Forêt*, p. 248, no. 153, 1270. Such donations to a nun are sometimes hard to distinguish from donations that were entry gifts or dowries. The confusion develops because in the thirteenth century monastic dowries were often described obliquely to avoid being censured as a forbidden practice. But some dowries are still undisguised, as is the eight pounds from Hugh of Bois Simon that is to go to the abbey within two months of his sister's profession: *Cartulaire du Lieu-Notre-Dame-lès-Romorantin*, pp. 40–41, no. 49, 1261.
12. *Cartulaire de Notre-Dame de Saintes*, pp. 37–38, no. 31, 1150.
13. *Cartulaire du Lieu-Notre-Dame-lès-Romorantin*, p. 102, no. 155, 1263.
14. Rouen, BD, Clairruissel 53 H, carton 1, MS. no. 29; Poitiers, BD, La Trinité, 2 H 2, liasse 30, ch. 1, art. 3.
15. *Recueil du Val-Saint-Georges à Salzinnes*, p. 208, no. 158, 1277, and Poitiers, BM, MS. 27, p. 163, 1253.

could be resolved by a papal exemption. The canny nuns of Salzinnes took this route, receiving permission from Pope Innocent IV to hold inherited property.[16] They may have broken the spirit of the rule, but they were then within the letter of church law.

Although monks held personal property during the central Middle Ages, the evidence suggests that nuns were much more likely to do so. This was largely because Continental religious women often received family inheritances—although not the personal grants from donors common for Anglo-Saxon nuns.[17] The concern of the kinship to see that daughters received their appropriate portion reflects both a growing interest in inheritance law and a response to the dwindling resources in the control of communities of religious women. Custom dictated that female descendants receive their fair share of the family goods, while at the same time the penury of many nunneries cried out for help. After all, it would not add to a family's prestige or spiritual reassurance to have its intercessors starving to death in ramshackle convents.

Medieval people took the afterlife very seriously: the days of life on this earth were few in comparison with all eternity. Concern to prepare for life after death pervaded society and was felt as strongly by monastic people as by secular women and men. Since being a monastic was not ipso facto a guarantee of salvation, nuns and monks wanted to be prayed for by their fellow monastics, which was ensured by writing the name of a deceased community member into the monastery's martyrology so there would be an annual prayer for that person's soul. In addition, however, monastics wanted to leave money for a pittance to be enjoyed by the community on the anniversary day. The inhabitants of a poor house were at a disadvantage in preparing for their own deaths, since they lacked funds for these ritual meals, and since nunneries sank below the medieval poverty line more quickly than did male houses, religious women had to scramble to find money. For instance, when the abbot of a wealthy abbey prepared for death, he simply diverted some monastic income to endow his pittance.[18] When the prioress of a dependent obedience worried about her salvation, no excess income could be siphoned off

16. *Recueil du Val-Saint-Georges à Salzinnes*, p. 120, no. 97, 1245.

17. Christine Fell, *Women in Anglo-Saxon England* (Bloomington: Indiana University Press, 1984), p. 123. Anglo-Saxon nuns received personal grants from donors, a practice uncommon for Continental nuns.

18. See, for example: *Cartulaire de la Trinité de Vendôme*, 3:142, no. 727, 1266, p. 161, no. 739, 1275, p. 184, no. 750, 1307.

from the priory for her sake; she herself had to buy the rents from a meadow for her anniversary celebration.[19]

But there was a further change in liturgy that added to the stress on the financial base of nunneries. The practice was growing during the twelfth century of celebrating masses for the souls of the departed in addition to or even instead of remembering their anniversaries with prayers and inclusion in a monastery's martyrology; the growing belief in purgatory, a place from which the soul of the departed could be extricated by suffrages, added to the importance of masses for the dead.[20] Only a priest could celebrate mass, which at the beginning of our period meant that both female and male monastics had to provide an ordained celebrant and pay him. However, during the central Middle Ages it became more and more common for monks to be ordained to the priesthood, so that by the end of the twelfth century the vast majority were priests. When anniversary masses were required for a patron or a member, one of a community of monks could perform the service. In contrast, when anniversary masses were required for a patron or a member of a nunnery, the nuns had to pay for a priest to be the celebrant.

A gender comparison of nuns and monks censured by Eudes Rigaud for infractions against the vow of poverty reveals that women were more apt to fail in this vow than were men. Four-fifths of the nunneries had individuals who broke their vow of poverty, while two-thirds of all male houses experienced such failings.[21] Owning property in spite of one's vow of poverty seems to have more commonly been a failing of nuns than of monks.

The pressure to obtain spiritual insurance in financially limited convents impelled community members to look to their families for financial help, and since families liked to earmark the wife's dowry for her children, and often particularly for her daughters, there was a natural feeling that certain income belonged by right to the girls in a family. Economic need coupled with customary practice made it likely that nuns during the central Middle Ages would hold pri-

19. Poitiers, BD, La Trinité, 2 H 2, liasse 93, ch. 1, art. 13.

20. See David Knowles, *The Monastic Order in England*, 2d ed. (Cambridge: Cambridge University Press, 1966), p. 468, and Jacques Dubois, "Office des heures et messe dans la tradition monastique," in *Histoire monastique en France au XIIe siècle* (London: Variorum, 1982), p. 75, for increase in the mass, and Jacques Le Goff, *The Birth of Purgatory*, trans. Arthur Goldhammer (Chicago: University of Chicago Press, 1984), for the development of the doctrine of purgatory.

21. The rate of infractions is 83 percent of female houses and 68 percent of male houses.

vate property. Visitors railed against this sin; but solving the underlying malaise of penury and its etiology was beyond even the most hardworking and well-intentioned prelate, although Eudes Rigaud tried by requiring that nuns' incomes be held only with the superior's knowledge.[22] Owning private property had come to be a survival technique for religious women, who were squeezed by shrinking institutional resources but often endowed with family inheritances.

The Vow of Chastity

The second vow taken by monastic women, the vow of chastity, usually receives the most modern attention because of reports like the following from Villarceaux:

> Philippa of Rouen [is ill famed of sexual activity with] . . . the priest at Chèrence, in the diocese of Chartres. Marguerite, the treasurer, is ill famed of Richard of Genainville, cleric. Agnes of Fontenay is ill famed of the priest at Guerreville, in the diocese of Chartres. La Toolière is ill famed of sir Andrew of Mussy, knight. All of them let their hair grow down to the chin, and put saffron on their veils. Jacqueline left the priory pregnant as a result of her relations with one of the chaplains, who was expelled because of this. Item, Agnes of Mont-Secours is ill famed of the same man. Ermengarde of Gisors and Joan of Hauteville came to blows. The prioress is drunk nearly every night.[23]

Medieval churchmen might well have heard such a sad account as fulfilling their worst expectations. In the minds of many of their contemporaries, medieval nuns were ripe to fall into sexual sins. In the ninth century a church council stated that "in some places the monasteries seem to be brothels."[24] In the twelfth century Ivo, bishop of Chartres, wrote scathingly that nuns in a particular monastery were prostitutes.[25] Homiletic literature written in the thirteenth and fourteenth centuries often was addressed to wayward nuns, who were seen as wont to sneak out to rendezvous with lovers.[26] The theme became a swelling melody during the fifteenth and

---

22. ER, p. 708.

23. ER, p. 49.

24. MGH, Concilia aevi Karolini 1, pars II (36) cap. XII, p. 713. This was the Second Council of Aix-la-Chapelle in 836.

25. Ivo of Chartres, Epistle 70, PL, 162:90.

26. Ruth Mohl, *The Three Estates in Medieval and Renaissance Literature* (New York: Columbia University Press, 1933), p. 352.

sixteenth centuries, particularly in England, leaving a profound impression of demoralization in nunneries.[27]

Many modern scholars are now conditioned by the chorus of medieval criticism, reinforced by examples of scandalous behavior like the one above, to expect to find that cloistered women in the Middle Ages lived in a world of monastic debauchery. Even a thoroughly sympathetic scholar like Eileen Power writes ruefully that religious women in late medieval England fell far below the "monastic standard" in maintaining their vows of chastity.[28] A recent book argues that "the wayward nun in medieval literature is the reflection of the one in the nunnery," a thesis the author patently fails to support with solid historical evidence.[29] How then are we to assess the vow of chastity taken by medieval nuns? Shulamith Shahar asserts that nuns' failure to live up to the ideal of chastity can be identified "from the homiletic literature of the period and from a more reliable source, namely the reports of bishops or representatives of orders who visited nunneries and subsequently instructed the abbess to correct the flaws."[30] When such episcopal reports are examined, one does indeed discover sexual scandals in nunneries. But are these shocking cases representative of general behavior so that the medieval convent deserves its ill repute as a den of licentiousness hiding behind a veil of piety? Are we reading reliable sources, or are religious women being presented as stereotypes? If medieval nuns committed offenses against the strict rule of celibacy, how commonly did this happen, and how did nuns' offenses compare with those committed by monks?

These questions can be addressed quantitatively to test the anec-

27. See Eckenstein, *Woman under Monasticism*, pp. 408–9, in which Archbishop Morton castigated the convents of Pré and Sopwell, and pp. 434–35, which describe the dissolution of convents so that their properties could be used to establish college foundations or to enrich the king's purse.

28. Eileen Power, *Medieval English Nunneries: c. 1275 to 1535* (Cambridge: Cambridge University Press, 1922), p. 471. Others are harsher in their judgments of nuns, painting their lives in premodern Europe as sexually promiscuous. See, for instance, Judith C. Brown, "Lesbian Sexuality in Renaissance Italy: the Case of Sister Benedetta Carlini," *Signs: Journal of Women in Culture and Society* 9(1984): 751: "Renaissance convents were notorious for their loose moral standards and their sexual license." A few modern scholars romanticize the virtue of premodern nuns: "Bref, la chasteté accorde aux femmes une vertu qui est rare chez les hommes; elle sauvegarde la pureté de leur corps avec celle de laur âme." See Parisse, *Nonnes au Moyen Age*, p. 173.

29. Graciela S. Daichman, *Wayward Nuns in Medieval Literature* (Syracuse: Syracuse University Press, 1986), p. xiii.

30. Shahar, *Fourth Estate*, p. 46.

dotal and often shocking stories of nuns' sexual behavior. Since reports of disreputable behavior in female monasteries become meaningful only when examined in context by comparing nuns' and monks' unchaste behavior, the sample must include monastics of both sexes. To achieve a comparative base for comparing the sexual activities of nuns and monks, I have used a data base created from the episcopal visitation record of Eudes Rigaud.

Archbishop Eudes's notes of twenty-one years of official visits have been used previously to assess how well monastics kept their vow of chastity; for instance, G. G. Coulton comes to the conclusion, using this material, that "the proportion of peccancy in nuns is more than double that of the monks."[31] He used the *Register* primarily for examples rather than for exact figures, however, and his findings are more anecdotally striking than historically accurate.

Eudes visited fourteen women's houses, sixty-one men's houses, and seven hospitals (three of which were predominantly women's institutions and are included here to make a total of seventeen female institutions) run by religious following at least some sort of monastic rule.[32] Sexual offenses for these houses were counted that included being ill famed, which meant there was a commonly held opinion that someone was living unchastely; being pregnant or known to have caused a pregnancy; bearing a child or fathering a child; having had an abortion or helping someone attempt abortion; and being involved in gay sexual behavior.

Three warnings should be kept in mind: All that the figures from the data base can do is to create one test case in which we can investigate nuns and monks in Normandy in the middle of the thirteenth century and their sexual lapses. Second, this study will not be able to come up with figures of actual sexual behavior; it can only produce a count of those who were found out. Third, we should ex-

31. Claude Jenkins, "A Thirteenth-Century Register: Odo, Archbishop of Rouen," *Church Quarterly Review* 101(1925): 80–123. Jenkins is unreliable: for example, he counts twenty-nine nuns charged with incontinence (p. 103). This figure is in error because he counts three nuns, whose designations are admittedly confusing, twice. See also G. G. Coulton, *Five Centuries of Religion*, vol. 2 (Cambridge: Cambridge University Press, 1929), pp. 224–25. Coulton too is unreliable: to cite just one of many errors, he says that the archbishop visited five nunneries outside his diocese, whereas he actually visited six: Almenèches in Séez, Aries in Avranches, Saint-Leger-des-Préau in Lisieux, Sainte-Marguerite de Gouffern in Séez, Saint-Sauveur in Evreux, and Sainte-Trinité at Caen in Bayeux.

32. I excluded visits to houses when Eudes came in other than his official capacity as visitor. The proportion of women's to men's houses in this comparison is 26 percent.

TABLE 1: Sexual Misbehavior in Houses of Nuns and Monks in Normandy

	Nunneries	Male Monasteries	Total
All monasteries			
Number	17	65	82
Percentage	21	79	100
Monasteries with offenses against the vow of chastity			
Number	8	25	33[a]
Percentage	24[b]	76[b]	100

[a]Thirty-three houses comprise 40% of all the houses in the sample.
[b]The percentage of nunneries with offenses (24%) is not statistically significant measured against the percentage of nunneries in the total number of houses (21%); nor is the percentage of male monasteries with offenses (76%) statistically significant in light of male houses' constituting 79% of the total. The number of houses with offenders is therefore consistent with the proportion of female and male houses in the sample, leading to the conclusion that gender does not predispose the members of a monastery to keep or break the vow of chastity.

pect that nuns' sexual activity would at the very least seem to be more common than monks', since in the days before reliable birth control, a woman's sexual activity could easily result in pregnancy, a difficult condition to hide. Therefore a higher proportion of male straying or of roughly equal sexual activity of nuns and monks would be particularly worthy of note. Table 1 summarizes the comparison of female and male monasteries.

Eight of the seventeen regular houses for women that Eudes visited had at least one incident in which a nun was sexually involved, but only three of those eight had serious problems.[33] The three female monasteries that were the settings for the most lurid events were Villarceaux, Saint-Saens, and Saint-Aubin. Saint-Aubin and Saint-Saens had somewhat similar patterns in that a very small number of misbehaving nuns created most of the trouble; Villarceaux has the dubious distinction of having been unique among all

33. The actual breakdown is two houses with one incident apiece, one house with three, two houses with four each, one with eleven, one with thirteen, and one with fourteen, for a total of fifty-one incidents. I have counted as one incident each entry in which Eudes notes "general scandal" or that "some" nuns were ill famed. Fifty-one incidents are more than the number of erring nuns (twenty-six) because an individual could be involved in more than one censure, and several instances of unchaste behavior by clerics or canons resident in nunneries were counted among convent incidents.

the religious institutions—whether female or male—that Eudes visited in having the most individuals cited for unchaste behavior in any one visit.

The example that opened the discussion of the vow of chastity is a quotation from the *Register*'s entry for the visit of July 9, 1249, to Villarceaux, a small rural Benedictine priory north of la Roche Guyon. At that time Eudes recorded that of the roughly nineteen resident nuns, ten—or better than half—were involved in sexual scandals. This sorry state of affairs was discovered in Eudes's very first visit to the priory, and during his subsequent ten visits he never again had cause to cite a single nun for even one slip from her vow of chastity. This is not to say that the religious of Villarceaux led blameless lives in every way after 1249; rather, despite continuing areas in which they needed correction, such as possessing private property and acting in a worldly way, their adherence to the chaste life seems to have been absolute. One reason for such a complete about-face may be that Eudes went out of his way to reform the house. The *Register* contains a copy of the letter of correction and admonition he sent to the prioress to be studied carefully and read aloud a minimum of once a month in chapter; it is a thoughtful, balanced letter intended to serve as a miniature rule of admirable brevity and inclusiveness:

> Brother Eudes, by God's permission archbishop of Rouen, etc., to his beloved daughters the prioress and convent of Villarceaux, greeting, etc. Since we found, during our recent visit to your priory, many things that needed to be corrected in the interests of the general welfare, and since we are bound by the command of our office to bring back these things to the status of the Rule, in so far as we can, we will and order above all that the Divine Offices, both in the daytime and at night, be celebrated regularly and at the proper hours as the Rule demands, and that they should be sung with modulation and as order demands; and as soon as the hour strikes all shall hasten at once to the church, unless they are sick or are excused by the prioress or her substitute. Item, we will and decree that the required silence be observed according to the Rule in the choir, the cloister, the dormitory and the refectory, and that there be no talking at all after Compline. Item, we will and decree that all shall sleep together in one dormitory at the same time and that all shall enter and leave it together, and that the keys of the dormitory and of the cloister shall be in trustworthy keeping, nor shall anyone

be permitted to enter the cloister until after Prime, and that suitable and competent inspectresses be appointed for the dormitory and such other places which pertain to the religious life.

Furthermore, we order that no lay or suspect person be received as a guest nor be permitted to sleep within the limits of the cloister. We strictly forbid any sister to leave the cloister without permission and without respectable companionship, nor shall such permission be granted without patent and reasonable cause. Item, we order that no one shall converse with any outsider or with any suspect person without permission and in the presence of some mature sister. We decree that no more saffron shall be placed on the veils, that the hair be not arrayed in vain curls, nor shall silver or metaled belts, or the skins of divers and wild animals be worn, nor shall the hair be allowed to grow down below the ears. Item, we forbid you to continue the farcical performances which have been your practice at the feast of the Innocents and of the Blessed Mary Magdalene, to dress up in worldly costumes, or to dance with each other or with lay folk, neither shall you eat outside the refectory, nor shall you invite any layfolk to eat with you in the refectory. Item, we will and decree that if a quarrel among the sisters should progress from words to blows, each shall be equally blamed and punished in proportion to the violence and malice of the delinquent, by her who shall preside at the chapter on the following day.

Item, until your numbers are reduced to a point consistent with the resources of the priory, we strictly forbid you to receive without permission any expelled sister, any sister who has left the priory without permission, or any novice; nor, in this matter, shall you even obey your abbess (of St-Cyr). We will and decree that every month, or at least every two months, the prioress shall make a faithful audit of receipts and expenditures, in the presence of three suitable and discreet sisters chosen by you in chapter and of the proctor or curator whom we shall give to you, and that twice a year, or at least once, a general audit of these items shall be made. We warn you collectively and severally that the common life which is to be observed in religion, in clothing, in food, and in other things is to be maintained; nor shall you of your own accord sell or give away any of those things which pertain to the common victualizing or clothing, and if you shall have received anything from friends, you shall apply it to the common use and not to your own. Item, we order and enjoin you to read this present letter in chapter at least once a month, and you may be assured that if we find you negligent in this respect we shall not with a benevolent eye overlook your faults but shall proceed all the more heavily against you with our hand. Given at Sausseuse, on the feast of the Exaltation of the Holy Cross, 1249.[34]

Six of the nuns' ten male sexual partners at Villarceaux were in holy orders, including three priests, one cleric, the prior of Gisors, and a resident chaplain. These men were all subject to the archbishop's discipline, and it is possible that Eudes took steps to reform the house by removing some or all of them. The chaplain had a particularly bad record, for he had made Sister Jacqueline pregnant so that she had to leave the priory, and then later had become involved with another nun, Agnes of Mont-Secours. Removing this chaplain went a long way towards reforming the priory, and this action may have been one of several Eudes initiated to discipline the clerics involved in affairs at Villarceaux. Whatever happened to bring Villarceaux back to a more decorous life-style, the archbishop stayed alert for danger to the nuns from clerics outside the priory: when Eudes visited the Abbey of Jumièges in 1267, he warned the abbot never again to drop in on the nuns of Villarceaux, since he was occasioning scandal by his familiarity.[35] A more cynical interpretation of the improvement in morals would be that the nuns of Villarceaux learned to be extremely discreet in their affairs, which may be true in part but seems unlikely as a blanket explanation for the priory's dramatic volte-face.

The second badly behaved nunnery, which we have already met— the Priory of Saint-Saens in the small town of Gournay—was a Benedictine dependent cell of the important male house of Saint-Wandrille. It was smaller than the average women's house, having only nineteen choir nuns at its largest. Nevertheless, for a modest-sized monastery it was responsible for a substantial amount of scandal, generating eleven incidents of unchastity discovered by Eudes in fifteen visitations scattered over eighteen years.

The records of the visitor's inquiries offer clues to the sources of much of the trouble; these causes can be classified roughly under either house administration or economics. No institution can func-

34. ER, pp. 49–50.
35. ER, p. 674.

tion smoothly if its leadership is inept or corrupt, and Saint-Saens had several key administrators who were failing not only to do their jobs but also to function as chaste role models for their flock. Eudes noted in 1259 that the prioress was "under suspicion" owing to her intimacy with Richard of Maucomble, who ate and even slept at the priory on occasion.[36] A year later this prioress was forced to retire because of ill health, and Joan Morcent was elected with Eudes's approval.[37] After a few years, however, the new prioress was cautioned for her intimacy with the priest of l'Hortier, with whom she was accused of having clandestine meetings.[38] But even the weight of Eudes's warnings and displeasure did not bring Prioress Joan to mend her ways, for she was still assumed to be involved with the priest four years later.[39] Immoral prioresses would have been bad enough had that been all; but besides having unchaste prioresses, Saint-Saens had unchaste priests. Eudes expelled one for sexual offenses in 1252 and ordered another removed two years later.[40]

The Priory of Saint-Saens also had the responsibility of administering a small, nonconventual cell or obedience, Sainte-Austreberte, about twenty-five kilometers away. The mother priory had to provide an administrator for this cell, which presented difficulties for a small priory with limited personnel. When Saint-Saens sent one nun—perhaps all that could be spared—as obedientiary to oversee the cell, this was in contravention of the Statutes of Pope Gregory, which decreed that no monastic should be in residence without a fellow; equally dangerous was having a single lay sister and brother alone together in the obedience instead of the safer accepted number of two of each sex.[41] Clearly this situation created the potential for inappropriate intimacy. Saint-Saens responded to the archbishop's censure and sent two choir nuns to Sainte-Austreberte; nevertheless, a few years later Eudes insisted they both be recalled to the mother priory, since there were inadequate funds to support them and he feared their living there "because of the danger."[42] A year later Eudes found the two were still in the little obedience and had

36. ER, p. 384.
37. ER, p. 430.
38. ER, p. 559.
39. ER, p. 687.
40. I believe the entries refer to two priests, although they can be read as referring to one priest who had defied Eudes's expulsion of 1252 and stayed on at Saint-Saens, occasioning a second order of expulsion in 1254. ER, pp. 158, 199.
41. The Statutes of Pope Gregory IX are included in ER, pp. 737–46. See p. 306 for the case of Sainte-Austreberte, where there was also one chaplain in residence.
42. ER, p. 430, "propter pericula."

not been recalled because, according to the prioress, one of the nuns, Mary of Eu, was extremely difficult, and the prioress "feared that if she returned, she would upset the whole community."[43] The prioress was using the obedience as a safety valve for siphoning off troublesome individuals, but the archbishop was not deterred and ordered the recall. Whatever the actual behavior of the two nuns who were in this tiny obedience, the possibility of their using the distance and lack of supervision for misbehaving deeply concerned Eudes.

Besides weak administrative personnel and problem-making responsibilities, both of which could generate a climate conducive to unchaste behavior, the general economic state of a monastery was a crucial determinative element. Poverty and trouble went hand in hand, and Saint-Saens—struggling economically—was so badly off that the priory could not even afford its own refectory but fed the nuns in the infirmary.[44] The roofs needed repair, and on one occasion Eudes made the interesting notation that their poverty was such that they were forced to eat meat, a diet that strikes us as the reverse of poverty rations.[45] The nuns clamored on several occasions for the right to increase their numbers so they could receive the much-needed entry gifts that postulants brought.[46] In fact the priory was in severe financial straits, with a meager 26 pounds as its mean net assets, less than half the mean net worth of 60 pounds for the whole group of Norman nunneries.

The third female religious house that experienced many cases of sexual misbehavior was Saint-Aubin, a small Cistercian priory in the countryside east of Rouen. Saint-Aubin at its largest numbered sixteen choir nuns, and just about every one of its fourteen visitation entries is marked with evidence of the priory's extreme poverty. The house was struggling for financial survival by trying every possible expedient. The nuns continually sought to expand their number so as to receive new entry gifts, apparently for the quick fix of the dowry despite the long-range added cost of another person to feed and clothe.[47] To realize income they tried taking in children to be educated and even sending some of the younger nuns out of the

43. ER, pp. 477–78.
44. RV, p. 170: "Non posssunt tenere refectorium, set (comedunt) per consortia in infirmaria."
45. ER, p. 513, p. 199. It may be that the meat was game donated by friends or relatives of the nuns.
46. ER, pp. 353, 430.
47. ER, pp. 225, 285, 364, 411.

cloister to earn money, both considered inappropriate measures by the church because of the resulting contact with the outside world.[48] The house had a heavy debt to the king, and many buildings were falling down around the inhabitants' ears.[49] In this state of financial brinkmanship, it is not surprising that we find fourteen incidents of sexual offenses—the highest number recorded for any one house.

One nun, Alice of Rouen, first appeared in the *Register* in 1255, ill famed of having borne a child fathered by a priest from Beauvais; a year later Eudes punished Alice for her behavior by taking away her veil, the equivalent of demoting a soldier to civilian status.[50] Apparently undeterred by this punishment, the next year Alice was still in residence and again "in grave fault" for loose sexual behavior.[51] When he visited four years after, Eudes recorded that Alice had conceived and borne another child since his previous visit, making her the mother of three children.[52] The lid blew off completely in 1261 when Alice and another like-minded nun, Beatrice of Beauvais, "led away by frivolity of soul . . . departed at the devil's instigation."[53] We hear no more of Alice in the *Register*, but we should not assume that silence means she never returned, since Beatrice, her confederate in sin, did come back and was received despite the archbishop's sharp enjoinder that both women be admitted only with his most particular consent. Alice may also have returned, but it is just as possible that she reverted to the secular life after leaving the cloister.

These cases illustrate the general rule that female lapses usually occurred when the monastic environment was a small, isolated, and financially strapped institution in which morale must have been low and life particularly hard[54] (see table 2). Such a qualitative read-

48. ER, p. 471.
49. ER, p. 569.
50. ER, pp. 226, 285.
51. ER, p. 319.
52. ER, p. 470.
53. RV, p. 471: "Animi levitate ducte, dyabolo exierant instigante."
54. These findings are echoed by a thirteenth-century episcopal letter containing a list of abuses to be discussed at an upcoming council. Written in 1227–28, probably by the bishop of Angers, the list includes the problem of isolated, rural women's priories, which were perceived to be the loci of sexual scandals. The bishop recommends consolidating these tiny houses into bigger monasteries of thirty or forty members. See Joseph Avril, "La province de Tours après le IVe concile du Latran: Les 'articuli missi archiepiscopo Turonensi,'" *Annuarium Historia Conciliorum* 6(1974): 299.

TABLE 2: Profile of Women's Monastic Houses in Normandy

	Nunneries with Sexual Offenses	Nunneries without Sexual Offenses	Mean for All Convents
Finances			
Mean debt	£6	—	
Mean assets	—	£119	£60
Mean size	25	41	35
Location (percentage in countryside)	71	29	—

ing of the *Register* is supported quantitatively by statistical analysis.[55]

Despite a natural expectation that the salacious anecdotes should be representative of most monastic behavior, the number of cloistered women and men who failed to keep their vows of chastity and were found out is strikingly small: only twenty-six nuns and forty-nine monks (see table 3). This is even more impressive in light of the biological realities that lead us to expect that nuns' offenses would be discovered much more often than those committed by monks. To discover whether the correlation between the figures has any mathematical meaning, I tested the numbers with the standard statistical tool known as a t-test. When this test is used to ascertain whether the number of female and male sexually active monastics has statistical significance—whether or not the 4 percent and 3 percent figures in the gender pools actually indicate a difference—the

55. Two-, three-, and four-way multivariable statistical analyses were run on the correlations of gender, order, size, mean net worth, location, incidence of sexual offenses, and numbers of those apprehended in breaking the vow of chastity. In the three-way statistical analysis, there is a 13 percent correlation between involvement in forbidden sexual activity and living in a poverty-stricken nunnery (one that had less than the mean assets for all female houses), compared with a 6 percent correlation between involvement in sexual activity and living in a poor male institution (one having less than the mean assets for other male houses). In addition, there is a 19 percent correlation between sexual activity and residing in small nunneries (those below the mean size for female houses), compared with only a 5 percent correlation between unchaste behavior and living in small male houses (those below the mean size for male houses).

conclusion is that the probability of unchastity for nuns and monks in this place and time was statistically the same.[56]

We can understand that poor administration, heavy responsibilities, and poverty might deform the monastic ideal, but exactly why one individual and not another became sexually active is not discernible from the kind of records available. In the final analysis, it is up to the individual monastic to decide whether to be celibate. One nun who chose to ignore her vow was Nicola of Rouen, who left her mark in Eudes's records of visitations to Saint-Saens. Nicola was probably from the city of Rouen, both on the evidence of her name and because her sister is mentioned as coming from there.[57] She became a choir nun at Saint-Saens and had a long-running involvement with Simon, the rector of the church in the village of Saint-Saens. The second child of this relationship was born at the priory of Saint-Saens on Ash Wednesday in 1259 with two village midwives in attendance; the baby was christened and the mother was churched, then the baby was sent off to be raised by Nicola's sister in Rouen.[58] This sounds like a situation that should have required

TABLE 3: Sexual Behavior of Individuals in Norman Monasteries

	Nuns	Monks	Total
All monastics			
Number	587	1,486	2,073
Percentage of total monastics	28	72	100
Individuals who broke			
the vow of chastity			
Number	26	49	75[a]
Percentage of erring monastics	35	65	100
Percentage of individual			
offenders compared with			
gender pools	.044[b]	.032[b]	

[a]Seventy-five monastics comprise only 4% of all monastics in this sample.
[b]The .012 difference between female and male offenders is not statistically significant.

56. The t probability for statistical significance in assessing gender as a determinative factor for monastic chastity is .188, which is not statistically significant at the .05 level.
57. ER, p. 560.
58. ER, p. 384.

severe penalties and even expulsion. Indeed, the prioress may have meted out heavy punishments and Nicola may have had to do heavy penance; yet five years later she was still in residence and had become cantress.[59] At this time she was recorded as being ill famed by the rumor of having had an abortion—an accusation the other nuns stoutly defended her against, saying that it "was falsely and untruthfully imputed to her." Although Eudes was apparently convinced that Nicola was innocent of that charge, he still strongly disapproved that she and her sister had joined Simon for dinner. Perhaps the aunt had brought the baby or news of its progress to the natural parents. Nicola passes out of the documents after 1264, but the fragmentary evidence of the *Register* makes it clear that she and Simon had developed some kind of enduring bond, that an extended family network had helped clear up the fallout from the relationship, and that the other nuns had not ostracized Nicola, nor had the archbishop expelled her permanently from her monastery.

Nicola's lover was a priest from the village. A nun did not have to look even that far afield for a potential sexual partner, since all nunneries were staffed by men who in their roles of chaplain, priest, lay brother, and overseer were in close day-to-day proximity to nuns. Contemporaries were often aware of the problem. The Premonstratensian Chapter General, for example, advised its abbots to limit the number of canons with access to the religious women as a way of protecting the nuns.[60]

Twenty-nine specific sexual partners of the nuns noted by Eudes can be named from the evidence of the *Register*; of these, nineteen were clerics, five were commoners, one was a knight, and four were of unclear status. Thus more than two-thirds of the nuns' known partners were clergy whom women monastics were obliged to have present in their cloisters owing to the male sacerdotal monopoly in the church. In some instances the religious women may have been unwilling recipients of men's sexual advances; the story of Christina of Markyate tells of her terrifying experience with Bishop Ralph Flambard, who tried to seduce her by getting her alone in his apartments and would have raped her had she not outwitted him.[61] Equally, men could and sometimes did enter nunneries in search of

59. ER, p. 560.

60. Carol Neel, "Their Too Frequent Cohabitation with Nobles and Other Men: Women in the Thirteenth-Century Order of Prémontré," paper presented to the Seventh Berkshire Conference on the History of Women, at Wellesley College, June 1987, p. 15.

61. *Life of Christina of Markyate*, pp. 40–42.

a woman. Jacques de Vitry uses an example in one of his sermons of a man's removing an unwilling nun from her cloister, and a saint's vita tells of a nun who had to call for help to chase out an unwanted admirer, who then resorted to the age-old weapon of blaming the victim, accusing her of immorality to protect his reputation and salve his wounded pride.[62] Even anchoresses, women living as enclosed hermits, were not always exempt from the unwanted advances of the clerics who ministered to them; there were times when these women "needed some protection from their protectors."[63] Although there is no way of knowing the figures, some of the sexual activity of religious women may have been unwilling, either through forcible rape or through intimidation.

To assess the stereotype of the scandalous nun, the sexual behavior of female monastics must be measured against that of monks. Of the monastic men Eudes Rigaud visited in Norman monasteries, forty-nine were censured for sexual activity. Their lapses from chastity occurred, however, in a much more random pattern of location and size of house than did those of the nuns. For instance, Bourg-Achard was a small house of Augustinian canons in the countryside west of Rouen. In 1253 Eudes visited and censured the prior, who was ill famed of involvement with two women, La Cornue and Alice of Bouquetot. It was also noted that in the past he had been involved with the mercer's wife.[64] Typically for monks, he was never again noted as erring, nor was another monk, Robert Macue, who was also ill famed on the same visit. Jumièges, one of the big, grand old Benedictine establishments in the environs of Rouen, had only one scandal, that of having a gay monastic couple in its midst; Eudes expelled both men, sending them separately to two monasteries "to expiate their offenses."[65] Some men's houses had multiple offenses against the vow of chastity—for example, Saint-Catherine, a good-sized Benedictine abbey in the city of Rouen, and Saint-Laurent, a small Augustinian priory in the countryside east of Rouen. Of the eleven monks censured in these two houses, all but two were one-

62. Jacques de Vitry, *Sermons*, p. 243, and Simenon, *Julienne de Cornillon*, pp. 44–45.

63. Ann K. Warren, *Anchorites and Their Patrons in Medieval England* (Berkeley: University of California Press, 1985), p. 61.

64. ER, p. 190.

65. ER, p. 3. The best discussion of gay relationships in the Middle Ages is John Boswell, *Christianity, Social Tolerance, and Homosexuality: Gay People in Western Europe from the Beginning of the Christian Era to the Fourteenth Century* (Chicago: University of Chicago Press, 1980).

time offenders only, and there was no evidence that any of them had formed long-lasting bonds with lovers.[66]

When all male institutions are considered together, no obvious correlations of size or location appear. Unchaste monks came from houses that were on average somewhat larger than the women's monasteries but varied radically in size from a high of ninety-two to a low of ten. The locations of men's houses with offenders were also more diverse than those of women: the men's houses were about half rural and half urban instead of being predominantly rural as were the women's.[67]

Further dissimilarities existed. Male houses, unlike nunneries, evinced no clear pattern of administrative difficulties. Of the forty-nine censured monks, ten were either abbots, priors, or subpriors—about one-fifth of all male offenders. But a loose-living head did not necessarily lead his whole flock into debauched behavior. In addition, only seven offenders were in small, nonconventual priories, which seems a low figure given the high number of men's monastic houses that were responsible for such tiny obediences and the freedom from centralized discipline in these cells. Monks in small priories were more often apprehended in gracious living with feather beds and broken fast days than in sexual activity; in contrast, the concern—if not necessarily the reality—expressed about nuns in obediences was always that they would fail in the vow of chastity, not of poverty. The sexual double standard of the medieval world was based on the belief that women were more carnal and lascivious than men.

The women who were sexually involved with monks are not usually fully identified, but of the 20 percent who are mentioned with some designation, only one was upper class. Monks' sexual partners tended to be women from the lower classes—for instance, the wife of a tradesman.[68] Also, they seem to have lived outside the monas-

66. ER, pp. 9, 184, 210, for Sainte-Catherine; pp. 76, 129, 224, 414 for Saint-Laurent.

67. I tested and had to discard other possible correlations for houses of nuns and monks. There is no relevant correlation of immoral behavior with any particular order; nor does the foundation date of a house—whether established in the early Middle Ages or during the twelfth-century reform enthusiasm or in the thirteenth-century— appear to set the stage for moral or immoral behavior; nor did whether a house was a priory or an abbey, dependent or independent, seem to dispose the residents to good or bad behavior.

68. When class is not specified but a woman is simply referred to by her first name or by a nickname, for instance "La Cornue" (ER, p. 190), I am assuming that she was from the lower classes. Marina Warner, *Joan of Arc: The Image of Female Heroism* (New York: Random House, 1982), p. 104, argues that nicknames went to indepen-

teries and often in another town rather than being resident in or next to the male houses. The relative freedom of movement possible to male monastics allowed them to find sexual partners at some distance from their house, which may have cut down on the lapses discovered by the visitor and made the number of monks who were apprehended as unchaste seem lower than it actually was.

There is one important gender similarity, however: monks, like nuns, were more apt to commit sexual offenses when living in poor monasteries, although for them the correlation is less striking. In fact, male houses with sexual violations were generally in debt, owing a mean of 18 pounds, whereas male houses that did not experience unchastity had a mean net worth of 394 pounds.

Although no overall pattern emerges to describe the institutional setting in which monks broke their vows of chastity, the character of their sexual activity was different from that of nuns in two ways. Most notably, engaging in gay sex was perceived as a sexual offense committed by male but not female monastics, although various councils, like that of Paris in 1212, did show some anxiety by legislating that nuns should not share a bed.[69] The *Register* contains two clear-cut cases and one possible case of gay monks recorded by Eudes.[70] In contrast, whatever the possible lesbianism of the Norman nuns, it either went undetected or, because of a phallic-centered definition of sexuality, failed to be defined as sexual activity. Second, most monks were one-time offenders or at least were found out only once.[71] Those who acted unchastely seem often to have done so impetuously rather than by entering into a relationship as the erring nun was apt to do. Perhaps this resulted from biological or social conditioning, but fear of discovery may also have influenced the short duration of most monks' liaisons.

The analysis of evidence from this data base suggests it would be an error to assume that most nuns and monks were unchaste or that sexual experimentation was the accepted norm. Most monastics, indeed the vast majority as far as the visitor could tell, were loyal to

---

dent women who often were "conducting their own affairs and often as not, making money at it."

69. Carl Hefele, *Histoire des conciles d'après les documents originaux*, trans. H. Leclercq (Paris: Letouzey, 1913), 5²: 108.

70. ER, pp. 2, 533, are clear-cut, and p. 715 is a possible case.

71. Twenty-six nuns were involved in 48 censured incidents for a mean of 1.84 events apiece, or rounded to 2 apiece. Forty-nine male monastics accounted for 63 censured incidents for a mean of 1.28 apiece or rounded to 1 apiece.

their vows of chastity. Punishments could be extremely harsh for those who erred, as in the case of Agnes of Pont from Saint-Aubin, whom Eudes ordered to serve in a leper house as retribution for having helped another nun first arrange a meeting with a lover and then try to procure an abortion.[72] Eudes wanted punishment to be a deterrent, and he urged one prior "to impose such a penalty upon" erring monks "that they and others would dread to be delinquent in the future."[73] Clearly this was not a laissez-faire atmosphere.

Thus Archbishop Eudes Rigaud, a visitor of exceptional perspicacity and industry, recorded data suggesting that better than 95 percent of the cloistered women and men in his ecclesiastical province (or 2,073 monastics) lived up to their vows of chastity. We have to conclude either that they were talented dissimulators or—and I believe this was the case—that at least at this time and in this place they led celibate lives with a high degree of success. Monastic men who were discovered having sexual relations numbered 49 out of 1,486 (or 3 percent), while 26 out of 587 (or 4 percent) of monastic women were censured for sexual offenses against the rules of their orders, a difference between nuns and monks that is too small to be statistically significant. Nuns therefore might be expected to fall short of their vows in about equal proportion to their male counterparts.

A bleak and isolated institutional setting was particularly destructive for nuns' religious resolve to adhere to their vows of chastity. In contrast, the type of monastic environment was not as formative for monks, whose lapses from chastity occurred randomly among big and little, urban and rural institutions.[74] Yet for both nuns and monks, a correlation existed between unchaste behavior and penuriousness, although it was significantly higher for nuns. One explanation for this correlation might be that the misbehavior of monastics disgusted patrons, who withdrew financial support so that disreputable houses became impoverished. The charters, however, do not support such a theory. Rather, patrons seem to have fol-

72. ER, p. 285.

73. ER, p. 434. Elkins, *Holy Women of Twelfth-Century England*, p. 146, says only one English nun was charged with bearing a child in the century; even when the nun of Watton is added, this suggests a phenomenally chaste convent population or, more likely, an underreporting of unchastity.

74. One further conclusion is that in contrast to the medieval sense that the city was Sodom, city life in thirteenth-century Normandy was not particularly corrupting for monastics: nuns were more apt to sin in the countryside than in the city, and monks fell into unchastity about equally in town and country settings.

lowed their own family and political strategies in almost total disregard for the existence of a sexual scandal.[75] Although proof of causality remains elusive, I suspect an appropriate reading of the evidence is that poverty and its attendant daily miseries constituted the most potent force that drove monastics to substitute emotional and sexual satisfaction for the ordered monastic life.

When nuns had affairs, they often entered into relationships, usually with local clerics, that lasted for some length of time rather than being short flings; therefore they were more likely than monks to be discovered and to be cited in the *Register* as repeat offenders. When monks erred, it was apt to be in hit-and-run fashion rather than in ongoing relationships, and with women who often lived at some remove from their monasteries (making discovery difficult). It appears that when monastics became sexually active, the nuns sought human intimacy more than the monks, who reduced the possibility of forming relationships by taking partners who were not local women and by seeing them rarely.

From time to time a small number of nuns and monks abandoned their vows and left the cloister. Leaving the monastery openly might seem more honest and admirable to us than furtive trysting with a lover, but to the medieval world it was a reprehensible denial of an oath rather than a temporary failure. Some may have been recalled by families who needed them; some ran away intending to marry. A certain "M," one of the nuns of Notre-Dame-aux-Nonnains, left her abbey in the early thirteenth century to move to Provence and marry a man from the south.[76] Yet even though she was forsworn, she was still a nun in the eyes of her contemporaries, and the pope and the abbess continued to talk of the possibility of her eventual return. Other nuns who ran away with men may actually have been abducted, as is possible in the case of Mabille of Châtillon, a nun of Holy Cross in Poitiers.[77] The bishop's letter decries the abduction of this nun as one of a series of crimes committed by his former canon, Bernard of Artige. Bernard is described as a violent troublemaker

---

75. For instance, the thirteenth-century charters from Saint-Saens do not show a significant drop in gifts corresponding to the scandal-ridden years: Rouen, BD, Saint-Saens, 56 H, carton 1. Yet there is evidence that some nobles might lampoon nuns for unchastity, as did the author of an early thirteenth-century poem; see Bouchard, *Sword, Miter and Cloister*, p. 229.

76. Paris, BN, MS. Moreau 1179, fols. 80r and v.

77. *Jean XXII (1316–1334) lettres secrètes et curiales relatives à la France, extraites des registres du Vatican*, ed. Auguste Coulon (Paris: Thorin, 1906), 1:175–77.

who forcibly carried off Mabille. Since the bishop is clearly on the warpath, he may be viewing an elopement as an abduction, although Mabille may indeed have been an entirely unwilling partner.

There were cases of sexual philandering, pregnancies, attempted abortions, and births as well as probable instances when men preyed on the inmates of thirteenth-century Norman nunneries. Looked at in context and compared with the behavior of monks, the individual cases remain, but the stereotype of convent debauchery dissolves. Sister Isabelle did have an affair with a priest, but in context she was one of a tiny minority of straying nuns who broke their vows of chastity, a minority equivalent in proportion to the equally unsubstantial number of monks who erred.[78] The depiction of dissolute medieval nuns must be questioned as possibly the result of wish fulfillment, projection, and hostility by both medieval and modern commentators more than a reflection of reality. Further, the bitterness of medieval critics may be partly explained by personal or corporate guilt, since most of the nuns' clerical denouncers must have known, as did Guibert of Nogent, about men like the priest who "was in the habit of having intercourse with a certain nun from a well-known family."[79]

The evidence of Archbishop Eudes's visitations cannot be used to prove that most nuns in our period abided by their vows of chastity; however, it does suggest that nuns in the central Middle Ages in northern France may well have been much more chaste than their critics would have us believe, and not significantly different from their male counterparts.

The Vow of Obedience

The third vow, that of obedience, was a muted but continuing challenge for monastics, both women and men. We have little evidence of the daily obedient behavior of professed monastics; most of what survives is documentation of the breakdown of obedience in the face of apparent poor leadership, which occurred both in nunneries and in male monasteries. The superior in a monastery had absolute power over everyone in the institution; as Abelard put it: "Complete control rests on the authority of a single person."[80] A good superior might demand total and willing acceptance of authority without much resistance from the flock; a bad superior could push monastics to sullen resentment or even open rebellion.

78. ER, p. 227.
79. Guibert of Nogent, *Memoirs*, p. 115.
80. *Letters of Abelard and Heloise*, p. 197.

In visiting the Cistercian nuns at Bondeville, Archbishop Eudes Rigaud reported "that the prioress was quarrelsome and of an evil tongue, that she had no idea how to maintain discipline, and that she was even scorned by the sisters."[81] A harsh and repressive regime at Bondeville led to rebellious behavior, as did the other extreme of an overly lenient rule, like that of the prioress of Villarceaux, whose gentle and muddled administration allowed her priory to disintegrate into chaos.[82] Convents were as apt to suffer under inept leadership as were male houses, but using the gender comparison from Norman visitations, the proportional instances of disobedience in women's houses were dramatically fewer than those in men's monasteries. Aside from the two mentioned, there were only three other cases in which Eudes specifically noted that the sisters were refusing to obey a superior: when the lay sisters at a hospital fought with their prior over pittances; when nuns at Saint-Aubin either refused claustral offices or unceremoniously dropped such responsibilities against the prioress's express orders; and when one noble nun, "Joan Martel was rebellious and disobedient and quarreled with the prioress" and then "rode out on horseback to see her relatives, clad in a sleeved gown made of dark material." To add insult to injury, she "had her own messenger whom she often sent to her relatives."[83]

Abbesses and prioresses generally did not have to cope with overt disobedience from the professed women in their institutions, but they might well have to deal with defiance from the men in their charge. Lay brothers, canons, and priests could add to the superior's headaches, as when Brother Oger refused to obey the prioress of Bondeville or when a disobedient priest had to be thrown out of the hôtel-Dieu at Pontoise.[84] Further, a whole college of canons could challenge an abbess, as we will see in the next chapter.

Disobedience and rebellion were common problems in the men's houses visited by Archbishop Eudes. When he questioned a community about the state of its house, complaints against the abbot or prior tended to come pouring in. In addition, Eudes had to contend with individual monks and canons whose disobedience was uncovered in the course of his inquiries. He punished the kitchener at Eu, who had defied the abbot for taking away his horse; he scolded Brother Henry at Corneville, who refused to take up the priory su-

<hr/>

81. ER, p. 237.
82. ER, p. 48.
83. ER, pp. 371–72, 712, 383.
84. ER, pp. 708, 613. A lay brother also acted disobediently at Saint-Amand (p. 734).

pervision ordered by his abbot; he chastised William, an English monk at Aumale, who was overtly rude to his abbot; in fact, Eudes records thirty-five cases of disobedience by monks and canons to male superiors.[85]

Some of these instances were caused by one particular rebellious person. Peter of Neubourg, a monk of Jumièges, was so infuriated by his abbot that he prepared a written indictment accusing Abbot Richard of being a forger, which he read when the visitor came for his inquiry.[86] He seems to have been a sole voice of defiance at that visit, but in other cases the entire congregation was up in arms against its head. The monks of Saint-Martin-de-Pontoise had reached such an angry impasse with their abbot that they had sent three of their number to Rome to appeal to the pope against him.[87] Things did not simmer down until a new abbot was elected three years later.

One of the most dramatic examples of how far disobedience could escalate in a male monastery occurred in 1266, when Eudes hurried to the Abbey of Eu "upon the complaint of many concerning the violent quarrel which had broken out between the abbot and community there."[88] Eudes listened to an outpouring of woes from the community and then retired to sleep on the problem. The next day he legislated many changes and finally privately "enjoined the abbot, and warned him secretly, to attend the community better than he had been doing and to behave with greater clemency towards the canons."

It seems that monks more often than nuns had to listen to exhortations to obey their superiors "in all legitimate and proper things as they were bound to do, or that otherwise" the visitor would "severely punish those . . . guilty of disobedience."[89] This may be partly a result of the visitor's expectations: men would be competitive and would chafe under the rule of obedience; women would be docile in the face of authority. In addition, cultural conditioning may have disposed women actually to be more obedient on the whole than men.

85. ER, pp. 54, 217, 386. The monks of Bourg-Achard, Envermeu, Jumièges, Mont-Deux-Amants, Saint-Lô, Saint-Martin, Bellencombre, Sainte-Catherine, Saint-Wandrille, Saint-Victor, and Ouville complained about their superiors once or on multiple visits.
86. ER, pp. 697–98.
87. ER, p. 389.
88. ER, p. 659. Also see p. 700 for the continuing conflict.
89. ER, p. 515.

When we compare the abilities of monastic men and women to hold to the demanding vows they had taken at profession, women seem to have been more often guilty than men of breaking the first promise by owning their own property; nuns and monks seem to have been equally good by and large about keeping the second promise to live chastely; and men were less successful than women in maintaining the third vow of obedience. The general outlines that emerge from what can be compared suggest that the religious women and men of northern France in the central Middle Ages were doing well overall in keeping their vows, and that being female or male did not automatically make it easier or harder to live by the rigor of the rule.

Spiritual Life
The Liturgy

"None of the nuns may be absent from the Canonical Hours, but as soon as the bell is rung, everything must be put down and each sister go quickly, with modest gait, to the divine office."[90] Thus does Abelard open his discussion of the offices in his letter to Heloise describing how her nuns should live. The daily repetition of the round of prayers that comprised the hours was the structure within which the monastic life took its form. If the vows taken at profession were the templates monastics used to shape their souls, then the *Opus Dei* was the regular maintenance for tooling the soul to perfection. Each day the nuns and monks of our period participated in a series of services of psalms and prayers that made up this divine work. The daily recitation of psalms that echo the full range of human emotions gave the monastic a powerful vehicle of expression, while the vigils served as a time to listen quietly for God's voice. Again and again the cloistered person chanted and recited the words from which to draw strength and against which to check personal growth or failings, while at the same time the corporate body of the monastery was reinforced by the shared chants and prayers. Centuries earlier Saint Benedict had written: "We believe that God is present everywhere and that the eyes of the Lord in every place behold the good and the evil; but let us especially believe this without any doubting when we are performing the Divine Office."[91] Ideally, it was in this belief that the *Opus Dei* was performed; human nature being what it is, it is certain that many nuns and monks—at least

90. *Letters of Abelard and Heloise*, p. 220.
91. *Rule of St. Benedict*, pp. 66–67.

on occasion—participated in the hours by rote, without contributing fervor or receiving comfort and support.

The offices, contained in monastic breviaries, were performed each day starting in the small hours of the night; the cycle began earlier in the summer than in the winter and varied in the usage of different orders and houses. Benedict had legislated a round of eight services: the night office or matins an hour or two after midnight, lauds at daybreak, and then prime, terce, sext, none, vespers, and compline throughout the day. To this was added chapter meeting after prime and at least one daily mass, usually after terce, making what amounted to ten services a day, with additions for Sundays and saints' feast days and for the deaths and anniversaries of members and those in confraternity.[92] It was this prayer wheel of praise and petitions that won respect and support from the world outside the cloister for "those who prayed."

Continually repeating words can lend them the strength of a mantra but can also render them boring and empty. Some medieval monastics grew weary of the divine office and tended to rattle off the prayers and chants. Archbishop Eudes was always alert to check how the offices were being performed. He scolded monastics for a hurried and sloppy performance of the hours when nuns and monks speeded up the tempo because they liked it fast or because they were rushed or tired.[93] He rejected the excuse that when a congregation was stressed—when many were sick or had just been bled—then the poor quality of performance was understandable and excusable.[94] Individual superiors of houses sometimes sympathized with such claims, equating the health that resulted from an adequate food supply with the monastics' ability to perform the *Opus Dei* well. Thus when the abbess of Saint-Sulpice visited all the dependent priories of her house, she ordered the male prior who attended to the finances at Locmaria to pay the nuns their dues lest the divine offices

92. Parisse, *Nonnes au Moyen Age,* p. 148, points out that not all nuns said the night offices during the Middle Ages. See Joan Evans, *Monastic Life at Cluny, 910–1157* (Oxford: Archon Books, 1968), p. 80 and passim, and Hunt, *Cluny under Saint Hugh,* pp. 99–114, for a detailed description of the process of liturgical accretion that affected Cluny as well as almost all other orders during the central Middle Ages.

93. The nuns of Saint-Amand sang too fast (RV, p. 15): "Aliquando cantant horas Beate Marie et psalmos suffragiorum, cum nimia festinatione et precipitacione verborum." They may have shared a style of performance with their neighboring confreres, the monks of Saint-Catherine, who also were cited for a hurried singing of the hours (ER, p. 9). The monks of Saint-Sever were also wont to rush through the chant (p. 276).

94. ER, pp. 306, 182.

suffer, an interesting case in which the interweaving of material and moral is apparent.[95]

Another failing, but one that Eudes found almost exclusively in nuns' performance of the chant, was to sing it "sine nota" instead of "cum bassa nota."[96] It is not clear what seemed objectionable to Eudes. The correct attention to chant was obviously demanding for all monastic choirs whether female or male, but though Eudes scolds monks for poor performances, only once does he object to the chant of men by urging that four canons should chant "cum nota."[97] One possible explanation is that he was criticizing inadequate knowledge of the notes. Perhaps the inhabitants of most nunneries but only one house of canons had failed to learn the plainsong settings thoroughly, or the women were not using polyphony improvised upon the plainchant.[98] To have had all but one group of men competently versed in the notes and polyphonic settings seems unlikely, although not impossible. A second explanation is that the criticism was of volume, not pitch. *Haut* was sometimes used to mean loud for medieval instruments, and *bas* to mean soft; in this case women may have tended to sing too loudly for Eudes's taste. The archbishop's reaction was perhaps colored by an unconscious negative reaction to the sound of women's voices, which church tradition believed to be erotic and provocative. The timbre of women's voices may have sounded shrill to him. Whatever lies behind this interesting difference, the perceived female failing to chant the offices to the visitor's satisfaction indicates one area in which female monastics seemed to their contemporaries to be falling short of their male counterparts.

One of the ways a monastery asserted its individuality and manipulated its environment was through the offices. From time to time, new celebrations for the dead in general or for a patron saint in particular were composed for and by houses. Sometimes these new ser-

95. *Cartulaire de Saint-Sulpice-la-Forêt*, p. 447, no. 245, 1341.

96. ER, pp. 48, 129, 182, 285, 306, 383, 477, 513, 559, 595, 628. He records of the nuns of Saint-Aubin: "Psallunt horas diurnas sine nota; iniunximus eis ut psallerent saltem cum bassa nota" (RV, p. 114).

97. ER, p. 227; RV, p. 208.

98. Anne Yardley, "Ful Weel She Soong the Service Dyvyne": The Cloistered Musician in the Middle Ages," in *Women Making Music: The Western Art Tradition, 1150–1950*, ed. Jane Bowers and Judith Tick (Urbana: University of Illinois Press, 1986), p. 17. Yardley suggests that nuns received a musical education inferior to that of monks. Her evidence seems primarily to be later English examples, which waters down its value for this study. I am indebted to Edward Roesner for the suggestion about polyphony.

vices responded to the translation of a relic to a new monastic home; sometimes they developed to emphasize the age or authority of a religious institution. The emergence of the office of Saint Leucon at Notre-Dame-aux-Nonnains may well have marked an effort by the nuns to strengthen their hand against the pope's imposition of a competitive house of canons on what they saw as their region of control. Notre-Dame had fought Pope Urban IV's rival foundation throughout the 1260s and 1270s, several times resorting to violence that finally brought excommunication down on their heads. The ban was eventually lifted in 1283, releasing the nuns from excommunication but failing to resolve the tension between them and the canons.

Since neither violence nor papal intercession had given the nuns back the authority they felt the canons had taken from them, Notre-Dame then tried something new by developing the office for Saint Leucon. The earliest manuscript of this service is dated 1287, although it is possible this could be a recension of an earlier document.[99] The timing, however, four years after the lifting of the ban, seems signally appropriate to be the first appearance of this office. Saint Leucon was a seventh-century missionary bishop in Troyes who was believed to have defeated paganism in the region and established Christianity in its stead. He also was credited with installing a community of religious women within the city walls, which foundation Notre-Dame claimed as that of its own original abbey. By associating their nunnery with the patron saint of the city and dating their own existence back to the seventh century, the nuns claimed a quasi-apostolic authority with which to counter the papal patronage of the foundation of Saint-Urbain. In this case the expansion of the hours at Notre-Dame represented a drive by a nunnery for greater religious and political power in the area.

The growing general importance of the mass during the central Middle Ages meant that its celebration in nunneries increased too. By the thirteenth century many donors wanted to institute memorial masses in a convent for themselves and their families. A few still followed the traditional custom and simply requested the prayers of religious women: the knight Geoffrey of Fougereuse gave Saint-Sulpice his property in 1237, asking that two nuns be assigned to pray for his and his ancestors' souls.[100] Some people covered

99. *Documents de Notre-Dame-aux-Nonnains*, p. 154. Lalore also explores the tradition of Saint Leucon as founder of Notre-Dame (pp. 151–55).

100. *Cartulaire de Saint-Sulpice-la-Forêt*, p. 195, no. 117, 1237.

themselves both with the old spiritual insurance of monastic prayers and also with the new, stylish protection of masses, but more
and more donors just wanted masses.[101] Patrons who had limited
resources to donate might merit only one collect in one mass; larger
endowments could fund annual celebrations of the mass or even the
ultimate return of a daily mass in perpetuity.[102]

As donors' needs for masses grew, the arrangements became more
complicated. Nunneries hired chaplains to say the masses for souls
of individuals who had contracted with them for one service or
more a year or made space available to donors for their own chaplains.[103] For instance, in 1234 a knightly couple gave the nuns of
Notre-Dame of Voisins the considerable annual income of thirty-
five pounds and ten solidi to support a chaplain. The abbess of Voisins assigned them one altar dedicated to the Virgin on the left side
in the nuns' church, where their chaplain could celebrate daily
masses for their souls after their deaths. Some donors went even
further and created not only the position for the chaplain but also
the chapel in which he could offer the daily sacrament.[104]

Making masses available was an expensive proposition. When a
nunnery accepted a donation and agreed that its donors would receive an annual mass, the institution was taking on a perpetual obligation, which inflation could make into a budget-breaking responsibility. For instance, in the mid-thirteenth century a donation of
thirty-five pounds annually funded daily masses, five pounds covered weekly masses, and one pound paid for a yearly mass. By the
end of the century the yearly mass had become more expensive,
however, necessitating a three-pound annual income.[105] A monas-

101. *Cartulaire de Saint-Sulpice-la-Forêt,* p. 285, no. 174, 1335, records a couple's
request for both nuns' prayers and masses. Gifts for masses started appearing at the
end of the twelfth century; for instance, Rouen, BD, Bondeville, 52 H, charter from
1191: "Concessit etiam ut tres misse cantentur in monasterio sanctimonialium que
statute erant in monasterio Bondeville cantari."

102. *Cartulaire de Saint-Sulpice-la-Forêt,* p. 176, no. 94, 1219; *Cartulaire du Lieu-
Notre-Dame-lès-Romorantin,* p. 15, no. 9, 1248; *Abbaye des Clairets,* p. 170, no. 78,
1292.

103. Nuns set up a clerk to say masses for the dead: *Cartulaire de Saint-Georges
de Rennes,* 10:36, no. 27, 1231; nuns give a priest a prebend to say masses: *Documents de Notre-Dame-aux-Nonnains,* p. 89, no. 128, 1200; nuns designate an altar
for a couple's chaplain: *Cartulaire de Notre-Dame de Voisins,* p. 119, no. 111, 1234.

104. Paris, BN, MS. lat. 11002, fols. 21v–22r.

105. *Documents de Notre-Dame-aux-Nonnains,* pp. 68–69, no. 101, 1240, records
a gift of one pound in annual rents for a yearly mass. When Marguerite, queen of
Jerusalem, endows an annual mass in 1292, she donates a three-pound yearly income:
Abbaye des Clairets, p. 170, no. 78, 1292.

tery that accepted a fixed-rent income still had somehow to fulfill its obligation to the donor even when decades later the endowment no longer covered the cost of paying the chaplain. Religious women were clearly at a considerable disadvantage compared with their monastic confreres, since at a pinch the monks who were priests could celebrate the masses themselves without paying an outsider as the nuns had to do. Indeed, a convent could feel the staffing problems acutely; at the Priory of Saint-Saens one of the nuns braved all the pollution taboos to assist the priest in celebrating the mass, probably owing to a shortage of male personnel.[106]

Liturgical practices at medieval monasteries grew more complex and numerous over the centuries. Houses developed special celebrations, like the nine that grew up at the Abbey of the Holy Cross in Poitiers. These included four celebrations for the founder and patron saint, Saint Radegunda, two for their great relic of the cross, and one each for Radegunda's close friends and supporters the poet Fortunatus, the nun Disciole, and Agnes, the first abbess.[107] Such liturgical events brought in income and fostered local pride and a sense of community in the members of the abbey.

One of the ceremonies in which nuns participated and that had long-term effects was the Easter play of the three Marys, which dramatized the story of the Marys going to the tomb and finding it empty. A very ancient trope, the *Quem queritis,* was the germ from which this liturgical drama grew. In its earliest ninth-century form it contained only four lines of dialogue:

> Whom do you seek in the sepulcher, O servants of Christ?
> Jesus of Nazareth crucified, O inhabitants of heaven.
> He is not here; he is resurrected as it was foretold.
> Go and announce that he is raised from the dead.

This was then followed by the introit of the mass.[108] During the central Middle Ages the *Quem queritis* was expanded into the *Visitatio sepulchri* and came to be performed in the office of matins rather than in the canon of the mass. It is from this small Holy Saturday playlet that modern theatrical performance eventually

---

106. ER, p. 199.

107. Robert Favreau, "Heurs et malheurs de l'abbaye, XIIe–XVe s.," in *Histoire de l'abbaye Sainte-Croix de Poitiers: Quatorze siècles de vie monastique,* Mémoires de la Société des Antiquaires de l'Ouest, 4th ser., 19 (Poitiers: Société des Antiquaires de l'Ouest, 1986), p. 138.

108. Diane Dolan, *Le drame liturgique de Pâques en Normandie et en Angleterre au Moyen Age* (Paris: Presses Universitaires de France, 1975), pp. 11–13.

grew, and it was monastic women and men who shaped this development from the dramatic to drama.

In its early form, as at Notre-Dame-aux-Nonnains, the playlet combined the talents of nuns, clerics, choirboys, and the entire membership of the convent.[109] The service manuscript of the abbey reads very like a script. First the costumes and setting are described and then the action. The entire convent bearing candles is assembled in the choir, and the clergy are before the high altar, on which rest holy water, the cross, censers, and candles. The priest is vested for mass, except he wears his choir cape instead of his chasuble; the deacon and subdeacons wear dalmatics and tunics.

Then the action begins, assisted by one nun who stands by as prompter, with a torch and a book to help out if anyone forgets the lines. The three Marys, three nuns wearing their habits, come before the altar, kneel, and recite the *Confiteor*; the clerics say the *Misereatur*. Each Mary then takes up her props: a box, a towel, and a candle that is lit by the prompter. The entire congregation then forms up in procession to conduct the Marys around the church to a pillar next to the altar of Saint Michael, where two little boys stand robed all in white to represent the angels. The Marys and the angels recite their lines in Latin, with the angels concluding, "He does not lie here, come and see." The angels lead the Marys to the altar of Saint Anthony, to which also process those carrying the cross, the holy water, the Gospels, censers, and candles. The congregation of nuns watches in silence. The Marys chant *Salve rex sabaoth* and then *Gloria sancte tibi*. The priest advances to the altar and elevates the chalice and Host, at which the cantress leads the nuns in chanting *Christus resurgens* and *Ex mortuis* as the church bells peal out the joyful gospel message of resurrection.

The playlet ends with the clergy processing carrying the Host, flanked by the two angels and followed by the Marys and the children's choir until they come before the congregation of nuns. The procession again chants the *Christus resurgens*, to which the cantress responds with *Dicant nunc*. The *Te Deum* is sung, and the clergy drape the high altar with cloth of gold.

To participate in this playlet, acting a part or as a member of the audience, must have been moving. The voices of women, boys, and

109. *Documents de Notre-Dame-aux-Nonnains*, pp. 198–200. The text is contained in fols. 301v–302v of the ordinarium of 1287. Different versions of the playlet developed at various houses: Holy Cross in Poitiers had one cleric acting the part of the angel and one nun acting that of Mary Magdalen. See Favreau, "Heurs et malheurs," pp. 139–40.

men raised in plainsong chant, the flickering light of candles and torches, incense, rich fabrics and precious stones on the silver chalice and Gospel book covers all contributed to the beauty and excitement of the service. Three women are the heroines of the action; it is they who go to minister to their dead Lord and first hear of his resurrection. Medieval religious women must have identified with those women of Galilee from so long before when the nuns acted in and watched this playlet every year; they must have felt their fellowship with religious men as they all, together, reenacted the crucial moment in Christian history.

Solemn processions were central to medieval monastic life: nuns and monks formed processions in church as part of the liturgy; they marched in procession as a weapon to subdue recalcitrant secular folk; they proceeded in formal order out of their cloisters to greet the bishop. The monastic community also processed to the graveyard with the body of one of its members or of a confrere. This was a signal honor for a layperson and was sometimes spelled out in a donation charter as an important spiritual benefit. Rocand gave the nuns of Saint-Georges his lands so that when he died his family would hand over his body to the nuns to be transported to their abbey for an interment honored "with a procession of nuns in the cemetery of Saint-Georges."[110] Burial processions of nuns sometimes left the nunnery with a corpse bound for another final resting place, as when the abbess and nuns of Salzinnes accompanied the funeral cortege of the saintly Juliana of Cornillon to its burial at the Abbey of Villers.[111]

Nuns did not take part in as many extraclaustral processions as monks did, and the nuns of some houses, particularly the later foundations, rarely if ever processed outside their walls. Ancient and powerful nunneries founded in the Merovingian period had been natural leaders of the religious life of their region; it was these houses that usually were able to continue the custom of joining the public liturgical life of their towns well into the thirteenth century. On Rogation Days, the three days preceding Ascension Day, the church held processions of chanting clergy and monastics. Nuns from houses like Holy Cross in Poitiers, founded in the seventh century, participated in the ceremonies.[112] On Monday the nuns marched to Sainte-Radegonde and Saint-Austrégisile; the next day

110. *Cartulaire de Saint-Georges de Rennes*, 9:270, no. 43, ca. 1070.
111. Simenon, *Julienne de Cornillon*, p. 90.
112. Favreau, "Heurs et malheurs," p. 140.

the monks of Saint-Cyprien came to their nunnery in procession, and after receiving them the nuns then joined them for the return trip to Saint-Cyprien; Wednesday the nuns again went out to make the solemn trip to the cathedral, the baptistry, Notre-Dame, and back to their own cloister. The nuns of Holy Cross were full and equal participants in the high moments of public religious fervor in the city of Poitiers.

During the twelfth century and increasingly in the thirteenth, the church attempted to repress nuns' participation in Rogation Day processions as well as other public ceremonies. In fact the constriction of any exterior liturgical observances could be severe. Archbishop Eudes Rigaud insisted as a means of ending "all matter for scandal" that the nuns of Montivilliers totally give up processing throughout their own church into the nave used by townspeople; instead, the nuns were to chant the prayers and antiphons usually sung in procession while standing in the privacy of their own choir.[113] The same sort of constriction affected the nuns of Saint-Amand, who in the mid-thirteenth century received a bull from Pope Innocent IV ordering them to cease all processions unless they received ecclesiastical authority to hold such a public liturgical display.[114]

Holy Things and People

Holy things in a monastery could attract attention or create disturbances. These relics, the physical remains of the greatest holy people of the church, were magnets that drew visitors and pilgrims seeking indulgences and cures to the church that housed them. Being the resting place for important relics increased visibility and income, since such prominence attracted recruits to swell the ranks of the order and pilgrims whose thank offerings to the saint filled the abbey's coffers. Abbess Imene of Salzinnes used her powerful ecclesiastical brother to obtain relics of the Eleven Thousand Virgins of Cologne for her house. The presence of these important holy remains lent prominence to the convent, which then became known as the nunnery founded to the "honor and praise of the blessed and glorious Virgin Mary, Saint George, Saint Michael, and the Eleven Thousand Virgins."[115]

---

113. ER, p. 538.
114. Rouen, BD, Saint-Amand, H 55, carton 1, 1355 vidimus of bull of Pope Innocent IV dated June 3, 1244.
115. *Recueil du Val-Saint-Georges à Salzinnes*, p. 235, no. 175, ca. 1300.

The acquisition of relics could actually reshape a monastery's persona. In the early twelfth century John, bishop of Orléans, gave the Abbey of Fontevrault a church dedicated to "Mariae Magdalenae de Hospitali."[116] Vauzelles believes this was a house that originally took in poor girls, but once the church was donated by the bishop the order moved to regularize it by sending out a colony of twelve nuns and a prioress to make the little foundation into a proper priory.[117] The priory became a respectable member of the order of Fontevrault but certainly not a particularly notable one. Then in 1267 King Louis IX acquired some important relics of Mary Magdalen, the bulk of which he donated to the Abbey of Vézelay, with the leftovers going to the bishop of Orléans. The bishop apparently wanted to enhance a local house and made the priory with its attribution to the Magdalen the lucky recipient. The nuns were also granted the right to celebrate he saint's feast day and to give pilgrims sixty-day indulgences for venerating the relics. The priory, which up to then had usually been referred to as the Hospicium, increasingly began to be called la Magdalene. Resident relics gave to the priory a new sense of itself.

Holy things were the objects most treasured by monasteries. What of holy people? Saintly nuns were conspicuous for their absence in the nunneries of northern France in the central Middle Ages. Of the two dozen plus convents I examined for this study, not one produced an indigenous saint in our period, and only one—Salzinnes—had a saintly resident inside its cloister for a time: Juliana of Cornillon lived temporarily at Salzinnes after riots in Cornillon drove her into exile.[118] She was helped and financed largely by the highborn and vigorous Abbess Imene, who first helped her establish herself in a house in Namur and later received her and her followers into the abbey itself. Juliana's presence does not seem to have been peaceful and serene: she acted as a storm center wherever she went. One can only conjecture that the nuns of Salzinnes, proud though they might be to give refuge to a holy woman, may have found her presence disruptive.

The work of other scholars corroborates the general rarity of saintly women in the central Middle Ages. Jane Schulenburg finds

---

116. Vauzelles, *Histoire de la Magdeleine-lez-Orléans*, pp. 205–6, no. 1.

117. Vauzelles, *Histoire de la Magdeleine-lez-Orléans*, pp. 10–15. If so, they were probably soliciting to support themselves. The charter describing the gift of relics is on pp. 227–28, no. 25, 1267.

118. Simenon, *Julienne de Cornillon*, pp. 75–89, deals with the years of her exile and death.

that between the years 500 and 1099, female saints numbered on average only 14.9 percent, peaking at 22 percent between 650 and 750 and dwindling to 10.6 percent in the eleventh century.[119] Weinstein and Bell find women making up on average 17.5 percent of the saints in their study—specifically, 8 percent of the saints in the eleventh century (their numbers differ from those of Schulenburg), 11.8 percent in the twelfth century, and 22.6 percent in the thirteenth century. They note that nuns were disproportionately few in the central Middle Ages; for instance, only 11 percent of the Benedictine saints from the eleventh and twelfth centuries were women.[120]

If indeed "saints reflect the popular collective religious mentality of the period," then does their absence from northern French convents indicate that nuns saw themselves as "morally and spiritually the weaker sex"?[121] Does the absence of holy nuns mean society perceived the nunneries as of little value? It is clear from the careful work of both of these studies that women never made up more than a small proportion (about 15 percent, or slightly less than one out of every seven) of those popularly seen as saints. This modest showing certainly might suggest that women's self-perception and society's evaluation of women were both less robust than were the self-image and view of men. In the patriarchal world of medieval Europe this would come as no surprise. Yet the absence of saintly women in convents of northern France in the central Middle Ages actually may demonstrate that sanctity was not the only religious ideal forming public opinion in the period. Overt community support existed for nunneries, which would make little sense if the sole criterion for religious success was to house saints. Since patrons and recruits continued to express enthusiasm for women's monasticism, there must have been ways this life satisfied social needs. Most nuns were not venerated as saints, but they were still respected as intercessors, valued as relatives, and needed for their many contributions to society. Whether or not a nun achieved holiness, her life of striving won admiration.

119. Jane Schulenburg, "Female Sanctity: Public and Private Roles, ca. 500–1100," in *Women and Power in the Middle Ages*, ed. Mary Erler and Maryanne Kowaleski (Athens: University of Georgia Press, 1988), p. 104.

120. Donald Weinstein and Rudolph Bell, *Saints and Society: The Two Worlds of Western Christendom, 1000–1700* (Chicago: University of Chicago Press, 1982), pp. 220–23.

121. Schulenburg, "Female Sanctity," p. 103, and Weinstein and Bell, *Saints and Society*, p. 235.

Monastics pursued their own perfection through the second spiritual activity of sacred reading, or *lectio divina*, in addition to their primary commitment to the *Opus Dei*. In Abelard's words addressed to the nuns of the Paraclete: "For the food of the soul and its spiritual refreshment is the God-given understanding of Scripture, . . . if you are unable to be kindled to such fervour of devotion, you can at least in your love and study of sacred Scriptures model yourselves on those blessed disciples of St Jerome, Paula and Eustochium."[122] Reading and study had spiritual value: such activities could and should make nuns grow toward their spiritual goal.

At the beginning of our period there is no doubt that choir nuns and monks—in contrast to lay sisters and brothers—had to be literate in Latin to be able to chant the liturgy. They were expected to read and learn from the Fathers, biblical commentaries, monastic contemplative writing, and the other works collected in their *armarium*, or monastic library. Eleventh-century nuns were literate or even highly educated: nuns like Pisomenna composed charters in the safety of the abbey or, like the unfortunate unnamed nun who was part of a heretical group in Orléans, repented of having been part of a sect "composed of members of the social and (in that as clerks they were *literati*) intellectual élite."[123] She would not have been admitted into this group had she not been an intellectual equal of the men.

To become a nun was to anticipate becoming literate or maybe even learned. When one father brought his daughter to Ronceray to be accepted as a nun, he required the house to educate her or, if she proved too dull, to allow him to substitute a brighter daughter in her place.[124] Learning to read was an integral part of the making of a nun. The context for this learning can be seen at Notre-Dame in Saintes during the twelfth century. The abbey maintained a school, five of whose senior students were sufficiently lettered to be present as witnesses for the signing of a charter; this school was presided over by a male schoolteacher, at least at times during the twelfth and thirteenth centuries.[125] Books were available in the *armarium*,

122. *Letters of Abelard and Heloise*, pp. 260, 269.

123. *Cartulaire de Saint-Georges de Rennes*, 9:263, no. 34, 1085: "Pisomenna qui hanc cartam composuit." Moore, *Origins of European Dissent*, p. 30.

124. *Cartulaire du Ronceray*, p. 246, no. 402.

125. *Cartulaire de Notre-Dame de Saintes*, p. 126, no. 202, 1148, lists "scolaribus vero Ermengarde, Sibilla, Leticia, Agnete, Petronilla de Birach." Reginald the "magister scholarum" is mentioned on p. 132, no. 208, 1141–66 and p. 157, no. 237, 1162. There is still a male teacher in the thirteenth century (p. 178, no. 274, 1220).

and one of the most important nuns, Agnes Morell, was the librarian in the mid-twelfth century. Nuns not only were literate but also were capable of composing charters, as did Rixende and also Galarda, the sacristan, who closed one charter with: "I, Galarda, sacristan of Notre-Dame in Saintes, wrote this charter and left the writing to those who come after me in perpetuity."[126]

Nuns could write more than legal charters; some penned poetry, examples of which survive in the *rotuli*. The following was composed by a member of the nunnery of Argenteuil:

> Flet pastore pio grex desolatus adempto:
>   Soletur miseras turba fidelis oves.
> Proh dolor! hunc morsu sublatum mortis edaci
>   Non dolor aut gemitus vivificare queunt.
> Ergo quid lacrime? avid tot tantique dolores
>   Prosunt? nil prodest hic dolor, imo nocet.
> Sed licet utilitas ex fletu nulla sequatur,
>   Est tamen humanum morte dolere patris.
> Est etiam gaudere pium, si vis rationis
>   Tristitie vires adnichilare queat.
> Mors etenim talis, non mors, sed vita putatur.
>   Nam moritur mundo, vivit et ipse Deo.
> Ores pro nobis; omnes oramus ut ipse
>   Xpistum
> Et nos ad   perveniamus. Amen.
>   vitam

> The shepherd gone, the sheep bereaved,
> Death's hungry jaws have caused this pain.
> Console the faithful lambs that grieve.

> No cries nor tears can life regain
> So why these tears? Why saddened face?
> Is there purpose to the pain?

> Such sorrow has no saving grace,
> In fact, it wounds the baser sort.
> Such is the nature of our race:

> A father's death does tear the heart.
> But joy does rise above the pain
> For reason takes the higher part,

126. *Cartulaire de Notre-Dame de Saintes*, p. 56, no. 56, 1100–17, p. 78, no. 86, 1174–1203: "Ego Galarda, sacristana Beate Marie Xanctonensis, hanc cartam inscripsi et posteris meis in perpetuo legendam reliqui."

And conquers sorrow by the claim
That death in fact is life reborn
For earthly death is heavenly gain.

So pray for us and we shall pray
That Christ himself shall come again
And we shall live in endless day. Amen.[127]

Some scholars argue that there was a significant loss of learning in the convents of the twelfth and thirteenth centuries, and others emphasize that religious women never had as high a level of cultural activity as did religious men.[128] There is indeed some evidence that the use of Latin in nunneries was on the decline in the thirteenth century. For instance, Archbishop Simon of Beaulieu preached to the canons of Clermont in Latin, to the monks at Saint-Jean d'Angély in French and Latin, and to the nuns of Holy Cross in Poitiers in French.[129] But many male houses were also experiencing an intellectual decline marked by losing their former scholarly enthusiasm and their fluency in Latin. Abelard castigates the monks of his day for intellectual sloppiness, the ability to read but not to understand, and more pride in the numbers of books they possess than in any real knowledge of their contents.[130]

Certainly some monks were struggling with Latin as much as were some nuns. The abbot of Saint-Georges, for example, played hooky during the offices and mass because he could not understand the lessons.[131] A survey of Archbishop Eudes's records reveals that on six occasions the archbishop specified that a house needed to obtain vernacular copies of either the rule or the Statutes of Pope

127. *Rouleau mortuaire du B. Vital, Abbé de Savigny,* ed. Léopold Delisle (Paris: H. Champion, 1909), p. 22, title 41. It has been suggested that this poem might actually have been written by Heloise. The translation is by Patrick T. McMahon, O. Carm.

128. Michel Parisse, *La Lorraine monastique au Moyen Age* (Nancy: Presses Universitaires de Nancy, 1981), p. 61: "La vie culturelle des religieuses fut, on ne guère en douter, moins dynamique que celle des hommes." This seems a difficult premise to support, since the cultural level of houses was unique to each institution, and convents like Notre-Dame in Saintes with a library, school, and literate nuns were surely a cut above places like the male monastery of Aumale, which needed the Statutes of Saint Gregory in French (presumably because the monks did not understand them in Latin) and where the monks had given up reading during meals in the refectory: ER, pp. 85, 566.

129. Mansi, pp. 279, 271, 170.

130. *Letters of Abelard and Heloise,* pp. 260–68.

131. ER, p. 571.

Gregory. Three male monasteries and two convents were ordered to acquire French texts, which suggests that in the mid-thirteenth century Latin fluency was a bit shaky among monastics of both sexes.

Towards the end of our period, however, there still were schools, books, and Latin literacy in some convents. Holy Cross kept a school for girls; the nuns of Voisins were happy to inherit eight books from an anchorite; and the nuns of Notre-Dame-aux-Nonnains and the Paraclete were still reading the Scriptures in Latin during meals in the refectory.[132] But keeping a high educational level became difficult for nuns, who as women were not able to take advantage of the university educations available to men. From the twelfth century on, as universities grew and proliferated, orders sent their brightest male monastics to become educated in university towns; this option was not open to any women, even those in nunneries. By the tail end of the Middle Ages, in the fourteenth and fifteenth centuries, the undereducation of nuns had become the norm; but although there was some slippage during our period of the central Middle Ages, many religious women were not yet far behind their confreres.

Besides performing the *Opus Dei* and *lectio divina*, the nun could strive for spiritual growth through asceticism; she might discipline her body with austerities, prime among which was fasting. Monasteries in the early Middle Ages had entirely abstained from meat and observed fast days in penitential seasons such as Lent. These practices had eroded significantly by the twelfth century, although the new reform orders, like the Cistercians, did reinstitute them.[133] Yet by the end of the century an austerity diet was not customary in most wealthy northern nunneries. In 1182 the nuns of Jully received a present of a vineyard from the countess of Nevers; the sale of the wine was intended to buy meat for the community.[134] This occasioned no outcry. In the mid-thirteenth century the nuns of the Abbey of Saint-Sulpice routinely ate meat three times a week with the full approval of the abbess.[135] Eating meat might be becoming more common in some monasteries, but it was still censured by Eudes in the mid-thirteenth century. It was, however, a particularly male offense in his Norman monasteries: 92 percent of all the archbishop's

---

132. Favreau, "Heurs et malheurs," p. 133; *Cartulaire de Notre-Dame de Voisins*, p. 135, no. 129, 1245; *Documents de Notre-Dame-aux-Nonnains*, pp. 220–21; there were similar lists of Latin readings from the Paraclete in the same period.

133. Bynum, *Holy Feast and Holy Fast*, pp. 40–42.

134. *Cartulaire de Jully-les-Nonnains*, p. 273, no. 51, 1182.

135. *Cartulaire de Saint-Sulpice-la-Forêt*, p. 224, no. 137, 1261.

criticisms of eating meat were of male houses, a striking predominance that may reflect Norman nunneries' relative poverty as much as their piety. Yet it was at this very same period and perhaps in reaction that holy women began increasingly to practice food austerities.

Caroline Bynum has investigated the role food played for women and the way women manipulated food. Holy and saintly women like Catherine of Siena, Mary of Oignies, and Angela of Foligno fasted to the point of starvation to control themselves and to influence the society around them.[136] Bynum's work raises the question of how far such behavior may have been an issue in the lives of unknown women: nuns who may have fasted and venerated the Eucharist without ever attracting outside attention; nuns who like the woman from the Fontevrist Priory of Borueul ate and drank nothing on Mondays, Wednesdays, and Fridays, and on the other days of the week ate extremely sparingly, never taking wine or meat. In the climate of the thirteenth century there may well have been other nuns for whom fasting was an important route to spiritual fulfillment but who never attained the public renown that led to recognition as a saint.

Another ascetic practice was total withdrawal from the world by becoming an anchoress, enclosed for life in a tiny cell. This life was not for everyone, but it seems to have particularly appealed to women. Ann Warren finds at least twice as many English female anchoresses as anchorites but suggests that there may have been fewer female recluses on the Continent, since more religious paths were available to women there than in England.[137] However, other studies have found women predominating as recluses in areas of France too.[138] Such people, determined to test and temper their spirituality with solitude, prayer, and contemplation, usually lived in tiny cells attached to a church, often a monastic church. Once enclosed in this anchorhold, the anchoress or anchorite was dead to the world and was never again to move freely.

Not all who yearned to be enclosed achieved their desire. There

136. Bynum, *Holy Feast and Holy Fast*, chaps. 6 and 7.

137. Warren, *Anchorites and Their Patrons*, pp. 19–22. In the twelfth century English anchoresses outnumbered anchorites five to three, and in the thirteenth century, four to one.

138. Paulette L'Hermite-Leclercq, "Reclus et recluses dans le sud-ouest de la France," in *La femme dans la vie religieuse du Languedoc (XIIIe–XIVe s.)*, vol. 23 of *Cahiers de Fanjeaux* (Paris: Privat, 1988), p. 281. Their numbers grew in the thirteenth century (p. 284). Huyghebaert, "Femmes laïques dans la vie religieuse," p. 359.

were practical barriers: the person needed the personal and spiritual fortitude to make a success of the venture, and an endowment was necessary for support. To fund the enclosure of his daughter at Saint-Pierre-aux-Nonnains in Metz, Wenhern donated a vineyard.[139] This father had the necessary resources, but since the endowment for a recluse was substantial, the inability to get funding may have kept some women from following this life. Another barrier for a professed monastic who wanted to take up life in an anchorhold could be getting permission from a superior to be released from claustral responsibilities. When a twelfth-century nun applied to Bernard of Clairvaux for advice and support in her quest to take up the life of solitude, the abbot responded that she should forgo her plan since "if you are one of the foolish virgins, the congregation is necessary for you; if you are one of the wise virgins, you are necessary for the congregation."[140] He followed up with dire warnings of the wolves in the woods that lay in wait for innocent lambs and reminders of her responsibility to the community. The letter must have deflated the nun's excitement, but we do not know if it deflected her or if she persevered in her desire for the solitary life.

Some nuns had to journey far off to find the enclosure where they wished to spend the rest of their earthly lives. Emma was professed in Normandy at the Abbey of Saint-Amand, where she must have developed a strong veneration for her monastery's patron saint. The actual relics of the saint were not in the convent, however, but were housed at the Flemish Abbey of Saint-Amand les Eaux d'Elnone. This abbey of monks had suffered a devastating fire in 1066 but managed to rebuild its church speedily so that the consecration took place only twenty-two years later, in 1088. The Norman nuns of Saint-Amand knew of the planned ceremony of consecration, and Emma must have conceived the idea, with the backing of her community, of going to the Flemish monastery to take up the anchoritic life close to the holy remains of her saintly patron at this time of special celebration. Apparently the monks accepted her plan, for archaeologists have recently discovered a lead plaque with the following inscription: "Here lies Emma, the recluse, a nun of the church of Saint-Amand in Rouen, who joyously moved here to the presence of the same saint. She lived here, serving God enclosed in this place for thirty-six years. Having died and been buried, she rests here. Emma died in the year 1124 of our Lord's incarnation, the fourth of

139. Paris, BN, MS. lat. 10027, fol. 39r.
140. Bernard, Epistle 115, PL, 182:261–62.

December."[141] Emma journeyed from Normandy to Flanders to find the enclosed life for which she hungered; Eve, an English nun from Wilton Abbey, traveled even farther in search of greater austerities. She went with a companion, Benedicta, across the English Channel to Angers to live a heightened ascetic existence with several like-minded people in the anchorhold of Saint-Laurent.[142] Eve stayed there with a companion, Petronilla, for perhaps twenty years and then moved to a cell attached to the Priory of l'Evière to live with the anchorite Hervé. At some subsequent time she was joined there by her niece, Ravenissa. The women borrowed books from abbeys in their region and were not above adding a little holy graffiti to a Gospel book from Holy Trinity, Vendôme: "Eve, a recluse made this sign of the cross in memory of her constancy to her vow, and Ravenissa her niece [made] that one."[143] Eve enters the historical record partly through the letter, the *Liber confortatorius*, written to her by her friend, Goscelin, who had been an intimate monastic confrere at Wilton before Eve journeyed to the Continent. She died at an advanced age about the year 1125.

This transplanted anchoress was extremely assertive about pursuing her dream: although she entered monastic life willy-nilly, given by her parents to Wilton Abbey at seven years old, she shaped her life to her needs, moving twice in search of what she wanted. In addition, although she sought a more austere day-to-day existence than she could find in a nunnery, she was never really alone: first Goscelin, then Benedicta and Petronilla, and finally Hervé and her niece were companions, and Goscelin was even a soul mate. Eve was literate and apparently continued *lectio divina* all her life. She must have been a charismatic individual—a nun attempting to achieve sanctity through asceticism, yet for whom human connections and intellectual activities were part of the enclosed world in which she spent her days.

Cloistering

Religious women pursued spiritual perfection behind the protective walls of their cloister; or at least that was the theory expounded in the writings of many of the important male monastic legislators, whose clear intent was to impose rigorous cloistering on monastic

141. Platelle, "Relations entre Saint-Amand et Saint-Amand d'Elnone," p. 84.

142. André Wilmart, "Eve et Goscelin," *Revue Bénédictine* 46(1934): 414–38, 50(1938): 42–83.

143. Vendôme, BM, MS. 2, fol. 1r. See my discussion of Eve and Hervé, in Johnson, *Prayer, Patronage, and Power*, pp. 163–64.

women. Claustration had two aspects: it could be both active, the absolute and permanent enclosure of a religious person within a monastery (no different theoretically from the enclosure of a recluse), or passive, the total exclusion of all outsiders from the monastery. Stephen of Obazine attracted both female and male followers in great numbers in the first half of the twelfth century. When the saint regularized these people into monastic communities, he enclosed the nuns in "perpetual claustration."[144] Abelard in his letter of direction to Heloise for the Paraclete warned that "solitude is indeed all the more necessary for your woman's frailty," adding sanctimoniously, "inasmuch as for our part we are less attacked by the conflicts of carnal temptations and less likely to stray towards bodily things through the senses." Thus he urged that all the necessary resources for a nunnery be encircled by its walls, "places where the sisters may carry out their daily tasks without any need for straying outside."[145] Thirteenth-century statutes for the nuns of Prémontré legislated punishments for any nun or lay sister who failed to observe claustration, and Jacques de Vitry, that champion of religious women, enthusiastically described nuns as living in absolute enclosure, sealed away from all outside contact.[146]

Passionate defense of enclosing holy women did not necessarily cloud the good sense of its supporters. The rather pragmatic precepts set out for the nuns of Fontevrault stated that nuns should never go out but acknowledged that they would sometimes have to leave their house; the rule therefore attempted to legislate seemly behavior with the requirement that two men—one religious and one secular—should always accompany any nun sallying out of her cloister.[147] Abbot Peter the Venerable wrote with enthusiasm of the absolute enclosure at the Cluniac nunnery of Marcigny, famous for its strict claustration from which no nun was ever to wander away; yet when faced with the real demands of the cellaress, his mother Raingarde, Peter acknowledged that she would have to venture out of the monastery to see to the various needs of the sisters.[148] Stephen of Obazine had legislated the tightest of rules for cloistering,

144. *Vie de St. Etienne d'Obazine*, pp. 98–99.
145. *Letters of Abelard and Heloise*, p. 196.
146. *Les statuts de Prémontré au milieu du XIIe siècle*, ed. Placidius F. Lefèvre and W. M. Grauwen, Bibliotheca Analectorum Praemonstratensium 12 (Averbode: Praemonstratensia, 1978), pp. 113–15, and Jacques de Vitry, *Historia occidentalis*, as quoted by Parisse, *Nonnes au Moyen Age*, p. 31.
147. Rule of Fontevrault, PL, 162:1079.
148. "De miraculis," PL, 189:889 D; Epistle 17, PL, 189:220 D.

yet when the nuns were visited in 1285, the archbishop had to warn them about slack attention to enclosure.[149] Theory might have to bend to practicality, but it persisted. Some acknowledged the difficulty, if not the outright danger, of strict cloistering; Humbert of Romans preached to nuns of the problems of enclosure, which could lead them to become gloomy, hungry for gossip, and lax in maintaining both active and passive claustration.[150]

Contemporary observers also recognized that following a monastic rule imposed enclosure on monks—at least in theory—just as it did on their female counterparts. Yet from the time of Caesarius of Arles (ca. 470–542), who had instituted the first rule intended particularly for women, religious leaders had invested the cloistering of nuns with greater importance than the enclosure of monks. In fact it was the rule of Caesarius that initiated "the vital importance of cloister to monasticism for women."[151] Some later writers, like the monk Idung in the twelfth century, defended the inequity of tighter cloistering for nuns than for monks, rooting the case in the authority of Saint Jerome, whose belief in the fundamental weakness of female nature led him to call for more stringent enclosure for women than for men.[152]

These are the voices of men. The women are mute on the subject of cloistering, even in the extraordinary case of Heloise. If we put clerical theories and legislation to one side, however, we can see that the nunnery walls served communities as permeable membranes rather than watertight seals. Neither active nor passive cloistering was absolute: religious women commonly left their houses on all sorts of errands, and those who were not community members entered the monastic precincts on all sorts of pretexts; much of this movement both in and out of monasteries was seen by nunnery of-

149. Mansi, p. 284.

150. Humbert of Romans, "De eruditione praedicatorum," in *Prediche alle donne de secolo XIII*, ed. C. Casagrande (Milan: Bompiani, 1978), pp. 142–43.

151. Donald Hochstetler, "The Meaning of Monastic Cloister for Women according to Caesarius of Arles," in *Religion, Culture, and Society in the Early Middle Ages: Studies in Honor of Richard E. Sullivan*, ed. Thomas Noble and John Contreni (Kalamazoo, Mich.: Medieval Institute Publications, 1987), p. 27.

152. Idung, "Argumentum super quatuor questionibus," ed. R. B. C. Huygens, *Studi Medievali*, 3d ser., 13(1972): 355–62. Jean Leclercq, "Medieval Feminine Monasticism: Reality versus Romantic Images," in *Benedictus: Studies in Honor of St. Benedict of Nursia*, ed. Rozanne Elder, Studies in Medieval Cistercian History 8 (Kalamazoo, Mich.: Cistercian Publications, 1981), p. 59 describes the case of the male Abbey of Valladolid, which King Juan I put under strict claustration in imitation of the cloistering of nuns.

ficials as licit, although some was judged illicit even by the nuns themselves.

The most commonly authorized reason for a nun to be out of her monastic retreat was to secure powerful support for her monastery. For instance, religious women outside the walls of their houses could be defending their communal privileges or temporal possessions, which often entailed seeking episcopal help. Abbesses often traveled to the bishop's palace for negotiations and litigation.[153] At other times nuns could be in search of spiritual aid, like the Fontevrist nun who traveled with her mother to the archbishop of Bourges to seek support for her extensive fasting. Sometimes the authority before whom the religious woman appeared was a secular lord.[154] But one way or another, the exigencies of their lives called on nuns to meet with authority figures.

The uncloistered nun was not always a suppliant. On many occasions she was assertively attending to business or looking out for her abbey's interests. Nuns strode around the fields walking boundaries with lay officials; they traveled considerable distances on abbatial business; they went to the family members of a donor to receive each relative's consent to a gift.[155] When a wounded count wanted to settle his affairs, he made a donation to the nuns of Saintes, and among the group of witnesses who crowded into his bedroom were four nuns; when a nunnery was in severe financial straits, as was Saint-Aubin in Normandy, two nuns left the abbey, apparently with the approval of the abbess, to raise funds for the impoverished community.[156]

Nuns also left their enclosures with the full support of their superiors to right wrongs done their communities. Canny abbesses might use the weapon of surprise by sending out legations to shame malefactors into compliance.[157] A dramatic case of how this worked occurred in the early twelfth century when the nuns of Notre-Dame in Saintes were locked in conflict with two brothers. News reached the convent that a man had died without having returned the tithe

153. Poitiers, BD, la Trinité, 2 H 2, carton 12, 2; and Paris, BN, MS. lat. 10027, fols. 45r and v.

154. *Cartulaire de Saint-Sulpice-la-Forêt*, p. 417, no. 220, 1138.

155. *Cartulaire de Notre-Dame de Saintes*, p. 80, no. 88, 1150, p. 64, no. 68, 1163; Poitiers, BM, MS. 27, p. 105, no. 109, 1161.

156. *Cartulaire de Notre-Dame de Saintes*, p. 85, no. 99, 1119–23; ER, p. 537.

157. *Cartulaire de Notre-Dame de Saintes*, p. 147, no. 227, 1100–1107, recounts how the abbess sent a nun accompanied by two abbey men to forbid a certain Radulf from taking monastic vows as his ploy for evading reparations to the abbey.

and woods he had stolen from the convent. The abbess seized the moment for confrontation, sending the nuns in stately procession to the church to confront his grieving brothers over the body of their dead sibling; dramatically bearding the opposition, the band of religious women won their point and then graciously promised commemorations for the souls of relatives as a sweetener for the bereaved brothers, who had lost not only a brother but also the property. The physical appearance of nuns outside their cloister, standing in the presence of the corpse, proved an invincible weapon in their battle to regain stolen property.

Abbesses who bore responsibility for the temporal and spiritual welfare of their communities were the most visible of all uncloistered women. Abbess Agnes of Barbezieux, head of Notre-Dame in Saintes, traveled to the Abbey of Saint-Jean d'Angély so that she could plead before the bishop in a case of contested property.[158] When a plea was settled for Holy Trinity in Poitiers, Abbess Petronilla and two of her nuns were present at the bishop's residence.[159] Superiors who made such appearances moved in state as befitted any great ecclesiastical power, so that all who saw them were struck by their physical presence outside the cloister.

Another reason nuns ignored precepts of claustration and left their abbey's precincts was to seek refuge in time of danger. When the canonesses of La Barre in Château-Thierry received a farm, it became a safe retreat from the city in wartime.[160] The ever-present danger of fire, which could be part of the horrors of warfare inflicted on noncombatants, was another common threat in the Middle Ages. Perhaps because of medieval people's inability to contain fire and the terror it therefore evoked, fire occurs in didactic stories of holiness.

In medieval tales of sanctity, a pious person might avert a conflagration as did Bishop Mellitus, who had himself borne into the path of an encroaching fire to shield the city of Canterbury with his frail body.[161] But what of a nunnery in the path of an advancing blaze? Since cloistered nuns were theoretically not to leave their convents, religious women could be burned alive while trapped in their monastic cage. The literary topos gets inverted in an interesting way in these tales: the holy nuns refuse all appeals to quit the cloister and

158. *Cartulaire de Notre-Dame de Saintes*, pp. 73–75, no. 82, 1174.

159. Poitiers, BD, la Trinité, 2 H 2, carton 12, no. 2, 1144.

160. "Abbaye de la Barre et son recueil," p. 151, no. 31.

161. Bede, *A History of the English Church and People*, trans. Leo Sherley-Price (Harmondsworth, England: Penguin, 1968), pp. 111–12.

seek safety as urged by their male advisers; the power of their commitment to their vows serves as holy asbestos, and they are miraculously protected.[162] Nunneries in some instances may have survived fierce fire storms, protected by stone buildings or other bulwarks. But when we turn to the documents of practice, we find mention of convents destroyed by fire in which some of the inmates perished and other occurrences where the only mention is of property loss.[163] When nuns died in a fire, it could have been an accidental tragedy rather than a voluntary martyrdom, although it is possible that some may have chosen to die rather than leave the cloister.

Not all the comings and goings of nuns were for necessary business or in search of refuge. Often when nuns went outside their abbeys without permission, it was either to see family or on personal or even clandestine trips. Nuns went to visit their relatives, and when illness struck it could be the nun who was called out of her monastery to nurse a sick relative; in fact, religious women remained more embedded in their families than monks and commonly visited at home.[164] In cases when nuns were censured by the official visitor for wandering, it is not always clear what they were doing to deserve opprobrium. But sometimes the circumstantial evidence makes it clear that a nun was illicitly meeting a lover or visiting her child.[165]

Even if religious women left their cloister precincts, was not that walled community at least off limits to those who were not community members? To the contrary, religious, lordly, and hospitable

162. This is a much-repeated story. Two famous examples are the steadfastness of the nuns of Saint-Jean in Arles, the congregation under the direction of Bishop Caesarius of Arles in the sixth century, and the Cluniac nuns of Marcigny, who refused to heed pleas to flee to safety. See Jean-Baptiste Thiers, *Traité de la clôture des religieuses* (Paris: A. Dezaillier, 1681), pp. 12–13, for not only the story but its continued hortatory use at the end of the seventeenth century; and see Peter the Venerable, "De miraculis," PL, 189:890 C and D.

163. The year after the fire of 1188 that devastated the nunnery of Notre-Dame-aux-Nonnains in Troyes, Count Henry reconfirmed his and his family's donations to the nuns, noting that he wanted "the nuns perpetually to hold this church and land, which I gave to them for the pressing accident to the ladies who perished miserably here in the fire of Troyes": *Documents de Notre-Dame-aux-Nonnains*, p. 12, no. 7, 1189. However, Saint-Amand in Rouen experienced two severe fires, one in 1136 and one in 1248, in both of which only property was lost: Rouen, BD, Saint-Amand H 55, carton 1, no. 3.

164. ER, pp. 212, 383, 386, 680 for visits to families, and p. 335 for going home to nurse a sick relative. Bitel, "Women's Monastic Enclosures in Early Ireland," pp. 19–20, also finds nuns continuing their connections with their families.

165. ER, pp. 560, 537.

responsibilities overrode the obligation to keep people out. The entry of a noble widow as a *conversa* at Jully and her gift to the abbey necessitated a veritable crowd of witnesses gathering in the chapter house.[166] The ratification of a gift Count Baldwin had made earlier brought him with twenty-eight male witnesses to the Abbey of Bourbourg to reaffirm his generosity "publicly in the church," and a few years later a comital court heard a case at Bourbourg "in the abbess's private chamber."[167] Nunneries also had to honor their obligations to serve ritual meals to those in their *societas,* or confraternity, so that Mainard, Achard, and their foresters had the right to bread and wine twice a year in the refectory of Notre-Dame in Saintes.[168] Perhaps the most intrusive and disruptive entries came as a result of monastic obligations to offer hospitality. What must it have done to the quiet of the cloister when in 1169 the nuns of Jully hosted Count Henry of Troyes traveling on pilgrimage to Vézelay with his entire train?[169]

In addition to the laypeople who visited cloisters with some particular purpose—as donors, witnesses, members of a *societas,* or travelers—there were many others who wandered in and out in a nonspecific way. Guibert de Nogent's mother not only freely entered her neighborhood nunnery but also convinced an elderly nun to leave and become her companion.[170] The visitation records of Archbishop Eudes Rigaud show that unwarranted lay and religious people routinely intruded into nunneries. A number of these inappropriate intrusions, at least 7 percent, were by relatives coming to visit the nuns, to eat in the refectory, or even to sleep at the monastery. Sometimes, however, the archbishop specifies that there were particularly unsavory sorts wandering around, like the two clerics and "a certain miller, named Frongnet" who were to be kept out of Saint-Aubin; at other times Eudes records that general procedures were lax: "The gate looking towards the fields is open too often; we ordered it

166. *Cartulaire de Jully-les-Nonnains,* p. 257, no. 3, 1128. The same situation occurred at Holy Trinity in Poitiers when a large crowd gathered for an oblation and a gift to the house: Poitiers, BM, la Trinité, MS. 27, p. 105, no. 109, 1161.

167. *Cartulaire de Notre-Dame de Bourbourg,* 1:12, no. 16, 1112, p. 33, no. 37, 1128–69.

168. *Cartulaire de Notre-Dame de Saintes,* p. 59, no. 59, 1107. This was quite a common abbatial gift to supporters; also see p. 62, no. 64, 1096–1107, and p. 63, no. 65, 1137.

169. *Cartulaire de Jully-les-Nonnains,* p. 268, no. 34, 1169.

170. Guibert of Nogent, *Memoirs,* p. 75.

closed."[171] Nuns had to be alert to specific troublemakers as well as maintaining general security.

Clearly, in actual practice religious women often did not live by the theory of enclosure, a reality that was true of nuns in southern France as well as of their northern sisters.[172] Nuns' behavior could have seemed particularly reprehensible to contemporaries, who perceived them as falling sadly below the standards and practices of religious men in adhering to enclosure. No sources are available for a broad comparison of cloistering by gender, but it is possible to compare monks and nuns in a representative sample using the data base constructed from the visitation register of Eudes Rigaud.

Looking first at the results for passive cloistering, Eudes had occasion to censure the presence of unauthorized people on 21 percent of his visits to Norman nunneries and 18 percent of his visitations to male houses.[173] This suggests that outsiders meandered into the cloisters of nuns and monks in roughly equal numbers and that the gender of the monastics had no statistical significance on their ability to bar outsiders. The slightly elevated proportion of censures for outsiders' entry into convents reflects the problem nunneries had in excluding people, because women's houses could always be entered by clerical men, whether or not these individuals belonged. Archbishop Eudes strenuously forbade the seemingly respectable abbot of Jumièges from paying inappropriate visits to one nunnery because of the scandal he was creating. To forbid entry to such an eminent ecclesiastic would have been extremely difficult for the nuns. The outsiders within convents may quite often have been those who forced their way in either by dint of birth or by authority of office.

In contrast to the figures for passive cloistering, the numbers from the data base for active cloistering are dramatically different by gender. Nuns were censured for unauthorized exits from their houses on 26 percent of Eudes's visitations to convents, and monks on only 11 percent of his stops at male houses.[174] These figures suggest that nuns either were more prone to wander than monks or were more

171. ER, pp. 676, 317.
172. Moreau, "Moniales du diocèse de Maguelone," p. 257: "La clôture a été observée avec une grande souplesse."
173. Nunneries had 27 censures out of 129 visitations, and male houses had 85 censures out of 467 visitations.
174. The numbers are 33 unauthorized cases of "wandering" by nuns out of 129 total visits, and 50 unauthorized cases of "wandering" by monks out of 467 total visits.

apt to be found adulterine for behavior that might escape notice in a monk. I think the evidence suggests that both were true. We have seen how necessary it was to the well-being of nunneries to have the ability to confront enemies and meet with friends. Indeed, those houses that had few qualms about violating claustration were the most prosperous.[175] Institutional success was not necessarily achieved at the expense of spiritual health, for poverty rather than wealth correlates with evidence of monastic decadence.[176]

All medieval people must have been aware of the presence of houses of religious women and men scattered around the country-side, and it would have been almost impossible not to have had feel-ings about these ubiquitous monastics. We might posit, therefore, that lay patronage of nunneries would have dwindled noticeably in the central Middle Ages in response to the casual comings and goings of nuns if the breaking of cloister offended a convent's lay neighbors. This did not occur. Donations and oblations to nunneries kept proportional pace with those to men's houses through the thir-teenth century. A drop is apparent in the late Middle Ages—the fourteenth and fifteenth centuries. This shrinkage was a response to multiple shifts in society, economics, and demography, however, not particularly to breaches of enclosure, which had been occurring for centuries. Indeed, a qualitative comparison of cartularies from wom-en's and men's monasteries shows a very similar pattern of dona-

175. The Paraclete, Notre-Dame in Saintes, and other such rich Benedictine houses were casual about cloistering and stayed prosperous and free of major scandals throughout the period. This is admittedly a chicken-and-egg problem: Did the free-dom to tend to exterior needs lead to well-being, or did wealth lead to enough power so that the nuns felt unconstrained by tight rules of claustration? Both are partly true, I suspect; the way external control led to conventual problems is apparent for the Abbey of Notre-Dame-aux-Nonnains in Troyes, which fell increasingly under epis-copal control and lost prestige and income in the thirteenth century. See Théophile Boutiot, *Des privilèges singuliers de l'abbaye de Notre-Dame-aux-Nonnains de Troyes* (Paris: A. Aubry, 1864), and Régis Rohmer, "L'abbaye bénédictine de Notre-Dame-aux-Nonnains de Troyes des origines à l'année 1503," in *Position des thèses de l'École des Chartes* (Mâcon: Protat Frères, 1905), pp. 123–29.

176. Multivariable analysis of all factors that might contribute to the decadence of Norman nunneries visited by Archbishop Eudes Rigaud produces poverty as the only independent variable that consistently is associated with deeply troubled houses. My research therefore reinforces Schulenburg's findings that claustration was a control mechanism that impeded women's achievement of spiritual autonomy by suggesting that this also holds true for the eleventh through the thirteenth centuries. Jane Schu-lenburg, "Strict Active Enclosure and Its Effects on the Female Monastic Experience (500–1100)," in *Distant Echoes*, vol. 1 of *Medieval Religious Women*, ed. John A. Nichols and Lillian Thomas Shank, Cistercian Studies Series 71 (Kalamazoo, Mich.: Cistercian Publications, 1984), p. 79.

tions and support, which shifts for both nuns and monks from large land grants to smaller gifts of dues and rents over the course of the central Middle Ages. Since it was in response to family and friends that nuns left the cloister or received visitors, these same lay supporters were not alienated by a loose interpretation of enclosure. In contrast, the ecclesiastical hierarchy responded angrily to breaches in the cloistering of nuns. It may be that religious women's casual attitude towards enclosure helped damn them in the eyes of male monastics, for from the mid-twelfth century on, hostility towards female houses and their inmates grew in many male orders.[177]

Modern historians interpret sources on the cloistering of medieval nuns in various ways, running the gamut from a complete acceptance that enclosure existed in reality just as it was described in the monastic legislation of the day to maintaining that cloistering existed in theory but not in practice.[178] In the case of northern France in the central Middle Ages, strict claustration was certainly more an ideal than a reality; many cases of movement in and out of cloisters are contained in the documents, some approved by the abbey superior, some against her will. How are we to assess the impact of casual cloistering? Would it lead to frivolity—or worse, lechery—as was feared?[179] A temperate scholarly voice comments that "those modern writers who interpret every violation of enclosure as evidence of a moral lapse forget that economic necessity often forced nuns to go outside their convents."[180] This argument, however, covers only business excursions outside the walls; I would expand the defense, since nuns had other legitimate and innocent needs for leaving the cloister beside the economic exigencies of their convents.

177. See, for example, the catalog of resistance to women in one male order: Thompson, "Problem of the Cistercian Nuns in the Twelfth and Thirteenth Centuries," pp. 227–52.

178. Stein, "Religious Women of Cologne," p. 22, believes in the actuality of cloistering as it appears in the legislation. So too does Louis Gaillard, "Géographie des fondations monastiques," in La Normandie bénédictine au temps de Guillaume le Conquérant (XIe siècle). (Lille: Facultés Catholique de Lille, 1967), p. 61. In contrast, Parisse, "Lorraine monastique, p. 60, asserts that "la clôture était plus théoretique que réelle." Leclercq, "Medieval Feminine Monasticism," p. 59, briefly investigates the complexity of harmonizing theory and reality.

179. See, for instance, the arguments of Daichman, Wayward Nuns, pp. 19–22, who accepts that the nuns who wandered physically strayed morally. The view of naughty nuns held by medieval moralists, she says, reflects "a prejudice against religious women that does not seem wholly unjustified, after all" (p. 167).

180. Boyd, Cistercian Nunnery in Mediaeval Italy, p. 109.

Some of the contradictions and confusions can be avoided if we separate the impact of cloistering on nunneries from its effect on the lives of individual nuns. Strict enclosure could devastate a convent. For instance, in investigating the decline she sees in women's monasticism from its early medieval heights to a low point in the mid-eleventh century, Jane Schulenburg indicts rigid claustration for damaging the economy of nunneries and perhaps also their ability to recruit oblates.[181] The need continued in the central Middle Ages for nuns to be at least partially free of cloistering in the best interests of their nunneries. If a convent could not send a member out to tend its business, it was hamstrung; the house became totally dependent on the ability and honesty of its male provosts. To entrust affairs to unsupervised personnel was to invite trouble. Faced with this dilemma, female superiors routinely left the cloister or sent delegates out on conventual business, and since the practice of enclosure forbade such behavior, monastic or episcopal overseers routinely denounced it.[182] Convent superiors felt that their members who went out on house business were not breaching the rules, but visitors did not always see nuns' absences in this same benign light. The interpretation of behavior becomes, at least in some instances, a judgment of a nunnery's autonomy. In fact, we can go even further and say that the real issue of claustration was social control—a control often resisted by female communities, which—judging by their own lights—saw many legitimate reasons for their extraclaustral activities.[183]

181. Schulenburg, "Strict Active Enclosure," p. 77. John Nichols also finds damage being done to later English Cistercian nuns by their close cloistering: "English Cistercian Nunneries and English Bishops." Other scholars' work supports the view that nuns were less enclosed in the earlier period and that this changed in the twelfth century. See Suzanne Wemple, *Women in Frankish Society: Marriage and the Cloister, 500 to 900* (Philadelphia: University of Pennsylvania Press, 1981), pp. 167–68, 173, who views cloistering as providing an unattainable ideal before the eleventh century. Also see Parisse, *Nonnes au Moyen Age*, p. 184, who argues for an intensification of female cloistering in the twelfth century. No full chronological study of the ebb and flow of the theory and practice of medieval cloistering has yet appeared; such work needs to be done.

182. ER, pp. 386, 518. Eudes forbids abbesses to give nuns permission to go out. The archbishop scolds the prioress of Saint-Aubin for having allowed two nuns to go out seeking alms—surely a respectable activity, but one to which he had not assented (p. 537).

183. One of the themes of monastic history is the continual efforts of monasteries to win exemption from episcopal control. This goal was pursued particularly strongly by nunneries. See, for instance, the discussion of forged exemptions by the nunnery of Montivilliers: Priem, "Abbaye de Montivilliers," pp. 155–57.

Although most convents defied cloistering because it inhibited their freedom, enclosure could have a positive meaning for the individual nun. From a modern perspective restriction of one's movements sounds repressive, but this was not necessarily true for medieval women. The records left by the lives of extraordinary women suggest that some of them eagerly sought the structure of a cloistered life. A young woman like the English nun Eve might so yearn for the austerities of enclosure that she would travel a considerable distance to become an anchoress. It is also possible that cloistering freed nuns from unwanted outside demands. A nun might have welcomed the news that her father needed her nursing skills at home, but perhaps her heart sank at what she perceived as an onerous duty. An abbess might have relished going to court to do legal battle with a neighbor over abbey property, or maybe she thankfully handed the litigation to her male provost. Within the cloister a woman's first concern was her own salvation, not the care of her kin. We cannot be sure, but for some women cloistering may have been useful insulation from an importunate world's demands. Finally, cloistering seems to have promoted communal sensibilities; separation from outside ties fostered shared responsibility and interdependence, building the group's awareness of its own identity. Thus the irony is that though strict enclosure often worked against the institutional well-being of convents, it may have helped to create a positive spiritual environment for individual nuns.

Theoretically, claustration was meant to free nuns by protecting them from evil outside their walls and inside themselves. The positive aspect of this theory may have been sincerely believed by individuals, but enclosing nuns also represented an anxious institutionalization of pollution fears, reinvigorated in the twelfth century as a defensive clerical response to reform. Nuns were to be both "imprisoned" and "dead to the world." [184] Society incarcerates the antisocial and disposes of the dead; criminals and corpses damage and infect society, not the other way around. The new rhetorical intensity about nuns that developed in clerical writing in the twelfth century sprang, I believe, from the increased emphasis on virginity and the imposition of celibacy on the clergy by its leaders.[185]

184. Peter the Venerable wrote that a nun "obsecrat ut apud Marciniacum perpetuo carcere claudat": PL, 189:217 B. He also wrote to Heloise that "laetareris (puellas) infra arcta septa domorum, etiam corporaliter beatae spei velut sepulcro jam conditas": PL, 189:350 B–C.
185. See Anne L. Barstow, *Married Priests and the Reforming Papacy: The Eleventh-Century Debates*, Texts and Studies in Religion 12, (New York: Edwin Mel-

The latter part of the eleventh century witnessed the battle between reformers and married clergy over clerical celibacy. Married
clerics regarded celibacy as an unwarranted innovation and hotly
defended the legitimacy of their wedded state. Nevertheless, the reformers prevailed at Second Lateran Council in 1139, and clerical
marriage was finally and irrevocably banned.[186] By midcentury the
clerics who had to minister to the growing numbers of nuns were
forced into celibacy; yet priests had to hear confessions and administer the sacraments to nuns they saw as threatening to their chastity. In response to the chafing demands on them, the clergy insisted
on rigid claustration of nuns, which served two purposes: strict enclosure made these tempting women as inaccessible as possible to
protect men from the pollution of arousal, and it allowed the clergy
to vent frustration by punishing nuns as the scapegoats for male
sexual feelings.[187]

The clerics who judged the nun outside her cloister as being at
risk saw the world through the biases of the ancients, to whom
women were inferior beings. Thus the clergy read women's nature
as weak and liable to corruption. These critics also misunderstood
the real needs and contributions of nunneries, seeing them as institutions that should be encapsulated from society rather than integrated into it. The criticism that medieval religious women ignored
claustration is valid: they continually bent and broke the rules of
enclosure. However, the further accusation that this behavior inevi-

---

len Press, 1982). Jean Leclercq, "Spirituality of Medieval Feminine Monasticism," in
The Continuing Quest for God, ed. William Skudlarck (Collegeville, Minn.: Liturgical Press, 1982), p. 131, asks if this later, stricter cloistering was influenced by contacts with the East. Some of the more hyperbolic statements are well known, such as
that of Abbot Conrad of Marchtal, who says the Cistercians rejected women because
"the wickedness of women is greater than all the other wickedness of the world . . .
we will on no account receive any more sisters . . . but will avoid them like poisonous
animals": Quoted by R. W. Southern, *Western Society and the Church in the Middle
Ages* (Harmondsworth, England: Penguin, 1970), p. 314.

186. Barstow, *Married Priests*, p. 1. She argues that to win the battle to control the
right ordering of society, the church had chosen to throw its priests into the fray with
the empire; priests would live by the most rigorous standard of chastity to show their
worthiness to be the leaders of society. Clerics found their new image uncomfortable
and prone to contradictions.

187. Mary Douglas, *Purity and Danger: An Analysis of the Concepts of Pollution
and Taboo* (Harmondsworth, England: Penguin, 1970), p. 149 and passim, discusses
pollution taboos as a response to social contradictions, and pp. 163–64 points out
that a high moral expectation leads to hypocrisy and thereby also to pollution behavior.

tably led the nun astray is unfounded; some nuns broke their vows when outside the convent, but the insistence that uncloistered nuns were acting immodestly, if not immorally, is off the mark.

Charters from nunneries show a laity remarkably unconcerned with either the passive or the active cloistering of nuns.[188] Nuns go out to visit their mothers; brothers come into the cloister to see their sisters; nuns deal constantly with the laity both inside and outside their convents. The laity does not protest such uncloistered activity, and secular benefactors continue eagerly to seek suffrages from religious women. If the laity who funded convents and supplied them with recruits was not threatened because women vowed to chastity were in touch with secular life, then perhaps the often hysterical rhetoric of clerics is unfounded.

CONCLUSION

The spiritual life of nuns during the central Middle Ages is notable for its commonality with that of monks: nuns and monks took the same three difficult vows, forswearing money, sex, and autonomy. They followed, as Peter the Venerable wrote to Heloise, "our common Rule, which belongs to us both."[189] Nuns and monks celebrated the same liturgy, learned the same psalms by heart, pooled their talents for liturgical drama, joined in solemn processions, revered the same or similar relics, read and even shared the same books, chose to be enclosed in anchorholds, and listened to the same canon of the mass.[190] They lived in conventual buildings that varied in response to dictates of their orders and finances but not their gender, and their abbesses and abbots carried similar croziers that reflected monastic authority (see fig. 4 as an example). But there also were significant gender variations in monastic spirituality.

Two major divergences between the religious life of nuns and of monks were either neutral or positive for women. The proportion of female saints shrank in our period compared with that of male saints, but apparently without damaging the female monastic life. The community surrounding a nunnery continued to respect nuns as seekers after sanctity even when it stopped short of attributing

---

188. In the thousands of monastic charters I have read from the central Middle Ages, I have found no trace of lay criticism of monastics for breaking strict claustration.

189. *Letters of Abelard and Heloise*, p. 286.

190. Yardley, "Ful Weel She Soong," p. 20, points out that the repertoire "varied not according to the gender of the inhabitants but according to the location and order of a particular house."

Figure 4. Crozier of the twelfth-century abbess of Notre-Dame in Saintes.
Courtesy of the Musée Archéologique de Saintes.

sainthood to them. A new route opened for the expression of female piety as the role of penitential food practices came to dominate female but not male spirituality.

Two other gender differences that grew during the central Middle Ages mark the developing second-class status that would clearly belong to nuns by the late Middle Ages. Claustration, intended in theory as protective enclosure for all monastics, evolved into an ambivalent means of attempting to control nuns, whose sexuality threatened the post-Gregorian strict priestly chastity. Nuns in our period treated rules of enclosure generally with benign neglect; but by the fourteenth and fifteenth centuries these rules would grow to be destructive to their conventual life and would become impossible in the early modern period. Finally, as the custom developed in the twelfth century for monks to take holy orders by being consecrated to the priesthood, male monastics became celebrants of the mass rather than joint witnesses with nuns to the sacrifice of the Eucharist. They became participants instead of onlookers. When the mass became increasingly important to church life during the thirteenth century, male monasteries were spared extra costs for outside priests, costs that became burdensome for nuns.

Professed medieval women and men shared an enormously rich spiritual heritage. Changes in the church and in society, reform of the clergy, sacralization of all the clergy, and growing hierarchical organization began to distort the commonality so that the sense of being equal laborers in the Lord's vineyard was replaced with male overseers and female underlings, a deformation of the original ideal of the monastic life as one for lay women and men.

5

THE STRUCTURE

THE VERY ESSENCE of the monastic life lay in community. Although a tiny minority of professed monastics chose to withdraw into the anchorhold, most participated in the corporate religious experience offered by monasteries. To create the communal life of the cloister required more than goodwill; leadership, authority, and resources were necessary building materials.

ADMINISTRATION
Female Leadership

The abbess of a rich house was usually an aristocratic and erudite women. We can picture her, elegant in her simple habit set off by an impressive jeweled pectoral cross and gilded crozier, sitting in a central, elevated position in the chapter house to rule over the convent as absolute authority to her nuns, lord to her tenants, feudal vassal to her secular overlord, and equal to the abbots of her order. The picture was different for the head of a small, modest nunnery, who may have worn a makeshift habit, might have lacked a chapter house in which to sit in state, and had no clout to exercise in the world outside the cloister. Scholars are generally agreed that these two pictures are accurate, but both need to be understood in the medieval context, where only a very small percentage of the population exercised any significant power.[1] The vast majority of society

---

1. Eckenstein, *Woman under Monasticism*, p. 152: "As abbess of one of the royal houses the princess certainly held a place of authority second to that of no woman in the land." Margaret W. Labarge, *A Small Sound of the Trumpet: Women in Medieval Life* (Boston: Beacon, 1986), p. 98: "The superiors were usually women of considerable social standing, used to power in their own right and enjoying its exercise. An abbess or prioress was an important person, not only in her own convent but also in the outside world." Shahar, *Fourth Estate*, pp. 37–38: "There were some, particularly in the rich nunneries with extensive land holdings, who wielded considerable powers in various spheres," and "some abbesses enjoyed extensive powers in the organiza-

belonged to the mass of those who labored rather than those who lived off that labor. To be the head of any monastery—small, medium, or large, rich, comfortable, or impoverished—was to join the tiny elite that ran medieval Europe. Second, although to an outside viewer the prioress of a little house with, say, fourteen nuns all living on meager rations may seem to be a superior without real power, she still occupied a position that had great meaning and influence for those thirteen other women. To be the head of any monastery was to have *auctoritas*, to control the lives of others for better or worse.

The women chosen as monastic superiors were almost universally aristocratic and even sometimes from the highest nobility.[2] For instance, Abbess Cecilia of Holy Trinity in Caen was the daughter of William the Conqueror, Abbess Adele of Saint-Georges in Rennes was the sister of the count of Brittany, and Agnes Barbezieux of Notre-Dame in Saintes was descended from the dukes of Aquitaine. Having a rich and powerful head could be enormously beneficial to a house. Abbess Philippa, daughter of the lord of Mirepoix, gave her house of Port-Royal five thousand pounds to build a new refectory and to buy a cross, a silver reliquary, a gold box for the Host, and a chalice.[3] Philippa was valuable to the institution, and whether an abbess was the daughter of a king, a duke, or a knight, her birth was enhanced by the dignity of the abbatial office, which combined in one position the symbols and perquisites of male ecclesiastical and secular power. Like her male confreres, a woman who was a monastic superior directed clerics and received homage and fealty from tenants.[4] Although the powers tended to be similar among superiors, however, the institutional role of the abbess varied at different houses. Penny Gold points out that the abbess at Ronceray shared power with the chapter of her nuns, whereas the abbess at Fontevrault included only the prioress in exercising administrative control.[5]

---

tional sphere in their own dioceses." However, "Smaller nunneries with financial burdens (and many such existed) held neither land nor the secular and ecclesiastical rights deriving from it."

2. Bouchard, *Sword, Miter, and Cloister*, p. 67. This was equally true for the southern abbey of La Celle: L'Hermite-Leclercq, *Monachisme féminin*, p. 217.

3. *Cartulaire de Porrois*, pp. 324–25.

4. Poitiers, BM, MS. 27, p. 199.

5. Penny S. Gold, "The Charters of Le Ronceray d'Angers: Male/Female Interaction in Monastic Business," in *Medieval Women and the Sources of Medieval History* ed. Joel T. Rosenthal, (Athens: University of Georgia Press, 1990).

Some female superiors may have been undistinguished or even inept. Others either came to office as forceful and capable individuals or developed into powerful women to be reckoned with. The position of abbess or prioress was not an easy one, and its demands and frustrations could easily overwhelm a weak personality. Putting up with physical attack was certainly not in an abbess's job description, but even that might come her way. When an explosive disagreement developed between the Abbey of Notre-Dame in Saintes and the lord of La Chaume over a boundary line, both parties wanted a settlement.[6] The lord sent his steward, William of Mauzé, to walk the line with the convent's provost, Arnold Faraon. The abbess, Agnes of Barbezieux, chose to be present in the fields to see that all was properly resolved. William and Arnold could not stay calm during the negotiations, and their basic dislike of each other exploded into a fight. Agnes stepped in to protect her steward, but the infuriated William was undeterred. He tore Arnold out of her defending arms, knocked her to the ground, and shouted insults at her. Although it probably was uncommon for an abbess to get such treatment, for the duke's daughter stepping gamely into a fight was as real a part of life as stepping with measured tread and downcast eyes in a liturgical procession.

Besides confronting the violent side of life, a convent superior had to have a strong constitution when defending her institution's rights. In the late eleventh century, the nunnery of Ronceray in Angers was trying to regain from the monastery of Saint-Nicolas parish rights they both claimed, in this case the right to bury the dead and receive a small burial payment.[7] Abbess Richilde chose to make a test case of what she claimed was the illegal burial of a workman's son in the monks' graveyard. She led a crowd of dignitaries and workmen to the cemetery and insisted on exhuming the corpse. When the body was dug up, it proved to be in a particularly smelly state of decomposition. Nothing deterred, Richilde prepared to have it carried back to Ronceray. Fervent entreaties from the dismayed church leaders eventually convinced her that she did not need to

---

6. *Cartulaire de Notre-Dame de Saintes*, pp. 80–81, no. 88, 1150. The interpretation of this charter has been almost as lively as the original exchange. Several scholars have argued that the abbess was actually raped in the fields, but Louis Audiat, "Agnes outragée," *Revue de Saintonge et d'Aunis* 5(1884–85): 232–36, presents a more reasonable interpretation with which mine agrees in general outline. Violence might be experienced by clerics as well as nuns; for instance, John had to pay a fine for hitting a cleric; *Cartulaire de Notre-Dame de Saintes*, p. 154, no. 234.

7. *Cartulaire du Ronceray*, pp. 41–42, no. 48.

process across town with a rotting corpse to make her point, and the body was hastily returned to its grave. The monks' chaplain was thus maneuvered into agreeing that he would refrain from administering sacraments in the parish.

Holding the position of abbess or prioress invested a woman with the potential to affect the church and society. The choice of who would be the superior of a house was therefore of interest to secular society and the ecclesiastical hierarchy as well as of gripping importance to the inhabitants of the monastery. Superiors were chosen in different ways at different monasteries, although the most common system was the nuns' election of one of their own number. Saint-Pierre-aux-Nonnains, an Ottonian foundation in Metz, received imperial confirmation from Otto II and Otto III of its right to elect its own abbess, but later houses were more apt to have election procedures set by the church than by secular lords.[8] Pope Nicholas II ordained in 1061 that when the abbess of Notre-Dame in Saintes died her successor was to be chosen by the diocesan bishop, local abbots, and the congregation of nuns. If no suitable candidate was available from among the nuns, they were to look outside Notre-Dame for a new superior.[9]

Fourth Lateran Council of 1215 regularized the modes of electing abbesses, making them identical to those for abbots and bishops.[10] The three authorized means of choosing a superior were by unanimous vote (divine inspiration), by a complex and unwieldy system of scrutators who questioned each elector and tallied the votes (scrutin), and by compromise among several candidates without a clear majority.[11] The actual election of the head of a convent was often a rich liturgical drama.

In the fall of 1297 the Abbey of Holy Trinity in Poitiers had lost its abbess and needed a new superior.[12] Marquisia, the claustral prioress, wrote to Walter of Bruges, the ordinary, to announce the death of Abbess Agnes and solicit his approval for electing a new abbess. After receiving his consent, the election was set for the Feast of the Apostles Simon and Jude. All the nuns who had a right to a voice in

8. Paris, BN, MS. lat. 10027, fols. 13r–16r.
9. *Cartulaire de Notre-Dame de Saintes*, p. 9, no. 4, 1061.
10. Parisse, *Nonnes au Moyen Age*, pp. 116–17.
11. Jean Gaudemet et al., *Les élections dans l'église latine des origines au XVIe siècle* (Paris: F. Lanore, 1979), p. 293.
12. Poitiers, BD, la Trinité, 2 H 2, liasse 4, ch. 2, art. 10, MS. no. 1, is the original letter from Prioress Marquisia detailing the process and announcing the election results to the bishop.

the election were called to the chapter house on that morning by the measured beating of a gong, and the mass of the Holy Spirit was celebrated. The assembled chapter humbly sang the *Veni Creator Spiritus* and then proceeded to the business of election. The nuns picked seven of their number and charged them with choosing an abbess before a candle burned down. They successfully arrived at a happy decision, designating Frances, the prioress of one of the abbey's dependent obediences. Sister Agnes de Milanges then made the announcement to the whole chapter, saying that Frances was "trained over a long time in honesty of speech and life and in spiritual things, and circumspect in the handling of temporalities." Since the candle had not yet guttered out and the electors were still empowered, Agnes then proclaimed Frances elected. The entire assembly filed into church to the high altar, where they sang the *Te Deum* in full solemnity.

Elaborate ceremonies also developed around the institution of a new monastic superior. For all women and men elected heads of regular houses, their blessing at the hands of a bishop—usually the diocesan except in cases of exempt houses, which could choose any bishop—was the necessary confirmation of election. After the episcopal blessing and consecration (see fig. 5), it was common for the new head to recite the oath of office and for the members of the community one by one, in order of their seniority and importance, to swear an oath of obedience to her. These oaths were embedded in liturgical pomp: first the clergy in festival robes bore the crucifix, holy water, and Gospels in procession, then the *Honor virtus* and the *Te Deum* were chanted to set the stage for the abbess's oath.[13] With her hand on the Gospels, the abbess then promised to guard the goods and privileges of the house, to lead the abbey according to its established customs, to provide for the nuns, and to protect them and accord them all their dues. They in their turn, with the claustral prioress leading off, swore fidelity to her. Abbess and nuns were then bound together to honor their vows and their oaths.

The freedom to choose their own superiors was one of the many autonomous rights that tended to erode toward the end of our period. Thirty-five years after Frances was elected, Holy Trinity lost an abbess and had to accept the bishop's nomination of an outside candidate, Matilda of Saint-Maur, a nun from Notre-Dame de Beaumont near Tours.[14] The ordinary's choice may well have been forced on

13. *Documents de Notre-Dame-aux-Nonnains*, pp. 184–85.
14. Poitiers, BD, la Trinité, 2 H 2, liasse 4, ch. 2, art. 10, MS. no. 3.

Figure 5. Abbess receiving her crozier from a bishop. Metz Pontifical, MS
298, fol. 82v. Fitzwilliam Museum, Cambridge.

Holy Trinity because of what he perceived as a lack of suitable candidates from the abbey, or it may have been part of his effort to establish his authority over the nuns or even to put in a friend or relative as abbess. Whatever his motives, the result was damaging to
the abbey's independence.

Contested elections could be deeply divisive and damaging to the
spiritual fabric of a monastery. Fiercely competitive elections occurred both in convents and in male monasteries, usually when two
candidates commanded roughly equal support. This happened at
Notre-Dame-aux-Nonnains in late May 1262.[15] After the death of
Abbess Matilda, the nuns gathered for an election but immediately
fell to bickering. Eventually they decided to use the compromise
system, which failed after an extended argument. After cooling off
overnight, they gathered again the next day and decided to switch to
the system of scrutin, choosing three nuns and two clerics to check
each vote and report to the chapter exactly what they found. The
vote was exceedingly close: thirty chose Ermengarde of Castell,
the treasurer, and twenty-seven voted for Isabelle, the infirmarian.
The majority proclaimed Ermengarde the new abbess, but the minority was enraged and appealed to Rome. After receiving the reports of the deputies he had designated to look into the conflict,
Pope Urban IV settled on the minority candidate, Isabelle, to be the
new abbess of Notre-Dame, a choice that clearly was unpopular

---

15. *Documents de Notre-Dame-aux-Nonnains*, pp. 116–18, no. 187, 1262, no. 189,
1263, record stages in this conflict. The full text of no. 189 is contained in Paris, BN,
MS. Moreau 1208, fols. 266r–268r.

with more than half the convent. It is no surprise that when this same pope installed his house of canons in Troyes, cheek by jowl with the convent, the nuns of Notre-Dame bristled at their rivals and led raiding parties on the canons' buildings.

Some superiors died in office, some resigned owing to ill health, and others were removed by pressure when they became incompetent. When a beloved head died, it could be a devastating blow to the residents of a monastery. An even broader community of folk, particularly those religious people who received a *rotulus* announcing the death, joined in the mourning and prayers for an eminent abbess or abbot. The death of Abbess Matilda of Holy Trinity in Caen in 1113 was announced by a circulating death roll that collected prayers and poems from many monasteries and chapters. A nun of Notre-Dame in Saintes who was designated as her abbey's spokeswoman to commemorate the abbess' death wrote of Matilda that "her flock is taught to know boundless grief from her death," drawing perhaps from similar pain the author had experienced when her own house lost its abbess.[16]

If sickness or infirmity proved more than transitory, the head was expected to resign, like Abbess Tiburge of Ronceray, who stepped down "not for moral fault but because of ill health and old age."[17] The prioress of Saint-Saens gave up her office when she could no longer execute her responsibilities, handing over her seal to the diocesan, who released her from her oath of office.[18] At other times the bishop had to step in and remove a superior who had become feeble but wanted to carry on, as Eudes Rigaud regretfully did with the failing Prioress Comtesse of Bondeville. (See fig. 2 for the seal of her successor.) The retired superior then had to be cared for by a pension or some other retirement scheme.

Pensions for retired monastic superiors could be either a fixed, annual payment or perquisites that the retired head continued to enjoy until they reverted to the house at her death. When Alice, the abbess of Notre-Dame-aux-Nonnains, stepped down, she kept the income from properties she had purchased (possibly with abbey funds), and the house guaranteed her an anniversary celebration for two pounds.[19] Further, the abbey provided her with a small cellar next to the cloister for storing her wine and gave her a meadow near

16. *Rouleaux des morts*, p. 242.
17. *Cartulaire du Ronceray*, p. 18, no. 16, 1073.
18. ER, p. 431.
19. *Documents de Notre-Dame-aux-Nonnains*, p. 98, no. 149, 1231.

the wine press. In contrast, the abbess of Bival, who retired a few years later, received from her house only a fixed annual pension of three pounds. This sort of social security looks paltry compared with the pension of thirty pounds a year the same monastery paid to one of its priests or with the pension of twenty pounds a year for Abbot William of Eu when he was put out to grass, with "a suitable companion" to care for him.[20] The elderly abbess or prioress might be well cared for in retirement, but often she ended her life in penury on a meager pension.

Community Size

The responsibility of an abbess or prioress to rule over a community of women could entail supervising from fewer than a dozen to close to a hundred choir nuns. The professed women serving in hospitals and almshouses generally had the smallest communities, ten to fourteen members, and the largest conventual bodies usually were those of the older Benedictine houses, with the thirteenth-century foundations falling in between. For instance, there were only ten sisters in the almshouse of Saint-Jean in Angers, whereas the Merovingian foundation of Notre-Dame-aux-Nonnains had an upper limit of sixty nuns and the new thirteenth-century foundation of Clarisses at Reims was kept at forty or fewer.[21] The average size of the women's houses in northern France in the central Middle Ages cannot be figured accurately, but one comparison comes from the Norman documents. Using the numbers from the visitations of Eudes Rigaud, we can arrive at averages and compare the sizes of women's and men's monasteries in the second third of the thirteenth century: the average Norman nunnery housed 35 nuns, and the average male house held only 23 monks, a somewhat surprising result, since most authors assume that convents were smaller than male houses. Not only were Norman nunneries bigger than their brother houses, they were significantly larger than their sister institutions across the Channel, which one estimate puts at slightly more than 20 nuns per convent.[22]

20. ER, p. 732, for the abbess's pension; p. 629 for the priest's pension; and p. 700 for Abbot William's companion and p. 727 for the abbot's pension.
21. *Cartulaire de Saint-Jean d'Angers*, p. cxx, no. 157, 1267–68. *Documents de Notre-Dame-aux-Nonnains*, p. 51, no. 70, 1231. De Sérent, "Ordre de Sainte Claire en France," p. 133.
22. Labarge, *Small Sound of the Trumpet*, p. 99. Careful work on relative sizes of female and male houses needs to be done by region and time period so that we can accurately chart the ebb and flow of the cloistered life. Bynum, *Holy Feast and Holy*

The difference in community size affected not only the type of monastic experience but also the quality of that cloistered life for the residents, a causal relationship recognized by medieval monastics and bishops. Indeed, directives to limit size or exhortations to increase numbers were a constant of monastic visitations as well as a continuing concern of the monastics themselves. General awareness existed that a monastery's economic base needed to harmonize with the size of the community. The hierarchy and the houses themselves limited the numbers of personnel according to the resources available.[23] It was common to find a house like Bourbourg keeping a girl but not vesting her in a novice's habit until a place opened for her.

The size of a community was also related to its moral and spiritual well-being. The church hierarchy had come to expect problems in tiny cells. The bishop of Rennes commanded Abbess Joanna to increase the number of nuns in the Priory of Locmaria as a means of improving the regular life in that house.[24] Other prelates also viewed tinkering with the size of a house as a solution to its problems. In the early thirteenth century the bishop of Angers suspected that a small congregation led not just to sloppy monastic performance but eventually to debauchery. He wrote to the archbishop in preparation for the Synod of Château-Gontier in 1231 to suggest that one item on the agenda should be increasing numbers in tiny priories, since those whose numbers dwindled to four or six nuns became loci for sexual philandering.[25] He wanted to see these cells consolidated into bigger houses of thirty or forty nuns.

It was all very well to urge increasing the size of convents, but if they did not possess the financial wherewithal to support larger numbers, the exhortations were pointless. Archbishop Eudes re-

---

Fast, p. 80, says that men's houses were richer and bigger than women's. I suspect from my evidence that women's houses were indeed fewer, in general poorer, but often slightly larger than their male counterparts. Indeed, it was their size that added to their financial problems. David Herlihy, *Opera Muliebria: Women and Work in Medieval Europe* (New York: McGraw-Hill, 1989), p. 62, comes up with different populations (33 nuns and 16.5 monks on average) for the houses Eudes visited.

23. See *Cartulaire de Jully-les-Nonnains,* p. 298, no. 144, 1279, and Parisse, *Nonnes au Moyen Age,* p. 107, for several examples. Such limiting of numbers also was common in convents in the south of France: Moreau, "Moniales du diocèse de Maguelone," p. 252, and L'Hermite-Leclercq, *Monachisme féminin,* p. 183.

24. *Cartulaire de Saint-Sulpice-la-Forêt,* p. 443, no. 243, 1244.

25. Avril, "Province de Tours," p. 298.

flected this economic reality in his continued arguments with Norman convents that wanted to grow and that he limited because of small endowments. The provincial Council of Pont-Audemer over which he presided passed a resolution that all monasteries should bring their numbers up to the maximum if their "resources have not been diminished."[26] The tension between financial limitations and the desire to keep up monastic numbers was widespread in the thirteenth century, but at the other end of the spectrum, monasteries had to resist pressure to take oblates they could not support.[27] Pressure from patrons could be extremely difficult to resist, and some superiors like the abbess of Salzinnes asked for and obtained papal permission to refuse new members.[28]

There was a pattern of fluctuation in size for monastic institutions during the Middle Ages. Some of the early foundations had begun life with very large congregations of one hundred nuns or more. Shrinkage of numbers or complete disappearance then occurred for many of these Merovingian or Carolingian monasteries in the difficult years of the tenth and early eleventh centuries. By the mid-eleventh century, a rebuilding and reconstituting of monastic houses was under way in Europe, although numbers often did not swing back to their earlier high levels. Numbers of choir nuns and monks stayed relatively constant during the central Middle Ages, with a slow dwindling as the fourteenth century approached. A precipitous fall in professions affected many houses during the late Middle Ages, when vocations and donations sagged badly. One house that seems simply to have deflated slowly across the years is the great abbey of Holy Cross in Poitiers. This nunnery housed two hundred nuns in its early years during the sixth century; in the early ninth century the roster had been cut in half to one hundred and then halved again to fifty in the thirteenth century. By 1472, only twenty-five nuns lived in the convent.[29]

The drying up of recruits to the monastic life is difficult to trace with confidence, but the figures from Eudes Rigaud's register again offer a rare chance to quantify, in this case, where the monastic drought hit hardest. The archbishop reported that the census of

26. ER, p. 325.
27. Rouen, BD, Saint-Amand, H 55, carton 1, 1265: Fulk puts enormous pressure on the convent to accept Joanna, daughter of Giles of Lokeron, without concern for the abbey's resources and size limitations.
28. *Recueil du Val-Saint-Georges à Salzinnes*, p. 122, no. 99, 1245.
29. Labande-Mailfert, "Débuts de Sainte-Croix," pp. 83, 131, 177.

monks was below par in eighteen male houses and two female houses he visited. That is, that 32.7 percent of the male monasteries were experiencing difficulties in staying at full strength compared with only 14 percent of nunneries with the same problem. The gender component of monastic recruitment is reinforced by looking at cases where there was pressure to get into monasteries: Eudes limited the numbers of female oblates in six nunneries and four male monasteries. Or to put it in percentages, the archbishop had to tell close to half of the convents (42.8 percent) in contrast to only 6.5 percent of the male houses) that they were too large or in danger of growing too large. The Norman case suggests that in the thirteenth century individual women as well as families with daughters continued to look favorably on the monastic life, whereas other vocations competed with the cloister for male oblates.

The Familia

The community a monastic superior ruled was often an odd assortment of individuals who made up the familia—those who answered to the monastery's orders and depended on it for their livelihood. It is extremely difficult to put those people into neatly labeled categories; in fact, although all monastic historians make some efforts to do so, from our modern vantage point it probably is impossible to pigeonhole tidily everyone who belonged to a monastery. However, it is possible to outline several general groupings by the functions of people found in the conventual familia.[30] Those for whom the institution existed were bound above all else to pray. They were the choir nuns or canonesses, professed women who took the triple vows when vested in the habit of their order.

The second great category was those whose principal activity was to contribute the sweat of their brows to make the nunnery run. This large, loose collection of working people included free and unfree serfs, salaried servants, those who commended themselves to the abbey, and various types of lay brothers and sisters. The serfs who belonged to an abbey generally worked as peasants raising crops and livestock; it was they who fed the monastic family. The superiors of convents acted as lords to their peasantry, overseeing the customs and dues from each tenant, controlling marriages of the un-

---

30. See *Prayer, Patronage, and Power*, pp. 36–49, in which I examine those who made up the familia of Holy Trinity in Vendôme.

free, rendering justice, and protecting tenants from the depredations of other lords.[31]

Salaried female servants tended to be maids living in the nunneries, while male servants were generally laborers or overseers, who might do very well for themselves, rising to be provosts who administered the convent's lands. Although the maids were housed in the monasteries, the more important male servants often had their own dwellings.[32] The authority and freedom some of these monastic officials enjoyed emboldened them to try and seize for themselves the income they administered. Arnold David was a servant of the Priory of Saint-Julien who oversaw the exploitation of its forests and exercised powers delegated to him by the nuns.[33] When he died, his opportunistic nephew tried to claim hereditary rights to the forests, which unjust claim the nuns defeated. This sort of challenge was a common problem monasteries had to counter.

Clear distinctions become impossible when we consider those who commended themselves to a house, because though some certainly belonged with workers and others with those who prayed, many seem to have melded the functions of praying and working. People who commended themselves to an abbey were usually seeking economic security and personal safety under conventual protection. Once that is said, little else is simple, since they had different needs and goals. Some commended themselves to a monastery to become part of the work force while remaining secular people, others to become lay sisters and brothers, or like a third group—which remained separate from the work force—to become semimonastic retirees, nuns or monks *ad succurrendum* who gave over all their goods and in return received a pension and housing.

Some charters specify the functions being assumed by a com-

31. See, for instance, the lists of customary payments of pigs and poultry at Christmas from two villages and relief and tallage owed by the inhabitants of another village: *Cartulaire de Notre-Dame de Saintes*, p. 100, no. 125, p. 102, no. 129, p. 101, no. 127. *Documents de Notre-Dame-aux-Nonnains*, p. 91, nos. 134, 135, p. 93, no. 139, record the exchanges between lords of serfs following servile marriages outside the convent's lands. *Cartulaire de Notre-Dame de Saintes*, pp. 146–48, no. 227, 1100–1107, records a settlement in which the abbey sought to protect its men from the viscount's men.

32. *Cartulaire de Notre-Dame de Bourbourg*, 1:24, no. 27, ca. 1120.

33. *Cartulaire de Notre-Dame de Saintes*, p. 140, no. 218, 1134. Quite commonly lay provosts or their relatives claimed hereditary right to own what they administered. This happened again to Notre-Dame when Hugh of Corme attempted to acquire control over abbey rights: p. 92, no. 112, 1134–51, p. 96, no. 118, 1141–51.

mended person. Mary Oubert, "wishing to provide for the salvation of her soul," gave herself and a house she owned into the service of Notre-Dame.[34] Mary entered conventual service but did not take vows. Jordan of Samaria gave himself together with all his goods, saving only twenty pounds for his daughter's dowry.[35] Jordan, a man of considerable substance, became a lay brother, probably because as an unlettered man he could not be accepted as a choir monk or canon. The widow Legarde took all her possessions, chattels as well as real estate, to les Clairets. After she died, her heirs claimed this had not been a permanent transfer of property. The abbey countered that Legarde "gave and conceded herself with all her movable and landed property to the abbess of les Clairets irrevocably and in perpetuity."[36] Legarde had come to the nuns as a pensioner who permanently transferred all property to the abbey in return for lifetime support.

Although in theory lay sisters (*conversae, sorores*) and lay brothers (*conversi*) were monastics who took truncated vows and wore habits, their primary function was to work rather than to pray. What prayers they said were by rote, since they were generally unlettered, and they sat in the nave of a monastic church, not in the sanctuary where the choir nuns or monks chanted the offices. Lay sisters inevitably performed physical labor. Some lay brothers were laborers or, like the brother at Saint-Amand, might be in charge of the bakery, but others acted for the nuns in various capacities outside the cloister, performing fealty in the name of the house and receiving settlements for the nuns.[37] When a nunnery had just a few *conversi* (Bondeville had only three, and Saint-Amand and Saint-Saens had only one apiece in the mid-thirteenth century), it became the superior's responsibility to see that these lay brothers confessed and received the Eucharist.[38] Having one brother in a convent meant an extra pair of strong arms but could also present a discipline problem for the superior.[39]

It had been part of the genius of the reforming Cistercian order

34. *Cartulaire de Notre-Dame de Saintes*, p. 67, no. 71, 1137–74, "se servicio . . . dedit."

35. *Cartulaire de Notre-Dame de Saintes*, p. 67, no. 71, 1137–74; Poitiers, BM, Fonteneau MS. 27, p. 157, "in fratrem et condonatum."

36. *Abbaye des Clairets*, p. 165, no. 74, 1289.

37. ER, p. 678; Paris, BN, MS. lat. 11002, fol. 24r; *Cartulaire de Notre-Dame de Bourbourg*, 1:140, no. 152, 1248.

38. ER, pp. 237, 677, 158.

39. ER, p. 734.

early in the twelfth century to institutionalize lay brothers as the work force of the monastery. Thus one would expect to find *conversi* at Cistercian convents. This is not always the case. For instance, in twenty-one years of visiting the Cistercian nuns of Bival and Saint-Aubin, Eudes never found lay brothers present. However, two Benedictine abbeys, Saint-Amand and Saint-Saens, each had one in their cloisters.

All sorts of people might want to become lay brothers. An extraordinary original charter from the mid-thirteenth century contains information about Richard of Pontoise, a convert from Judaism, who became a *conversus* at the nunnery of Saint-Amand on condition that the convent would support his wife, Oda, and daughter, Joanna, whom he would be leaving without any income.[40] Somewhere along the line the nuns waffled on the agreement to pay the family the promised upkeep, but Richard did not give up easily. He went to the ordinary's court and won his case, forcing the abbey to pay him reparation of five pounds and to support his wife and daughter with payments of two pounds a year. In Richard's case an adult convert wanted to become a lay brother, but his family responsibilities made it impossible for him to take up the monastic vocation he desired without help from the nuns.

In many instances, however, the line was not at all clear between those who gave themselves into service, those who took vows as lay sisters and brothers, and those who became pensioners. For instance, Hardoin Michoz of Quinçay and his wife, Richilde, gave themselves and all their goods to the Paraclete with the stipulation that when one of them died the other would be able to take the habit as a lay brother or sister.[41] Clearly Hardoin and Richilde started by entering the family of the Paraclete as other than professed monastics. But were they becoming servitors or pensioners? Their considerable wealth suggests that probably they were entering as the latter. In another case Odo of Chardonelles vowed himself, his wife, and his five children all to la Magdeleine-lez-Orléans, where he assumed the habit.[42] What did his wife and children become? How could he take the habit while married if his wife did not also profess? Even more enigmatic is the stipulation of a donor to Bondeville that "my

40. Rouen, BD, Saint-Amand, H 55, 1249. Text edited: Le Cacheux, *Histoire de Saint-Amand*, pp. 259–61.
41. *Cartulaire du Paraclet*, p. 244, no. 272, 1264: "Petentes ulterius, quod, altero ipsorum sublato de medio, illi qui supervixerit habitum religionis predicti monasterii, tanquam fratri converso, vel sorori converse."
42. Vauzelles, *Histoire de la Magdeleine-lez-Orléans*, p. 213, no. 9.

Genevieve be able to have one room in the aforementioned house in which she can remain the rest of her life."[43] Genevieve may have been an old and respected nurse, a discarded wife or even concubine, or perhaps an aging mother. Whoever she was, in practice it did not really matter; Genevieve was accepted by the nuns of Bondeville into an institution flexible enough to accommodate all sorts of people.

What is more, although monasteries attempted to make concrete their ties to people and their acquisition of property, what was set could always be undone and readjusted. Once commended to a house in whatever niche, individuals and their goods were intended to be an irrevocable part of the monastery, yet this could be re-negotiated. A determined commended person, like Eremburge du Plessys-Gassault, was able to leave the royal Abbey of Maubuisson in 1275, which capitulated by releasing her and some of her property (although it kept part of her landed donation as its part of the settlement).

An attempt to distinguish some of the indecipherable members of conventual familiae can only dead-end in a byway of vague identities, but it also demonstrates the appeal of the monastic route that welcomed diverse travelers. All sorts of arrangements and contingencies could be negotiated, all sorts of people could be accommodated within an abbey's walls. If we take one nunnery as an example, in June 1255 the Cistercian house of Bondeville had inside its walls thirty nuns, five lay sisters, two young novices, three lay brothers, three clerics, maidservants, some secular children who were being educated, and some of the prioress's family members.[44] Of all these people, the ones who presented the greatest danger were the male clergy.

The Male Clerics Attached to Convents

Male ecclesiastics, whose function was to serve nuns rather than to labor for them like the *conversi*, provided essential sacramental, administrative, and financial services for nunneries in the Middle Ages. These clerics came from both the regular clergy, monks and canons who followed a rule, and from the secular clergy, priests who did not live by a monastic rule. There was no set formula for the kind and number of clerics that should be attached to a convent, but

43. Rouen, BD, Bondeville, 52 H, carton 1, 1281. In 1290 Robert became a monk at Bondeville, so his tie to the nuns was strong.
44. ER, p. 237.

a common pattern was to have one priest/confessor for every fifteen
to twenty nuns. In practice, however, female houses continually operated without sufficient clerical support, and one of the common
recommendations of Archbishop Eudes when visiting nunneries
was for the nuns to get another priest.[45]

Priests came to serve nunneries both as oblates and as adults who
joined the familia. Garnier Chape was dedicated to the Paraclete
with the gift of a house, but other families secured a position for a
son by donating to a nunnery the wherewithal to create a future
clerical position to be reserved for their kin.[46] When the church of
Saint-Silvain was given to the nuns of Notre-Dame in Saintes, the
family retained the right to name one of its relatives as the parish
priest.[47] To be a cleric attached to a convent carried the same status
as serving a male monastery, so that prominent families sought such
positions for their sons.

Large, rich nunneries sometimes had an entire chapter of canons
that served their needs and depended on them financially. Holy Trinity in Poitiers had a most impressive (and also most troublesome)
clerical support system in the thirteen canons of Saint-Pierre le
Puellier: Notre-Dame in Saintes was ministered to by the chapter of
canons of Saint-Pallais just outside their abbey walls; and the
wealthy Abbey of the Holy Trinity in Caen made do with a chapter
of only four canons. Usually even important and well-to-do nunneries had four clerics or fewer attached to them as full-time members
of the community, but it was not uncommon for a penurious convent to arrange with an outside cleric to be its part-time confessor.

No matter how cleverly they handled their affairs, convents could
not make do without clerics, for whom no substitutions were allowed. As religious communities they absolutely required the sacramental services of male clergy for their own members, since without a priest there could be no confession and no mass. When
monasticism developed in the early centuries of the Christian era
this presented no hardship for monasteries, because Christians generally took communion only once a year. But by the central Middle
Ages mass was celebrated at least once a day in monasteries, necessitating at least one resident priest. In addition, most monastics received communion once a month, requiring monthly confession for
each member of the congregation. One hard-pressed community, the

45. ER, pp. 127, 225, 447.
46. *Cartulaire du Paraclet*, p. 247, no. 277, 1266.
47. *Cartulaire de Notre-Dame de Saintes*, p. 106, no. 139, ca. 1117.

nuns of Saint-Saens, could not afford to take on its own confessor, so it arranged with the almoner of Saint-Victor to come in to hear confessions, probably once a month.[48]

The second need for clerics came about because most monasteries were responsible for parish churches, each needing a priest/vicar to administer the sacraments of the Eucharist, baptism, marriage, and burial for the parishioners. The nuns assumed responsibility for supporting these clergy. The prioress of Saint-Silvain provided a house right behind the convent for Rainald, the vicar serving parishioners.[49] The building was meant for storing bread and wine, not as a living space, but the prioress acknowledging the volatile situation in the Saintonge in the early twelfth century, agreed that Rainald could use it in wartime as a safe place to live.

Negotiations over the nuns' expectations of the priest and over his need for support could be very sticky. Ansold, a priest of the convent of Notre-Dame-aux-Nonnains, was responsible for ministering to the parish that used the nave of the nuns' church as its parish church. He complained that he had to celebrate more masses than was just.[50] A compromise was worked out whereby the abbess agreed that her chaplain would take over three or four of the daily masses in the abbey church when Ansold asked for his help. In addition, the chaplain would assist with parochial needs, visiting the sick, purifying women after childbirth, baptizing babies, and whatever else proved necessary.

The third area that needed priestly attention—and it was the final burden that tore the purses of many female houses—was masses for the dead. The growing enthusiasm for having masses said for the souls of the departed had led to an exponential increase in donations and requests for masses. Providing the clerics to keep up with these needs was a challenge. The donors gave annual rents to pay for the masses, but these fixed rents lost value with inflation so that monasteries came to be celebrating masses at a financial loss. What is more, as masses proliferated, clergy sought to lighten their load by doubling up and counting masses for the dead as satisfying a convent's requirement for daily claustral mass. When the canons and nuns of Faremoutiers disagreed over this practice, they had to turn to an outsider for adjudication. The settlement supported the can-

48. ER, p. 513.
49. *Cartulaire de Notre-Dame de Saintes*, p. 125, no. 198, 1104–17.
50. *Documents de Notre-Dame-aux-Nonnains*, p. 45, no. 59, 1226.

ons, so that when they celebrated mass for a recently deceased dignitary, this service counted as the nunnery's daily mass.[51]

Ordained men also served nunneries as clerks and administrators, although their status as priests was not crucial to these roles. Because the convent's clerics were already present, they slipped easily into working as the archivists and secretaries who did the abbey's paperwork and as the officials who settled its conflicts and oversaw its affairs.[52] When the church enforced strict active cloistering on religious women, it became crucial for a nunnery to have male officials who could deal with the outside world.

One nunnery that had an unusual system was the Breton house of Saint-Sulpice-la-Forêt, a large, rich institution with five good-sized priories. Saint-Sulpice functioned with a pair of executives in each of its houses: a prioress and a prior exercised control in each dependent house, and even in the mother abbey itself the abbess was joined by a prior (sometimes called rector).[53] The priors acted as administrators and represented the nuns in legal cases. Although they were powerful, in all things they were under the final authority of the abbess. For example, when the archdeacon made official visitations, he was to correct the brothers in a priory three times; if that failed, he was to denounce erring brothers to the abbess, not to the prior.[54] When Amice, "a person of good conversation and life, and born of a legitimate marriage," the sister of one of the priors, "desired to serve God virtuously in the religious habit," it was up to the abbess to decide whether to take her in.[55] Even though the prior exercised considerable authority, he was not able to accept an oblate; only the abbess could do that, since Saint-Sulpice's resources and administrative structure existed entirely "for the work of the nuns."[56]

A clerical support system carried a high price tag. Priests expected and often received generous support from monasteries, as did the thirteenth-century chaplains of Bourbourg. The priest who served as chaplain of Bourbourg lived very well indeed in the house that

51. Paris, BN, MS. n.a. lat. 928, p. 100.

52. *Cartulaire de Notre-Dame de Saintes*, p. 95, no. 116, 1150; *Cartulaire du Paraclet*, p. 210, no. 231, 1239, p. 232, no. 257, 1255.

53. *Cartulaire de Saint-Sulpice-la-Forêt*, p. 224, no. 137, 1261. In a later charter, p. 447, no. 245, 1341, he is called "priori vel administratori" instead of rector.

54. *Cartulaire de Saint-Sulpice-la-Forêt*, p. 438, no. 240, 1238.

55. *Cartulaire de Saint-Sulpice-la-Forêt*, p. 444, no. 243, 1244.

56. *Cartulaire de Saint-Sulpice-la-Forêt*, p. 135, no. 59, 1152, p. 142, no. 62, 1156.

was provided for him as a vicarage just outside the abbey's court-yard.[57] He had an annual income of fourteen pounds, generously augmented by substantial supplies of grains, produce, and animals as well as pasturage for cows and one hundred herrings in the two strict fast times of Advent and Lent. Another priest attached to the same house had the resources to build several buildings on lands belonging to the nuns in Gravelinghes, and yet another rented a con-vent house where he lived comfortably with his wife.[58] Certainly the clergy supported by impoverished houses had to make do on less than those employed by rich abbeys. Nevertheless, by the thirteenth century priestly status generally commanded a respectable income, and the many other opportunities available to clerics meant that monasteries had to offer competitive remuneration to attract really good candidates or else settle for the less lettered and less capable priests.

Struggling nunneries tried various expedients. The impoverished house of Saint-Saens even had one of its nuns assist the priest at the mass, presumably because no deacons or subdeacons were on the convent payroll. During the same visitation when Eudes censured this practice, he also noted that Saint-Saens had only one priest, Dom Luke, who was the confessor as well as the celebrant. Since he had a terrible reputation as a womanizer, the visitor ordered the nuns to sack him and find a new priest. Probably this was easier said than done by a poor convent with little to offer. The presence of second-rate priests in poor nunneries contributed to spiritual and moral necrosis, a decay that could not be halted with orders and punishments in place of the badly needed financial remedy.

Appointment of clergy to fill convents' needs generally lay with the female superior. She exercised, at least in theory, full control over the hiring and firing of male clerics. In the day-to-day life of the medieval church this meant that priests had to come as job seekers before a few monastic women, abbesses and prioresses whom they then served, knowing they could be fired if they failed to satisfy their female bosses. The abbess of Notre-Dame-aux-Nonnains chose candidates to present for the parishes in her domain, as did the abbess of Bourbourg for the priories dependent on her house; the nuns of Saint-Avit appointed the chaplain of Saint-Denis to hold his position at their pleasure; the prioress of Bondeville had control over

57. *Cartulaire de Notre-Dame de Bourbourg*, 1:160–61, no. 169, 1260–80.

58. *Cartulaire de Notre-Dame de Bourbourg*, 1:112–13, no. 117, 1219, p. 162, no. 171, 1262.

the priests in her priory's subject parishes.[59] This was a recognized and accepted part of ecclesiastical life. As late as 1333 a papal notary formally warned eight newly hired priests that they served at their abbess's will and that she had full power to remove them if they proved unsatisfactory.[60]

The right of presentation could dispose of valuable livings and therefore might be hotly contested. The abbess of Notre-Dame in Troyes had *ius patronatus,* the right of presentation, for Saint-Jean in the city's marketplace. This living of Saint-Jean was immensely profitable for its vicar, as evinced by the seventy pounds he turned over annually to the abbey as its share of the parish income.[61] Clergy energetically sought such lucrative positions, while the monasteries that controlled them acted with equal force in keeping intact the right of appointment. The Priory of Bondeville mounted a spirited defense and won its claim to present the vicar to the church of Guerris when the privilege was assailed by the hospital of Mary Magdalen.[62] Such litigation did not endear religious institutions to each other, but the diminution in financial support by the thirteenth century made monasteries grimly determined to fight for control of their resources.

Monasteries not only paid clerics who provided sacramental services, they also had to support them after they became too old and infirm to perform their jobs. For a male monastery, caring for elderly secular priests was a chore and might involve paying out pensions to retired clergy. At a pinch, however, nonmonastic clerics could be incorporated into the preexisting old-age support system for elderly monks. Nunneries had little choice but to provide annual pensions for their retired clergy, since failing priests certainly could not be cared for in the nuns' infirmary. Pensions might be paid grudgingly or even sporadically when a house harbored ill feeling towards an outgoing priest. In other cases nunneries committed themselves to princely pensions for clergy.[63] When the financially fragile Priory of Bival agreed to a pension of thirty pounds for a priest, this extrava-

59. *Documents de Notre-Dame-aux-Nonnains,* pp. 9–10, no. 5, 1188, p. 12, no. 8, 1190, p. 132, no. 206, 1284; *Cartulaire de Notre-Dame de Bourbourg,* 1:197–98, no. 204, 1284; Cuissard, "Abbaye de Saint-Avit," pp. 174–75; ER, p. 467.

60. *Cartulaire de Notre-Dame de Bourbourg,* 1:215–52, no. 244, 1333.

61. *Documents de Notre-Dame-aux-Nonnains,* p. 44, no. 58, 1225, pp. 46–47, no. 62, 1227. Also see p. 122, no. 197, 1267, and p. 132, no. 206, 1284.

62. Rouen, BD, Bondeville, 52 H, carton 1, 1280.

63. ER, p. 462. Also see p. 532 relating that Eudes has punished the cleric for receiving the pension, not the nuns for giving it.

gant sum might have reflected the nuns' affectionate regard. But the visitor later punished the cleric for taking such a lavish amount, which suggests that the priest may have conned the nuns into more of a commitment than was prudent.

The clergy who worked for nunneries as priests, confessors, clerks, and administrators swore to obey the superior but often found themselves at loggerheads with her. Disagreements took many forms. When superiors and the vicars of dependent parish churches fell out, the apportioning of *donationes altaris*, parishioners' offerings, was often at issue. Two canons had to arbitrate a settlement between the nuns of Saint-Pierre-aux-Nonnains and their vicar for the parish of Arancey.[64] The vicar's share was set at a ninth of the tithes, a third of the offerings received at Easter, Pentecost, and Christmas, and a third of the *donationes altaris*. Even the nitty-gritty was divided up: the priest was entitled to half of the offerings of bread as well as half of the candles parishioners donated to the church.

Although many of the conflicts between female conventual authorities and the male clerics under their control involved income, fighting over remuneration often was just one salvo in a more diffuse war over power. The canons of Saint-Pierre le Puellier waged an endless guerrilla offensive against the nuns of Holy Trinity in Poitiers, primarily over who was to control the symbols and perks of authority (see fig. 6). The Church of Saint-Pierre had originally been given to the nuns in the tenth century, but it is not clear whether it derived its name from having originally housed religious women or simply from being under their control.[65] In either case, it came to be the home for the college of canons who served the nuns.

Nuns and canons skirmished over prebends, customary meals, pensions, and the jots and tittles of liturgical practice in the two houses.[66] Two major attempts to settle all the inflammatory issues occurred in July 1268 and on January 25, 1335. The first settlement recorded by Bishop Hugh of Poitiers reviewed old battle lines and drew up new ones. The touchy subject of prebends was renegotiated

---

64. Paris, BN, MS. lat. 10027, fols. 34v–35v.

65. Poitiers, BD, la Trinité, 2 H 2, liasse 1, ch. 1, no. 11, is a vidimus of the original royal diploma of King Lothar, confirming Saint-Pierre's gift to the nuns.

66. Poitiers, BD, la Trinité, 2 H 2, liasse 14, ch. 8, art. 1, contains the charter from about 1220 concerned with prebends, a papal letter of 1265 about pensions, and a charter from 1294 dealing with customary meals. It also contains the extensive and detailed settlement of July 1268. The settlement of 1335 is recorded in Poitiers, BM, Fonteneau MS. 27, p. 239.

Figure 6. View of the Abbey of Holy Trinity, Poitiers. Phot. Bibl. Nat. Paris.

so of the thirteen positions available, six were to go to priests and the rest to deacons and subdeacons; the abbess alone was to invest and install all the canons, and she appointed the *custos*, the canons' financial official, who could be any candidate she wanted as long as he was a clerk who could read and sing. Further, she had the authority to present any of the canons to vacant positions in city churches.

The canons' foremost responsibilities were to celebrate mass in

the nuns' church on all double feasts and to divide up the performance of the mass at other times with the secular clerics attached to
the abbey. At Christmastime the canons paid the abbess annual
dues of five pounds in recognition of their dependence on her. In
addition, they had other solemn liturgical duties that they also
viewed as privileges. Competition was keen among all the clergy in
the nuns' service to be the most visible and indispensable clerics
at the major public festivals of the church. The canons had claimed
the right to participate in the burials of all the nuns and to bless the
water and the paschal candle for the nuns' Easter vigil. The settlement of 1268 guaranteed them both privileges. Also, it spelled out
exactly what rights the canons had to bear abbey treasures in the
yearly high festive processions of the church. On the Purification of
the Virgin, three canons could process to the nuns' church, vest, and
then take up the abbey's cross, the psalter of Lady Adele, and the
abbey's portable altar. But for this feast other chaplains of the abbey
had the right to carry the nuns' reliquary. Bearing these treasures,
the canons then joined the procession of nuns circulating through
the city visiting other specific churches. On Palm Sunday the procession was further enriched by more canons carrying two Gospel
books, candles, and censers. On Tuesday of the Rogation Days, the
canons could share in the nuns' *mandatum*, the ceremony in which
the abbess—in imitation of Christ—washed the feet of twelve poor
people.

The enjoyment of these liturgical services did not come free; they
cost the Abbey of Holy Trinity a hefty outlay of funds to reimburse
every sacramental act of the canons, be it celebrating a mass or bearing a banner in a procession. No participation, no matter how slight,
went without remuneration. The canon who celebrated a daily mass
at the nunnery received bread and wine, and the deacon who read
the epistle went home with bread. The canons received larger
amounts of bread and wine when they served during a festival mass.
The canon who carried the crucifix with a relic of the true cross in
it during the Rogation Day procession received two loaves of bread,
two measures of wine, and a penny for his efforts. The abbess paid
each canon whenever he took part in a service, although he also
received set cash payments at five times during the year.

In addition, the abbess had to assume all the expenses of keeping
up the canons' Church of Saint-Pierre le Puellier. The list of what
this entailed is staggering, ranging from masonry and roof repair
through supplying necessary liturgical vessels and vestments to providing straw for the church floor at festival vespers, charcoal for the

censers, and wax candles for services. The abbess's care for her canons followed them even to the grave, since she donated the silken shrouds to cover their bodies.

The canons of Saint-Pierre represented a luxury for the nuns of Holy Trinity. Sacramental services could be obtained for significantly less by using secular clerics who did not need to maintain their own church. Also, hiring individual clergy who lived apart from each other was less apt to result in a united clerical front, a veritable union of clergy that lobbied and agitated for higher pay, more status, and less work. To control the canons' tendency to operate on their own, it was imperative for the abbess to impress her authority on them. Three times a year, on the anniversary of the dedication of the Church of Saint-Pierre and on Tuesday and Wednesday of Rogation, the abbess and claustral prioress went to Saint-Pierre for services. The abbess had the right to sit in the first stall on the right with her abbatial crozier (see fig. 4 for an example), set up before her while the prioress sat in the first stall on the left as a visual statement of their power over the canons. After the service on Rogation Tuesday, the crozier and the nuns' reliquary were laid on the canons' high altar until the Wednesday service. The abbess kept the keys to the church overnight as a symbol of her authority over the canons and to safeguard the nuns' treasures.

The lengthy and elaborate settlement worked out in 1268 did not end the canons' pressure for more income. Another agreement was executed in 1335 to resolve continuing difficulties. Much of the thirteenth-century agreement was repeated, but the balance of power between nuns and canons shifted toward the men, who acquired greater power in two city churches, more property, and larger reimbursements for some of their sacramental services. Most telling, however, was that on the dedication day for the Church of Saint-Pierre and on the two Rogation Days, the abbess came accompanied by her priest to sit in state during the canons' services, with her priest—rather than the claustral prioress—occupying the first stall on the left. In addition, the keys to the church no longer jingled symbolically at her waist for twenty-four hours but went to the male guardian of the relics. A religious woman might wield power over religious men, but in the fourteenth century her autonomous authority was watered down to half-strength.

The conflict between the nuns of Holy Trinity and their canons continued over decades but never erupted through the polite surface to become a real confrontation. The same cannot always be said, for instance, about the relationship between the canons and the nuns of Holy Cross, also in the city of Poitiers. On several occasions these canons completely ruptured relations by refusing sacraments to the nuns.[67] Recognizing such potential difficulties, one nunnery, the Cistercian house of Salzinnes, devised a strategy to mitigate problems: the convent kept its number of clerics to an absolute minimum by using lay brothers whenever possible. Lay brothers represented the house for receiving donations, at sales, and for legal settlements.[68] Priests still had to perform the sacraments at Salzinnes, but there was no autonomous group of canons to challenge the abbess's control.

The clergy could feel deep antipathy for religious women. Much of the resentment expressed about nuns might be unconscious anger at women who directed male clergy, although in most of the vituperative writing it is hard to find the actual link. One satiric poem, however, seems so near the subject it lampoons that it may be reasonable to suggest the author was attached to the house. This poem, "The Council of Remiremont" was written in Latin in the mid-twelfth century, ostensibly about a court of love that is held by the canonesses of Remiremont to decide whether clerks or knights are better lovers.[69] The nuns are richly dressed and full of worldly wisdom. The directing lady sums up that (no surprises here) priestly lovers far outstrip their knightly competition. What is quite startling is the poem's use of nuns' proper names, several of which, like Elisabeth de Faucogney, can be verified as the names of real nuns in the abbey's obituary. Although knights lose out to clerks, it is really the religious women who are the poet's prey, victims he mauls thoroughly with trenchant satire. If this piece is an example of how deep could run the currents of male clerics' hostility towards the religious women they served, then clerical criticism of nuns needs to be taken with a pinch of salt.

Institutional conflicts and individual bitterness did not stop some religious folk from developing friendships; some priests forged warm ties to their nunneries. Nicolas of Dixmude, a clerk of Bourbourg, left his house to the nuns to celebrate his anniversary in the convent

67. Labande-Mailfert, "Débuts de Sainte-Croix," pp. 96–97.
68. *Recueil du Val-Saint-Georges à Salzinnes*, p. 171, no. 137, 1264, p. 194, no. 151, 1257, p. 102, no. 83, 1240. Not all Cistercian nunneries chose this route; Lieu-Notre-Dame-lès-Romorantin, for instance, had canons attached to it: *Cartulaire du Lieu-Notre-Dame-lès-Romorantin*, p. 17, no. 11, 1245, p. 76, no. 113, 1262.
69. Michel Parisse, "Le concile de Remiremont, poème satirique du XIIe siècle," *Pays de Remiremont* 4(1981); 10–15.

he had served for year.[70] Other priests came to be dearly loved by the congregations of nuns they served. This feeling could even break through the workaday language of a charter, as when Baldwin Tristram, "our beloved cleric," is named as his convent's representative.[71]

Generally, during the twelfth and thirteenth centuries nuns deflected the hostile challenges from dependent clergy, but towards the end of our period, in the increasingly chilly climate of the late thirteenth century, they lost some of their prerogatives to the clerics who ministered to their sacramental needs and whose ability to say masses often made them the recipients of ten times greater bequests than those received by nuns.[72]

JURISDICTIONS

Within the cloister, among an abbey and its dependent priories, and in the outside world, monasteries exercised a variety of jurisdictions. In the smallest of these three spheres—that is, inside each monastic house—the superior and monastic officeholders divided up power and responsibility into discrete jurisdictions. The same thing happened on a larger scale both between a mother house with only a few dependent priories and within a full-blown order. Finally, the monastery had to define the area over which it held juridical jurisdiction within society at large.

Monastic Decentralization

In the early eleventh century, monastic jurisdiction in all three of these spheres fell predominately to monastic superiors. The abbess or abbot existed as the embodiment of the institution and hence acted with a good deal of autonomy for the congregation. By the end of the thirteenth century, the chapter as the corporate expression of the institution shared control more actively with the superior, whose role was changing from personifying the group to acting as CEO with some similar and some divergent interests. In 1068 Abbess Hodierna of Saint-Georges settled a conflict over a former donation of property, acting on her own but in the interests of her community; but by 1252 when the Abbey of Voisins settled a disagreement with a local baron, the bishop heard the case with the

---

70. *Cartulaire de Notre-Dame de Bourbourg*, 1:192, no. 200, 1282.

71. *Cartulaire de Notre-Dame de Bourbourg*, 1:162, no. 171, 1262.

72. *Cartulaire de Porrois*, pp. 273–74.

abbess appearing "for herself, and Brother Gosbert of Voisins, representing the convent of Voisins."[73] Abbess and nuns were allies, but the former no longer automatically acted for the chapter, which existed as a separate entity. Our time frame spans the important development of ideas about corporate identity, which in the case of monastic chapters became more self-conscious and assertive during the twelfth century. Thus by 1137 the abbess of Notre-Dame in Saintes "could not give or sell any church property except with the consent of the whole chapter."[74]

In the most contained sphere of the monastery itself, monastic officeholders, such as claustral prioress, sacristan, librarian, cellaress, infirmarian, chantress, and almoner, took responsibility for particular areas of monastic life. In theory the administrative posts existed as parts of a whole, but in actuality they tended to become compartmentalized and autonomous. The decentralizing of finances actually began in the eleventh century and became general monastic practice by the middle of the twelfth century.[75]

The offices and their directors acquired separate incomes. Anne, the almoner at Ronceray in the early twelfth century, had the responsibility of exploiting particular lands to produce charitable income for the abbey.[76] With the advice of two local men from the city of Angers, Geoffrey and Marcher, she decided to plant a vineyard. But direct exploitation by the nuns proved too expensive and extremely unprofitable, so again with the backing of the congregation and the input of Geoffrey and Marcher, she made a new plan to lease the land to local peasant farmers. Twenty-one men took on strips of the land, agreeing to pay tithe and *cens* (rent) to the nuns and to use the abbey's winepress for the harvest. These men were acquiring only partial control over the land, which Anne emphasized by requiring each farmer to promise that he would sell back only to Ronceray. (Geoffrey and Marcher were among the new vintners, which might suggest that their advice had been other than impartial, since they wanted to share in this new venture.)

The economic realities of the twelfth and thirteenth centuries abetted the tendency towards monastic compartmentalization. Do-

73. *Cartulaire de Saint-Georges de Rennes,* 9:259, no. 30, 1068, and *Cartulaire de Notre-Dame de Voisins,* p. 5, no. 5, 1252.

74. *Cartulaire de Notre-Dame de Saintes,* p. 136, no. 213, 1137.

75. Johnson, *Prayer, Patronage, and Power,* pp. 52–53. R. Génestal, *Rôle des monastères comme établissements de crédit étudié en Normandie du XIe à la fin du XIIIe siècle* (Paris: A. Rousseau, 1901), pp. 168–72.

76. *Cartulaire du Ronceray,* p. 21, no. 22, ca. 1115.

nors no longer could lay their hands on large tracts of land with which to endow houses, so they were quick to shift from making general gifts of real estate to donating specific income to a particular administrator or for a specific purpose. The countess of Bar gave the income from Ceton "for the work of the infirmarian of the nuns" of the Abbey of les Clairets.[77] The dying count of Nevers willed five pounds income to the nuns of Crisenon, a perfectly respectable gift when earmarked as it was for the purchase of chemises, but small potatoes as a general endowment.[78]

The fragmentation of monastic authority also received encouragement from inside the cloister, since despite the vow of poverty the acquisitive instinct died hard. Even if one could suppress it personally, it often popped up professionally as a drive to enrich and empower the office rather than the individual. The hunger for power must have been particularly acute among medieval monastics, who had sworn to give up all property and its control. Monastic officials tended to create petty fiefdoms that they then hotly defended, as did the cellarer who squabbled with the treasurer of the male Abbey of Holy Trinity in Vendôme over income and the assumption of costs by their respective offices.[79] The compartmentalized income structure did not necessarily trail internal discord in its wake. The prioress of Jully received a bequest from the count of Bar-sur-Seine, which she readily handed over to the nun chamberlain to buy cloaks for the congregation.[80]

The real issue—the one destructive of the monastic ideal—was the disintegration of the common life that followed administrative and economic decentralization.[81] By the late Middle Ages monastic women and men often slept in their own rooms instead of in one large dormitory. This required building individual cells, which occurred at some but not all houses. Much more commonly, monastics ate alone, in small groups, or in the infirmary where the meals intended for the ill were more palatable than usual refectory fare. When Archbishop Eudes Rigaud visited the nuns of Almenèches in 1260 he noted that "the refectory often remained deserted, that is to say, they did not eat there as a body, but ate meat here and there in the rooms, in sociable groups of twos and threes. Several of them

77. *Abbaye des Clairets*, p. 103, no. 29, 1230.
78. Bouchard, *Sword, Miter, and Cloister*, p. 183, n. 34.
79. *Cartulaire de la Trinité de Vendôme*, 2:400, no. 549.
80. *Cartulaire de Jully-le-Nonnains*, pp. 285–86, 1219.
81. Lawrence, *Medieval Monasticism*, pp. 222 ff., and Favreau, "Heurs et malheurs," pp. 134–35.

194   ORGANIZING STRUCTURE

had their own rooms"; he "advised them to eat and live in common, and to give up their individual rooms."[82] Eudes discovered similar problems in male monasteries. The monks of Saint-Lô ate in their rooms and compounded the offense by indulging in meals of great sumptuousness, thus paining their ascetic visitor. He "forbade any of them to eat or drink in any place other than the refectory, the infirmary, or the prior's chamber."[83] In one house, Saint-Martin in Pontoise, the monks had created a cozy little bar for themselves and christened it "Bernard's Room," where they liked to gather to drink and chat.[84] Eudes was incensed and ordered the superior to put a quick stop to their monastic happy hour.

Although it is customary for critics to bewail the slippage of the monastic common life in the later Middle Ages, it was more a symptom than a cause of decline. Indeed, the monks of the Chartreuse, who have managed to maintain a particularly demanding and undeformed eremitical life in the mountains above Grenoble since the late eleventh century, eat and sleep apart except for a festive shared meal on Sundays and feast days. Perhaps the strain of complete communality—one common dormitory and shared communal meals—was itself responsible for some of the decay that set in among the monasteries of late medieval Europe, and those nuns and monks who drew a bit apart from each other were naturally seeking a respite from total togetherness.

Dependent Houses

The second jurisdictional sphere tied dependent monasteries to their mother priory or abbey. Such a pattern was wholly foreign to the original intention of monastic framers, who had conceived of each monastery as an independent and autonomous unit.[85] That early template had been discarded, however, in Carolingian and Ottonian periods of rejuvenation, when reformers purged houses of errors and then made the reformed institutions dependent on the reforming monastery. In the tenth century the Cluniac order initiated its famous model of dependent priories under the control of the mother abbey, a model that became widely known and was exten-

82. ER, p. 424. A Cluniac visitor in the late thirteenth century found in the Midi the same problem of eating and sleeping separately: *Visites des monastères de l'ordre de Cluny de la province d'Auvergne en 1286 et 1310,* ed. Alexandre Bruel (Paris: Collection de Documents Inédits sur l'Histoire de France, 1891), p. 20.

83. ER, p. 222.

84. ER, p. 309.

85. Knowles, *Monastic Order in England,* pp. 134–36.

sively copied. Dependent houses could be large and complete institutions, small priories, or even tiny cells or obediences. In all cases they had some reliance on the mother house, although this could be minimal.

In theory the parent monastery was expected to be an abbey, ruled over by an abbess or abbot, but even priories could and did control other houses, which were usually the small obediences. To be an abbey carried important status lacking to a priory, and pressure was often exerted by the monastics themselves or by important patrons to elevate a priory to abbatial standing. In 1175 the founder of the Priory of Bival, Hugh de Gournay, had his priory of nuns recognized as an abbey to protect it from interference by a powerful local abbot. Other priories like Bival's daughter house, the Priory of Bondeville, kept claiming abbatial status and attempted to help its case along with a little clumsy forgery, changing the word "prioress" to "abbess" on later documents.[86] Bondeville finally succeeded in making good that claim in the middle of the seventeenth century.

A mother house most commonly acquired dependencies through donations from patrons or by turning a property gift into a small obedience where a few of its nuns could oversee exploitation of the land. Small groups of monastics also moved from their own institution to colonize a new house when a donor had the urge to establish a monastery. The colony could be as small as the four Clarisses who started Longchamp in 1261 or the more traditional twelve monastics with a superior, in imitation of Christ and the apostles.[87] Colonization of a house was sometimes intended to create a dependent for the parent monastery, although more often the colony was meant to be autonomous.

The Abbey of Notre-Dame, a large, wealthy Benedictine nunnery in Saintes, controlled a number of smaller houses. At the time of its foundation, Notre-Dame received from its founders sixteen churches with their surrounding lands plus the monastery of Saint-Pallais, which became the home for its college of canons.[88] As the nuns organized their holdings, they designated some of these ecclesiastical properties as priories. The last two priories to take shape as

86. See, for example, the first line of Rouen, BD, Bondeville, 52 H, carton 1, MS. dated 1260.
87. De Sérent, "Ordre de Sainte Claire," p. 134.
88. *Cartulaire de Notre-Dame de Saintes*, p. 4, no. 1, 1047. The nuns acquired the Priory of Saint-Silvain independent of the founders: Paris, BN, MS. Périgord 35, fols. 140r–142v, as well as the Priory of Saint-Julian, which was under Notre-Dame's authority by 1098 (p. 139, no. 217, 1098).

such were the Church of Notre-Dame in Vix, in the thirteenth century, and Notre-Dame in Mon Polin, in the first half of the fourteenth century.[89] In addition, some of these priories were parent institutions to parish churches, such as the Priory of Saint-Sornin in Marennes, which had five dependent parish churches to staff, fund, and oversee. In all, the nuns of Notre-Dame had the responsibility for nineteen ecclesiastical properties in addition to the mother abbey in Saintes.

Agnes of Burgundy and her husband Geoffrey Martel, count of Anjou, were the founders of Notre-Dame and had been present for the dedication of the new Saintongeais nunnery in 1047. At this time they had just returned from attending the imperial coronation of Henry III and his wife, Agnes, Agnes of Burgundy's daughter and namesake. At that time Agnes and Geoffrey had reconfirmed all the convent's property and privileges, including the lands of Marennes north of the River Seudre, which were part of their original lavish gift.

The founders were treating Marennes as a one-size-fits-all gift item, since in the 1030s they had given it to another monastery, their previous monastic foundation for men, Holy Trinity in Vendôme. In the first round of this donation, they gave the monks half of both the cultivated lands and the newly assarted fields in Marennes, a holding that Agnes later rounded out by buying the monks the other half of the Marennes farmland for the then mind-boggling sum of three hundred pounds.[90] After the comital couple built the nunnery, they worked out a swap with Holy Trinity, giving the monks other property and churches closer to them in exchange for the Marennes holdings, which went to the nuns. The nuns came out on top in the exchange.

The area of Marennes on the Atlantic coast opposite the island of Oléron consists today, as it did in the Middle Ages, of swampy, low-

89. The house book of the abbey contains the necrology: Yale University, Beinecke Library, MS Marston 25, fols. 1r–44v. The bulk of the entries are in one hand, A, from the early fourteenth century, with its latest entry from 1333. The second hand, B, makes its first entry in 1344 in black ink. No mention is made of priory status for either Vix or Mon Polin in the cartulary, whose latest charter is dated 1220. Two prioresses of Vix are commemorated in the necrology: Emmelina (fol. 19v) in hand A, and Isabella (fol. 24r) in hand B. The likelihood is therefore that Vix became a priory after 1220 but before 1333. An entry for a prioress of Mon Polin occurs first in hand B (fol. 28v), suggesting that Mon Polin was raised to the status of a priory only in the fourteenth century.

90. *Cartulaire de Notre-Dame de Saintes*, p. 154, no. 235, before 1047.

lying salt flats that are a delta of the Seudre River. It is still useful property in modern times, but in the medieval centuries it was immensely valuable for its salt, harvested from the extensive salt pans, and the catches of seafood taken from its inlets and canals. Establishing a priory from which a group of nuns could direct the exploitation of these rich Atlantic resources was of great financial value for Notre-Dame.

Since the gift of Marennes specifies that Agnes and Geoffrey were donating a church with lands rather than a preexisting priory, it is likely that what the nuns acquired was originally a parish church, which they rebuilt along with claustral buildings soon after the abbey's foundation in 1047. The rebuilt and enlarged plant became, as the Priory of Saint-Sornin, the focus of Notre-Dame's activities in the delta region. The Romanesque church building of Saint-Sornin exists today, just north of national route 728 on the way to the town of Marennes. Its facade has been extensively modified, but its early interior still reflects the strong Saintongeais architectural idiom. The original eleventh-century flat chevet and some of the most interesting early capitals in the region are intact. At the crossing are two energetic wrestlers and a Daniel, dramatically confronting the lions. The single barrel-vaulted nave now has two added aisles. The easternmost end of the south aisle is angled towards the altar in the same way as at Saint-Pallais, the church of the nuns' canons, suggesting that in the twelfth century when the aisles were added, a sense of planning unity existed for the entire family of Notre-Dame's buildings. The priory's six parish churches were in surrounding villages of the salt-marsh region. One, Saint-Lawrence in le Gua, still has its impressive twelfth-century Romanesque tower. Although Saint-Sornin was only one of the Abbey of Notre-Dame's outposts, and a dependent one at that, its wealth and self-confidence show in its architecture.

Saint-Sornin's activities recorded in twelfth-century charters reveal the considerable stature and relative self-determination that such a monastic dependency could enjoy. The cartulary for Notre-Dame includes thirty-seven twelfth-century charters from Saint-Sornin. Of these only four (10.8 percent) show the hand of the central administration at work in the priory's actions; in almost 90 percent of the priory's dealings, the prioress of Saint-Sornin operated on her own. Even when the abbey was represented in transactions in Marennes, as for instance when Prioress Eremberge settled a contretemps over an illegal oven, it was with the abbess acting as witness rather than as participant.[91] The prioress did have a male prior working for her, but apparently more as her helper than as a business manager, since only once is he named in this run of charters.[92]

Three successive prioresses worked diligently in the first three-quarters of the century to maintain and expand Saint-Sornin's economic base. In the early part of the century, Benedicta was prioress and began the process of buying up property by acquiring part or all of four mills and a saltworks.[93] Next came Hylaria of Mornac, the daughter of Lord Helias of Mornac, the castellan of Mornac, a region just below the mouth of the Seudre River. Lord Helias, "because his daughter, Hylaria, was consecrated there to God," endowed the priory grandly with mills, fishing and hunting rights, pasturage, vineyards, salt flats, and two serfs; having a noblewoman in a monastic position of leadership tended to bring such benefits to the institution, but it might also involve a house in nepotism, as it did when Hylaria subsequently named her brother custodian of the saltworks, in thanks for his confirmation of their father's gift.

Prioress Hylaria built on Benedicta's acquisitions, buying gardens in Le Gua near one of Saint-Sornin's parish churches and receiving a gift of tithes in the same village.[94] She brought income to the priory by using her influence to talk the count of Poitou into donating tithes from fields, vineyards, woodlands, and marshlands to Saint-Sornin, and she defended the endowment from unjust claims of men as well as rebuilding after violent storms washed away mills in the floodplain.[95] She purchased for the sum of two pounds land that one of her successors, Prioress Eremberge, later rented out for an annual *cens* of four solidi, a rate so low that the investment would produce no profit for ten years.[96]

Eremberge of Périgord, who presided over Saint-Sornin in the third quarter of the century, came from much farther afield than Hylaria, which may explain why she was not able to use family and friendship to enrich the priory. She, however, also purchased land, tithes, and mills and saw to it that buildings were erected on four of the

91. *Cartulaire de Notre-Dame de Saintes*, p. 156, no. 237, 1162.

92. *Cartulaire de Notre-Dame de Saintes*, p. 174, no. 270, ca. 1148–71.

93. *Cartulaire de Notre-Dame de Saintes*, p. 159, no. 241; pp. 160–61, nos. 144, 145, 146, p. 170, no. 260.

94. *Cartulaire de Notre-Dame de Saintes*, p. 172, no. 266, ca. 1119–34, p. 171, no. 264, after 1119.

95. *Cartulaire de Notre-Dame de Saintes*, p. 170, no. 263, after 1119, p. 171, no. 265, 1119–22, p. 170, no. 261.

96. *Cartulaire de Notre-Dame de Saintes*, pp. 172–72, no. 268, 1146–71.

priory's properties.[97] Although she could not keep up with Hylaria's record of acquisitions, she put her energies into consolidation by having customary rents and services recorded, and she did so in such a way that she was seen as "Good Lady Eremberge."[98]

Electing a prioress could be in the hands of the nuns in either the mother house or the dependent house. When the dependent house was clearly just an extension of the parent institution, control stayed with the parent, which like the convent of Montivilliers could elect the prioress of its obedience, Saint-Paul's, or like the abbess of Holy Trinity in Poitiers, could simply appoint the new superior of Saint-Julian's.[99] Trouble between members of a monastic family often developed over defining where the power lay, which could be resolved by sharing jurisdiction when parent institution and offspring each had a strong sense of self-importance.

An interesting example of a monastic daughter with the clout to demand, and receive, privileges from the mother house was the Abbey of Pommeraye. In the mid-1100s Countess Herlesende decided to found her own nunnery and asked Abbess Heloise of the nearby convent of the Paraclete to concede to her the region of the Pommeraye; Heloise complied and helped structure the new abbey of Pommeraye, thereby gaining some control over it.[100] An arrangement was worked out whereby the first abbess of Pommeraye was elected at the Paraclete by the nuns of Pommeraye, but it was agreed that future abbesses would be elected at Pommeraye itself. Once a year the abbess of Pommeraye had the right to attend a chapter at the Paraclete, and once a year the head of the Paraclete could go to the daughter abbey to correct faults in its chapter. This rather unusual agreement evolved because Pommeraye had abbatial status yet owed a debt to the parent house. Over a hundred years after its foundation, Pommeraye still was sending a delegation of four of its senior nuns to the Paraclete to announce the election of one of its members as abbess of Pommeraye.[101]

The Paraclete experienced hostility in its turn from its own priories over their rights in the election of the abbess of the Paraclete. The priories objected vociferously that they were disfranchised by

97. *Cartulaire de Notre-Dame de Saintes*, p. 168, no. 257, before 1171.

98. *Cartulaire de Notre-Dame de Saintes*, p. 169, no. 258, before 1117; p. 173, no. 269, ca. 1146–71, p. 168, no. 257, before 1171: "Bona domina Ymberga Petragoricensis, dum priorissa de Maremnia."

99. ER, p. 361; Poitiers, BM, Fonteneau MS. 27, p. 255.

100. Paris, BN, MS. Baluze XLVI, pp. 143–44.

101. *Cartulaire du Paraclet*, p. 228, no. 251, 1251.

the practice of limiting the right to participate in the abbatial election to the nuns of the mother house.[102] They took their complaints to the episcopal court and won a compromise ruling by which each priory was to send seven nuns with its prioress to join seven nuns of the Paraclete as electors of a new abbess. In jockeying for the upper hand with its priories, the Paraclete failed to exclude them from its own electoral process but held on to the right to dictate their size and to exercise visitation rights over them.[103]

The responsibility of visiting another monastery imposed an obligation on a monastic superior but balanced it with great power: the right to punish and reform. Even in the equivocal case of Pommeraye, the abbess of the Paraclete retained the right to visit. This right carried with it a lot of hard work. For instance, when she was visiting dependencies, Abbess Joanna of Saint-Sulpice had to listen to extensive grumbling at the Priory of Locmaria about the cheese-paring ways of the rector at that house.[104] Once all the dirty linen of a monastery was aired, the visitor's real chores began when she attempted to reform vice, reward virtue, find solutions to insoluble problems, and heal the divisiveness that often wrenched communities apart. Less taxing for the superior of the parent monastery was the need to appoint clergy to dependent priories.[105] This offered the abbess or abbot an opportunity to reward friends and support relatives, a continuing concern for all members of medieval society.

The haphazard endowment practices of medieval donors were ruled much more by what the givers wanted to donate than by what the recipient institutions wanted to receive. The resulting pattern of holdings from which a monastic house had to wring its income was usually widespread and often inhospitable to centralized management. A loosely federated system of dependent priories situated in the major far-flung properties evolved to control and exploit the economic possibilities of these lands. This system worked financially as a management strategy, but much more important, it satisfied the localism of medieval sensibilities.

The prolific knightly family of Gardona lived during the early twelfth century in what is now the village of Gardonne on the Dordogne River west of Bergerac in Périgord. For this family the nearby

102. *Cartulaire du Paraclet*, p. 233, no. 258, 1255.

103. *Cartulaire du Paraclet*, pp. 215–16, nos. 238–39, 1244.

104. *Cartulaire de Saint-Sulpice-la-Forêt*, pp. 223–35, no. 137. Not all visitations sapped the visitor, but the tendency of superiors to procrastinate suggests that the responsibility was seen as onerous: ER, p. 435.

105. *Cartulaire de Notre-Dame de Bourbourg*, 1:197–98, no. 204, 1284.

Priory of Saint-Silvain served as a spiritual home. No matter that Saint-Silvain was only a dependent priory of the Abbey of Notre-Dame in Saintes; the rich and powerful—but too distant—mother abbey had no claim on the loyalties of the Gardona family. Because Saint-Silvain was the neighborhood monastery, the whole family became involved with it as nuns, donors, and supporters.[106] For example, within a few decades at least three of its women served the priory as nuns, and nine family members made donations for their burials at Saint-Silvain. When Lord Ebrard of Gardona wanted to make amends for the violence his grandfather had inflicted on property in Périgord belonging to the Abbey of Notre-Dame in Saintes, he made a donation for his soul and that of his grandfather not to the mother abbey but to its local priory, Saint-Silvain.[107] Notre-Dame was too far away to be practical for a burial site or a court hearing, but more important, it did not command the loyalty of the major regional families as did the neighboring nuns of Saint-Silvain.

Legal Jurisdiction

The proceeds from administering justice constituted one of the major sources of lordly income in the Middle Ages. Since monasteries exercised juridical lordship in the person of their superior, they enjoyed its financial benefits, although quite often they had to defend their legal turf from challenges.

During the summer of 1253 Oliver, lord of Tinteniac, seized one of the men of the Abbey of Saint-Georges for thievery committed in his domain.[108] Abbess Agnes of Erbreé protested vigorously on the part of her convent that Oliver did not have jurisdiction over abbey personnel, to which he countered that she was misinformed and that he had been exercising such justice in his own lands for forty years. Both sides were adamant, and the case had to be heard by the seneschal of Rennes, who worked out a division of authority. His solution was to create a joint jurisdiction for Tinteniac. Both sides appointed an *allocatus,* a sort of bailiff, to seize suspected criminals and bring them before a common court for trial. Each *allocatus* then informed the other side that a trial was set, but the trial proceeded even if the other lordship did not send a representative. The cost of imprisoning a thief was to be covered by the miscreant's own goods or, if the criminal owned nothing, the abbey and the overlord of Tin-

106. Paris, BN, Périgord, MS. 35, fols. 138r–139v; *Cartulaire de Notre-Dame de Saintes,* pp. 121–25, nos. 183–86, 188, 199.
107. *Cartulaire de Notre-Dame de Saintes,* p. 123, no. 192, before 1117.
108. *Cartulaire de Saint-Georges de Rennes,* 10:44, no. 34 A, 1253.

teniac had to share the expense. In noncapital cases, the abbey received all the criminal's goods. In capital cases when the condemned woman or man came from outside the abbey's lands, the two lordships shared the goods equally. The jurisdiction for executions by hanging was in the hands of the lord of Tinteniac.

Odd though it may seem to modern sensibilities, medieval monasteries usually had prisons, although such facilities may have been ad hoc affairs. Indeed, in the early Middle Ages, secular rulers sometimes remanded prisoners to abbatial prisons, since they often had none of their own, and in our period nunneries like Saint-Georges and Jully had their own lockups for malefactors apprehended by monastic officials.[109] Monasteries also used their prisons to punish their own members. The convent of Bival incarcerated some of its nuns for severe misbehavior, probably in an ordinary cell that could be locked, but this sort of punishment may not have seemed very severe to the offender; for instance, when two monks of Saint-Catherine in Rouen were imprisoned by their abbey, they sat around singing "dissolute songs," to the dismay of Archbishop Eudes Rigaud.[110]

Medieval legal jurisdiction distinguished between high justice, the responsibility to hear capital cases, and low justice, the adjudication of all other cases. The division along these lines of high justice to secular courts and low justice to ecclesiastical courts seems a natural one, since the church was bound by the Gospels not to shed blood and so could not handle capital crimes. Assertive abbesses did not necessarily see it this way, however; Abbess Agnes of Holy Trinity in Poitiers claimed high justice in the town of Segondigny, a claim contested by Alfonse, the count of Eu.[111] A hearing by the bishop and deacon of Poitiers settled the claims, as we might expect, by allotting low justice to the abbey and high justice to the count. The court also awarded the count the right to collect the taille (an arbitrary seigneurial levy on serfs), and other taxes in the area. Alphonse's victory was almost absolute, since a modest limit of sixty solidi (three pounds) plus one penny was set for the fines the abbey could levy. Agnes must have been chagrined.

Feelings about the infringement of juridical authority ran high,

---

109. *Cartulaire de Jully-les-Nonnains*, pp. 299–300, 1309.
110. ER, pp. 252, 118.
111. Poitiers, BD, 2 H 2, liasse 96, ch. 5, art. 6, 1269. Some convents exercised high justice; for instance, *Cartulaire de Notre-Dame de Saintes*, pp. 75–76, no. 83, 1174.

and great care had to be taken to respect rival jurisdictions. In Brittany the Abbey of Saint-Georges shared tenure of the island of Arz in the Gulf of Morbihan with the monks of Saint-Gildas-de-Rhuys (ill famed for posterity by Abelard's bitter indictment). Saint-Georges had a priory on the island, and some of the priory's peasants had become embroiled in a disagreement with a local priest.[112] The prioress must have notified her abbess that trouble was brewing and that abbatial clout was needed to help settle the battle over local rights. Abbess Agnes determined that the most powerful support of the abbey's rights would come from Peter, the comital seneschal, so she asked him to travel to Arz "to contribute his advice" in the case. The seneschal's charter describing this situation survives, and in it Peter takes great pains to emphasize that Arz is not under his or the count's jurisdiction, so that he is serving strictly as a legal adviser—not a judge—at the court of the abbess and prioress. Peter may have been a particular friend to the nuns or simply learned in the complexities of law; in any case, he accepted the request to contribute advice in the case while scrupulously defining his advisory role.

Monasteries had their own courts in which either the superior heard cases with the advice of lords temporal and spiritual or such men officially appointed as judges heard cases in the superior's name:

> Idercius had affirmed that he had hereditary right to some land of Notre-Dame and that Abbess Florence took from him what was known to be hereditary. Because of this seizure, Idercius came with his friends for judgment on the appointed day in the lady abbess's court in Saintes. Idercius saw, however, that he would not profit by the judgment, and in the presence of Bishop Ramnulf and Peter the archdeacon, he put himself in the mercy of the lady abbess.[113]

After conferring with the ecclesiastical and feudal luminaries she had gathered, Florence settled the case by granting Idercius a fief that he was allowed to hold during his lifetime. The abbess heard this case and delivered a verdict herself. In another instance from the same period and at the same abbey, two knights who seized the keys to a mill that had been part of Helias of Mornac's donation were called before the abbess's court, where they were judged by a panel

112. *Cartulaire de Saint-Georges de Rennes*, 10:42, no. 32 A, 1251.
113. *Cartulaire de Notre-Dame de Saintes*, p. 91, no. 111, 1100–1107.

of four judges: a royal provost, a castellan, an archpriest, and a canon of one of the local monasteries.[114]

Winning a legal claim required that a litigant travel to the court in the first place, bring witnesses to substantiate testimony, field oath helpers if necessary, and act with great confidence if faced with a juridical ordeal. It was important that a judge understand the psychology of a defendant, as did Abbess Florence when faced with Andrew of Trahent, a monastic official who had stubbornly claimed ownership of monastic customs over a long period of time.[115] The abbess sent Andrew notification of the court date, and he came to the abbey with his supporters on the appointed day. He must have been horrified to discover that he was to undergo trial by boiling water to prove the truth of his claim and that two huge cauldrons were already bubbling briskly in the convent church. Then Andrew, "seeing the absolute determination of the abbess to undertake the judgment, felt fear and did not dare to set himself against the lady in a dangerous trial." He retracted his claims and gratefully accepted the abbess's kindness in waiving the fine.

The same pressure worked with other ordeals when the defendants were bluffing in pursuit of some gain. Two men claimed the right to an abbey provostship through marriage.[116] Abbess Agnes, "knowing their claim to be risible . . . and trusting in God for justice," commanded the two to appear in court to undergo trial by battle. Their courage failed them, and they meekly gave up the claim, swearing in the abbess's hands to drop their case.

If one compares the legal administration of abbesses and abbots, they seem very alike. But might female judges be expected to show more mercy than their male counterparts? One case seems at first glance to support that possibility. The bishop of Orléans heard a case between the nuns of Voisins and Stephen of Genvriac.[117] The nuns charged that "Stephen had buried alive a certain woman thief, that is to say, in the land of the nuns next to the Abbey of Voisins, in prejudice and wrong to the nuns." Might this not be an expression of the nuns' horror at the grisly execution or the severity of the sentence for thievery? Not so; in fact, what was at issue was the nuns' desire to defend their own jurisdiction, since Stephen was poaching on their turf. The bishop worked out a compromise in which the nuns gave Stephen a piece of land eighteen feet by twelve alongside

114. *Cartulaire de Notre-Dame de Saintes*, p. 163, no. 250, ca. 1166–67.
115. *Cartulaire de Notre-Dame de Saintes*, pp. 148–49, no. 228, 1100–1107.
116. *Cartulaire de Notre-Dame de Saintes*, p. 93, no. 113, 1134–51.
117. *Cartulaire de Notre-Dame de Voisins*, pp. 5–6, no. 5, 1252.

the road and next to the woods as a place where he could erect a gallows. Stephen and his wife and brother-in-law promised in exchange to forswear any further efforts to exercise justice on the nuns' lands. The nuns of Voisins sound exceedingly hard-boiled, but religious women did at times express sensibilities about the results of medieval justice. Abbess Margaret of Faremoutiers successfully petitioned the king to have his official move the site for executions from right outside the convent's front gate, for the "horrible spectacle of the gibbet itself and the intolerable problem of the smell of rotting corpses hanging" bothered the nuns.[118] Individual abbesses or abbots might be particularly gifted at getting at the truth, individual monasteries might dispense justice in a particularly evenhanded way, but a monastic superior's exercise of juridical authority depended on how rich, elite, and powerful the monastery was rather than on the gender of its inhabitants.

Conclusion

In the hierarchical world of the Middle Ages, the bulk of administrative power within a monastery of nuns or of monks belonged to the superior, who in the eleventh century acted for the community and by the thirteenth century acted with the community. Outside the monastery the superior was a person of importance, one who wielded *auctoritas*. A medieval abbess was capable of facing down an army of clerics and workmen over a stinking corpse. She was often the chief executive of an elaborate pyramid of dependent houses and the judge presiding over a trial by combat or by boiling water. She approved loans and mortgages and struggled to maximize income and contain expenses. One scholar has even suggested that during the eleventh century she may have enjoyed greater independence than her fellow abbots, who were "answerable to more outside people and pressures."[119]

Those under her rule were often a motley collection of people, some professed, some employed, some in retirement, and the clerics who performed the sacraments. These clerical men represented a continuing challenge to conventual leadership; some became good friends and servitors of the nuns, but many others wanted much

---

118. André Galli, "Faremoutiers au Moyen Age VIIe–XVe siècle," in *Sainte Fare et Faremoutiers: Treize siècles de vie monastique* (Faremoutiers: Abbaye de Faremoutiers, 1956), p. 50.

119. Mary Skinner, "Abbesses in Action in Carolingian and Cluniac France," paper presented at the Seventh Berkshire Conference in Women's History, Wellesley College, June 1987, p. 17.

from the nuns they served and sometimes repaid them with excessive monetary demands, hostility, or too intimate relations with those sworn to chastity.

Regular houses were part of various jurisdictions. Interior partitions developed between offices of a monastery; exterior ties bound many houses into larger family networks of monasteries; and regionally every monastery was part of the system for administering justice. Monasteries grew ever more inwardly fragmented and compartmentalized over the central Middle Ages. Monastic officers came to have their own jurisdiction over some part of the monastery, like the infirmary or the food stores of the house, and rival monastic fiefdoms sometimes developed, to the detriment of the community. Paralleling this complicated decentralization of individual houses were the intricate relations of different houses as mother and daughter or elder and younger sister.

A consideration of the structure of medieval convents reveals both the unique opportunity these houses afforded to women and the dangerous faults in the system. Just by existing in the central Middle Ages, nunneries provided an arena in which women could exercise administrative and legal abilities. Abbesses and prioresses functioned as the powerful heads of their communities, elected by their fellow nuns. In no institution other than monasticism could women participate so fully in shaping their own lives. This is not to say medieval monasticism was democratic: far from it. In the nunnery, however, although birth added to prestige, offices were not determined solely by class, and a woman's ability could help her rise to a prominent position. The convent was the only institution in which a woman might direct the women and men under her care as a result of her election to power rather than owing solely to her birth.

6

THE FINANCES

I NSTITUTIONS —even those devoted to prayer—need income to exist, a need that creates immediate tension for monasteries committed to voluntary poverty. The uneasy solution that developed was to distinguish the individual from the corporate. Thus, although monastics were sworn personally to giving up the ownership of property, their monasteries were the greatest landowners of the early Middle Ages, and by our period they were still substantial holders of real estate. There are many studies of monastic financial affairs, particularly of land management by monks.[1] Few studies, however, deal with women's houses, because of both a past lack of scholarly curiosity about nunneries and a daunting dearth of manorial and estate records from women's houses. Much of the valuable current work in English is concentrating on women and their secular work in late medieval and early modern Europe, but French scholars are beginning to venture into the world of monastic women and their economic activities.[2]

1. Jean-Pierre Kempf, *L'abbaye de Cherlieu, XIIe–XIIIe siècles: Economie et société* (Vesoul: Société d'Agriculture, Lettres, Sciences et Arts de la Haute-Saône, 1976); Edmund King, *Peterborough Abbey, 1086–1310: A Study in the Land Market* (Cambridge: Cambridge University Press, 1973); J. A. Raftis, *The Estate of Ramsey Abbey* (Toronto: Pontifical Institute of Mediaeval Studies, 1957); Eleanor Searle, *Lordship and Community: Battle Abbey and Its Banlieu, 1066–1538* (Toronto: Pontifical Institute of Mediaeval Studies, 1974), for example, all deal with land management.

2. Most notable among the new Continental studies is L'Hermite-Leclercq, *Monachisme féminin*. Important English-language works include Bennett, *Women in the Medieval English Countryside*; Martha Howell, *Women, Production, and Patriarchy in Late Medieval Cities* (Chicago: University of Chicago Press, 1986); Merry Wiesner, *Working Women in Renaissance Germany* (New Brunswick, N.J.: Rutgers University Press, 1986); Hanawalt, *Women and Work in Preindustrial Europe;* and Lindsay Charles and Lorna Duffin, eds., *Women and Work in Pre-industrial England* (London: Croom Helm, 1985).

Since one of the purposes of my book is to investigate attitudes about religious women, material on the finances of nunneries might seem out of place. After all, money seems practical and concrete, remote from the subtlety of minds and feelings. Yet looking into the purses of nunneries reveals much about those who carried them: of how the world outside the cloister evaluated nuns and of how religious women envisioned who they were.

ECONOMIC ACTIVITIES

One of the ironies of the religious life for women is that it inadvertently broke many patriarchal rules, notably in the areas of economic management and administration. For instance, the direction of *Innenwirtschaft*, or household economy, traditionally is women's responsibility in most preindustrial societies, and as monasteries became large and complex in the early Middle Ages, nuns expanded this overseeing to include caring for the work of both servants and lay sisters and brothers, the planting and harvesting of gardens and orchards, and the storage and allotment of food supplies, wine, and clothing. Although theoretically confined to the cloister, monastic women also took responsibility for that area traditionally assigned to men, the *Aussenwirtschaft*, or field economy. By the central Middle Ages it had become uncommon for nuns to labor in the fields; indeed, no indication of their manual labor surfaced in the records I used. But even when male provosts and bailiffs worked for a convent, final responsibility and authority rested with the nuns.

The convents of our period typically derived income from two sources: exploiting the land and manipulating money. Monasteries tended in general to be rather good land managers. By the central Middle Ages the exploitation of land had become very sophisticated and involved both direct working of demesne lands (lands kept by a medieval lordship for its own direct use) and receiving indirect benefits of dues and services from dependent peasants. Handling money to generate income, on the other hand, came less easily to monasteries—both of nuns and of monks—although particularly Montivilliers and Notre-Dame in Saintes used considerable business acumen to generate income.

Land and Its Exploitation

The demesne lands of a monastery were plowed, planted, and harvested by servants and by peasants who owed corvée, work days, to their lord. The peasant families that held tenure of farms like those of Andrevenea and Malmiro owed the nuns who were their lords *opera manuum*, or corvée.[3] This work was used to bring in the crops from the lands directly managed by the monastery. But by the central Middle Ages the era when a monastery might profitably farm huge tracts of its own lands was over. A monastery might begin its own planting of a vineyard and then recognize that the yields would be better if the land was leased to peasants to work directly, in exchange for rent paid to the abbey as lord as in the case of Ronceray's vineyard. By the end of the eleventh century, nuns and monks had turned over the bulk of their real property to semidependent peasant farmers, who worked their farms and gave part of the harvest back to their lords.

The twenty-three holdings of Vix owed the nunnery of Notre-Dame substantial supplies of oats and hay over the course of a year, as well as fifteen hens and loaves of bread, sixteen days of carting goods or ferrying personnel to the mother abbey, and dues from the sale of pigs and sheep totaling twenty-five solidi and one penny.[4] Since these holdings were over a hundred kilometers away from the mother house, converting the dues that had originally been in kind as piglets and lambs into cash payments was practical, as well as requiring days of carting service or the use of horses to transport nuns and their servants at this far-flung property to and from the home abbey. Dues owed were usually arrived at logically. Thus coastal properties often owed customs that included catches of fish or eels, while holdings in forested areas paid loads of firewood or contributed honey. A part of whatever the tenants could glean from their lands had to be returned to the monastic lordship as payment for the tenure.

But the system had obvious flaws, the most common being that those who farmed the land and sweated to get the most they could from fields, forests, and fisheries came to think of the farms as their own, not as tenements held from a lord. Thus it happened that a tenant like the Breton farmer Guidifen could claim he held land freely as inherited property and not as a tenement.[5] The nuns imprisoned him for a year until he came to his senses, for such claims threatened the fabric of their lordship. As landlords in this case as in others, religious women were notably firm and unsentimental.

A number of social and economic shifts in the central Middle Ages led to a decreasing peasant population tied to servile tenancies.

3. *Cartulaire de Notre-Dame de Saintes*, pp. 113–14, nos. 154–55.
4. *Cartulaire de Notre-Dame de Saintes*, pp. 151–53, no. 231.
5. *Cartulaire de Saint-Georges de Rennes*, 9:250, no. 21, after 1054.

With fewer peasants owing corvée to a monastic lordship and with a money economy growing stronger and more sophisticated, monasteries had to evolve with the rest of society if they were to survive. This many of them did by converting properties from tenancies owing work service and dues to rental properties owing cens.[6] This was easier for some houses than for others. In general the urban monasteries seemed quicker to perceive the advantage and more apt to have appropriate holdings than did rural houses. The Paraclete and Notre-Dame-aux-Nonnains, two nunneries in the orbit of the great fairs of Champagne, were particularly canny about maximizing income in this way.

Some of the earlier rental property of the Paraclete was small and brought in negligible returns: two arable fields yielded five solidi and ten pennies, and a piece of a vineyard produced two barrels of red wine a year.[7] But the nunnery began to turn more of its holdings into rental income with good returns, like those from its property in the town of Châtel de Nogent. The nuns rented out this space, which was bounded by the grange of Michael Hall, the place of Colet Morot, and the public bakery, to Martin le Chopins and his wife Margaret.[8] Martin and Margaret agreed to pay an annual rent of ten solidi to the nuns each Easter; this high return of half a pound for a small space suggests this was commercial space where the couple's business was expected to flourish. Another couple rented a farm with sixty arpents of arable land from the Paraclete, paying the high rent of ten pounds a year.[9] After the couple's death, the farm was to revert to the abbey and could not be inherited by the heirs. The nuns were on to a good thing; much greater value could be gained by renting this farmstead than by settling it on a servile tenant.

A danger to the landlord was that inflation would make low, fixed rents unprofitable. If monasteries were alert to this problem, they could and did renegotiate the rents, but clearly this required both the financial expertise to recognize that an inflationary spiral was outstripping rent levels and the stature to talk the tenants into accepting higher rents. When Abbess Stephanie took office at Notre-Dame in Saintes in 1220, one of her early actions was to look over the rental levels set by her predecessor, Abbess Aldeburge. Unfortunately, the cartulary of her abbey comes to an abrupt end with just

6. Little, *Religious Poverty and the Profit Economy*, p. 183, defines *cens* as the "obligation to pay an annual return from a property."

7. *Cartulaire du Paraclet*, p. 254, no. 288, 1270, p. 265, no. 302, 1290.

8. *Cartulaire du Paraclet*, p. 266, no. 303, 1292.

9. *Cartulaire du Paraclet*, p. 269, no. 307, 1295.

three charters dating from her first year in office.[10] But since all three are involved in some way with reexamining income, it is probable that Stephanie was launching a concerted attack on low-yield holdings. She required new rental fees from John of Oleron of five solidi (up from three solidi) for an oven and eighty cuttlefish (up from fifty) for a moor; the new abbess seems to have begun her reign with a vigorous move to increase revenues by avoiding old cens that were "a grievous burden and prejudice" to the abbey. Not all abbesses had the experience or the ability to improve their finances. In 1281 Pope Martin IV warned the Norman Abbey of Saint-Amand that it should call in leases and raise rents to deal with its financial crisis.[11] The cartulary entries do not show such a response. Were the nuns of Saint-Amand not particularly adept at handling finances, or were they loath to gouge tenants? We cannot tell.

Monastic women and men did not have time to tend to all the workaday details of managing their property at the same time that they fulfilled the *Opus Dei*. Servants, serfs, and hired officials took up the slack for monks as well as for nuns. When Archbishop Eudes Rigaud visited the monks of Saint-Martin in Pontoise, he was horrified at the muddle he uncovered.[12] The prior was trying to run two houses at once, and the monks had gotten into a terrible state, having been saddled by debts and lacking even enough food to sustain themselves. Eudes sent his own brother Adam and another cleric back to try and sort out the mess, and then a few weeks later he wrote the abbot a sizzling letter, ordering him to fire clerics and hire "a cleric or a secular priest, whose aid and counsel he should use in handling the temporal affairs of his abbey." When monastics bungled their finances, they needed a new business manager.

Monks generally used employees to deal with a wide variety of routine affairs, not only as a desperation measure when they were mired in mismanagement. For instance, the monks of Holy Trinity employed provosts, one of whom seems to have felt warmly enough about the men he served to make donations to them, while the monks of Saint-Pierre, Corbie, and Watten appointed procurators to act officially for them in legal and business affairs.[13]

10. *Cartulaire de Notre-Dame de Saintes*, pp. 177–79, nos. 274–75, 1220, settles tithes, which are both "ad opus abbatisse"; p. 179, no. 276, 1220, renegotiates the cens.

11. Le Cacheux, *Histoire de Saint-Amand*, p. 65.

12. ER, pp. 355, 357.

13. *Cartulaire de la Trinité de Vendôme*, 2:369, no. 529, 1151; *Cartulaire de Notre-Dame de Bourbourg*, 1:103, no. 104, ca. 1208, p. 172, no. 181, 1270.

Women's houses also had male provosts and procurators acting for them. Brother Odo, the priest of the convent of Saint-Rémy in Senlis, acted as procurator for the nuns in a quarrel adjudicated in Paris, and the procurator for Voisins acted in the nunnery's name to collect a legacy left to the abbey.[14] The men designated to handle nunneries' affairs acted in the same sorts of cases and with the same kind of powers as did those who worked for male monasteries. This point is worth emphasizing, since the use of such officials was a monastic rather than a purely female strategy for managing property.

Banking and Trade

Women's houses also joined actively in the money markets of their day when possible, lending money, buying rents, and making profits out of trade. The lending of money by monastic institutions may seem inappropriate to modern people, who feel that those dedicated to God's service should be above the mundane business of charging interest. Such a view, however, romanticizes the medieval monastic house, which was an institutional entity, necessarily encumbered with all the financial, legal, and social responsibilities and involvements of any substantial institution. But even if we accept that monasteries managed money, surely they should not lend money at interest when the church forbade usury? Whatever Rome's fulminations, monasteries routinely served as credit institutions.[15]

Both medieval male monasteries and nunneries issued mortgages on land or on income, usually to people of the upper ranks of society. Different practices evolved in various parts of northern France. In Normandy, for instance, the monastic mortgage was popular in the eleventh and twelfth centuries but was on the way out by the beginning of the next century; however, it was still an active type of loan, particularly on the collateral of tithes, in much of the rest of the area during the thirteenth century.[16] A typical transaction was that of the Abbey of Lieu-Notre-Dame-lès-Romorantin, which lent fifty pounds to the knight Philip Tenerius against a mortgage on half the tithe due on his vines of La Landoniere.[17] His overlords agreed, and

14. Paris, BN, MS. lat. 11002, fol. 31r; *Cartulaire de Notre-Dame de Voisins*, p. 98, no. 94, 1248.

15. Little, *Religious Poverty and the Profit Economy*, p. 179. For a general treatment see Benjamin Nelson, *The Idea of Usury from Tribal Brotherhood to Universal Otherhood*, 2d ed. (Chicago: University of Chicago Press, 1969).

16. Génestal, *Rôle des monastères,* p. 84.

17. *Cartulaire du Lieu-Notre-Dame-lès–Romorantin*, no. 94, p. 66, March 1232, is the record by the bishop of Orléans of the mortgage, and no. 93, p. 66, May 1232, records the consent of the count and countess of Chartres to the arrangement.

his family recorded their consent to the arrangement, which meant that half the tithe would be paid directly to the convent until Philip redeemed the loan. Not all those who negotiated mortgages with convents were, however, from the noble ranks of society; some came from the wealthy burgher class, as did the three siblings Peter, William, and Eremburge, who mortgaged an entire tithe to the nuns of Voisins for sixty-seven pounds.[18] In general, monastic mortgages tended to be offered to a somewhat restricted group of the wealthy but issued from a broad range of houses. For instance, both Lieu and Voisins were Cistercian houses, which were as common among the monasteries lending money as the old-line Benedictine institutions.

Usually the charters do not mention what need impelled a borrower to approach a monastery for a mortgage, except when someone needed cash to go on pilgrimage, and sometimes the language intentionally obfuscates the real activity. Robert Tarzate, a clerk, lacked the resources to finance a trip to Jerusalem in 1166; his mother and four brothers agreed to mortgage a vineyard tithe to the Abbey of Notre-Dame in Saintes to obtain some ready cash.[19] The transaction was made more palatable—perhaps because the borrower was a cleric—by phrasing it as a gift of the tithe to pay for the illumination of the church, yet Robert received from the abbess twenty solidi on the collateral of the family property.

Although mortgages in the region of northern France tended to fund only those from the upper levels of society, there were exceptions. The Abbey of Notre-Dame sometimes invested capital in mortgages for simpler folk. For instance, Abbess Agnes of Barbezieux used a flexible, multifaceted approach to settle a complicated wrangle with one family, which included granting them a mortgage of four pounds on their lands.[20]

But nunneries could embark on bold financial ventures, making speculative loans to peasants based on their probable increased income. Matilda, abbess of Bourbourg in the early thirteenth century, negotiated a loan to a group of *hospites*, free peasants, to ditch and drain some newly assarted or cleared land.[21] She lent them one hundred pounds on the surety of pledges from three men, Folcran, Balg, and Tristram, and one woman, Alvidim, the widow of a knight. The

18. *Cartulaire de Notre-Dame de Voisins*, no. 29, p. 31, 1222. See other examples of monastic mortgages for tithes: *Cartulaire du Paraclet*, p. 163, no. 165, 1221, and Paris, BN, MS. lat. 10997 fols. 16r–17r.

19. *Cartulaire de Notre-Dame de Saintes*, p. 49, no. 45, 1166.

20. *Cartulaire de Notre-Dame de Saintes*, p. 87, no. 102, 1168.

21. *Cartulaire de Notre-Dame de Bourbourg*, 1:110–11, no. 114, 1218.

terms of the agreement were that the debt was due in a year, and if
the borrowers could not pay back the loan in full by Saint George's
Day of the following year, the abbey could seize and hold the goods
of the pledges. However, the charter acknowledges the difficulty of
draining and reclaiming land by giving the *hospites* a few years of
grace on the interest: they did not have to pay cens while involved
in the ditching project or for the first two years after its completion.

The convent may well have been taking a risk, since the four
pledges, identified without surnames, probably were of modest
means. If the borrowers defaulted on the debt, seizure of their property might well have barely covered the loan, causing the abbey to
lose money. On the other hand, Bourbourg was investing capital in
long-term improvements of its lands, which if the group of farmers
was knowledgeable and hardworking, would pay off in higher cens
for the future. The monastery that lent money may have taken a
chance with its capital, but when it made loans to peasants the risk
was generally taken for the sake of improving property.

Less risk was involved when monastics allowed a tenant to mortgage property to a third party. John of Doillet was burdened with
heavy debts, so with the consent of the abbess of Notre-Dame-aux-
Nonnains, from whom he held his land, he mortgaged his property
to his cousin Herbert for fifty-five pounds.[22] John had four years'
grace to redeem his lands; if he failed to come up with the money
in that time, the abbess could pay the debt and take over the property. This clause put the nuns in a strong position, which was bolstered by the further stipulation that if the rent of forty solidi due
from the tenement was not paid on time, the abbess could seize the
property and its income until satisfaction was received. Third-party
loans on land held from a monastery could be carefully negotiated
to be safe for the institution and potentially lucrative if the borrower
failed to repay in time.

During the thirteenth century monasteries in northern France became for all practical purposes agricultural banks by buying up cens,
or perpetual rents.[23] Some of these were "old rents" paid by a third
party, while the rest—and these came to dominate this market—

22. *Documents de Notre-Dame-aux-Nonnains*, p. 19, no. 16, 1205.

23. Génestal, *Rôle des monastères*, chap. 4, deals with the perpetual rents, and it is
he who terms monasteries "véritables banques agricoles" (p. 211). Although these
sales were by nature a type of loan, they were also really permanent: a charter from
La Presle that records the sale of rents by a couple to a bourgeois of Reims contains
the promise that the sellers will never try to buy back the rent: Carré, "Ste. Marguerite de la Presle," 5(1893): 352–53, no. 59, 1277.

were "new rents" paid directly by the landowner. Monastic houses bought the new rents from peasants, who were often under their own lordship, for a lump payment that allowed the landowner to invest in improvements. For example, Martin Riche, a villein, and his wife, Juliana, sold rents of fourteen solidi to the Abbey of Saint-Amand in 1217 for the sum of seven pounds.[24] This is a rate of 10 percent interest, just above the average for Saint-Amand's purchases of rents of 9.88 percent. Let us theorize that before this transaction Martin and Juliana had harvested from their fields enough to have seed for the following year, as well as grain to feed their family, and also a small surplus to sell. If they used the seven pounds to pay for intensive fertilization of their fields, their harvest would have increased markedly, so that after setting aside grain for seed and for their own bread, they could pay the abbey the annual rent of fourteen shillings and have a more substantial surplus to sell.

Peasants ventured into these contracts with the expectation of increasing their yield, and monasteries anticipated reliable payments that would fund particular needs such as charitable responsibilities, the purchase of nuns' habits, or repairs to their buildings. When all went well, the farmer increased his income and the monastery regularized its operating funds. The danger to the borrower was that if productivity did not increase, the monastery could seize cattle and impose fines; the danger to the lender was that it could tie up too much capital so that no liquid assets were available to pay for rebuilding after a fire, to meet expensive court costs, or to cover other such exigencies that required cash. However, these transactions became so common in the thirteenth century that they probably were most often mutually satisfactory.

The sale of old rents was less common and probably less constructive; when the knight William de Fraxino sold some rents from one of his own manors, he probably did not reinvest the nine pounds he received from the nuns of Saint-Sulpice in improving the lands of that manor, farmed by one of his tenants.[25] William received a quick cash fix, but if he frittered away the nine pounds, his economic state would be worse after the loan than before it, since he had forfeited the steady income of the rents.

Although in the lending and borrowing of money convents were often the institutional source of funds, sometimes it was they who needed to borrow. Both nunneries and male houses were forced from

24. Rouen, BD, H 55, Cartulary of Saint-Amand, fols. 35v–36r.
25. *Cartulaire de Saint-Sulpice-la-Forêt*, p. 250, no. 155, 1270.

time to time to obtain loans using lands or liturgical objects as collateral. Eudes Rigaud had occasion to scold both the nuns of Bondeville and the monks of Eu for pawning chalices when they were desperate for funds, and the incidence of floating loans does not seem to have been significantly higher for nunneries than for male houses.[26] It is interesting that at the same time that Bondeville was hocking its plate, it was busily buying up perpetual rents, so that its being poor may have been as much a function of overinvestment and cash flow problems as a matter of real penury.[27] A dwindling cash flow accounts for the need of the nuns of Notre-Dame-aux-Nonnains to pawn a censer to a laywoman in 1216, since two years later they were buying up property for 111 pounds.[28] To be driven to borrowing by a financial shortfall was not, however, the plight of nunneries alone. Indeed, the famous case of Cluny's indebtedness underlines that even the most eminent of houses could be impelled to borrow money.[29]

The economic activities of monasteries included direct interactions with borrowers and lenders, since religious houses, particularly in rural areas, were primary sources of credit; but monasteries had a hand in commerce as well as banking. Most often an abbey profited from trade through taxes or dues on the merchants or their merchandise, most commonly by levying tolls at vulnerable points in trade routes such as valleys, bridges, and ferries, as well as by imposing tolls on traffic passing by its walls.[30] Religious houses, like the lay nobility, had acquired the royal power to tax during the breakdown of the centralized Carolingian monarchy in the ninth century. In addition, monasteries continued through our period to receive donations from benefactors of their rights to tolls on the transportation of goods. The noble family of Sequin Beraud gave the

26. ER, pp. 337, 113. Villarceaux pawned a book of homilies and some silk copes when the house was short on funds (p. 209).

27. Rouen, BD, Notre-Dame de Bondeville, 52 H, carton 1, is full of charters recording thirteenth-century monastic purchases of property and perpetual rents. For instance, eleven charters for the 1250s survive, all recording purchases made by the abbey: six are purchases of land, and five are purchases of rents. By the 1270s, of the seven charters that are extant, one is for buying land and the other six are for purchasing rents.

28. *Documents de Notre-Dame-aux-Nonnains,* pp. 28–29, no. 33, 1216, p. 31, no. 38, 1218.

29. Little, *Religious Poverty and the Profit Economy,* pp. 68–69.

30. Jean-Marc Bienvenu, "Recherches sur les péages angevins aux XIe et XIIe siècles," *Moyen Age* 12(1957): 209. This article describes the general use of tolls as well as quantifying the exact particulars of tolls in the county.

nuns of Notre-Dame the right to collect river tolls on the Charente
River both coming and going from Saintes to Taillebourg.[31] Such a
gift was extremely valuable, since the deplorable state of the roads
in twelfth-century France made river transportation the preferred
choice where available. By the thirteenth century the donations had
shrunk, and instead of getting the right to tax travelers and merchandise, monasteries usually received an annual cash payment
from a toll, like the twenty solidi given the nuns of Notre-Dame-
aux-Nonnains from the toll of Cantumerule.[32]

Monasteries near the Atlantic Ocean benefited from the development of seagoing trade. Saint-Sulpice's priory of Locmaria on the
coast had rights over the sale of ships in the harbor; the Abbey of
Montivilliers, which was adjacent to Le Havre on the English Channel, had economic rights over the maritime commerce developing
in the port of Harfleur.[33] Hall and Sweeney argue persuasively that
Harfleur served as a significant port for the wine trade and probably
for whaling from early in the eleventh century; they suggest that
Montivilliers may have played a part in this important commercial
growth. Certainly the Abbey of Montivilliers was much involved in
business in its area and had a hand in developing the cloth and
leather industry in western Normandy.[34]

If a religious house happened to be in a coastal region such as the
deltas of the Gironde and Charente rivers, it could be part of the
vital and lucrative salt trade. The Saintongeais Abbey of Notre-
Dame owned many salt pans and kept close tabs on this property.
The value of the salt-producing boggy areas meant that claims and
seizures were not uncommon and that they were often a subject of
litigation. The archbishop of Bourges and the bishop of Saintes recorded the settlement in favor of the abbess of Notre-Dame in one
such case where salt pans given the abbey by the widow Maximillia
had been seized by Urso Porchareu.[35] When the date was set for the
case, both parties came with their friends. The prelates' words in
the charter have a sound of weary resignation: "What more? the narrative of the abbess having been accepted and the response of Urso

31. *Cartulaire de Notre-Dame de Saintes*, pp. 62–63, no. 65, 1137.
32. *Documents de Notre-Dame-aux-Nonnains*, p. 21, no. 20, 1208.
33. *Cartulaire de Saint-Sulpice-la-Forêt*, p. 436, no. 239, 1224; Edwin Hall and
James Ross Sweeney, "The 'Licentia de Nam' of the Abbess of Montivilliers and the
Origins of the Port of Harfleur," *Bulletin of the Institute for Historical Research*
52(1979): 1–8.
34. Aubert, "Abbaye de Montivilliers," p. 12.
35. *Cartulaire de Notre-Dame de Saintes*, pp. 154–55, no. 236, 1137.

having been heard, we judged the investiture of the land to the abbess" and witnessed the payment by Urso of one hundred cuttlefish to the abbess as reparation.

Monasteries situated inland, away from the coast or any sizable and navigable rivers, missed out on the benefit of the maritime and commercial activities linked to water trade. But even a religious house in an agrarian setting might find ways of entering into the commercial life of its area. One way was through building and operating ovens, forges, and mills. The exercise of banal lordship by many monasteries gave them the power to create monopolies. Lords could demand that their tenants pay for baking bread in the lord's oven, shoeing draft animals at the lord's forge, and grinding grain in the lord's mill. Mills were particularly profitable, and in the eleventh and twelfth centuries mills were an important type of gift to monasteries. But by the thirteenth century the donations were more often part of the dues generated by a mill rather than the whole mill itself. The count of Nantes made a grant to the nuns of Saint-Sulpice in 1149 that included several mills, but the economic picture had changed by the next century so that gifts like one in 1226 from the count of Saint-Pol to the nuns of Pont-aux-Dames of ten measures of grain from a mill were becoming common.[36]

Since mills were valuable, they—like salt pans—were often a source of contention. The nuns of Bondeville brought suit against Giles, their local lord, for building two fishponds on a stream above one of their mills.[37] The ponds lowered the waterpower so the mill no longer ground effectively and added insult to injury by reducing the harvest of eels. Arbitrators chosen by both sides resolved the conflict by insisting that the ponds be removed but requiring the nuns to pay the lord fifteen solidi for the labor of tearing them down.

From time to time nunneries became involved in finances at the most fundamental level—minting money and setting standards—as did the Abbey of Notre-Dame in Saintes, which received the gift of minting rights from its founders, Agnes and Geoffrey Martel.[38] This was a privilege enjoyed by few monasteries, however, even those of rich monks.

Monasteries within towns benefited from the commercial life of

36. Paris, BN, MS. fr. 4669, fol. 48r; *Cartulaire de Saint-Sulpice-la-Forêt*, p. 134, no. 58, 1149.

37. Rouen, BD, Notre-Dame de Bondeville, 52 H, liasse titres généraux, French copy of charter from February 1268.

38. *Cartulaire de Notre-Dame de Saintes*, p. 3, no. 1, 1047.

the urban environment, particularly from local markets and fairs. Even the most modest trading was potentially taxable. The nunnery of Saint-Georges in Rennes enjoyed an ancient custom in the mid-eleventh century of receiving one bottle of wine for each tun of wine sold in the abbey's cemetery, where the town held its market.[39] Real estate in the marketplace could also generate good income, such as a stall in the local market or even just a shop window looking out on the marketplace.[40] If a monastery could exercise enough power in a rich trading area, as did Notre-Dame-aux-Nonnains in Troyes, it could be "the primary recipient of the increasing economic benefits of the great fairs held in Troyes."[41]

In sum, medieval monasteries—those peopled by women as well as by men—participated in the monetary and commercial activity of their region. Whether the house was perched on a rocky Breton shore, nestled in the rolling fields of Normandy, or set in the bustling market town of Troyes, it shared in the economic transactions of its time and place. Yet by the thirteenth century the inhabitants of northern France were beginning to expect convents to be poorer than men's monasteries, for nuns to be "*pauperes moniales.*"[42] Were there external signs of female conventual penury? Was this perception on the part of contemporaries accurate?

Economic Woes in Convents

These questions are difficult to answer, since a definite response requires access to complete financial records for a significant number of medieval women's and men's religious houses—a luxury not available. The invaluable *Register* of Eudes Rigaud again allows gender comparisons, this time of conventual finances. In the notes from most of his visitations, Eudes recorded the income and debts of each house. By subtracting money owed to a house from its assets and then finding the mean sum for all convents and all male monasteries visited by the archbishop, we can derive figures for the mean net worth of all the houses of women and of men. The mean worth was 60 pounds for nunneries and 394 pounds for male monasteries; thus the resources of nunneries were a slim 15 percent of what male

39. *Cartulaire de Saint-Georges de Rennes*, 9:231, no. 7, ca. 1050.
40. Paris, BN, MS. lat. 11002 fol. 34v, and MS. lat. 10997, fol. 51v.
41. Geary, "Saint Helen of Athyra and the Cathedral of Troyes," p. 152.
42. Rouen, BD, Notre-Dame de Bondeville, 52 H, carton 1, undated charter of Andulf of Bracheio.

houses received. Since the Norman convent were generally bigger than their brother abbeys (convents had a mean size of 35 and male houses of 23 members), this disparity suggests that Norman nuns in the mid-thirteenth century were living in virtual penury.

Another source that allows a financial comparison of monasteries by gender is the list of taxable ecclesiastical communities compiled for the count of Flanders in 1294.[43] As England and France jockeyed with each other, Guy, count of Flanders and vassal to the French king, prepared to guard his shores so that no armaments could be shipped to the English. To fund this effort he planned to collect taxes, although whether he ever did is not known. What survives is the tax list with its assessments. The list includes seventy-five male monasteries and twenty-eight nunneries, each with a tax assessment. The average assessment for the male monasteries is sixty-six pounds, but for convents it is only twenty-four pounds, 36 percent of the men's average tax, suggesting that those who drew up the list were aware that nunneries had the significantly smaller resources.

These data are supported by other evidence. For instance, only Norman nuns kept schools as a means of bringing in revenue, a practice much denounced and rejected by the visitor.[44] Also, the fees Norman houses paid to Eudes reveal the financial difference by gender. Of the sixty-one men's monasteries he visited, three (or only 4.9 percent) had their procuration costs remitted at some time because of poverty, whereas two of the fourteen women's convents (or 14 percent) were given the same consideration when in an impoverished state. (Hospitals are not counted, since they did not have guest rooms and pay procuration.) Yet it is startling that when the mean sum of all procurations are calculated by gender, women's and men's houses shared the same mean payment of eight pounds.[45] Despite the straitened circumstances of female monasteries, this is clearly one of the financial burdens they had to bear equally. Also, what procuration a house could afford may reflect what cash it had on hand more than its actual assets or income; for example, procuration was remitted sometimes for very wealthy abbeys like Holy

43. See the edited source: Charles Piot, "L'armament des côtes de Flandre en 1294," *Compte Rendu des séances de la Commission Royale d'Histoire*, 4th ser., 11(1883): 169–77. The value of this source is such that I am using it even though some of the monasteries it encompasses are not in the francophone region of Flanders.

44. ER; see, for example, pp. 369, 471.

45. Cheney, *Episcopal Visitation of Monasteries in the Thirteenth Century*, p. 114, reports an estimate that procurations ranged from six to nine pounds.

Trinity in Vendôme when they were experiencing cash-flow problems.[46]

More telling, perhaps, is where the archbishop tended to stay while doing his quality-control rounds. Generally he put up at a monastic institution either the night before or after the actual visitation, but he invariably bypassed staying the night at a few particular houses. Four monasteries that never housed the visitor—including two men's houses, Pré and Saint-Ouen, and two convents, Bondeville and Saint-Amand—never paid any procuration because Eudes was so close to either his home base in Rouen or his comfortable manor at Déville that he routinely stayed at one of these. However, there were also two more convents not close to his home or his manor at which the archbishop never spent the night: Bival and Saint-Aubin. Instead, when visiting them he put up for the night at any of several nearby male monasteries. Why, out of all seventy-five monasteries (discounting the four already accounted for) were only two—and those of women—never hosts for the visitor? The most likely answer is that neither had a guesthouse. Since even small and modest houses could usually find some sort of accommodations—albeit simple—for the archbishop, the inability of two convents to put up their ecclesiastical overlord suggests that their facilities must have been truly rudimentary.

What income and property did it take to support a house of nuns? This is another question impossible to answer, since the size, location, age of the buildings, and commitments to charity and hospitality all created the financial needs of a monastery. The tiny Cistercian Priory of Saint-Saens housed sixteen nuns in 1257.[47] These women and the priory familia lived on income in coin and in kind from tenants, augmented by what was produced on their own demesne lands. During the year they took in a little over 144 pounds, seventy-four muids of grain, 220 chickens, and 1,100 sheep, all from dues and cens owed by tenants. Their demesne lands included 245 arable acres, 115 of which were planted in grains and legumes. The remaining 130 must have been fallow, which suggests they were using a two-field rotation system, since it is roughly half their total holdings. The nunnery owned fifty-seven sheep, eighteen cows, and a number of plow animals: twelve plow horses and a four-ox plow team. In addition, Saint-Saens had two mills, milling and straw

46. *Cartulaire de la Trinité de Vendôme*, 3:18, no. 646, 1205.
47. ER, p. 306.

rents, some woods, and the right to pasture pigs in forest lands. That is the sum total of all the priory's assets—barely sufficient to support the inhabitants of the convent. Part of the difficulty Saint-Saens experienced may have resulted from its scant eight acres of pasturage for stock; these few acres were insufficient to feed its animals, so the priory was forced to buy hay for winter fodder. Also the house had no vineyards or orchards, so the nuns were constrained to purchase wine and cider, and no fisheries, so they had to buy fish. By 1257 they had incurred a debt of over 234 pounds (almost twice their annual income in coin), and in May of that year they had run out of wine and were down to two muids of grain in the storehouse to last them until the August harvest.

Four years later the worsening financial state of the house forced the nuns to sell off some woodland property for 350 pounds on the installment plan: 120 pounds down, 230 pounds to come later.[48] This was a risky business, dependent on being able to collect the rest of what was owed them. One year later they had been paid only 40 pounds more on the woods, and six years later they were still waiting for the full payment.[49] Even more dangerous was that by disposing of some of their income-producing property they inevitably reduced their assets. But what threatened the little priory's very existence was its inability to be self-sufficient. The nuns had to purchase fodder, fish, wine, and grain, whose costs were increasing while their income was decreasing owing to a diminution of assets.

All this information was carefully recorded by that indefatigable visitor, Archbishop Eudes Rigaud. Indeed, he was apparently constitutionally unable to go to a monastery simply as a guest, for when he traveled to the Paraclete in Champagne to install his sister Maria as the new abbess, he carefully drew up a record of all the convent's possessions at the time that Maria computed with her bailiff. The Paraclete's property included income of 180 pounds, eighty-five muids of grain, and one cask of white wine. This is not dramatically larger than the income of the poverty-stricken house of Saint-Saens, and it is certain that the Paraclete housed a bigger population than did the Norman priory.[50] The big difference between the two houses is that the Paraclete had much livestock at the abbey and at its four

48. ER, p. 478.

49. ER, pp. 513, 729.

50. Although there is no record of how many nuns were at the Paraclete in the middle of the thirteenth century, ten were present at the computing, and three of the abbey's dependent priories had been limited to twenty-five or twenty nuns: *Cartu-*

granges: 23 horses, 43 oxen, 35 asses, 49 pigs, 44 cows, and 605 sheep. Thus, although the Paraclete's income in coin and grain was only marginally bigger than that of Saint-Saens, the livestock, particularly its sheep, helped make the nuns in Champagne much richer than their Norman counterparts. Since the Paraclete seems to have been financially healthy, it is probable that the demesne being farmed for the nuns was equally extensive, included vineyards and fishponds, and was substantially larger than the modest demesne of Saint-Saens.

Nunneries were not alone in experiencing straitened finances in the thirteenth century; many male monasteries were also hurt by inflation operating within the growing commercial life of the period to compound problems for the conservative, land-based resources of regular houses.[51] The ordinary expenses monasteries had to meet were many: hired laborers and repairmen had to be paid; habits, shoe, and food that could not be produced in house had to be bought. Particularly in the spring, if the previous harvest had not been abundant and the winter stores were depleted, a house had to use its cash resources or borrow to buy grain. Further, emergency expenses arising from the need to rebuild after a fire or flood could burden a monastery with cruel debts. Something of the weight of multiple financial responsibilities on a monastery comes through in the terse summary of the economic troubles of the nuns of Bondeville:

> These are the debts of the house, from the statement drawn up in the presence of the community. Two hundred twenty pounds in cash, and two muids of barley; servants' (wages) for harvest time; item, they have only enough oats to last until seeding time. They use at least sixty-eight mines of wheat a month; item, in the cellar they have six casks of wine and two of cider; item, they do not think that the buildings can be repaired for (less then) eighty pounds of Tours; item, after Easter it will be necessary to purchase for the house all victuals but bread, peas, and legumes.[52]

---

laire du Paraclet, p. 183, no. 196, 1229, p. 216, no. 238, 1244, p. 216, no. 239, 1244. One would suspect, therefore, that the mother abbey would house at least twice as many nuns as one of its large priories, or fifty choir nuns at the minimum.

51. Robert S. Lopez, *The Commercial Revolution of the Middle Ages, 950–1350* (Englewood Cliffs, N.J.: Prentice-Hall, 1971), p. 162, points out that debased coinage and heightened living costs added to financial problems.

52. ER, p. 338.

Even the most ordinary monastic practices could begin to backfire when an inflationary spiral hit, as it did in the thirteenth century. For example, inflation damaged the common monastic practice of paying pensions to retired superiors, favorite priests, and donors who had given a substantial gift as a means of securing social security at the house. An inflationary period meant that annual fixed pensions became less and less valuable, discouraging donors from becoming pensioners or *ad succurrendum* monastics at monasteries. Religious houses received most of their income from fixed rents and customs, so paying out pensions was painful enough that some houses sought and gained exemptions from fulfilling these obligations. The nuns of Saint-Avit were able to inveigle Pope Innocent II into allowing them to renege on pensions that they were finding extremely burdensome.[53] There was no way out, however, of responsibility for one's own personnel, who might live to a ripe age and need care in their dotage.

Charitable responsibilities also could not be ducked; they were at the very heart of the monastic ideal, but they too were usually predicated on a fixed sum of money. The countess of Chartres donated twelve pounds to the nuns of Lieu to pay for eucharistic wine, the celebration of her anniversary, and the feeding of a poor person annually on that occasion.[54] As food costs rose this income unfortunately stayed constant, a situation that repeated itself over and over again in the funding of monastic charity. But other financial commitments of monasteries—like paying procuration to their visitors and assessed taxes to their overlords—went up with an inflating economy, even when their incomes remained fixed.[55]

When we seek to understand the poverty of monastic institutions, it is necessary to discount some evidence that reflects short-term cash-flow difficulties rather than abject poverty. Thus, when Saint-Amand was busily buying up cens, while at the same time complaining of financial disaster, the nuns were actually short on disposable assets but long on invested ones. Certainly when a nunnery

53. Cuissard, "Abbaye de Saint-Avit," p. 172. Other houses did the same thing by getting a local prelate to dispense them from paying pensions: *Recueil du Val-Saint-Georges à Salzinnes*, p. 156, no. 125, 1253.

54. *Cartulaire du Lieu-Notre-Dame-lès-Romorantin*, p. 12, no. 5, 1230.

55. Procuration fees for Eudes's visitation expenses included coin, hay for the horses, wood, beds, and bedcovers; thus these costs reflected the local costs of commodities rather than a house's ability to pay: ER, p. 121. No procuration amounts were recorded until 1255, after which they are mostly recorded until 1269; they show what seems to be a response to local prices, since fees were low in 1255 and 1256, rose between 1257 and 1262, and declined again in the next few years.

used a major chunk of capital to purchase land, like the 360 pounds paid for such a purpose of Port-Royal, this could leave it temporarily in a tight spot.[56] When such situations are filtered out, however, there still is the likelihood that nunneries in northern France were in worse financial shape than their male confreres by the thirteenth century.

Explanations for the economic woes of women's houses have not always been convincing, particularly the "they brought it on themselves" attitude.[57] Indeed, monastics who behaved stupidly and rashly may have squandered their property; those who shocked the community might have lost the respect and donations of patrons, although this does not seem to have been the case. In fact, the common belief that convents got into financial trouble owing to their sins may have been helped along by the propaganda of those greedily eyeing their assets. Emphasizing the general breakdown of regular life in a convent certainly was a good ploy if a house of monks wanted to take it over. Who would question the decision to suppress a small, poor, debauched convent of nuns? Those eager to take over the nunnery could argue that if the convent were truly beyond hope, it was simpler to disband its inhabitants and put the conventual assets in monks' hands than to try to reform such a bad nunnery; also, it was more profitable for the monks to take over the nuns' assets than to be forced to assume the expenses of reforming the community.[58]

Although women's and men's monasteries suffered under many of the same economic pressures during the later Middle Ages, women's institutions had one notable extra expense that was not usually a problem for their male counterparts; it is this commitment that most seriously harmed their finances and their morals: nuns had to hire male clerics to say masses, hear confessions, and handle the sacramental needs of the monastic and the parochial communities. Priests had to be paid, fed, pensioned, and dealt with day to day, which could involve delicate negotiations about their duties as well as possible chaperonage to protect the chastity of the women they

56. *Cartulaire de Porrois*, p. 215, no. 227, 1244.

57. Henri Vendel, "Etude sur l'abbaye d'Almenêches de sa fondation à l'an 1599," in *Positions des thèses de l'Ecole des Chartes* (Paris: A. Picard, 1921), p. 116, concludes that "la pauvreté du monastère est due surtout aux désordres des religieuses."

58. *Cartulaire de Jully-les-Nonnains*, pp. 253–54. The monks of Molesme annexed the possessions of Jully and closed the convent in 1456 because they maintained the nunnery was beyond hope. Galli, "Faremoutiers," p. 42: "Il était souvent plus facile de supprimer un monastère de moniales que de le réformer."

served. The sacramental disability of religious women left them open to the costs of maintaining clerics—costs that depleted their economic resources and could damage their professions.

The flip side of this development was that priestly communities of monks, canons, or secular priests who were free of this major expense could generate income by celebrating masses themselves, thereby doubling the economic gap between women's and men's houses. The economic inequities of women's sacramental disability are of enormous importance in understanding the past, and they continue today to create a two-tiered monastic system. A French monastic who sits on his order's budget committee reported to me that a male monastery of forty monks generates from their stipends for celebrating masses alone 40 percent of the total income of a neighboring nunnery of seventy nuns.

CONCLUSION

The very nature of medieval monasticism—its recruits, endowment, and mission—led the institution to participate as fully in the economic life of its society as it did in the religious and social life. If large pieces of land were changing hands, as they were in the eleventh century, monasteries became their recipients.[59] If needy folk wanted to use their property as collateral for a mortgage, monasteries lent capital. If buying up perpetual rents seemed a wise investment, monasteries acquired such income. If water trade and transportation expanded, monasteries on the riverbanks and the coast became part of that activity. Nunneries generally behaved no differently from male houses in all these interactions in the economic life of their community. And when inflation, growing population, and an accelerated money economy began to hurt conservative landowners, nunneries as well as male monasteries felt the pinch. In one way and in one way only did houses of women consistently suffer more financial burdens and fewer financial opportunities than their brother monks. Nuns could not administer the sacraments, so they had to assume the considerable cost of staffing their houses with male clerics, an expensive and often troublesome obligation that started a slow financial decline for convents that can be observed clearly by the thirteenth century.

59. Big pieces of land were also the norm for convents in the South during the eleventh century: L'Hermite-Leclercq, *Monachisme féminin*, p. 59.

PART III
ASSESSMENTS

7

RELIGIOUS PERSON RATHER

THAN WOMAN

WHAT WAS THE SELF-PERCEPTION of the cloistered medieval nun? Did she see herself first as a woman, or as a monastic, or perhaps as a member of her natal family and of her class? Was her identity a combination of these views? Second, by what means did she form her self-image? The issue of gender looms large to modern scholars as we read the diatribes of some male clerics or look back in history searching for the first stirrings of feminist consciousness. Nevertheless, the nuns who peopled the cloisters of nunneries from Therouanne to Saintes, from Nantes to Metz in the central Middle Ages probably saw themselves less consciously as women than as religious persons who happened to be female. In fact, female monastics seem to have recognized their wholeness as people who were at one and the same time women dedicated to the service of God and members of a family of birth—positioned, therefore, both in the church and in a class in society. A concentration on gender—or on its denial—was not primary to their self-definition, despite the insistence of certain highly visible and vocal male religious reformers and organizers that nuns had to reject their female nature to live the religious life. The Fathers had an enormous impact on attitudes in the church throughout the Middle Ages. Jerome, whose works were found in most monastic libraries, was the quintessential critic of female sexuality: "You must act against nature or rather above nature if you are not to exercise your natural functions, to weed out your own root, to harvest no fruit save that of virginity, to turn from the nuptial bed, to abhor contact with men, and to live in the body as if without a body."[1] Yet despite this tradition that exhorted religious women to despise and deny their female selves, medieval nuns did not ground their identity in either an affirmation or a denial of their gender; rather, since the realities of their lives in a nunnery

1. Jerome, Epistle 130, PL, 22:1116.

229

called on them to integrate their gender into the role of religious persons and of family members, nuns in the central Middle Ages synthesized a unified sense of self.

In attempting to uncover how ordinary medieval religious women perceived themselves in the absence of their own words, we have two helpful approaches: we can look at medieval society's attitudes and at nuns' behavior. First, we can assess the opinions of those around them to see how nuns were perceived, and since the surrounding world mirrored back to nuns their self-image, this became a reinforcing action in which self-confidence begat respect, which in turn bolstered self-confidence. Second, we can consider how nuns behaved in certain circumstances on the theory that the way people act is more of an index of what they think about themselves than what they say.

POSITIVE IMAGES
The Nun's Sense of Self

For religious women, the feeling of being a complete and worthy person began with their monastic profession; in the view of one twelfth-century commentator, they "rose to the holiness of nuns" on taking the veil.[2] It was a transformation of the individual woman into someone sharing a corporate monastic identity. Many of the women who became nuns in the Middle Ages had been offered to their convents as girls, leaving the institution of the family for the institution of the monastery. Early in the formative stages of their lives they had been separated from the models of their older, secular female relatives and had adopted the more senior nuns in their house as new people to emulate. In addition, the education of the novices drew on the monastic tradition they had joined, and since the history and literature of monasticism universally presented the story of the professed life through the lives and miracles of its male founders and heroes, religious women naturally learned of and identified with the experience of monks. Thus many nuns took cues on adult behavior less from their mothers than from the senior nuns of their house and the male tradition of their training.

The proportion of young, impressionable novices to mature entrants professing at convents was high at the beginning of our period. By the end, however, it seems to have shifted so that older entrants were the more sizable group. This change may partly explain the

---

2. *Libellus de diversis ordinibus et professionibus qui sunt in ecclesia*, ed. and trans. Giles Constable and Beryl Smith (Oxford: Clarendon Press, 1972), p. 5.

decline in nunneries' fortunes during the thirteenth century as older women brought to conventual life expectations shaped by secular society rather than by the monastic community.

Dedicating their lives to raising a perpetual anthem of praise to God made nuns particularly revered by their contemporaries. But even more important, they vowed themselves to chastity, and as brides of Christ became the virgins most fit to walk at the head of the procession of the Christian host. In their continence they imitated the Virgin Mary or even, in one formulation, the church.[3] The rich tradition of the nun as espoused of Christ gave professed women a unique and valued status in the Middle Ages. What this must have done to offset the other negative stereotypes we can only surmise but must not discount.

Their religious status was reinforced by the high social class of some nuns, particularly the superiors in many nunneries, whose birth imbued them with immense self-confidence. In the early eleventh century, for example, Adele, abbess of Saint-Georges in Rennes and sister of the count of Brittany, boldly opened an important charter with the words: "I, Adele, handmaiden of the handmaidens of Christ" "ego Addela, ancillarum Christi ancilla", thereby proudly assuming for herself the formula of extreme humility used by the pope.[4] Although only a few nuns in a given house might be from ducal or comital families, all their sister nuns benefited from the reflected social status of these great ladies. Elevated birth made noble nuns feel worthy of respect, and the presence of highborn nuns lent an aura of aristocratic power to the institutions where they were housed. Birth and its perquisites of power and prestige helped religious women form strong identities. But even in houses where most members were from the *petite noblesse* and where there were also many daughters of burgher families, other factors helped shape positive self-images for medieval nuns.

Daily, even hourly, the nun's positive image was reflected and reinforced by her interactions with both secular and religious people, who treated her not as a second-class monastic but as the equivalent of a monk. Lay and ecclesiastical patrons gave support and donations to both religious women and men who shared their family and class ties, and relatives visited their cloistered female and male kin. Bishops endowed, taxed, and oversaw nuns much as they did monks, and abbots shared confraternity and relics as well as circulating *rotuli*.

---

3. *Cartulaire de l'Yonne*, p. 398, no. 248, 1145.
4. *Cartulaire de Saint-Georges de Rennes*, 9:237, no. 12, 1032.

Male clerics sought the prayers of nuns and could ask, as did Peter the Venerable, "that you will think me worthy to be remembered, and will pray for the mercy of the Almighty upon me."[5] Even important church councils could be held at a convent, as was the Council of Jouarre in 1133–34.[6]

The interactions between community and convent were not always respectful and dignified; but even when a community was angered by the actions of a nunnery—as when the townspeople rioted in response to the destruction of a bawdy house by the nuns of Salzinnes—it was clear that the nuns were to be reckoned with.[7] To their neighbors, religious women were landlords or landholders, patrons or clients, protectors or judges, the source of charity, prayers, and comfort. In other words, medieval nunneries fulfilled a number of religious and social functions in their society: they were useful institutions whose members contributed to the well-being of the community. When, for instance, a patron gave the nuns a donation that funded anniversary prayers for his death and social services for the poor, the donor, the nuns, and society all benefited from the exchange.[8]

Society's View of Nuns

The interactive convent as described above does not conform to the picture of tightly cloistered medieval nunneries sketched by Georges Duby, who writes that "the main function of such houses was to keep a close watch over those who lived there and, to a lesser degree, to educate them." He describes convents as somewhat rude finishing schools in which girls were kept virginal and from which nubile young women were extracted when families wanted to make marriage alliances. He states further that although nuns performed the *Opus Dei*, their prayers were not valued, since "effective orisons came from male mouths only."[9] How accurate is Duby's description?

5. *Letters of Abelard and Heloise*, p. 286.

6. Jean Quéguiner, "Jouarre au XIIe et au XIIIe siècles," in *L'abbaye royale Notre-Dame de Jouarre*, 2 vols. (Paris: Bibliothèque d'Histoire et d'Architecture Chrétiennes, 1961), 1:91.

7. Simenon, *Julienne de Cornillon*, p. 83.

8. See, for example, the gift of Thomas, dean of the chapter of Saint-Aubain: *Recueil du Val-Saint-Georges à Salzinnes*, p. 159, no. 129, 1257.

9. Duby, *Knight, the Lady and the Priest*, p. 260. This is the same conclusion reached for English nuns by Janet Burton, who says that nuns' "prayers were somehow less effective than those of men." Janet Burton, "The Yorkshire Nunneries in the Twelfth and Thirteenth Centuries," *Borthwick Papers* 56(1979): 2.

Nunneries certainly included among their functions the warehousing and educating of females, but the documents show that they were more than holding tanks. Charter after charter records the gifts and petitions made to women's houses by medieval people seeking to share in the nuns' prayers. The gift of a parish to the abbess and convent of Saint-Georges in Rennes, for example, was made in 1034 by Count Alan, who sought the remission of his sins and the reward of eternal life "through the intercession of the saint and the prayers of the holy nuns."[10] Such sentiments are expressed over and over again, but though they might be suspected of masking a desire for more worldly rewards, in many cases the only benefit received was what was requested: the nuns' prayers. In the midtwelfth century when Count Henry of Champagne was on pilgrimage to Vézelay, he stopped at the convent of Jully-les-Nonnains to visit its nuns—women, he says, renowned for their holiness.[11] The count confirmed all the nuns' holdings in Bar-sur-Aube, and in return he received the gift of their prayers and their annual celebration of his anniversary.

At the close of the thirteenth century the concern to help nuns and to receive their prayers continued to motivate gifts to convents. The countess of Alençon records in one charter that "having heard of the good reputation of the religious women, the abbess and convent of Voisins, a Cistercian house in the diocese of Orléans, I went there to recommend myself to the ladies and to request their prayers for us to God . . . and so that we should merit to be partakers in the prayers and in the good works, which they do for their benefactors, gave . . . to the nuns . . . one hundred shillings of annual and perpetual rent."[12]

Enthusiasm for the suffrages of religious women remained a constant of monastic patronage throughout the central Middle Ages, particularly at times of crisis. When severe illness threatened the son of the count and countess of Nevers, the family turned to those they saw as best able to intervene for his recovery, the nuns of Jully-

10. *Cartulaire de Saint-Georges de Rennes*, 9:240, no. 15, 1034.
11. *Cartulaire de Jully-les-Nonnains*, p. 268, 1169.
12. "Sachent tuit que comme nous, couvetanz et queranz suffrages d'oroisons à Notre-Seigneur, entendue la bonne renommée de religieuses fammes, l'abbeesse et le convent de Voisins, de l'ordre de Citeaus, en la dyocise d'Orliens, fussiens venue audit lieu, pour nous recommender au dittes religieuses et pour requerre leur oroisons pour nous a Notre-Seigneur . . . et pour ce que nous deservissiens estre parconière des prières et de leur bonnes euvres, que elles font pour leur bienfetteurs donnasmes . . . cent solz": *Cartulaire de Notre-Dame de Voisins*, pp. 35–36, no. 34, 1289.

les-Nonnains.[13] The boy made a donation to the abbey in the hope that the prayers of its holy women would help to cure him. Like the comital family of Nevers, medieval people generally trusted in the intercession of religious women, whom they respected because they believed in the efficacy of nuns' suffrages. Layfolk wanted their daughters to enter convents as oblates, they wanted to be buried in the graveyards of nunneries, and they hoped for charity and sick care from nuns when they were in need; but above all, they requested and valued the nuns' prayers and protection. Pierre Cotheu made a gift to the canonesses of La Barre in 1303, saying that he was "full of respect for their probity and honesty and wanted to benefit from their prayers day and night." [14]

The presence of religious women made an imprint on the naming customs of a region, so that an important abbess or foundress often created a vogue for her name. Thus the name Heloise became popular in Champagne both for secular women and for those who entered the cloistered life a generation after the death of the great abbess.[15] In contrast, in the records of the Saintonge, in the region around the convent of Notre-Dame founded by Agnes of Burgundy, the name Heloise is absent but the name Agnes is common.[16] To name a child for a highborn figure remembered for her holiness and power must have carried a certain cachet; whether or not such name choices were made consciously, they reflect something of the psychological impact a nunnery and its important members had on the local community.

The image of themselves as worthy people focused most clearly for nuns through interactions with people outside the cloister. Whatever the type of contact between religious women and secular society, it often originated through family connections. Stout bonds of blood tied both lay and clerical people to relatives who were members of convents. Those medieval people whose sisters, aunts, cousins, and mothers had taken the veil felt connected to their female kinfolk and did whatever they could to ensure the welfare of the nunneries housing them. Family loyalty, therefore, added to the nuns' positive feelings about themselves.

13. *Cartulaire de Jully-les-Nonnains*, pp. 272–73, 1181.
14. Abbaye de la Barre et son recueil," p. 170.
15. *Cartulaire du Paraclet*, p. 93, no. 75, 1186: Heloise, wife of Lord Milo; p. 96, no. 80, 1192: Heloise, lady of Nangis; p. 143, no. 135, ca. 1211: Heloise, nun of the Paraclete; p. 197, no. 216, 1237: Heloise, niece of the abbess of the Paraclete; p. 222, no. 246, 1249: Heloise de Chalete, a nun at the Paraclete.
16. *Cartulaire de Notre-Dame de Saintes*, passim.

One paradoxical reason for medieval society's admiration of nuns applied uniquely to monastic women. Nuns inspired an inflated esteem because they were believed to be overcoming greater natural odds than were their male counterparts. Since women were seen as less than men in the order of nature, female monastic profession made nuns better than men in the order of grace. After all, did not everyone recognize with Abbess Heloise that women were "the weaker sex whose frailty and infirmity is generally known?"[17] When a woman denied herself the joys of love and family, the church viewed her renunciation of sexuality as more onerous than it was for a man because of her perceived inherent weakness and naturally stronger sex drive. The nun therefore was due greater honor than the monk for entering the cloistered life. That respect found expression in language. Monk in Latin is *monacus*, and nun is often rendered as its feminine equivalent, *monaca*, or as *monialis*. Another Latin word for nun, *sanctimonialis*, derives from *sanctimonium*, which means holiness or piety. But to the people of the Middle Ages, *sanctimonialis* naturally meant "holy nun" (*sancta monialis*), a bit of etymological creativity decried by modern scholars but one that correctly reflected a reality for medieval people.[18] No equivalent word existed for monks.

Another clue that shows the special reverence accorded to nuns is found in episcopal leave-taking. Before a prelate embarked on a pilgrimage, he was supposed to ask the congregations in his care to give permission for his absence. Eudes Rigaud followed this rule before leaving Normandy in 1269 to join King Louis IX's crusading host. Of the seven houses in his province to which he specifically applied for permission, four, or better than half, were female establishments, even though convents constituted only about one-fifth (21 percent) of all the monasteries under his care.[19] To be a nun was to be considered an especially holy type of monastic whose prayers and permission had value for a pious prelate.

This holiness was visibly reinforced in the community's consciousness by the clothing worn by religious women. Nuns wore habits and veils that were unique to their status as professed people. When financial troubles afflicted a convent, the nuns sometimes

---

17. *Letters of Abelard and Heloise*, p. 163. Bynum, *Holy Feast and Holy Fast*, p. 217, points out: "The medieval church itself elaborated a kind of functional inferiority of women to complement the physiological and ontological inferiority elaborated by earlier philosophical and theological tradition."

18. Parrise, *Nonnes au Moyen Age*, p. 126.

19. ER, p. 734.

had to make do with clothing that did not conform to the habit; this was censured by the visitor, however, since the habit was a necessary sign to the outside world and reminded the wearer of her special position. Archbishop Eudes details what the sisters in the leper house of Salle-aux-Puelles are to wear: "The raiment and clothing shall be according to that of your order and uniform, to wit, a russet mantle, and each sister shall receive a tunic and super-tunic every other year. Let them have warm mantles, and new ones every other year."[20]

Monks also wore habits to mark their special role in the church and in society. But the tradition of consecrated virgins taking the veil was perhaps the oldest liturgical vesture in the Christian tradition, while the veil itself, the outward sign of inward chastity for the professed woman, remained the one distinctively female part of the nun's habit. Thus the monastic habit worn by a religious woman marked her out as belonging, along with all monks, friars, and canons, to "the orders and professions that are in the church"—the only such profession open to women—and her veil indicated her special femaleness within those orders.[21]

In the later Middle Ages the English mystic Margery Kempe received the command from Jesus to dress all in white, the color of sexual purity; Margery cared passionately about her white garments, which were for her "an extension of herself, a measure of the recognition accorded her in the public domain."[22] Clothes are, as Margery recognized, a public statement, and no period in history was more aware of this reality than the Middle Ages, which developed elaborate sumptuary laws to use clothing as a mark of class, age, marital status, and religion.[23] Indeed, the nun's habit told her and her surroundings that she was special.

20. ER, p. 116.

21. The phrase comes from the twelfth-century book *Libellus de diversis ordinibus et professionibus qui sunt in aecclesia*, which covered monks, hermits, and canons and was intended to deal with nuns and anchoresses in a second part that never was finished.

22. Janel M. Mueller, "Autobiography of a New 'Creature': Female Spirituality, Selfhood, and Authorship in the Book of Margery Kempe," in *Women in the Middle Ages and the Renaissance: Literary and Historical Perspectives*, ed. Mary Beth Rose (Syracuse: Syracuse University Press, 1986), p. 161. See the discussion of clothing by Clarissa W. Atkinson, *Mystic and Pilgrim: The Book and the World of Margery Kempe* (Ithaca, N.Y.: Cornell University Press, 1983), pp. 50–51.

23. See, for example, the work of Diane Owen Hughes, "Distinguishing Signs: Earrings, Jews and Franciscan Rhetoric in the Italian Renaissance City," *Past and Present* 112(1986): 3–59, and her "Sumptuary Law and Social Relations in Renaissance Italy,"

Two Miraculous Events

But in light of the misogynist tone of much ecclesiastical writing, can we really say that monastic women saw themselves in positive terms, which a respectful outside world mirrored back to them? Considerable indirect evidence suggests they did. A careful reading of two miracles—which I have already mentioned in passing—in which nuns are found acting and reacting as religious people will illustrate a number of the ways religious women viewed themselves.

The Relic That Would Not Move

The first of these two miracles took place in Poitou, in the closing years of the eleventh century when a calamitous drought afflicted the area. "The fiery ardor of the sun fiercely burnt up the land of Aulnay and everything in it: castles, villages, houses, cornfields, vineyards, and meadows, everything green."[24] Chales, the viscount of Aulnay, advised by "honest men of his land," organized a penitential pilgrimage in which the relics of Saint Just would be conveyed to the great abbey of Saint-Jean d'Angély, eighteen kilometers away. The procession of barefoot penitents headed southwest bearing the reliquary through the parched fields. The penultimate stop on their journey before crossing the Boutonne River to reach Saint-Jean d'Angély on the other side occurred at the Priory of Saint-Julien, a dependent house of the nuns of Notre-Dame in Saintes. The bearers deposited the reliquary on the altar, and prayers were said. When the service had concluded, the procession made ready for its ultimate destination, but it proved impossible to budge the relics from their place on the altar. Fear swept through the assembly; the crowd in the church began to bewail their sins and fervently to promise repentance. Those in the procession made a second reverent but unsuccessful effort to move the reliquary. This failure convinced the people that they were experiencing God's wrath, and a tumult of anguished voices imploringly asked the cause of this divine punishment. At this highly charged moment, the chaplain and Prioress Lethoidis responded that the judgment was directed at the viscount for oppressing the people of the region. Thus publicly brought to account, the lord and those of his barons who had accompanied him

in *Disputes and Settlements*, ed. John Bossy (Cambridge: Cambridge University Press, 1984), pp. 69–99.
24. *Cartulaire de Notre-Dame de Saintes*, pp. 139–40, no. 217, 1098.

swore on the altar to mend their ways and to stop depriving the people of their rights and possessions. The relics were then easily moved, and the procession continued joyfully to the Abbey of Saint-Jean d'Angély.

This miraculous tale is recounted in the viscount's charter of June 22, 1098. In the charter the viscount confirms to the abbess of Notre-Dame in Saintes his promise, made in the Priory of Saint-Julien, that all the rights and possessions of the people of Aulnay will be respected. His imminent departure on the First Crusade is the occasion for this confirmation, sworn before the abbess and her "flock of holy nuns." This charter reveals ways the world saw religious women and ways they saw themselves.

The nuns played an important role in the eyes of their contemporaries in this highly emotional drama. First, the procession chose to stop at their priory. Either someone organizing the pilgrimage thought that a stop at Saint-Julien's might be efficacious in the crisis or else someone at the front of the procession spontaneously turned in to the priory church. In either case, a priory of nuns must have seemed like an appropriate and beneficial stopping place. Then the interpretation by Prioress Lethoidis and her chaplain of the relics' immovability was received respectfully by the barons and people in the church; no one questioned the authority of a woman to interpret miraculous happenings, and indeed in this charter she is mentioned by name but the chaplain is not. Neither did the viscount and his followers offer any self-defense or rebuttal to what must have seemed an infringement upon their prerogative to run roughshod over the countryside. Finally, the viscount later came before the assembled nuns of Notre-Dame to reconfirm his good behavior. He may have done so because, as was often the case, he needed monastic funding for his crusading venture, or he may have wanted the powerful protective prayers of the nuns for his dangerous undertaking; most probably he wanted both money and religious protection. He need for financial and spiritual support could have been satisfied by the many rich and famous male monasteries in the region, yet he chose to humble himself before religious women to receive the help he needed.[25] The value of the nuns at Saintes was self-evident to

25. The viscount passed over a number of monasteries of monks that were right in the vicinity. The monastery nearest the viscount's castle was a Benedictine priory in Aulnay. Next closest was Saint-Jean d'Angély, a major institution. In the city of Saintes, about a thirty-kilometer ride from his lands, were the great male houses of Saint-Eutrope and Saint-Vivien, while a bit farther to the north was the famous Abbey of Saint-Maixent.

Viscount Chales: they had been host to a miracle, the prioress had not feared to bring him to heel, and the abbey had the resources to outfit him and his men and to sustain them with suffrages through the dangerous adventure ahead.

The tale of the "sticky" relics also demonstrates the self-confidence and assertiveness of Prioress Lethoidis. She stepped forward in the midst of the anxious outcry to point an accusing finger at the baron whose violent behavior had brought down on them all the judgment of God. Yet she did not act alone: Lethoidis by her birth and her position felt empowered to be the interpreter of God's will; but as a religious woman, she linked herself with her chaplain and male counterpart, since as a nun she saw herself working with—not separate from—the male clergy. Lethoidis was a woman of sense, who judiciously did not overstep the bounds of medieval sensibilities, but she was also a woman of courage, prepared to challenge a tyrannical noble.

An Attempted Suicide

A second miraculous occurrence, which can be used to illuminate the identity of religious women as perceived by themselves and others, took place in Normandy in 1107. This event is described in extraordinary detail and with almost clinical clarity by Abbess Marsilia of the Abbey of Saint-Amand in Rouen in a letter she wrote to Abbot Bovon of Saint-Amand in Elnone.[26] The letter recounts how a local noblewoman's insecurity had been fueled by cruel gossip that her husband no longer loved her and had become involved with another woman. Whatever the truth of these rumors, they added to the wife's misery, and she plunged into acute depression, becoming suicidal. Her family brought her to the nuns' church of Saint-Amand, where they hoped she would be helped by the saint. After she had stayed in the church for a week, her caretakers decided that a cure might be effected by immersing her in holy water. The night before this was to be done, she was to sleep on a cot placed in front of the saint's altar. Those who had brought her retired, leaving guards to watch over her. During the night she pretended to be quite rational, thus reassuring the guards, who fell asleep. When she was sure no one was awake, the woman arose. Dressed only in her chemise, she climbed up the wall, tied one end of her veil to the capital on a column, and with the other end made a noose for her neck. Then

26. Valenciennes, BM, MSS. 500, 502. Transcribed by Platelle, "Relations entre Saint-Amand et Saint-Amand d'Elnone," pp. 104–6.

she leaped down with such force that the veil sliced into her flesh and blood spurted onto the wall.

Sometime after midnight one of the guards woke to find the woman's bed empty. He hunted feverishly and finally found her dead, hanging by the neck. His cries of horror soon brought the nuns, who joined in his lamentations. Candles were lit, and the body was cut down. Three nuns "who were braver or more audacious than the others, since it was nighttime," left the abbey and went to inform the archdeacon of the tragedy. His first response was that as soon as possible, even before daybreak, the nuns should throw the body into some ditch; however, he followed the nuns back to the church. Rather than shun the corpse of the wretched woman, the nuns hovered around the body. One drew close and was overjoyed to discover breath and life returning to the poor woman. For twenty-four hours they watched over her. She could not speak, and in her derangement she needed four strong men to keep her from harming herself. The next day her first words as she woke were: "Holy Lady, pious Mary, Mother of God, help me!" She called for a priest, confessed, and was completely restored to health and well-being.

This incident occurred at the convent of Saint-Amand because the woman's husband and relatives chose it instead of one of the four major competing male monasteries in Rouen at that time. Their choice was positive, not ruled by any feeling that it would only be appropriate to take a sick woman to stay in a house of nuns; sex segregation was not the norm when it came to cures, even when it meant that a sick woman might sleep at a shrine in a monks' church for an extended period.[27] In part the family members were hoping that the saint's dominion over demons would prevail, and in part they were responding to the reputation for power and sanctity enjoyed by the nuns of the abbey.

Indeed, the nuns' behavior showed they were worthy of the family's high regard. The guard who found the dead woman did not show the wit to cut her down; that happened only after the nuns arrived on the scene. Next, it was not the men on the scene but the nuns who went for help. Once the archdeacon arrived he proved useless, simply washing his fastidious ecclesiastical hands of a body that could not be buried in consecrated soil. It took the compassion and keen observation of one of the nuns to detect life in the woman. Since the body of a suicide is naturally a gruesome sight, and since

27. See Ronald C. Finucane, *Miracles and Pilgrims: Popular Beliefs in Medieval England* (London: J. M. Dent, 1977), pp. 76 ff., for such examples.

the archdeacon had made the church's judgmental position painfully clear, the nuns showed enormous courage and self-confidence in not distancing themselves from the upsetting and unholy corpse. The behavior of the religious women in whose church a tragedy was narrowly averted—or miraculously reversed—suggests that they saw themselves as actors rather than as merely acted upon.

The letter that contains the account was addressed to the abbot of a Flemish monastery dedicated to the same saint, Saint Amand, as was the convent where the miracle took place. Abbess Marsilia wrote to Abbot Bovon so that he could add her abbey's miraculous story of their shared saint to the collection of miracles Bovon had already assembled. It is clear that Marsilia knew the stories of Saint Amand's other miracles and was aware that the Flemish monks were composing a collection.[28] Not only was the abbess literate and in the mainstream of monastic networking, but she also did not hesitate to feel that she and her nuns had something worthy to bring to the attention of a house of monks. Her letter is sturdy evidence of the abbess's assurance that she is writing to a peer.

These two stories recounting miraculous events stand outside the literary tradition of medieval miracles. The description of the immovable relics occurs in an economic document recording a vow. Nowhere is the word "miracle" used; in fact, it is the villain of the piece—the viscount—not the nuns, who relates the story as an explanation for why he is reaffirming his promise before departing for the Holy Land. The tale is recounted in a straightforward manner that eschews any supernatural explanation.

The account of the failed suicide attempt is told in the words of a nun, Abbess Marsilia, writing to her confrere in Flanders. Marsilia's self-interest is apparent, for she opens by saying that she is sending a miracle to be inserted in the collection being compiled by Abbot Bovon in honor of their common patron saint. Her telling of the events is, however, remarkably different from most miracle stories, since its intent is to present the raw data, the facts of the case, rather than to editorialize and moralize. The abbess probably assumed that Bovon would add the flourishes and didactic message once he had the facts in hand. Since both of these tales served a practical purpose, they recount what happened in a vivid and unselfconscious tone.

---

28. Platelle, "Relations entre Saint-Amand et Saint-Amand d'Elnone," pp. 93–96, convincingly argues that the abbess was aware of and in touch with the tradition of Saint Amand and the activities of the monks of Saint-Amand-Elnone.

The reporting of these two events is probably accurate. It is in a charter issued not by the nuns but by the nobleman who was brought to account by the event that we encounter the unmovable relics, but we do not know why they refused to budge. Did someone manipulate the reliquary to make it heavy, and if so, who was responsible, and how was this achieved? Was the crowd so hysterical with anxiety in the face of a life-threatening drought that some sort of group hysteria occurred? Was it a miracle? There is no way of answering these fascinating questions, and as Caroline Bynum points out, it is irrelevant since it is the medieval perception of what happened that can best illuminate the past for us.[29] What we can say is that a prioress confidently used the occurrence to protect the people of the region.

It is also highly likely that the woman who tried to kill herself did return to life and rationality. Ronald Finucane has investigated a number of explanations for medieval cures, among which he numbers miraculous "revivals from death."[30] He notes that coma and drastically suppressed respiration could masquerade as death; when the victim began to breathe and regained consciousness, onlookers interpreted the event as a miracle. Even today, emergency medical personnel learn to check an apparently dead patient with great care to avoid tragedy. Why the woman revived was of great importance to medieval people, but for an investigation of the self-image of medieval nuns, behavior is more revealing and valuable than are explanations for her recovery. The actions of the nuns demonstrate that they were sure enough of themselves to cut down and tend the body, saving the woman who otherwise might well have asphyxiated in a drainage ditch.

Medieval monastics were not above exaggerating and manufacturing miracles as well as stealing holy relics to enhance their monasteries.[31] It is possible that the nuns of Notre-Dame in Saintes and Saint-Amand in Rouen embroidered their miracle stories after the fact or even engineered the events. But at the very least, simply by proclaiming that a miracle had touched a monastery, the nuns actively publicized their abbey. It is also worth noting that in a world whose "bounds of reality included the unseen in a way alien to mod-

29. Bynum, *Holy Feast and Holy Fast*, p. 8.

30. Finucane, *Miracles and Pilgrims*, pp. 73–82.

31. Benedicta Ward, *Miracles and the Medieval Mind: Theory, Record, and Event, 1000–1215* (Philadelphia: University of Pennsylvania Press, 1982), p. 215; Finucane, *Miracles and Pilgrims*, pp. 29–30; Patrick J. Geary, *Furta Sacra: Thefts of Relics in the Central Middle Ages* (Princeton: Princeton University Press, 1978), pp. 158–59.

ern thought,"[32] the participants in the two dramas may have acted in all sincerity, whatever their behavior.

These two accounts present nuns as their supporters want them seen. But not all religious women were calmly focused on the well-being of others. Some medieval nuns were simply too inept or timid to be of any use in a charged situation. These women generally do not surface in the documents. Other nuns acted courageously with a strong belief in the rightness of their cause, as did the nuns of Notre-Dame, who processed across the city of Saintes to beard an enemy as he kept watch over the body of his brother. When the nuns swung into action, the townsfolk, clerics at the Church of Saint-Eutrope where the confrontation took place, and the miscreant himself all beheld religious women emboldened by their status. In this case the nuns acted confidently and stayed within the bounds of sanctioned behavior, but at other times religious women clearly behaved inappropriately. During the extended conflict of the nuns of Notre-Dame-aux-Nonnains and the papacy over the Church of Saint-Urbain in Troyes, twice the nuns and their followers physically attacked the hated church; once they barred the archbishop of Tyre's access; and finally they became so heated that they threatened the prelate in the open street. The public nature of the conflict meant that no one in town could have failed to see the nuns acting in the belief that they were worthy opponents of the church hierarchy. Indeed, nuns could intimidate men by their fury, as did the nuns of Montivilliers, who when battling for their exemption refused to listen to the prelate's preaching, indignantly marched out on him, and then returned to scare him with threatening gestures. The church judged all such rebellious behavior as sinful and punished it. Yet the nuns acting as a corporate body seem to have felt confident that they were defending the rights and ancient customs of their institutions. Whatever the justification or lack thereof for the nuns of Notre-Dame-aux-Nonnains and Montivilliers, they were able to forcefully make known their feelings. These nuns, like Prioress Lethoidis and the sisters at Saint-Amand, were women to be reckoned with as either protectors or adversaries.

In other cases, like that of the best-known French nun of our period, Heloise, the documents sometimes present a contradictory picture, but one that can be resolved through the lens of behavior. This woman, the compelling heroine of one of the West's most powerful love stories, seems vivid and assertive when the reader first

32. Ward, *Miracles and the Medieval Mind*, p. 33.

meets her in Abelard's story of their tragic love; but later, in a letter Heloise wrote to Abelard requesting a rule for her nuns, she sounds anxious and needy, repeatedly referring to herself and her nuns as weak and as requiring special masculine consideration and help. Abelard, unable to ignore her appeal, responded with a rule that specified, among other particulars, that the nuns of the Paraclete should be strictly cloistered and have an abbot placed over them, a change that would have removed the abbess's autonomy.[33] Yet if we compare Abelard's rule with the actual organization of the Paraclete, we find that Heloise and her nuns did not follow his rule. This divergence led John Benton to argue that the famous correspondence between the former lovers was a forgery.[34] A simpler explanation, and one in line with her behavior as a competent abbess, would be that Heloise had asked Abelard for a rule more to manipulate him into reviving contact with her than to obtain his help. Her letter struck just the right note of entreaty to snare her wary former lover and husband into continuing their correspondence and their collaboration. Indeed, looking at Heloise's behavior rather than at her words demonstrates how a nun's real self may be seen more clearly in actions than in words. She reestablished contact with Abelard yet continued to run the Paraclete as its sole head. In addition, the reflection of regional admiration in local naming patterns and of ecclesiastical respect in Abbot Peter the Venerable's letters to Heloise, whom he respectfully begs to pray for him, complete the picture of an assertive and successful abbess.[35]

CONCLUSION

The confident behavior of the religious women of Notre-Dame and Saint-Amand was the norm for their cloistered sisters in northern

33. *Letters of Abelard and Heloise:* "Historia calamitatum," pp. 57–106, is the narrative; letter 5, pp. 159–79 is Heloise's request; letter 7, pp. 183–269, contains Abelard's rule.

34. John Benton, "Fraud, Fiction and Borrowing in the Correspondence of Abelard and Heloise," in *Pierre Abélard—Pierre le Vénérable: Les courants philosophiques, littéraires, et artistiques en Occident, au milieu du XIIe siècle,* Colloque International de Cluny, 1972, 546 (Paris: Editions du Centre National de la Recherche Scientifique, 1975), p. 474. Benton's argument is based on painstaking scholarly investigation, and although before his death he dropped his challenge to the authenticity of the correspondence, Georges Duby is now again raising questions. Whether or not the letters are interpolated, it seems to me that by applying Ockham's razor, we can explain a major problem of the rule without recourse to philological and chronological complexities.

35. *Letters of Abelard and Heloise,* pp. 277–84, 285.

France. When Abbess Emma of Faremoutiers went to Meaux to take an oath whose wording had already been agreed upon with the bishop, she did not hesitate to refuse to swear when she found the wording changed to the detriment of her abbey.[36] The argument over the correct wording raged until midday, when the bishop gave in— worn down by the assertive abbess—and administered the oath as she required. At the turn of the twelfth century the doors had not yet begun to close against nuns, as they would from the mid-twelfth century on. Society revered its religious women and provided liberally for them as it did for their brother monks. For instance, both Saint-Amand and Notre-Dame had been founded by noble couples who had also established houses of monks. Jocelin, lord of Arques, and Emmeline his wife founded Saint-Amand in Rouen, probably in the year 1030.[37] They also instituted the Benedictine house of Saint-Catherine in Rouen for monks at about the same time. Agnes of Burgundy and her husband, Geoffrey Martel, count of Anjou, founded the house of Notre-Dame in Saintes.[38] Fifteen years earlier they had established Holy Trinity in Vendôme as a house for Benedictine monks.[39] Neither foundress was establishing a convent with an eye to reserving its direction for herself or for her daughter, although Agnes did retire to Notre-Dame, where she ended her days as a nun.[40] In both cases, as in most foundations of nunneries, the patrons were instituting a convent as they would a monastery for men. Medieval people saw houses for both sexes as valuable; after all, nunneries would accept the patron's female relatives, while men's houses would accept their benefactor's male kin.[41]

A more negative image of religious women was embedded in the ecclesiastical literature, however. Canonists and monastic regula-

36. Galli, "Faremoutiers," pp. 45–46.

37. *Répertoire des abbayes et prieurés de Seine-Maritime: Ouvrage collectif publié à l'occasion de l'année des abbayes normandes* (Rouen: Archives Départementales de Seine-Maritime, 1979), pp. 105–6. Le Cacheux, *Histoire de Saint-Amand*, pp. 36–39.

38. *Cartulaire de Notre-Dame de Saintes*, pp. 1–5, no. 1, 1047.

39. *Cartulaire de la Trinité de Vendôme*, 1:55–60, no. 35, 1040. Although the earliest charter for the foundation of this house is dated 1040, the decision to found the abbey was taken in 1032. Johnson, *Prayer, Patronage, and Power*, pp. 9–23.

40. New Haven, Beinecke Library, Yale University, Kalendarius liber, Marston MS. 25, fol. 39v, records the celebration of Agnes's anniversary, noting that she was "venerabilis Agnes Aquitanie comitissa et huius ecclesie monaca."

41. Scholars tend to note that there were many fewer convents for women than monasteries for men. I suspect this had less to do with social acceptance of and respect for nunneries than with demographics and marriage patterns.

tors through the ages had developed a theoretical formulation that defined women through their sexuality. When considering the status of nuns, they focused all their attention on dealing with that sexuality and its dangers by concentrating on the vow of virginity, the age for profession, the protection of nuns, questions of monastic discipline, and cloistering.[42] It was as if the canonists inhabited a psychological space in which they defined female reality only by woman's biology, so that they could see other aspects of femaleness only if that bodiliness were negated by virginity. Until the twelfth century, monastic women lived in a different—but just as real—psychological space, in which they defined themselves by their useful spiritual and social activities; they knew that society relied on them for charity, justice, loans, burial, and prayers. This functional image lasted over the early medieval period and into the central Middle Ages because it had the affirmation of those around the convent, whose attitudes and affections reinforced the positive picture. The two differing psychological spaces coexisted. But as the value of being a monastic paled in the later twelfth and the thirteenth century in the presence of the growing importance of being a priest, the nun's self-definition as an integral part of the social fabric started to unravel. By the late medieval period religious women's psychological space had been compressed, but despite the restrictions—or perhaps because of them—they had fashioned a new self-image, at least for their elite, as spiritual or even mystical beings.[43]

Religious women of the twelfth century who chastised bullying barons and were active in the miraculous restoration of the dying were participating in a secular tradition that accepted and revered them and their way of life. The documents of practice overwhelmingly demonstrate that contemporaries cared about houses of women, and cared without particularly distinguishing nuns as less worthy than monks. Abbess Elizabeth of Salzinnes in Namur reflects something of that syncretic rather than separatist attitude when she refers to herself as "Sister Elizabeth, humble minister

42. Jacqueline Rambaud-Buhot, "Le statut des moniales chez les pères de l'église, dans les règles monastiques et les collections canoniques jusqu'à XIIe siècle," in *Sainte Fare et Faremoutiers: Trieze siècles de vie monastique* (Faremoutiers: Abbaye de Faremoutiers, 1956), pp. 149–74.

43. There is a good deal of interest in these late medieval religious women, and also considerable variation on interpreting their lives and writings. See, for instance, Bynum, *Holy Feast and Holy Fast,* and Elizabeth Petroff, *Consolation of the Blessed* (Millerton, N.Y.: Alta Gaia, 1980).

[*ministera*] of the monastery of Saint-George."[44] She uses the word *minister,* usually applied to male clerics in lower orders, in its feminine form. Such usage occasioned no shock, for indeed in the eyes of her contemporaries she was not radically different from her male counterparts.

But she and her sister nuns *were* different, and they knew it. In ways they received a disproportionate share of respect; in ways the misogynist rhetoric of the Fathers made them suspect. Whatever negative attitudes existed, however, were often dispelled by acting in concert with their confreres. Prioress Lethoidis confronted the viscount with her chaplain, and the nuns of Saint-Amand asked advice of their male superior. The harnessed joint energies and efforts of nuns and male clerics not only helped legitimize religious women but also worked synergistically to the advantage of society. The warm response religious women received reinforced their solid self-image, which deemphasized gender differences but did not deny their gender. Abbess Marsilia writes to Abbot Bovon speaking for her nuns, who she says are "different as to their sex but equal in their monastic profession," when compared with his monks of Saint-Amand in Elnone.[45]

The positive identity of nuns at the turn of the twelfth century grew out of their role as brides of Christ and was reflected and refracted by the contemporary respect felt for them as religious people who performed important functions in the medieval world. It was this acceptance of nuns by themselves and by society as worthy human beings that explains in part why throngs of adult women in this period sought the monastic life. By taking the veil, women could leave behind many of the "infirmities" of their sex to become "our good friends" to their neighbors; in the cloister they could find a satisfying and integrated self-image.

44. Elisabeth refers to herself as "ego soror Elisabeth, humilis ministera conventus Beati Georgii": *Recueil du Val-Saint-Georges à Salzinnes,* p. 22, no. 19, 1220.

45. "Congrum est enim, ut, sicut in castris regis eterni, etsi sexu dissimiles, proposito tamen equales, sub uno eodemque patrono militamus, ita de virtutum ejus triumphali preconio ad honorem Dei unanimiter congaudeamus": Platelle, "Relations entre Saint-Amand et Saint-Amand d'Elnone," p. 104.

8

CLOSING THE DOORS

THE FAMILY MODEL

THE FAMILY ORIENTATION of medieval monasticism contributed powerfully to the satisfaction that life provided for nuns and monks and helped keep it a viable option for many centuries. While the Christian spiritual ideal created the mission of the professed life, the human family model structured its daily sense of community. People related to each other by blood carried their solidarity into the cloister and also supported the nuns from outside. Relatives went into convents with other kin as choir nuns and as lay monastics. At times kin entered the world of the cloister together: it was not particularly remarkable when an entire family of seven commended itself to a convent, so that the parents and five children entered the familia as a coherent family group. Women within the cloister tended to share in their families' tradition of patronage. For instance, when it became Audeardis Lespeingnole's turn to profess as a sister at the almshouse of Saint-Jean in Angers, she moved into the room left vacant by her recently deceased sister Marie.[1] The community at Saint-Jean took over the functions of Audeardis's natal family by promising to provide for her as long as she lived with daily distributions of one measure of wine, two rolls, and plenty of cooked food as well as an annual income of four pounds. Through such agreements the natal family routinely became intertwined with the monastic family.

Even if one's relatives did not enter the monastery to serve in some capacity, a woman brought her relatives with her into the prayers of the nunnery. The necrology of the Paraclete remembers "our master, Peter Abelard," "Peter Astrolabe, the son of our master Peter," "Hersende, the mother of Lady Heloise, our abbess," "Canon

---

1. *Cartulaire de Saint-Jean d'Angers*, pp. cxiii-iv, no. 148, 1259.

Fulbert, the uncle of Lady Heloise." The family connections that include the husband, illegitimate son, mother, and vengeful uncle of Heloise, the first abbess of the house, are even stretched to bring into the prayer family Peter the Venerable, who sent the body of Abelard to the nuns of the Paraclete: "Abbot Peter of Cluny, by whose permission our church has the body of our master Peter."[2] Blood relatives, connections by marriage, and those woven into the community by loving concerns—all are tied together in the prayers of the nuns of the Paraclete.

Family bonds created strong loyalties within the cloister. When the nuns of Notre-Dame-aux-Nonnains challenged the creation of the Church of Saint-Urbain in Troyes, three sets of sisters spearheaded the resistance. Unlike modern monastic orders, which sometimes legislate family quotas, medieval orders had no limit on the number of siblings who could be professed in a house at one time. Indeed, most houses of religious women seem to have believed that receiving members of the same family strengthened a convent. Such a commitment to perpetuating family connections emboldened the nuns of Saint-Saens to defy the visitor's ban against expansion by giving letters to four of their members, promising acceptance to a niece of each of the four. Personal connections mattered to medieval nuns, and the strongest of all such ties was kinship.

The very structure of the monastic life took the family as its model. The necrology of the Paraclete commemorated its first abbess as "Heloise, the mother of our monastic community."[3] Just as a kin group assumed responsibility for its members, so the convent cared for its own from their entering the cloister, through old age, until reception into paradise. Friendships were forged between monastic sisters that paralleled those between blood sisters. A nun was consoror, fellow sister, to her abbess.[4] Caring could be so strong that it transcended the grave, bringing dead nuns back to the convent in dreams or visions to visit their favorite fellow nuns.[5] Concern for the souls of one's monastic sisters was strong. Nuns bought income

2. *Cartulaire de Paraclet*, pp. 465, 471–73.
3. *Cartulaire de Paraclet*, p. 466.
4. *Cartulaire de Saint-Georges de Rennes*, 9:284, no. 58, 1068–85.
5. *Vie de Saint Etienne d'Obazine*, pp. 104–6. Sharon Farmer, "Personal Perceptions, Collective Behavior: Twelfth-Century Suffrages for the Dead," in *Persons in Groups: Social Behavior as Identity Formation in Medieval and Renaissance Europe*, ed. Richard C. Trexler (Binghamton, N.Y.: SUNY Press, 1985), pp. 231–39, examines the miracles as a result of suffrages in *De rebus gestis in Majori Monasterio* for clues to how the monks of Marmoutier felt and acted individually as well as corporately.

to ensure that the anniversary of a deceased nun would be celebrated.[6] Claustral sisters cared for each other corporately as well as individually. When the widow Mathea entered the religious life as a sister at the almshouse of Saint-Jean, she drew up a will that set aside money for her burial and bequests to many worthy institutions.[7] The bulk of her inheritance she left to "the brothers and sisters of the said monastery," designating that it go for pittances, pilgrimages, and beautification of the house.

There was a downside to the fictive kinship that existed in the cloister, since the bonding in medieval convents could also lead to some bitter fights. Monastics' quarrels, those of monks as well as nuns, could have the particular nastiness that characterizes family squabbles. Nuns battled over who owned which chickens as well as over more serious problems like contested elections.[8] Sometimes several quarrelsome individuals within a house turned it into an armed camp by picking fights, enlisting others on their side, and then waging a war of stubborn silence. Monastics who refused to speak to each other were certainly not living in charity.[9] In one case the visitor, like a peacemaking parent, tried to enforce forgiveness and harmony by insisting that the feuding sisters make up "to the extent of kissing each other on the mouth," and he attempted to forestall a rematch by forbidding them "ever to mention the cause of their disagreement under pain of excommunication."[10] The interior life of the religious house could disintegrate so totally that physical violence erupted, as when Ermengarde of Gisors and Joan of Hauteville were reduced to pummeling each other.[11] The erosion of family community occurred in houses of both religious men and religious women, so quarreling and violence do not seem to have been specifically gender linked. Rather, people who lived close together in the cloister might care a great deal about other members of the community but also nurse resentments exaggerated by lack of privacy. Family members resent and compete with each other as well as loving one another.

6. Poitiers, BM, la Trinité, MS. 27, p. 161; also see *Cartulaire de Notre-Dame de Bourbourg*, 1:198, no. 205, 1285.

7. *Cartulaire de Saint-Jean d'Angers*, pp. cxvii-cxix, no. 154, 1265.

8. ER, pp. 629, 681.

9. ER, p. 214. Cases of monks' not speaking to each other also occurred. See, for example, the monks of Aumale, p. 251.

10. ER, pp. 226–27, 207.

11. ER, p. 49; this was unusual, since nuns usually limited their quarrels to trading words, not blows. Monks also came to blows on occasion (see pp. 313–14).

Although most monastic women forswore husband and children, giving up both the joys and the burdens of being wife and mother, their world remained lively. The zesty ingredients of the monastic family included both strong family connections and new contributions from professed sisters, seasoned with the friendship of male clerics in their house and a dash of cosmopolitanism from ties to a far-flung order. But as the twelfth century wore on, the monastic recipe lost some of its savor as the male orders began to cut dependent nunneries out of the shared richness of the monastic family.

Breakdown

To change the metaphor, the essential family glue of medieval monastic life was slowly coming unstuck in the central Middle Ages. Monasticism in general suffered from competition with the friars, the universities, and the increased civic assumption of charity. But the monastic life for women—though not for men—was also limited and even suppressed from inside the institution.[12] The movement of male orders to divest themselves of the *cura monialis* began during the twelfth century and became general in the thirteenth. The Premonstratensian order separated its nuns from its monks in 1134 and, after much lobbying, received from Pope Innocent III in 1198 the bull *De non recipiendis sororibus* (About Not Having to Receive Sisters), giving them the right to refuse entry to women.[13] The Cistercians began to worry about the large numbers of women who, often on their own initiative, had taken up the Cistercian customs in the late twelfth century. The order generally ignored their existence until the early thirteenth century, when it began to recognize some of the nunneries by legislating restrictions. In 1220 and even more stringently in 1228 the Cistercian order moved to ban new convents, although there were local variations in this pattern; for instance, there was a spurt of foundations of female Cistercian houses in the diocese of Sens in the first half of the thirteenth cen-

12. Brenda Bolton, "Mulieres Sanctae," in *Women in Medieval Society*, ed. Susan Mosher Stuard (Philadelphia: University of Pennsylvania Press, 1976), pp. 141–58. The time frame for shrinkage in nunneries may have been different in the South; for instance, La Celle had its highest population of nuns in the thirteenth century: L'Hermite-Leclercq, *Monachisme féminin*, p. 218. Elkins, *Holy Women of Twelfth-Century England*, chaps. 6 and 8, demonstrates a slowing of enthusiasm for women's monastic foundations coupled with growing criticism in the second half of the twelfth century.

13. See Gold, *Lady and the Virgin*, pp. 78–93, for a good overview of this process of limitations followed by exclusions.

tury, which came to an end a few decades later with the 1251 agreement that the order could deny entry even to new convents supported by the papacy.[14]

Although women joined in the great enthusiasm for the new orders of the Franciscans and the Dominicans in the early thirteenth century, the friars were extremely ambivalent about regularizing female branches within their structures. Prouille, a convent for nuns founded by Dominic himself as his first monastery, had to wrestle for half a century to obtain a place in the order.[15] Despite resistance from abbots and chapters of men, the church supported the incorporation of women into the two mendicant orders. But because the Franciscans were dedicated to total poverty and begging to support themselves, while the Dominicans were committed to preaching against heresy, it seemed inappropriate to the male hierarchy for women to participate in the public aspects of these two orders. Thus the Poor Clares, the female branch of the Franciscans, and the female Dominicans became simply two more types of cloistered—and very tightly cloistered at that—monastic women. The church's expectation that religious women would be cloistered smothered the initial excitement women had felt for the apostolic life of Francis and Dominic.

How can we make sense out of this growing resistance and antipathy? What was going on? Would that there were one answer! What I find is a complicated, multifaceted process. The change in women's monastic life is not marked by a clear fault line between positive and negative experience; it cannot be dated with precision; it cannot be located with absolute accuracy on the map. But it was real, and it was only the tip of the iceberg of the declining status of women in late medieval Europe. The slow erosion of women's monastic profession shows in the records as a gradual loss of stature over the three hundred years of our study, although the more rapid decrease in numbers and prestige of religious women comes in the later Middle Ages. Religious women's autonomy was under attack: nunneries were losing the right to choose their own superiors, and

14. Thompson, "Problem of the Cistercian Nuns," p. 238. Constance Berman, "Fashions in Monastic Patronage: The Popularity of Supporting Cistercian Abbeys for Women in Thirteenth-Century Northern France," paper presented at a meeting of the Western French History Society, October 1989.

15. Micheline de Fontette, "Les dominicaines en France au XIIIe siècle," in *Les religieuses en France au XIIIe siècle*, ed. Michel Parisse. Conference Proceedings of l'Institut d'Etudes Médiévales de l'Université de Nancy II and CERCOM, 1983 (Nancy: Presses Universitaires de Nancy, 1985), pp. 100–104.

superiors were having to take more extensive and binding oaths of obedience to diocesans. Religious women's control of their clerics was slipping, just as the keys to the canons' church, symbolically held by the abbess of Holy Trinity in 1268, had fallen to the possession of a male cleric by 1335. Religious women's authority faded as their education failed to keep pace with clerical university training; once they lost their facility in Latin, there would be precious few Heloises corresponding with abbots of Cluny. Religious women's spiritual power waned when their liturgical processions and solemn oath ceremonies were confined within convent walls, away from society, and their prayers for the dead were eclipsed by masses celebrated by priests.

In the beginning of our period, religious women—in fact all women—had been treated differently in theory and in fact: in theory cloistered women were derivative and dangerous creatures formed from Adam's rib. But in fact they saw themselves and were seen by society at large as sharing with men the vital institutional and spiritual life of the cloister. By the end of our period, theory and fact had moved closer together, so that the negative view of women more closely approximated their diminished status in the regular life. Changes in demography, the family, social and economic patterns, the church, and group consciousness all intertwined to squeeze the vitality out of all women's experience and particularly women's monastic experience.

Demography and the Family

Population increased dramatically in Europe during the central Middle Ages because of several interacting forces. Warmer and drier weather accompanied by agrarian innovations—improved crop rotations, new plowing techniques, the increased use of protein-rich legumes—occurring from the ninth to the eleventh century made possible a demographic increase and a concomitant economic speedup evident at the beginning of the central Middle Ages.[16] Parents had more children who survived, at least until they left a mark in the records. We can find large families in royal marriages: Peter of France (fifth son of Louis VI) and Elizabeth had twelve children, Saint Louis and his wife Margaret had eleven. Numerous children

16. Georges Duby, *The Early Growth of the European Economy: Warriors and Peasants from the Seventh to the Twelfth Century*, trans. Howard Clarke (Ithaca, N.Y.: Cornell University Press, 1974), p. 71: "The demographic impulse has to be placed in its [the pattern of development's] centre."

254 ASSESSMENTS

were also born to less illustrious parents, so that in our period having seven or eight children became relatively common.[17] By the twelfth century large families were affecting society. For instance, an excess of knightly younger sons, the *juvenes*, led to changes in culture as society responded to the surfeit of violent young men by siphoning them off into dangerous activities.[18] They became the crusading hosts, the tournament participants, the mounted troops, but also the appreciative audience for courtly love poetry. Many of their sisters filled the newly founded or renovated convents. But what is particularly important for understanding women's status is that the sex ratio—the number of females relative to the number of males within the population—increased dramatically. Although we cannot prove there was such a change, many scholars believe the sex ratio tipped in favor of women during the central Middle Ages.[19] Some indices of this change show in documents of practice. For instance, in an advocacy list from the Abbey of Bourbourg dated to the second half of the thirteenth century, there are 54 women out of a total of 78 people: women make up 69 percent of the total.[20] Even if

17. *Cartulaire de Saint-Georges de Rennes,* 9:267, no. 39, 1063: seven children; 10:18, no. 12 A, 1203: eight children. *Cartulaire du Lieu-Notre-Dame-lès-Romorantin,* p. 80, no. 116, 1237: seven children; pp. 93–94, no. 140, 1266: seven children. *Cartulaire de Jully-les-Nonnains,* p. 280, no. 71, 1202: seven children; p. 282, no. 81, 1210: eight children. Since daughters are often not listed in medieval records and some children would have died young, the evidence for large families seems very strong.

18. Duby, "In Northwestern France: The 'Youth' in Twelfth-Century Aristocratic Society," pp. 198–209.

19. Bynum, *Jesus as Mother,* p. 182, n. 33, cites a string of works all noting the increased numbers of women in the central Middle Ages. Martha Howell et al., "A Documented Presence: Medieval Women in Germanic Historiography," in *Women in Medieval History and Historiography,* ed. Susan Mosher Stuard (Philadelphia: University of Pennsylvania Press, 1987), pp. 116, 112, examines the established opinions about the female preponderance. Duby, *Early Growth of the European Economy,* p. 29, notes that before the climate change and its associated improvements in harvests, "Among the adult population death struck especially hard at young mothers." David Herlihy, "Life Expectancies for Women in Medieval Society," in *The Role of Woman in the Middle Ages,* ed. Rosmarie Morewedge (Albany: State University of New York Press, 1975), p. 11: "There is, in other words, a body of scattered but consistent comment which indicates that between the early and the late Middle Ages, women had gained a superiority over men in life expectancy." Vern Bullough and Cameron Campbell, "Female Longevity and Diet in the Middle Ages," *Speculum* 55(1980): 317–25, make a persuasive case that improved diet led to a decrease in deaths of women from anemia and therefore led to an imbalance in the sex ratio as women outlived men. Robert Fossier, *Histoire sociale de l'Occident médiéval* (Paris: Armand Colin, 1970), p. 132, is alone in arguing that the sex ratio changed in the opposite direction.

20. *Cartulaire de Notre-Dame de Bourbourg,* 1:224–26, no. 222, ca. 1250–1300.

women had not come to outnumber men in society, however, many of the contemporary commentators believed they did. Albert the Great, seeking a cause for the preponderance of women, explains that they outlive men because they "work less, and are not so much consumed."[21] The perception that numbers of women were increasing and that women were demanding space in convents created anxiety and hostility in male commentators even if it was not true.

In addition, and partly in response to demographic shifts, the family changed its composition. David Herlihy argues in *Medieval Households* that the age for first marriages was the middle to late twenties for both women and men in the early Middle Ages. The pattern then changed in the central Middle Ages, when the age for a woman's first marriage dropped to the early teens, in contrast to her husband's which remained the later twenties.[22] The dowry custom, which in the early Middle Ages had been a nuptial gift from the groom to the bride, in our period was replaced by large dowries paid by the bride's family to the groom. These shifts, he suggests, reflect the decreasing valuation of females. It cost a family dearly to "unload" a daughter.

Further, if women's work status is linked to their economic contributions to the family as Martha Howell argues, then a decline in their economic production would aggravate their loss of value to the family and to society.[23] This occurred in the late medieval and early modern periods when the family, the group in which women had worked constructively, ceased to be a viable economic unit. When the family was a unit of production working together to raise crops and produce basic necessities, women's contribution was needed and valued, and their status was enhanced; when the corporatism of guild structures replaced the family as an economic entity, women's status declined.

Since monastic institutions were intricately interwoven with family structure, social and economic changes in the family and in production from the mid-twelfth century chipped away at the stature, recruitment, and income of monasteries. The changes hurt men's houses, but they seriously wounded and sometimes killed fe-

21. Herlihy, "Life Expectancies for Women," p. 11.
22. Herlihy, *Medieval Households*, pp. 103–10.
23. Martha Howell, "Women, the Family Economy, and the Structures of Market Production in Cities of Northern Europe during the Late Middle Ages," in *Women and Work in Pre-industrial Europe*, ed. Barbara A. Hanawalt (Bloomington: Indiana University Press, 1986), p. 201. Herlihy, *Opera Muliebria*, also shows the erosion of women's work opportunities and status.

male houses. A society geared to the family as defining all phases of life was being replaced by new structures. Interestingly, it was during the thirteenth century that monastics first began to take new names on entering the religious life—a change that seems to echo the rupture of the ancient alliance of kinship and cloister.[24] In the next centuries the monastic would be less important to the natal family, and the family would be less important to the cloistered person. The world of the knight, the nun, and the monk was giving way to the world of the friar and the merchant.[25] The first was aristocratic and gave a woman some share of its space by virtue of her birth; the second was bourgeois and limited the woman to the home. This new medieval world rewarded those who made money outside the home and those who preached in church and the marketplace. Women were barred from such public activity.

The separation of women's sphere of influence from men's tended to follow the public/private dichotomy.[26] Jane Schulenburg tracks this development and sees it already in process for religious women between 500 and 1100.[27] But the polarity grew stronger and more insistent in the centuries that followed. The inner and outer definitions of society—home as the appropriate place for a woman and marketplace and church square for a man—continued and became more binding on women over the centuries. In the late Middle Ages a woman's purity and domestic skills were lauded in treatises written by men to shape females into docile wives; the Goodman of Paris reminds his audience of the danger of immoral behavior: "And wot you that riches, beauty of form and face, lineage and all other virtues be all perished and wiped out in a woman that hath any stain or suspicion against one of these virtues aforesaid."[28] The public/ private dichotomy was paralleled by ecclesiastical authorities' efforts to subject nuns to more rigorous cloistering. The good nun was the cloistered nun whose purity reflected well on the church, just as

24. Bouchard, Sword, Miter and Cloister, p. 62, n. 51.

25. Little, Religious Poverty and the Profit Economy, pp. 200–202, suggests this dichotomy but without including nuns.

26. Susan Mosher Stuard, "A New Dimension? North American Scholars Contribute Their Perspective," in Women in Medieval History and Historiography, ed. Susan Mosher Stuard (Philadelphia: University of Pennsylvania Press, 1987), p. 93.

27. Schulenburg, "Female Sanctity," pp. 102–25.

28. The Goodman of Paris, trans. Eileen Power (New York: Harcourt Brace, 1928), p. 105. Also see another such hortatory treatise, this one addressed to a noble female audience: Le livre du Chevalier de la Tour Landry, ed. Anatole de Montaiglon (Paris: P. Jannet, 1854).

the good wife reflected well on her husband. A terse Spanish proverb embodies such thinking: "La mujer honrada, la pierna quebrada y en casa" ("The honorable woman is locked in the house with a broken leg"). Women's behavior can damage the reputation of the men associated with them, but the reverse is not true.

Changes in the Church

In addition to the new social and economic patterns that were taking shape in the central Middle Ages, the church too experienced change when in the middle of the eleventh century a wave of reform and renewal swept over it. Although called the Gregorian Reform, it was already several decades old before Gregory VII ascended the papal throne in 1073. The impact of the new ideas was profound, since they sought to redefine ultimate authority in the world and to separate the clergy from the laity.[29] The reform affected nuns who had since the early church shared lay status with monks, both being separate and distinct from the priestly orders.[30] But in the process of redefining society into those people in clerical orders and those secular folk outside of orders, religious women increasingly were lumped with the laity instead of with their fellow monastics as more and more monks became priests. The sacralization of monks shattered the symmetry of female and male monasticism, making nuns second-class monastics.

A second change that diluted the impact of religious women on society was the advent of the friars in the early thirteenth century. These mendicant orders competed with the older monastic foundations for recruits and gifts. The Franciscans occupied the moral high ground previously enjoyed by the Cistercians and other reformed orders of the twelfth century. The Dominicans became the highly educated elite, used by the papacy as inquisitors. Both groups of friars were extremely visible within society, since they preached in public. Women who joined these two orders, however, entered cloistered convents very like the houses that had preexisted the friars. Ironically, the Poor Clares and female Dominicans, despite the innovations of their founders, offered women nothing new; instead, the

29. Gerd Tellenbach, *Church, State and Christian Society at the Time of the Investiture Contest*, trans. R. F. Bennett (New York: Harper, 1959), pp. 126–61. Moore, *Origins of European Dissent*, p. 78.

30. Dubois, *Histoire monastique en France au XIIe siècle* (London: Variorum, 1982), p. 68.

female branches of the two orders simply increased the number of traditional monasteries that needed lay support.

The competition of the mendicants caused problems for established monasteries. When the friars crowded a strong and self-confident house, the fur flew. The Dominicans who settled in Troyes made the mistake of building in the city near the nunnery of Notre-Dame-aux-Nonnains, home to the formidable nuns who earlier had resisted a papal foundation.[31] Abbess Isabelle, incensed by these new encroachments, called out her troops—her brother, Sir Guy of Saint-Fale, and the sergeants and men of the abbey—and led these armed supporters to break into the Dominican priory. When townfolk gathered to gawk or remonstrate, they were summarily dumped in a ditch. The next day the town provost with his sergeants attempted to protect the Dominicans, but he too quailed before the abbess and her troops when they broke into the friars' cloister and trashed it to make their point. Such aggressive resistance to the new orders is rare, but it suggests something of the hostility established houses felt toward the new orders. The final act in this minidrama was a royal directive for two of Philip IV's men to settle the conflict. The Dominicans were refused the right to expand into the nuns' grounds or to enlarge the portal, but the nuns had to make reparation for their vandalism and repair the broken wall.

The mendicants were joined in the thirteenth century and increasingly in the later Middle Ages by a host of other competitors for charitable patronage: beguines (laywomen who took simple vows and lived alone or with a few other women), recluses, hospitals, leper houses, colleges, civic charities like bridge and road repair, the poor, endowments of dowries for poor girls, and chantry priests who said masses for the testator's salvation. The will of the widow Mathea is representative of the expanding range of bequests in the thirteenth century. Now that she is widowed Mathea has decided to enter the monastic community of the Hospital of Saint-Jean. She makes bequests to that institution, and also to the Franciscans, the Dominicans, three houses of religious women and one of monks, two leper houses, two churches for rebuilding projects, the poor, and several servants and friends. The Franciscans get ten pounds, the Dominicans receive five pounds, and then there is a big drop as the nuns, monks, and leper houses get between ten and twenty solidi each (one-half to one pound).

31. See *Documents de Notre-Dame-aux-Nonnains*, pp. 138–39, no. 211, 1307, for the story of the attack. Also see p. 139, nos. 212–13, 1307 for the settlement.

Not only was there a proliferation of good causes that might claim the donor's attention, but inflation meant bequests did not stretch as far. In the mid-eleventh century, Agnes of Burgundy had spent 875 pounds to endow Notre-Dame in Saintes; when Queen Blanche of Castille founded the Abbey of Maubuisson in 1241, she laid out 25,000 pounds.[32] Few founders had the lavish resources of the queen; by the end of our period, even patrons who wanted to contribute to the upkeep of a monastery could seldom marshal sums capable of rebuilding part of an abbey or refurbishing convent buildings. It became customary, therefore, to sprinkle small sums around among many worthy institutions instead of endowing one monastery with a major bequest.

During the thirteenth century the older monasteries lost their chic to the new mendicant orders and began to feel the pinch. Too many hungry hands were reaching out for the available resources. Particularly hard hit were the women's convents, which could not hold their own against the highly visible and fashionable friars. What is more, the nunneries were always vulnerable to a takeover by monks if some excuse could be found to make such a move defensible. It is very hard to discern whether such seizures were justified, but I strongly suspect that they were generally political and economic in nature rather than moral and spiritual. Not only were new institutions and civic needs competing with the nuns for patronage and support, but also bishops were actively bringing monasteries under their control in the central Middle Ages.[33] Thus the nunneries were challenged laterally by friars and other charities and repressed vertically by the consolidation of episcopal power.

Changes in beliefs and devotional practices also had an impact on the fortunes of monastics. The laity were becoming more involved in spiritual exercises as large crowds of city folk gathered several times a week to hear the mendicants preach. In addition, during the thirteenth century lay women and men began routinely to say the rosary, patterned repetitions of the *Pater Noster* and the *Ave Maria*.[34] Devout women and men who said their rosaries may well have felt less need to petition and pay for monastic prayers.

32. See my article, "Agnes of Burgundy: An Eleventh-Century Woman as Monastic Patron," *Journal of Medieval History* 15(1989): 93–104, n. 17. For Blanche, see Dutilleux and Depoin, *Abbaye de Maubuisson*, p. 4.
33. Giles Constable, "The Authority of Superiors in the Religious Communities," in *La notion d'autorité au Moyen Age: Islam, Byzance, Occident*, Colloques Internationaux de la Napoule, 1978 (Paris: Presses Universitaires de France, 1982), p. 196.
34. Little, *Religious Poverty and the Profit Economy*, p. 211.

The dependence of religious women on the priesthood increased in our period. The replacement in 1228 of monastic confession, which was not dependent on the presence of a priest, by penance, which necessitated his actions, added one more way convents required priestly intervention.[35] Whereas a nunnery had once been able to get by with paying only one priest, by the thirteenth century it might need three to handle its increased sacramental needs. But even more pressing was the demand for masses for the dead, which could be celebrated only by a priest. With the doctrine of purgatory in place by the 1200s, people both inside and outside the church wanted the suffrages and masses that would help their souls and those of family members escape the fires of divine punishment. Pressured by the desire to rescue beloved souls from torment, the laity preferred to establish masses with monks, most of whom by the end of our period were priests, or with secular priests and friars rather than with nuns.[36]

The Xenophobic Reaction

Religious women's status was dented and diminished by the broad social, economic, and ecclesiastical changes of the central Middle Ages that were accelerated by a subtle yet critical change in the thinking of medieval people. This shift in *mentalité* occurred during the twelfth century when western Europe's self-confident growth and expansion failed to carry the Second Crusade to a successful conclusion. In an elegantly constructed article, Giles Constable demonstrates that the crusade actually comprised a number of thrusts at the Levant, coupled with separate campaigns against the pagan Wends and the Almoravids.[37] Pope Eugenius III and Saint Bernard orchestrated this multifaceted attack on the enemies of Christendom. The signal lack of success—indeed, the humiliation of the Western forces—is reflected in the writings of contemporaries, who fix on different scapegoats: human sin, the crusaders' failings and sinfulness, the forces of nature, the Saracens, betrayal by Franks in the East, or infighting among the leaders. Whatever causes were blamed, the West was forced to recognize that its pride and glory, its

35. Leclercq, "Medieval Feminine Monasticism," p. 61.

36. Jean-Loup Lemaître, "Nécrologes et obituaires des religieuses en France," in *Les religieuses en France au XIIIe siècle*, ed. Michel Parisse, Conference Proceedings of l'Institut d'Etudes Médiévales de l'Université de Nancy II and CERCOM, 1983 (Nancy: Presses Universitaires de Nancy, 1985), p. 165.

37. Giles Constable, "The Second Crusade as Seen by Contemporaries," *Traditio* 9(1953): 213–79.

crusading hosts, could not prevail against the enemies of Christ. The awareness of failure dealt a decisive blow to Western optimism, and from about 1150 on the West began to show a defensive xenophobic reaction. Those groups holding beliefs or demonstrating behavior outside the norms for western Europe began to feel this adverse response turned against them.

The timetable varies, but the direction is clear: somewhere between the late eleventh century and the late twelfth, the empowered majority began to feel growing suspicion of those different from themselves, a process that accelerated in the late Middle Ages.[38] The first to bear the brunt of the hostility toward outlanders were the Jews of the Rhineland, who found themselves in the path of the unruly crusaders on their way to liberate the Holy Land in 1096; in contrast to the violent attacks the Rhineland Jews experienced, most of French Jewry escaped the slaughter because of bribes paid to the crusaders.[39] Robert Chazan points out that in fact the Jews living in France fared well in urban commerce and developed their own institutions for self-government in the eleventh and twelfth centuries. He describes a flourishing French Jewish community that nevertheless lived in an uneasy limbo, since "the twelfth century was an especially active period in the gestation of deep-seated animosities."[40] Trouble was brewing for the Jews of France, who would by the end of the century experience arbitrary confiscations and expulsions whenever the crown needed money.

The Franks had seen Muslims as enemies from at least as early as the eighth century, but latent fear and hostility were whipped into a frenzy by the preaching of crusades starting in 1095. R. W. Southern discerns a subtle shading in the thinking and behavior of Christians toward their Islamic adversaries.[41] He describes an age of ignorance in the early Middle Ages, followed by a century of reason and hopefulness in the twelfth century, lasting until the end of the thirteenth century when, with the fall of Acre in 1291, all positive feelings

38. I owe the genesis of this argument to Giles Constable's article "The Second Crusade as Seen by Contemporaries" and to John Boswell's book *Christianity, Social Toleration, and Homosexuality.*

39. See Shlomo Eidelberg, ed., *The Jews and the Crusaders: The Hebrew Chronicles of the First and Second Crusades* (Madison: University of Wisconsin Press, 1977); Robert Chazan, *European Jewry and the First Crusade* (Berkeley: University of California Press, 1987).

40. Robert Chazan, *Medieval Jewry in Northern France: A Political and Social History* (Baltimore: Johns Hopkins University Press, 1973), p. 46.

41. R. W. Southern, *Western Views of Islam in the Middle Ages* (Cambridge: Harvard University Press, 1962).

were extinguished. Other scholars revamp his three-part scheme and dating but agree that fear and hatred of the Muslim enemy increased in the later part of the central Middle Ages.[42]

Perhaps the most insidious enemies inspiring fear and hatred in the central Middle Ages were the heretics, those people who were felt to have consciously chosen to deny the beliefs and practices of Christianity. Although some learned heresies existed in the early medieval period, it was during the eleventh and twelfth centuries that popular heresy was born.[43] Church and secular authorities came together in the thirteenth century to crush the largest of medieval heretical movements: the Albigensians in Languedoc.[44]

John Boswell suggests that the rising hostility against gay men in the latter part of the twelfth century was one more current in this tide of more general distrust of "the Other." He discerns a repressive reaction against homosexuality following a flowering of gay culture from about 1050 to 1150; the new antagonism against gay men crystallized officially in a judgment of Third Lateran Council in 1179, the first general council of the church to legislate penalties for homosexual acts.[45] In the twelfth and thirteenth centuries, gay men were lumped first with the Muslims and then with another feared and hated group, heretics.[46] The revulsion against gays crescendoed

42. Ronald C. Finucane, *Soldiers of the Faith: Crusaders and Moslems at War* (New York: St. Martin's Press, 1983), p. 157, marks the period from about 1095 to 1200 as the time of "outspoken, often wild, verbal attack upon Moslems and their religion." He cites a Dominican missionary's growing "sense of anxiety" about 1300 (p. 167). Benjamin Z. Kedar, *Crusade and Mission: European Approaches toward the Muslims* (Princeton: Princeton University Press, 1984), p. 35, specifically challenges Southern's view of the early age of ignorance and argues that in the thirteenth and fourteenth centuries many medieval theorists accepted the linkage of the sword and the Word as a means to subdue the Saracens.

43. Moore, *Origins of European Dissent,* p. ix. Moore sees heresy in our period as social dissent. In contrast, Jeffrey Burton Russell, *Dissent and Reform in the Early Middle Ages* (Berkeley: University of California Press, 1965), pp. 233–34, dates the origins of dissent to the eighth century and sees the causes as more religious than social.

44. See Walter L. Wakefield, *Heresy, Crusade and Inquisition in Southern France, 1100–1250* (Berkeley: University of California Press, 1974), which presents a revisionist view arguing that the Albigensian Crusade did not destroy a flourishing southern culture, that the great lords of the south were indifferent to either religion, and that the damage to Languedoc was speedily repaired.

45. Boswell, *Christianity, Social Tolerance, and Homosexuality;* chap. 9 describes the free expression of gay culture, and chap. 10 deals with the reactionary climate against minority groups.

46. Boswell, *Christianity, Social Tolerance, and Homosexuality,* pp. 278–86. The Orléans code is mentioned on pp. 289–90.

into the thirteenth century, when a law code drawn up by the school at Orléans decreed draconian punishments for homosexual behavior.

Other marginal groups also experienced a growing reaction against them. The association of lepers with sin, particularly with sexual depravity, made these unfortunate souls some of the most despised outcasts in the medieval world. Their segregation from the rest of society was legislated by Third Lateran Council.[47] But the worst outrage was inflicted on them in the early fourteenth century when King Philip V accused them, together with the Jews, of poisoning wells. Philip, like some of his predecessors, was in need of money and used this slander as an excuse to confiscate the endowments of leper houses in the South after many of their inmates had been burned to death.

Fear of the poor as dangerous and sinful was general by the beginning of the thirteenth century and accelerated in the late Middle Ages.[48] Yet at the same time, giving to the poor was a charge laid on every Christian. Thus paupers occupied a strange niche in medieval culture: they inspired fear yet symbolically represented Christ. In our period, charity for the poor first was embedded in monastic observances that were primarily liturgical practices; then, during the thirteenth century, much of the care for the poor began to pass to civic institutions like hospitals and almshouses run by town governments.

The "distinct hardening of attitudes," the rejection of dissenting voices, marked the closing down of societal flexibility in the 1140s and 1150s.[49] The largest group to be marginalized by this rigidity and exclusivity in the twelfth century in the West was women. Even though by the mid-twelfth century women may well have outnumbered men, their proportional numbers did not earn them dominance in institutions of power and wealth; they remained on the margins of social control systems. Their huge numbers protected them from being physically driven to the outskirts of society as were the smaller groups, but ironically, their real or perceived numerical advantage may have helped earn them hostility—a resentment dif-

47. Saul Nathaniel Brody, *The Disease of the Soul: Leprosy in Medieval Literature* (Ithaca, N.Y.: Cornell University Press, 1974), p. 64; see pp. 92–93 for their treatment by Philip V.

48. Michel Mollat, *The Poor in the Middle Ages: An Essay in Social History,* trans. Arthur Goldhammer (New Haven: Yale University Press, 1978), pp. 112, 251–54.

49. Moore, *Origins of European Dissent,* p. 254.

ferent in intensity but not in nature from that aimed at other marginalized groups. Willy-nilly, religious women reaped the harvest of
distrust along with their secular sisters.

This shift in the status of medieval nuns does not happen all at
once, nor does it occur in any absolute fashion. What we have been
examining is a slow evolutionary process, not a rapid revolutionary
change. Religious women in the eleventh century lived and wor-
shiped in a generally friendly religious and secular environment; by
the thirteenth century the religious climate was suspicious yet the
secular environment was still friendly. By the late Middle Ages, religious women existed in an environment that cared little about
them; their numbers would decrease rapidly, foundations would be
gobbled up by male houses, existing nunneries would sag deeper
into debt, and their intellectual and spiritual life would erode. The
constriction of the regular cloistered life for religious women nar-
rowed their options; whether the new expressions to which women
turned—intense mystical experience and the often fierce denial of
physical needs—were positive or not depends heavily on individual
scholarly interpretation. There is, however, general unanimity that
the shift occurred.[50] When women and men shared the institution
of monasticism with some semblance of equality, participants and
structure flourished. But when gender symmetry was lost, nuns became a nuisance rather than an asset, and their position deterio-
rated. The decline in numbers and stature of religious women was
important in itself; it also stands near the beginning of a more general decline in women's status that, I believe, is not reversed in the
West until the nineteenth century.

50. Peter Dronke, *Women Writers of the Middle Ages: A Critical Study of Texts
from Perpetua (+203) to Marguerite Porete (+1310)* (Cambridge: Cambridge University Press, 1984), p. 202, defines the change as one of an "increased subjectivity." Bell
and Bynum see the new subjectivity as positive. Bell, *Holy Anorexia*, p. 117: "Holy
anorexics did in fact break out of the established boundaries within which a male
hierarchy confined female piety, and thereby established newer and wider avenues for
religious expression by women more generally." Bynum, *Holy Feast and Holy Fast*,
p. 296, argues even more strongly for the positive interpretation of extreme food practices among holy women: "Women saw themselves not as flesh opposed to spirit,
female opposed to male, nurture opposed to authority; they saw themselves as human
beings—fully spirit and fully flesh." Others are more cautious, Petroff, *Consolation
of the Blessed*, p. 41: "Their physical austeries were often horrifying; in many accounts, the girls' refusals to eat look very much like anorexia nervosa and for this
reason some scholars have suspected that they felt a deep aversion to mature sexuality."

CONCLUSION

The tail end of medieval monasticism in the later Middle Ages is not very edifying; this was often true for monks and usually true for nuns. But I do not want to end on such a dreary note. I have chosen to study some three hundred years to see what change over time could be perceived in women's monastic vocations, and to better understand the perceptions of those vocations during the central Middle Ages. In the process, the extreme polemical positions fall by the wayside. There is no use sentimentalizing the medieval nun: she is not best represented by saccharine Sunday school images, on her knees, eyeballs rolled heavenward. She could be as tough as any man: imprisoning dishonest stewards and dealing with a neighbor's crude form of capital punishment, demanding that serfs pay their fines, attacking encroaching neighbors, and disciplining unruly patrons. She is equally ill served by a dogged feminist attempt to prove she was part of a self-conscious female subculture.[51] The medieval nun did not see herself first and foremost as a woman; to expect she would is to think anachronistically. Nor was she—in the spirit of porn films about nurses or stewardesses—a member of a group of women who, once free from chaperonage, would become lustful lovers. Some of her sisters slipped from the rigor of the rule, but by and large she was not a naughty nun.

Without the distorting stereotypes, we find that what she was in her world, she was in her own right, not as a substitute for a man.[52] Contemporary secular folk wanted her prayers and supported her way of life. Contemporary ecclesiastics accepted her as one of them in the earlier part of our period. The author of a twelfth-century book about monastics intended to discuss religious women but apparently never finished his work (a fate not unknown to scholars!). In his introduction he sets out his plan: "Then similarly we shall revert to women, who lead an eremitical life, rising to the holiness of nuns, and to those who sweetly take up Christ's yoke with holy men or under their guidance."[53] Indeed, in the twelfth century it was very possible for a nun to take up the yoke *with* her confreres.

Brenda Bolton raises an interesting question, asking why the in-

51. Newman, *Sister of Wisdom*, p. xv, also finds no evidence of a female subculture in twelfth-century Germany.
52. Bennett, *Women in the Medieval English Countryside*, p. 160, describes how peasant women were at best only surrogates for men.
53. *Libellus de diversis ordinibus*, p. 5.

creased numbers of women seeking a religious vocation did not generate a new order specifically for women in the early thirteenth century.[54] She is positing that nuns would have wanted an order framed
exclusively for women which, however, would have seemed pointless to them. They did not think of binary exclusivity, an either/or
ideal in the regular life, but rather envisioned a joint endeavor of
women and men, living and working in symmetrical systems. Partly
this mind-set is due to the absolute necessity for religious women
to rely on priests for the sacraments, which was a fundamental
weakness of the medieval convent; but partly it grows out of the
great shared strength of monastic women and men, who partook of
a common vision of equality in the order of grace.

Substantive differences did exist between religious women and
men. They boil down to three critical disparities: monks could be
ordained to the priesthood while nuns could not; women were more
tightly cloistered than men; and women's houses were generally
poorer than men's. It is highly probable that the ability of monks to
take priestly orders explains in good part the growing economic gap
between nunneries and male monasteries, while the ever more
stringent cloistering of nuns seems to grow out of the fears and resentments toward marginal people that proliferated in the end of the
twelfth century. But though many male authors could not resist the
duality of black and white, evil and good, female and male, "Eva
espina, Maria rosa," by and large, before the midpoint of the twelfth
century the pragmatic reality was that nuns and monks shared a
parallel, a symmetrical life.[55] Abelard addressing the nuns of the
Paraclete probably is speaking for most of his fellow monastics
when he says: "In name and profession of continence you are one
with us."[56]

54. Bolton, "Mulieres Sanctae," p. 143.
55. Saint Bernard's duality of thorny Eve and blooming Mary quoted by Shahar,
Fourth Estate, p. 42, n. 5.
56. *Letters of Abelard and Heloise*, p. 184, a sentiment worlds apart in feeling but
only a few decades distant from the "general suspicion of female character" that
Bynum notes in thirteenth- and fourteenth-century treatises for religious women.

APPENDIX A

THE TWENTY-SIX FEMALE MONASTERIES STUDIED

Diocese and Location	Name[a]	Order	Date Founded
Namur (Namur)	Val-Saint Georges, Salzinnes (Salsinia)	Cistercian	1111
Therouanne (Ther-ouanne)	Notre-Dame de Bourbourg (Broburgense)	Benedictine	ca. 1099
Rouen (Le Havre)	Notre-Dame de Monti-villiers (Montivillarium)	Benedictine	682
Rouen (Rouen)	Saint-Amand (S. Amandus)	Benedictine	ca. 1030
Rouen (Gaillefon-taine)	Clairruissel (Clarus Rivus)	Fontevrist	1140
Rouen (Pontoise)	L'hôtel-Dieu, Pontoise (Domus Dei Pontisare)	Augustinian	ca. 1190
Rouen (Pontoise)	Notre-Dame-la-Royale, Maubuisson (Malus Dumus)	Cistercian	1241
Rennes (Rennes)	Saint-Georges (S. Georgius)	Benedictine	11th c.
Rennes (Rennes)	Saint-Sulpice-la-Forêt (S. Sulpitius)	Benedictine	12th c.
Soissons (Château-Thierry)	La Barre (Barra)	Augustinian	1210
Meaux (Crécy-en-Brie)	Pont-aux-Dames (Pons Dominarum)	Cistercian	1226

Diocese and Location	Name[a]	Order	Date Founded
Troyes (Troyes)	Notre-Dame-aux-Nonnains (B. Maria)	Benedictine	657
Troyes (Nogent-sur-Seine)	Paraclete (Paracletus)	Benedictine	1129
Troyes (Bar-sur-Aube)	Notre-Dame de Basse-Fontaine (Bassus Fons)	Premonstra-tensian	1143
Sens (Sergines)	Notre-Dame la Pommeraie (Pomeraya, Pomerium, Pomaria)	Benedictine (Paraclete)	1151
Sens (Sens)	Mont-Sainte-Catherine (Mons S. Catharinae)	Clarisse	1248
Chartres (Château-dun)	Saint-Avit (B. Avitus, Castrodunense)	Benedictine	1045
Chartres (Theil)	Les Clairets (Claretum, de Claretis)	Cistercian (Savigny)	1204
Orléans (Orléans)	La Magdeleine-lez-Orléans (BVM de Hospitium)	Fontevrist	ca. 1113
Orléans (Meung-sur-Loire)	Notre-Dame de Voisins (Vicinis)	Cistercian	1213
Orléans (Orléans)	Lieu-Notre-Dame-lès-Romorantin (Locus B. Mariae)	Cistercian	1250
Angers (Angers)	Notre-Dame la Charité, Ronceray (B. Maria Caritatis, Andegavensis)	Benedictine	1028
Angers (Angers)	Saint-Jean, Angers (Elemosinaria B. Johannis)	Augustinian	1166
Mctz (Metz)	Saint-Pierre-aux-Nonnains (Insula Metensis)	Benedictine	598
Poitiers (Poitiers)	Sainte-Trinité (S. Trinitatis)	Benedictine	965
Saintes (Saintes)	Notre-Dame de Saintes (B. Maria Sanctonensis)	Benedictine	1047

[a]Latin name in parentheses.

APPENDIX B

LIST OF MONASTERIES FROM THE REGISTER OF EUDES RIGAUD
(WOMEN'S HOUSES, MEN'S HOUSES, AND HOSPITALS)

Name	Status	Order	Average Number of Residents	Diocese	Number of Visits
WOMEN'S HOUSES					
Almenèches	Abbey	Benedictine	41	Séez	3
Aries	Priory	Benedictine	15	Avranches	1
Bival	Abbey	Cistercian	33	Rouen	14
Bondeville	Priory	Cistercian	40	Rouen	10
Lisieux	Abbey	Benedictine	32	Lisieux	4
Montivilliers	Abbey	Benedictine	57	Rouen	15
Saint-Amand	Abbey	Benedictine	48	Rouen	11
Saint-Aubin	Priory	Cistercian	14	Rouen	14
Sainte-Marguerite	Priory	Benedictine	24	Séez	1
Sainte-Trinité, Caen	Abbey	Benedictine	71	Bayeux	3
Saint-Léger	Abbey	Benedictine	45	Lisieux	4
Saint-Saens	Priory	Benedictine	16	Rouen	15
Saint-Sauveur	Abbey	Benedictine	62	Evreux	4
Villarceux	Priory	Benedictine	20	Rouen	11
MEN'S HOUSES					
Aumale	Abbey	Benedictine	17	Rouen	10
Beaulieu	Priory	Augustinian	12	Rouen	16
Beaumont en Auge	Priory	Benedictine	13	Lisieux	4
Beaumont le Roger	Priory	Benedictine	8	Evreux	4
Bec	Abbey	Benedictine	79	Rouen	8

Name	Status	Order	Average Number of Residents	Diocese	Number of Visits
Bernay	Abbey	Benedictine	21	Lisieux	4
Bourg Achard	Priory	Augustinian	11	Rouen	14
Conches	Abbey	Benedictine	27	Evreux	4
Cormeilles	Abbey	Benedictine	26	Lisieux	4
Corneville	Abbey	Augustinian	9	Rouen	12
Croix Saint-Leufroy	Abbey	Benedictine	20	Evreux	4
Envermeu	Priory	Benedictine	11	Rouen	15
Eu	Abbey	Augustinian	29	Rouen	14
Fontenay	Abbey	Benedictine	22	Bayeux	3
Graville	Priory	Augustinian	11	Rouen	15
Grestain	Abbey	Benedictine	29	Lisieux	4
Hambye	Abbey	Benedictine	19	Coutances	3
Ivry	Abbey	Benedictine	16	Evreux	4
Jumièges	Abbey	Benedictine	50	Rouen	18
Lessay	Abbey	Benedictine	34	Coutances	3
Longues	Abbey	Benedictine	20	Bayeux	3
Longues Priory	Priory	Benedictine	8	Bayeux	1
Lyre	Abbey	Benedictine	46	Evreux	3
Mont Deux Amants	Priory	Augustinian	13	Rouen	15
Montebourg	Abbey	Benedictine	34	Coutances	2
Montmorel	Abbey	Augustinian	15	Avranches	3
Mont Saint-Michel	Abbey	Benedictine	40	Avranches	3
Ouville	Priory	Augustinian	11	Rouen	15
Pré	Priory	Benedictine?	17	Rouen	6
Rocher de Mortain	Priory	Benedictine	10	Avranches	2
Sausseuse	Priory	Augustinian	13	Rouen	16
Sainte Barbe-en-Auge	Priory	Canons	35	Lisieux	4
Sainte-Catherine	Abbey	Benedictine	29	Rouen	17
Saint-Etienne	Abbey	Benedictine	62	Bayeux	3
Sainte-Etienne le Plessis Grimoult	Priory	Augustinian	16	Bayeux	3
Saint-Evroult	Abbey	Benedictine	33	Lisieux	4
Saint-Fromond	Priory	Benedictine	14	Coutances	3
Saint-Georges Bohon	Priory	Benedictine	7	Coutances	3
Saint-Georges de Boscherville	Abbey	Benedictine	22	Rouen	17
Saint-Hymer	Priory	Benedictine	11	Lisieux	4
Saint-Laurent	Priory	Augustinian	15	Rouen	15

Name	Status	Order	Average Number of Residents	Diocese	Number of Visits
Saint-Lô	Priory	Augustinian	18	Rouen	19
Saint-Martin Pontoise	Abbey	Benedictine	22	Rouen	15
Saint-Martin Séez	Abbey	Benedictine	32	Séez	2
Saint-Ouen	Abbey	Benedictine	55	Rouen	14
Saint-Pierre Dives	Abbey	Benedictine	35	Séez	3
Saint-Pierre Lierru	Priory	Augustinian	9	Evreux	3
Saint-Pierre Préaux	Abbey	Benedictine	31	Lisieux	4
Saint-Sauveur le Vicomte	Abbey	Benedictine	26	Coutances	3
Saint-Sever	Abbey	Benedictine	17	Coutances	3
Saint-Sulpice	Priory	Benedictine?	8	Evreux	3
Saint-Taurin	Abbey	Benedictine	24	Evreux	4
Saint-Victor	Abbey	Benedictine	18	Rouen	13
Saint-Vigor Cerisy	Abbey	Benedictine	35	Bayeux	3
Saint-Vigor le Grand	Priory	Benedictine	13	Bayeux	2
Saint-Wandrille	Abbey	Benedictine	39	Rouen	16
Tréport	Abbey	Benedictine	21	Rouen	13
Troarn	Abbey	Benedictine	41	Bayeux	3
Val	Abbey	Augustinian	13	Bayeux	3
Valmont	Abbey	Benedictine	25	Rouen	14
Voeu	Abbey	Augustinian	26	Coutances	3
		HOSPITALS			
Bellencombre Priory/leper hospital Run by Prior	Hospital	?	7 (3 sisters, 4 canons)	Rouen	2
Caen, hôtel-Dieu Priory/hospital Run by prior	Hospital	?	16 (10 sisters, 6 canons)	Bayeux	2
Mont-aux-Malades Priory/leper hospital Run by prior	Hospital	Augustinian	26 (16 sisters, 10 canons)	Rouen	6
Neufchâtel, hôtel-Dieu Priory/hospital	Hospital	?	8 (4 sisters, 4 canons)	Rouen	9

Name	Status	Order	Average Number of Residents	Diocese	Number of Visits
Pontoise, hôtel-Dieu					
Priory/hospital	Hospital	Augustinian	16	Rouen	6
Run by prioress and			(12 sisters,		
rector			4 canons)		
Sainte Mary Magdalen,					
Hôtel-Dieu Rouen					
Priory/hospital	Hospital	?	37	Rouen	8
Run by prioress and			(23 women,		
prior			14 canons)		
Salle aux Puelles					
Priory/leper hos-	Hospital	?	2	Rouen	5
pital			(1 sister,		
Run by prioress and			1 canon)		
prior for "advantage					
of sisters"					

Number of convents: 14
Total number of nuns: 518
Average convent size: 37

Number of monasteries: 61
Total number of monks: 1,443
Average monastery size: 23.6

Number of hospitals and leper houses: 7
Total sisters: 69
Total canons: 43

Average size for all religious women's houses: 35
Average size for all religious men's houses: 23

Cumulative totals for Norman religious represented in the *Register* of Eudes Rigaud:
monastic women, 587; monastic men, 1, 486

GLOSSARY

Ad succurrendum nun or monk: person who took the habit in old age or illness to be cared for at a monastery until death

Advocate: person designated protector of a monastery

Almoner: monastic official who dispensed a monastery's almsgiving

Almshouse: poorhouse

Alod: freehold land

Anchoress: woman living as an enclosed hermitess

Anchorite: man living as an enclosed hermit

Armarium: monastic library

Arpent: roughly an acre of land

Cartulary: a book of collected documents usually dealing with legal and economic transactions of a monastery

Cellaress: monastic official who procured and oversaw a monastery's food supplies

Cens: annual rent on property paid by a landholder to a landowner

Chantress: monastic official in charge of choral service and production of books

Cloistering: (passive) barring of nonmonastics from the house; (active) prohibition of monastics from exiting the house

Computation: periodic, formal accounting by a monastery's leaders

Confraternity: union of prayer and privileges between individuals and monasteries or between monasteries (also called *societas*)

Conversa (-ae): lay sister

Conversus (-i): lay brother

Corvée: work days owed by a peasant to a lord or lordship

Cura monialium: overseeing of and clerical support for a nunnery by male clergy

Decana (-ae): monastic official who served as vice abbess

Demesne land: land kept by a medieval lordship for its own use

Diocesan: bishop of a diocese

Documents of practice: pragmatic legal, economic, and institutional records that reflect the world as it was

273

Documents of theory: prescriptive and hortatory records that show the world as the writer thought it should be

Donationes altaris: parishioners' offerings to priest who performed sacraments and officiated on feast days

Dowry, for monastics: entry gift given monastery when a nun or monk joined an order

Exemption: freedom for a monastery from episcopal control and oversight

Familia: Group of people who answered to a monastery's orders and depended on it for their livelihood

Gradual: hymn sung between the reading of the Epistle and the Gospel

Hagiography: writing of saints' lives

Hospes (-*itis*): free peasant

Indulgence: remission of punishment granted a penitent for performing acts such as going on crusade or on pilgrimage

Infirmarian: monastic official in charge of the infirmary

Ius patronatus: right to name a priest to a benefice

Lectio divina: monastics' regular daily reading and meditation on sacred texts

Mandatum: ceremony of washing the feet of twelve people in memory of Christ's washing his apostles' feet

Martyrology: calendar of saints' feast days, to which were added the death dates of people to be remembered in monastics' daily prayers

Muid: measure of grain

Novice: woman or man who has entered a monastery but has not yet taken final vows

Obedience: small, dependent monastic community with fewer than eight monastics

Oblation: offering oneself or a child to serve God as a nun or monk

Opus Dei: divine offices, or the hours; eight services of prayers and psalms celebrated throughout each day by nuns and monks

Ordinary: bishop with ordinary jurisdiction over a diocese

Panchart: document containing a collection of related documents

Pittance: extra serving of food or wine, received by each monastic to celebrate a festive occasion

Procuration: customary fee paid by a monastery to the official visitor

Regular clergy: ecclesiastics who follow a rule

Rogation Days: three days before Ascension Day

*Rotulus (-*i*):* monastic chain-letter scroll, circulated among religious institutions to announce the death of an abbess or abbot

Sacristan: monastic official with responsibility for care of altar and vestments and care and repair of church

Secular clergy: ecclesiastics who take holy orders but do not follow a rule

Sester: measure of grain

Taille: an arbitrary seigneurial levy on serfs

Tithe: tax assessment of one-tenth income due to local parish

Visitor: cleric who makes periodic official visitations to secular and regular clergy in his diocese

Vita (-*ae*): written life of medieval saintly person

Note on medieval money: The silver penny, (*denarius/denier*), was the only Western medieval coin. Twelve pennies equaled one shilling (*solidus*), and twenty shillings equaled one pound. The shilling and pound were not coins but money of account designations. A mark equaled thirteen shillings and four pennies, or two-thirds of a pound.

SELECTED BIBLIOGRAPHY

PRIMARY SOURCES
Manuscripts

Archives Départementales de Charente-Maritime, La Rochelle
  H 75, 76, 77
Archives Départementales de Seine-Maritime, Rouen
  H 51, 52, 53, 55, 56
Archives Départementales de la Vienne, Poitiers
  2 H 1, 2 H 2
Beinecke Library, Yale University, New Haven
  MS. Marston 25, Kalendarius liber
Bibliothèque Municipale de Poitiers
  MS. 430
  Collection Fonteneau, MSS. 24, 25, 27, 27³, 80
Bibliothèque Municipale de La Rochelle
  MSS. 128, 129, 130
Bibliothèque Municipale de Saintes
  MSS. 507, 576e
Bibliothèque Nationale, Paris
  MSS. lat. 9220, 9234, 9894, 10027, 10028, 10944, 10997, 10998, 11002, 12665, 12667, 12682, 12700, 12754, 12755, 12759, 12780, 13758, 16309, 17140, 18402
  MS. n.a. lat. 928
  MSS. fr. 4669, 4194, 12052, 19836, 20909, 24714, 26480
  Collection Baluze, MSS. 38, 46, 75
  Collection Champagne, MS. 17
  Collection Duchesne, MS. 20
  Collection Gaignières, MSS. 17029, 20898, 20909, 20913, 20917
  Collection Lespine, MS. 34
  Collection Périgord, MSS. 34, 35, 41
  Topographie de Champagne, MS. 24

Printed Works

"L'abbaye de la Barre et son recueil de chartres." Edited by Alexandre-Eusèbe Poquet. *Annales de la Société Historique et Archéologique de Château-Thierry* 58(1884): 117–77.

L'abbaye du Pont-aux-Dames (ordre de Cîteaux) assise en la paroisse de Couilly, 1226–1790. Edited by Claude H. Berthault. Meaux: Librairie le Blondel, 1878.

Abbaye royale de Notre-Dame des Clairets: Histoire et cartulaire par le vicomte de Souancé, 1202–1790. Edited by Joseph-H.-H.-J. Guillier de Souancé. Vannes: Lafolye, 1894.

Carré, E., ed. "Histoire et cartulaire du prieuré de Notre-Dame et Ste. Marguerite de la Presle." *Revue de Champagne et de Brie,* 2d ser., 4(1892): 5–27; 5(1893): 20–54, 348–68, 432–49, 508–14.

Cartulaire de l'abbaye cardinale de la Trinité de Vendôme. Edited by Charles Métais. 5 vols. Paris: A. Picard, 1893–1904.

Cartulaire de l'abbaye de Basse-Fontaine. Edited by Charles Lalore. *Collection des principaux cartulaires du diocèse de Troyes,* vol. 3. Troyes: Thorin, 1878.

Cartulaire de l'abbaye de Maubuisson (Notre-Dame-la-Royale). Part 1. *Chartes concernant la fondation de l'abbaye et des chapelles.* Edited by Adolphe Dutilleux and J. Depoin. Pontoise: L. Paris, 1890.

Cartulaire de l'abbaye de Notre-Dame de Bourbourg. Edited by Ignace de Coussemaker. 3 vols. Lille: V. Ducoulombier, 1882–91.

Cartulaire de l'abbaye de Porrois, au diocèse de Paris, plus connue sous son nom mystique de Port-Royal. Edited by Adolphe de Dion. Paris, 1903.

Cartulaire de l'abbaye de Saint-Georges de Rennes. Edited by Paul de la Bigne-Villeneuve. *Bulletin et Mémoires de la Société Archéologique du Département d'Ille-et-Vilaine* 9(1875): 129–311, 10(1876): 3–327.

Cartulaire de l'abbaye de Saint-Sulpice-la-Forêt, Ille-et-Vilaine. Edited by Pierre Anger. Extract from *Bulletin Archéologique d'Ille-et-Vilaine,* 1911, 1–473.

Cartulaire de l'abbaye du Paraclet. Edited by Charles Lalore. Vol. 2 of *Collection des principaux cartulaires du diocèse de Troyes.* Paris: Thorin, 1878.

Cartulaire de l'abbaye du Ronceray d'Anger (1028–1184). Edited by Bertrand de Broussillon. Paris: A. Picard, 1900.

Cartulaire de l'abbaye royale de Notre-Dame de Saintes de l'ordre de Saint Benoît. Vol. 2 of *Cartulaires inédits de la Saintonge.* Edited by Thomas Grasilier. Niort: L. Clouzot, 1871.

Cartulaire de l'abbaye royale du Lieu-Notre-Dame-lès-Romorantin, de l'ordre de Cîteaux publié d'après l'original avec introductions, notes et appendices. Edited by Ernest Plat. Romorantin, 1892.

Cartulaire de l'hôpital de Saint-Jean d'Angers. Edited by Célestin Port. Paris: J.-B. Dumoulin, 1870.

Cartulaire de l'hôtel-Dieu de Pontoise. Edited by J. Depoin. Pontoise: Société du Vexin, 1886.
Cartulaire de Notre-Dame de Voisins de l'ordre de Cîteaux. Edited by Jules Doinel. Collection des cartulaires du Loiret 3. Orléans, 1887.
Cartulaire du prieuré de Jully-les-Nonnains. Edited by Ernest Petit. *Bulletin de la Société des Sciences Historiques et Naturelles de l'Yonne* 34(1880): 249–302.
Cartulaire général de l'Yonne. Edited by Maximilien Quantin. Auxerre: Perriquet et Rouillé, 1854.
Chibnall, Marjorie, ed. *Charters and Customs of the Abbey of Holy Trinity, Caen.* Records of Social and Economic History, n.s. 5. London: Oxford University Press, 1982.
Cuissard, C., ed. "Sommaire de chartes de l'abbaye de Saint-Avit de Châteaudun." *Bulletin de la Société Dunoise Archéologique, Histoire, Sciences et Arts* 9(1897–1900): 169–200.
"Documents inédits pour servir à l'histoire de l'abbaye de Sainte-Croix de Poitiers." *Revue Mabillon* 9(1913): 50–87, 259–82.
Documents sur l'abbaye de Notre-Dame-aux-Nonnains de Troyes. Edited by Charles Lalore. *Mémoires de la Société Académique d'Agriculture, des Sciences, Arts et Belles-Lettres du Département de l'Aube.* 3d ser., 11(1874): 5–236.
Guibert of Nogent. *Self and Society in Medieval France: The Memoirs of Abbot Guibert of Nogent (1064?–c. 1125).* Edited with an introduction and notes by John F. Benton. New York: Harper and Row, 1970.
Jacques de Vitry. "Quatre sermons *ad religiosas* de Jacques de Vitry." Edited and introduced by Jean Longère. In *Les religieuses en France au XIIIe siècle,* edited by Michel Parisse. Nancy: Presses Universitaires de Nancy, 1985.
Le Grand, Léon, ed. "La règle de l'hôtel-Dieu de Pontoise." *Mémoires de la Société de l'Histoire de Paris et de l'Ile-de-France* 17(1890): 95–144.
The Letters of Abelard and Heloise. Translated by Betty Radice. Harmondsworth, England: Penguin, 1974.
Libellus de diversis ordinibus et professionibus qui sunt in aecclesia. Edited and translated by Giles Constable and Beryl Smith. Oxford: Clarendon Press, 1972.
Life of Christina of Markyate, ed. C. H. Talbot. Oxford: Clarendon, 1959.
McLaughlin, T. P. "Abelard's Rule for Religious Women." *Mediaeval Studies* 18(1956): 241–92.
Malicorne, J. *Documents et courte notice sur l'abbaye de Bival du douzième siècle jusqu'en 1789.* Rouen: L. Gy, 1897.
Nusse, C. "Charte de fondation d'un hôtel-Dieu à la Bare, transformé plus tard en abbaye (1211)." *Annales de la Société d'Historique et Archéologique du Château-Thierry,* 1874, 191–92.
Parisse, Michel. "Le concile de Remiremont, poème satirique du XIIe siècle." *Pays de Remiremont* 4(1981): 10–15.
Piot, Charles. "L'armement des côtes de Flandre en 1294." *Compte Rendu*

des Séances de la Commission Royale d'Histoire de Belgique, 4th ser., 11(1883): 169–78.

Recueil des chartes et documents de l'abbaye du Val-Saint-Georges à Salzinnes (Namur) 1196/7–1300. Edited by E. Brouette. Cîteaux-Commentarii Cistercienses, Studia et documenta 1. Achel: Abbaye Cistercienses, 1971.

Rigaud, Eudes. *The Register of Eudes of Rouen*. Edited by Jeremiah F. O'Sullivan. Translated by Sydney M. Brown. Columbia Records of Civilization 72. New York: Columbia University Press, 1964. Originally published as *Regestrum visitationum archiepiscopi Rothomagensis: Journal des visites pastorales d'Eude Rigaud, archevêque de Rouen (1248–1269)*. Edited by Thomas Bonnin. Rouen: Auguste Le Brument, 1852.

Rouleau mortuaire du B. Vital Abbé de Savigny. Edited by Léopold Delisle. Paris: H. Champion, 1909.

Rouleaux des mortes du IXe au XVe siècle recueillis et publiés pour la Société de l'Histoire de France. Edited by Léopold Deslisle. Paris: J. Renouard, 1866.

The Rule of St. Benedict. Edited and translated by Justin McCann. Westminster, Md.: Christian Classics, 1972.

Statuts d'hôtels-Dieu et de léproseries recueil de textes du XIIe au XIVe siècles. Edited by Léon Le Grand. Paris: A. Picard, 1901.

Vauzelles, Ludovic de. *Histoire du prieuré de la Magdeleine-lez-Orléans de l'ordre de Fontevraud*. Paris: J. Baur, 1873.

Vie de Saint Etienne d'Obazine. Text established and translated by Michel Aubrun. Clermont-Ferrand: Institute d'Etudes du Massif Central, 1970.

Visites des monastères de l'ordre de Cluny de la province d'Auvergne en 1286 et 1310. Edited by Alexandre Bruel. Paris: Collection de Documents Inédits sur l'Histoire de France, 1891.

SECONDARY SOURCES

Andrieu-Guitrancourt, Pierre. *L'archevêque Eudes Rigaud et la vie de l'église au XIIe siècle, d'après le "Regestrum visitationum."* Paris: Sirey, 1938.

Aubert, Yvonne. "L'abbaye Notre-Dame de Montivilliers au diocèse de Rouen des origines au XVIe siècle." In *Position des thèses de l'Ecole des Chartes*. Nogent-le-Rotrou: Daupeley-Gouveneur, 1939.

Aubry, Pierre. *La musique et les musiciens d'église en Normandie au XIIIe siècle, d'après le journal des visites pastorales d'Odon Rigaud*. Paris: H. Champion, 1906.

Audiat, Louis. "Agnes outragée." *Revue de Saintonge et d'Aunis* 5(1884–85): 232–36.

Avril, Joseph. "La province de Tours après le IVe concile du Latran: Les 'articuli missi archiepiscopo Turonensi.'" *Annuarium Historiae Conciliorum* 6(1974): 291–306.

———. "Les fondations, l'organisation et l'évolution des établissments de moniales dans le diocèse d'Angers (du XIe au XIIIe siècle)." In *Les religieuses en France au XIIIe siècles,* edited by Michel Parisse. Nancy: Presses Universitaires de Nancy, 1985.

Barstow, Anne L. *Married Priests and the Reforming Papacy: The Eleventh-Century Debates.* Texts and Studies in Religion 12. New York: Edwin Mellen Press, 1982.

Bell, Rudolph M. *Holy Anorexia.* Chicago: University of Chicago Press, 1985.

Bennett, Judith M. *Women in the Medieval English Countryside: Gender and Household in Brigstock before the Plague.* New York: Oxford, 1987.

Berman, Constance. "Women as Donors and Patrons to Southern French Monasteries in the Twelfth and Thirteenth Centuries." In *The Worlds of Medieval Women: Creativity, Influence, Imagination,* edited by Constance Berman, Charles Connell, and Judith Rothschild. Morgantown: West Virginia University Press, 1985.

Bitel, Lisa M. "Women's Monastic Enclosures in Early Ireland: A Study of Female Spirituality and Male Monastic Mentalities." *Journal of Medieval History* 12(1986): 15–36.

Blanc, Colette. "Les pratiques de piété des laïcs dans les pays du Bas-Rhône aux XIe et XIIe siècles." *Annales du Midi* 72(1960): 137–47.

Bolton, Brenda. "Mulieres Sanctae." In *Women in Medieval Society,* edited by Susan Mosher Stuard. Philadelphia: University of Pennsylvania Press, 1976.

Boswell, John. *Christianity, Social Tolerance, and Homosexuality: Gay People in Western Europe from the Beginning of the Christian Era to the Fourteenth Century.* Chicago: University of Chicago Press, 1980.

Bouchard, Constance. *Sword, Miter, and Cloister: Nobility and the Church in Burgundy, 980–1198.* Ithaca: Cornell University Press, 1987.

Boyd, Catherine. *A Cistercian Nunnery in Mediaeval Italy: The Story of Rifreddo in Saluzzo, 1220–1300.* Cambridge: Harvard University Press, 1943.

Bullough, Vern, and Cameron Campbell. "Female Longevity and Diet in the Middle Ages." *Speculum* 55(1980): 317–25.

Bynum, Caroline Walker. *Jesus as Mother: Studies in the Spirituality of the High Middle Ages.* Berkeley: University of California Press, 1982.

———. *Holy Feast and Holy Fast: The Religious Significance of Food to Medieval Women.* Berkeley: University of California Press, 1987.

Caille, Jacqueline. *Hôpitaux et charité publique à Narbonne au Moyen Age de la fin du XIe à la fin du XVe siècle.* Toulouse: Privat, 1978.

Carré, J.-B.-E. *Notice historique sur le prieuré de Gérigny de l'ordre de Prémontré au diocèse de Reims (1130–1789) avec plans et pièces justificatives inédites.* Reims: P. Michaud, 1885.

Cheney, C. R. *Episcopal Visitation of Monasteries in the Thirteenth Century.* Manchester, England: Manchester University Press, 1931.

Constable, Giles. "The Second Crusade as Seen by Contemporaries." *Traditio* 9(1953): 213–79.

Daichman, Graciela S. *Wayward Nuns in Medieval Literature.* Syracuse: Syracuse University Press, 1986.

Darlington, Oscar. *The Travels of Odo Rigaud, Archbishop of Rouen (1248–1275).* Philadelphia: University of Pennsylvania Press, 1940.

De Fontette, Micheline. "Les dominicaines en France au XIIIe siècle." In *Les religieuses en France au XIIIe siècle,* edited by Michel Parisse. Nancy: Presses Universitaires de Nancy, 1985.

De Ganck, Roger. "The Integration of Nuns in the Cistercian Order, Particularly in Belgium." *Cîteaux: Commentarii Cistercienses* 35(1984): 235–47.

Desmarchelier, Michel. "L'architecture des églises de moniales cisterciennes: Essai de classement des différents types de plans." In *Mélanges à la mémoire du Père Anselme Dimier,* edited by Benoît Chauvin. Architecture Cistercienne 3. Arbois: Benoît Chauvin, 1982.

De Sérent, A. "L'ordre de Sainte Claire en France pendant sept siècles." *Etudes Franciscaines,* n.s., 11(1953): 133–65.

Distant Echoes. Vol. 1 of *Medieval Religious Women.* Edited by John A. Nichols and Lillian Thomas Shank. Cistercian Studies Series 71. Kalamazoo, Mich.: Cistercian Publications, 1984.

Dolan, Diane. *Le drame liturgique de Pâques en Normandie et en Angleterre au Moyen Age.* Lettres et Sciences Humaines de l'Université de Poitiers 16. Paris: Presses Universitaires de France, 1975.

Douglas, Mary. *Purity and Danger: An Analysis of the Concepts of Pollution and Taboo.* Harmondsworth, England: Penguin, 1970.

Dubois, Jacques. "Office des heures et messe dans la tradition monastique." In *Histoire monastique en France au XIIe siècle.* London: Variorum, 1982.

Duby, Georges. "In Northwestern France: The 'Youth' in Twelfth-Century Aristocratic Society." In *Lordship and Community in Medieval Europe,* ed. Fredric L. Cheyette. New York: Holt, Rinehart, and Winston, 1968.

———. *The Knight, the Lady, and the Priest: The Making of Modern Marriage in Medieval France.* Translated by Barbara Bray. New York: Pantheon, 1983.

Dutilleux, Adolphe, and J. Depoin. *L'abbaye de Maubuisson (Notre-Dame-la-Royale): Histoire et cartulaire publiés d'après des documents entièrement inédits.* 4 vols. Pontoise: A. Paris, 1882–85.

Duval-Arnould, Louis. "Les aumônes d'Aliénor, dernière comtesse de Vermandois et dame de Valois." *Revue Mabillon* 60(1984): 395–463.

Eckenstein, Lina. *Woman under Monasticism.* New York: Russell and Russell, 1896; reissued 1963.

Elkins, Sharon. *Holy Women of Twelfth-Century England.* Chapel Hill: University of North Carolina Press, 1988.

Favreau, Robert. "Heurs et malheurs de l'abbaye, XIIe–XVe s." In *Histoire de l'abbaye Sainte-Croix de Poitiers: Quatorze siècles de vie monastique*. Mémoires de la Société des Antiquaires de l'Ouest, 4th ser., 19. Poitiers: Société des Antiquaires de l'Ouest, 1986.

Galli, André. "Faremoutiers au Moyen Age VIIe–XVe siècle." In *Sainte Fare et Faremoutiers: Trieze siècles de vie monastique*. Faremoutiers: Abbaye de Faremoutiers, 1956.

Gaussin, Pierre-Roger. "Les religieuses de la congrégation de la Chaise-Dieu." In *Les religieuses en France au XIIIe siècle*, edited by Michel Parisse. Nancy: Presses Universitaires de Nancy, 1985.

Gazeau, Roger. "La clôture des moniales au XIIe siècle en France." *Revue Mabillon* 58(1974): 289–308.

Geary, Patrick. "Saint Helen of Athyra and the Cathedral of Troyes in the Thirteenth Century." *Journal of Medieval and Renaissance Studies* 7(1977): 149–75.

Génestal, Robert. *Rôle des monastères comme établissements de crédit étudié en Normandie du XIe à la fin du XIIIe siècle*. Paris: A. Rousseau, 1901.

Gold, Penny Schine. *The Lady and the Virgin: Image, Attitude, and Experience in Twelfth-Century France*. Chicago: University of Chicago Press, 1985.

Hall, Edwin, and Ross Sweeney. "An Unpublished Privilege of Innocent III in Favor of Montivilliers: New Documentation for a Great Norman Nunnery." *Speculum* 49(1974): 662–79.

———. "The 'Licentia de Nam' of the Abbess of Montivilliers and the Origins of the Port of Harfleur." *Bulletin of the Institute for Historical Research* 52(1979): 1–8.

Hanawalt, Barbara A., ed. *Women and Work in Preindustrial Europe*. Bloomington: Indiana University Press, 1986.

Herlihy, David. "Life Expectancies for Women in Medieval Society." In *The Role of Woman in the Middle Ages*, edited by Rosmarie Morewedge. Albany: State University of New York Press, 1975.

———. *Medieval Households*. Cambridge: Harvard University Press, 1985.

———. *Opera Muliebria: Women and Work in Medieval Europe*. New York: McGraw-Hill, 1989.

Histoire de l'abbaye Sainte-Croix de Poitiers: Quatorze siècles de vie monastique. Mémoires de la Société des Antiquaires de l'Ouest, 4th ser., 19. Poitiers: Société des Antiquaires de l'Ouest, 1986.

Hunt, Noreen. *Cluny under Saint Hugh, 1049–1109*. Notre Dame, Ind.: University of Notre Dame Press, 1968.

Huyghebaert, Nicolas. "Les femmes laïques dans la vie religieuse des XIe et XIIe siècles dans la province ecclésiastique de Reims." In *I laici nella "societas christiana" dei secoli XI e XII*. Miscellanea del Centro di Studi Medioevali 5. Milan: Catholic University of the Sacred Heart, 1968.

Jenkins, Claude. "A Thirteenth-Century Register: Odo, Archbishop of Rouen." *Church Quarterly Review* 101(1925): 80–123.

Jobin, Jean-Baptiste. *Histoire du prieuré de Jully-les-Nonnains avec pièces justificatives.* Paris: Bray et Retaux, 1881.

Johnson, Penelope D. *Prayer, Patronage, and Power: The Abbey of La Trinité, Vendôme, 1032–1187.* New York: New York University Press, 1981.

————. "Agnes of Burgundy: An Eleventh-Century Woman as Monastic Patron." *Journal of Medieval History* 15(1989): 93–104.

Jordan, W. C. "The Cistercian Nunnery of la Cour Notre-Dame de Michery: A House That Failed." *Revue Bénédictine* 95(1985): 311–20.

Kealy, Thomas. *Dowry of Women Religious.* Canon Law Studies 134. Washington, D.C.: Catholic University of America, 1941.

Knowles, David. *The Monastic Order in England.* 2d ed. Cambridge: Cambridge University Press, 1966.

Labande-Mailfert, Yvonne. "Les débuts de Sainte-Croix." In *Histoire de Sainte-Croix de Poitiers: Quatorze siècles de vie monastique.* Mémoires de la Société des Antiquaires de l'Ouest, 4th ser., 19. Poitiers: Société des Antiquaires de l'Ouest, 1986.

Lawrence, C. H. *Medieval Monasticism: Forms of Religious Life in Western Europe in the Middle Ages.* London: Longman, 1984.

Le Cacheux, Marie-Josèphe. *Histoire de l'abbaye de Saint-Amand de Rouen des origines à la fin du XVIe siècle.* Caen: Société d'Impression de la Basse-Normandie, 1937.

Le Cacheux, Paul. *L'exemption de Montivilliers.* Caen, 1929.

Leclercq, Jean. "Medieval Feminine Monasticism: Reality versus Romantic Images." In *Benedictus: Studies in Honor of St. Benedict of Nursia,* edited by Rozanne Elder. Studies in Medieval Cistercian History 8. (Kalamazoo, Mich.: Cistercian Publications, 1981).

————. "Feminine Monasticism in the Twelfth and Thirteenth Centuries," and "The Spirituality of Medieval Feminine Monasticism." In *The Continuing Quest for God,* edited by William Skudlarck. Collegeville, Minn.: Liturgical Press, 1982.

L'Hermite-Leclercq, Paulette. "Le monastère de La Celle les Brignoles (Var) au XIIIe siècle." In *Les religieuses en France au XIIIe siècle,* edited by Michel Parisse. Nancy: Presses Universitaires de Nancy, 1985.

————. *Le monachisme féminin dans la société de son temps: Le monastère de La Celle (XIe–début du XVIe siècle).* Paris: Editions Cujas, 1989.

Lemarignier, Jean-François. *Etudes sur les privilèges d'exemption et de juridiction ecclésiastique des abbayes normandes depuis les origines jusqu'en 1140.* Paris: A. Picard, 1937.

Little, Lester K. *Religious Poverty and the Profit Economy in Medieval Europe.* Ithaca, N.Y.: Cornell University Press, 1978.

Lorcin, M.-T. "Retraites des veuves et filles au couvent: Quelques aspects de la condition féminine à la fin du Moyen Age." In *Annales de démographie historique*, edited by L. Henry. Paris: Librairie de la Nouvelle Faculté, 1975.

Lynch, Joseph H. *Simoniacal Entry into Religious Life from 1000 to 1260: A Social, Economic and Legal Study*. Columbus: Ohio State University Press, 1976.

Metz, René. *La consécration des vierges dans l'église romaine: Etude d'histoire de la liturgie*. Paris: Presses Universitaires de France, 1954.

Mews, C. J., and C. S. F. Burnett. "La bibliothèque du Paraclet du XIIIe s. à la Revolution." *Studia Monastica* 27(1985): 31–68.

Moore, R. I. "Family, Community, and Cult on the Eve of the Gregorian Reform." *Transactions of the Royal Historical Society* 30(1980): 49–69.

———. *The Origins of European Dissent*. Oxford: Basil Blackwell, 1985.

Moreau, Marthe. "Les moniales du diocèse de Maguelone au XIIIe siècle." In *La femme dans la vie religieuse du Languedoc (XIIIe–XIVe s.)*. Cahiers de Fanjeaux 23. Toulouse: Privat, 1988.

Newman, Barbara. *Sister of Wisdom: St. Hildegard's Theology of the Feminine*. Berkeley: University of California Press, 1987.

Nichols, John. "English Cistercian Nuns." In *Distant Echoes*. Vol. 1 of *Medieval Religious Women*, ed. John A. Nichols and Lillian Thomas Shank. Cistercian Studies Series 71. Kalamazoo, Mich.: Cistercian Publications, 1984.

La Normandie bénédictine au temps de Guillaume le Conquérant (XIe siècle). Lille: Facultés Catholiques de Lille, 1967.

Oursel, Raymond. *Une fondation flamande aux carrefours des chemins de pèlegrinage: Le grand hôpital d'Aubrac*. Annales de l'Ecole des Hautes Etudes de Gand 9. Ghent: Imprimerie Van Doosselaere, 1978.

Parisse, Michel. *La Lorraine monastique au Moyen Age*. Nancy: Presses Universitaires de Nancy, 1981.

———. *Les nonnes au Moyen Age*. Le Puy: Christine Bonneton, 1983.

———. "Les Bénédictines de Lorraine et leurs documents nécrologiques." *Studia Anselmiana* 574(1985): 249–61.

Pernoud, Régine. *La femme au temps des cathédrales*. Paris: Stock, 1981.

Pibrac, Anatole du Faur Cte. de. *Histoire de l'abbaye de Voisins ordre de Cîteaux, diocèse d'Orléans*. Orléans: H. Herluison, 1882.

Pierre Abélard—Pierre le Vénérable: Les courants philosophiques, littéraires, et artistiques en Occident au milieu du XIIe siècle. Colloque International de Cluny, 1972, 546. Paris: Editions du Centre National de la Recherche Scientifique, 1975.

Platelle, Henri. "Les relations entre l'abbaye Saint-Amand de Rouen et l'abbaye Saint-Amand d'Elone." In *La Normandie bénédictine au temps de Guillaume le Conquérant (XIe siècle)*. Lille: Facultés Catholique de Lille, 1967.

Priem, Georges. "L'abbaye royale de Montivilliers." In *La Normandie bén-*

édictine au temps de Guillaume de Conquérant (XIe siècle). Lille: Facultés Catholiques de Lille, 1967.

Quéguiner, Jean. "Jouarre au XIIe et au XIIIe siècles." In *L'abbaye royale Notre-Dame de Jouarre*. 2 vols. Paris: Bibliothèque d'Histoire et d'Architecture Chrétiennes, 1961.

Rambaud-Buhot. "Le statut des moniales chez les pères de l'église, dans les règles monastiques et les collections canoniques jusqu'à XIIe siècle." In *Sainte Fare et Faremoutiers: Trieze siècles de vie monastique*. Faremoutiers: l'Abbaye de Faremoutiers, 1956.

Les religieuses en France au XIIIe siècle. Edited by Michel Parisse. Conference Proceedings of l'Institut d'Etudes Médiévales de l'Université de Nancy II and CERCOM, 1983. Nancy: Presses Universitaires de Nancy, 1985.

Renouard de Bussière, Marie-Théodore. *Histoire des religieuses dominicaines au couvent de Sainte-Marguerite et Sainte-Agnès à Strasbourg*. Strasbourg: L.-F. Leroux, 1860.

Répertoire des abbayes et prieurés de Seine-Maritime: Ouvrage collectif publié à l'occasion de l'année des abbayes normandes. Rouen: Archives Départementales de Seine-Maritime, 1979.

Rohmer, Régis. "L'abbaye bénédictine de Notre-Dame-aux-Nonnains de Troyes des origines à l'année 1503." In *Position des thèses de l'Ecole des Chartes*. Mâcon: Protat Frères, 1905.

Roisin, Simone, "L'efflorescence cistercienne et le courant féminin de piété au XIIIe siècle." *Revue d'Histoire Ecclésiastique* 39(1943): 342–78.

Rollet, J. "Relevé de chartes, donations, et titres divers relatifs à l'abbaye de la Barre." *Annales de la Société Historique et Archéologique de Château-Thierry* 107(1883): 64–93.

Saint-Denis, Alain. *L'hôtel-Dieu de Laon, 1150–1300*. Nancy: Presses Universitaires de France, 1983.

Sainte Fare et Faremoutiers: Trieze siècles de vie monastique. Faremoutiers: Abbaye de Faremoutiers, 1956.

Schulenburg, Jane. "Female Sanctity: Public and Private Roles, ca. 500–1100." In *Women and Power in the Middle Ages*, edited by Mary Erler and Maryanne Kowaleski. Athens: University of Georgia Press, 1988.

Shahar, Shulamith. "De quelques aspects de la femme dans la pensée et la communauté religieuses aux XIIe et XIIIe siècles." *Revue de l'Histoire des Religions* 185(1974): 29–77.

———. *The Fourth Estate: A History of Women in the Middle Ages*. Translated by Chaya Galai. London: Methuen, 1983.

Simenon, G. *Julienne de Cornillon*. Brussels: Presses Universitaires de Belgique, 1946.

Stein, Frederick Marc. "The Religious Women of Cologne: 1120–1320." Ph.D. diss., Yale University, 1977.

Thompson, Sally. "The Problem of the Cistercian Nuns in the Twelfth and Thirteenth Centuries." In *Medieval Women*, edited by Derek Baker. Studies in Church History, Subsidia 1. Oxford: Basil Blackwell, 1978.

Vendel, Henri. "Etude sur l'abbaye d'Almenêches de sa fondation à l'an 1599." In *Positions des thèses de l'Ecole des Chartes.* Paris: A. Picard, 1921.

Verdon, Jean. "Notes sur le rôle économique des monastères féminins en France dans la seconde moitié du IXe et au début du Xe siècle." *Revue Mabillon* 58(1975): 329–43.

———. "Les moniales dans la France de l'Ouest aux XIe et XIIe siècles: Etude d'histoire sociale." *Cahiers de Civilisation Médiévale* 19(1976): 247–64.

———. "Recherches sur les monastères féminins dans la France au sud aux IXe–XIe siècles." *Annales du Midi* 88(1976): 117–38.

Weinstein, Donald, and Rudolph Bell. *Saints and Society: The Two Worlds of Western Christendom, 1000–1700.* Chicago: University of Chicago Press, 1982.

Wilmart, André. "Eve et Goscelin." *Revue Bénédictine* 46(1934): 414–38, 50(1938): 42–83.

Yardley, Anne B. "Ful Weel She Soong the Service Dyvyne": The Cloistered Musician in the Middle Ages." In *Women Making Music: The Western Art Tradition, 1150–1950,* edited by Jane Bowers and Judith Tick. Urbana: University of Illinois Press, 1986.

INDEX

Abbesses
—authority of, 167; ebbing of, 253; shared with chapter, 191–92
—election of, 169–71; contested, 171
—and oaths: to bishop, 64, 245; of office, 170
—office of: pension for, 172; recruitment of, 95; retirement from, 72, 172–73
Abduction of nuns, 125, 130
Abelard: advice for Heloise, 90, 130, 133, 144, 244, 266; criticized monks' learning, 146; and enclosure for nuns, 151; gave Paraclete to Heloise, 89–90; in martryology, 249
Abortion, 114, 124
Adele, abbess of Saint-Georges, Rennes, 26, 51, 167, 231
Adele, countess of Apulia, 78
Adele, countess of Poitiers, 38
Adeline, abbess of Montivilliers, 83
Adrian IV, pope, 83, 85
Ad succurrendum nun or monk, 29, 177, 224
Advocate of monastery, 44–45
Agnes, abbess of Holy Trinity, Poitiers, 169, 202
Agnes of Barbezieux, abbess of Notre-Dame, Saintes, 75, 167; gave mortgage, 213; as judge, 204; and violence, 168
Agnes of Burgundy: at dedication of Notre-Dame, Saintes, 196; donated Marennes to nuns, 197; donated mint, 218; endowed Notre-Dame, 259; joint founder of Holy Trinity, Vendôme, 245; joint founder of

Notre-Dame, 34, 61; name popular, 234
Agnes of Erbrée, abbess of Saint-Georges, Rennes, 201, 203
Agnes of Mount-Secours, nun of Villarceaux, 112, 118
Alan, count of Brittany, 26, 233
Alcuin, 96
Aldeburge, abbess of Notre-Dame, Saintes, 210
Alfonse, count of Eu, 202
Alice, abbess of Bourbourg, 42
Alice, abbess of Montivilliers, 83
Alice, abbess of Notre-Dame-aux-Nonnains, 172
Alice of Rouen, nun of Saint-Aubin, 121
Almshouses, 39, 50, 173. *See also* Hospitals
Anchoress, 125, 149–50. *See also* Emma, nun of Saint-Amand; Eve
Anchorite, 101
Anselm of Bec, 33

Banal dues, 218
Beatrice, first abbess of Montivilliers, 36
Beguines, 55, 258
Benedictine Rule, 3, 50, 56, 69
Bernard of Clairvaux, Saint, 4, 96, 260
Bertrand de Got, archbishop, 68
Bishops: consecrated monastics, 63; and oath to nuns, 65; and responsibility to monastics, 62; visitations by, 67–74, 84–85
Blanche, countess of Champagne, 38
Blanche of Castille, queen of France, 38, 41, 52, 63, 259
Bleeding, 134

Size of monasteries. *See* Monasteries, size of
Statutes of Pope Gregory, 69, 119
Stephanie, abbess of Notre-Dame, Saintes, 210
Steven of Obazine, 89, 151
Suicide, attempted, 240
Synod of Château-Gontier (1231), 174

Thérèse of Lisieux, Saint, 21
Third Lateran Council (1179), 262–63
Tiburge, abbess of Ronceray, 172
Tolls, 216–17
Trial by fire, 204

Unchastity. *See* Sexual activity
Urban IV, pope, 86–88, 136, 171

Veils for nuns, 230, 236; blessed, 63; dyed with saffron, 117; taken away, 121
Veronica, Saint, 21
Villarceaux, Priory of: bad prioress of, 131; scandals at, 116–18

Violence: of monks, 250 n; against nuns, 57, 168; of nuns, 112, 243, 250
Visions, 249
Visitation, by abbess, 200
Visitatio sepulchri, 138–40
Vitalis of Mortain, 25
Vocation, false, 29
Vows, monastic: breaking of, 15, 28, 131–32; of chastity, 112–30; no more than three, 106; of obedience, 130–33; of poverty, 107–12

War: Angevin-Capetian, 44–45, 57–58, 83; localized, 57; retreat from, 154, 182
Widows, 28–29, 37, 55, 57, 109
William the Conqueror, 36, 82
William Helias, 76
Wills, 56, 258
Women: as marginalized group, 263; options for, 17; as weaker sex, 235
Work: by married women, 255; by nuns, 107, 208